BERKELEY

AN INTERPRETATION

BERKELEY

AN INTERPRETATION

Kenneth P. Winkler

CLARENDON PRESS · OXFORD
1989

Oxford University Press, Walton Street, Oxford OX2 6DP

Oxford New York Toronto
Delhi Bombay Calcutta Madras Karachi
Petaling Jaya Singapore Hong Kong Tokyo
Nairobi Dar es Salaam Cape Town
Melbourne Auckland
and associated companies in
Berlin Ibadan

Oxford is a trade mark of Oxford University Press

Published in the United States
by Oxford University Press, New York

British Library Cataloguing in Publication Data
Winkler, Kenneth P.
Berkeley : an interpretation.
1. Irish philosophy. Berkeley, George,
1685–1753
I. Title
192
ISBN 0–19–824907–1

Library of Congress Cataloging in Publication Data
Winkler, Kenneth P.
Berkeley : an interpretation / Kenneth P. Winkler.
Includes index.
1. Berkeley, George, 1685–1753. I. Title.
B1348.W56 1989 192—dc19 88–25116
ISBN 0–19–824907–1

Set by Hope Services, Abingdon

Printed and bound in Great Britain by
Biddles Ltd, Guildford and King's Lynn

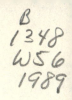

to Janie and Becky

PREFACE

THIS book on Berkeley is an interpretation: an exposition of his arguments, an assessment of their significance, and an explanation—inevitably partial—of their content and form. My explanations are proposed as hypotheses: I argue that Berkeley's writings are shaped by concerns they do not always acknowledge, and in such cases I defend my hypotheses as plausible explanations of a range of texts. I have tried throughout to make Berkeley's arguments as plausible as I can. This brings, I hope, a kind of understanding—the understanding that comes when we comprehend a belief by seeing how we ourselves might be brought to hold it.

My topics and their arrangement are a bit unusual. Berkeley wrote to Percival that in *A Treatise concerning the Principles of Human Knowledge* he 'omitted all mention of the non-existence of matter in the title-page, dedication, preface, and introduction', so that 'the notion might steal unawares on the reader, who possibly would never have meddled with a book that he had known contained such paradoxes' (*Works* VIII, p. 36). The point, he confided in his notebooks, was to help the truth to glide insensibly into the soul (*Philosophical Commentaries* 185). Of course anyone meddling with *my* book does so precisely because of the paradoxes. But for a reason closely related to Berkeley's I postpone paradox for as long as possible. There is no real discussion of the non-existence of matter until Chapter 6. In the first five chapters I concentrate instead on topics which may seem remote from immaterialism: intentionality (Chapters 1 and 2); necessity (Chapters 3 and 4); and intelligibility (Chapter 5). My hope is that when I arrive in Chapter 6 at the views for which Berkeley is most famous, they will seem natural rather than outrageous. I do this partly because understanding a philosophical view is not so different from being convinced by it. 'I wonder not at my sagacity in discovery the obvious tho' amazing truth', Berkeley wrote of immaterialism. 'I rather wonder at my stupid inadvertency in not finding it out before. 'tis no witchcraft to see.' (*Philosophical Commentaries* 279.) What made it difficult to see was not inadvertency, but the fact that immaterialism, like most things we call obvious, is obvious only against a certain background. In Chapters 1 to 5 I try to fill that background in. Some of the consequences of immaterialism are discussed in Chapters 7, 8, and 9.

This is a sympathetic presentation. I do offer criticisms, but I spend at least as much time defending Berkeley against criticisms made by others. Philosophical ideas cannot be understood or elucidated unless they are seen at work, and their author is not the only one with a right to decide what that work should be. As Joseph Butler wrote in the Preface to his *Fifteen Sermons*, ideas in philosophy 'never are in themselves determinate, but become so, by the train of reasoning and the place they stand in'. An approach to Berkeley that is itself an argument—sometimes with Berkeley, sometimes with other commentators—is also justified by Berkeley's character as a philosopher. Argument is Berkeley's medium: he uses it not only to persuade, but to expound and clarify. I have tried to follow his example.

A first draft of the bulk of this book was written in 1982–3, when I was an Andrew W. Mellon Faculty Fellow in the Humanities at Harvard University. I am grateful to the Mellon Foundation and Harvard University for their support, and to Richard M. Hunt, Director of the Mellon Fellowship Program, for his encouragement and help. I am also grateful to the Department of Philosophy at Harvard for its hospitality, as well as for the opportunity to teach its course on the British Empiricists. Chapter 3 is based on a paper originally written in 1981, when I was awarded a Summer Stipend from the National Endowment for the Humanities; I gratefully acknowledge the Endowment's support. Grants from Wellesley College twice supported the typing of the manuscript, first in 1984 and again in 1987.

An earlier version of parts of Chapter 2 appeared as 'Berkeley on Abstract Ideas' in *Archiv für Geschichte der Philosophie* 65 (1983), 63–80; section III of that paper appears here as an appendix to the chapter. A somewhat different version of Chapter 5 was published as 'Berkeley on Volition, Power, and the Complexity of Causation' in *History of Philosophy Quarterly* 2 (1985), 53–69. Parts of Chapter 7 were published as 'Unperceived Objects and Berkeley's Denial of Blind Agency' in *Hermathena* 139 (1985), 81–100, and reprinted in David Berman (ed.), *George Berkeley: Essays and Replies*, Dublin, 1986. At scattered locations in Chapters 1, 2, and 6 I have borrowed sentences, and in two or three places paragraphs, from the introduction to my edition of Berkeley's *Principles*, published by Hackett Publishing Company of Indianapolis and Cambridge, Massachusetts in 1982.

While working on the book I had useful conversations or exchanges of letters with many people, among them Jonathan Adler, Michael Ayers, Owen Flanagan, Eckart Förster, Daniel Garber, Paul Hoffman, Edwin McCann, David Raynor, Ian Tipton, Cass Weller, and John Yolton. I am grateful to them all. Michael Ayers, Charles McCracken, Robert McKim, David Raynor, Ian Tipton, and Margaret Wilson were kind enough to provide detailed comments on earlier versions of some of the material. Drafts of chapters were delivered as papers at the Berkeley Tercentenary Conference in Dublin, and at meetings of the American Philosophical Association and the Royal Institute of Philosophy. I am grateful to my commentators—Margaret Atherton, George Pitcher, Ian Tipton, and Stanley Tweyman—for their replies. Conferences sponsored since 1979 by the International Berkeley Society were also important occasions. I am acutely conscious of the debt I owe to earlier writers on Berkeley, many of whom are criticized, sometimes persistently, in the pages that follow.

This book is dedicated to my wife, Janie Penn, and to our daughter, Rebecca Penn Winkler; I thank them both for their support and love.

CONTENTS

BIBLIOGRAPHICAL NOTE

FOR Berkeley's writings I have used A. A. Luce and T. E. Jessop (eds.), *The Works of George Berkeley, Bishop of Cloyne*, 9 vols., London, 1948–57. When I quote from the *Philosophical Commentaries*, the notebooks Berkeley kept in 1707–8, I generally include his marginal signs. The plus sign marks material Berkeley decided not to use (see Luce's *Berkeley and Malebranche*, London, 1934, pp. 187–8; his remarks in *Works* I, p. 4, and on pp. xxv–xxvi of his diplomatic edition of the *Commentaries*, London, 1944; and his note on pp. 229–33 of George H. Thomas's edition of the *Commentaries*, Alliance, Ohio, 1976). Berkeley's own explanations for some of the remaining signs are as follows:

I	Introduction
M	Matter
P	Primary and Secondary Qualities
E	Existence
T	Time
S	Soul; Spirit
G	God
Mo	Moral Philosophy
N	Natural Philosophy

These explanations appear at the beginning of Notebook A (*Works* I, p. 50; Thomas p. 50). For an explanation of the multiplication sign and the numbers sometimes placed within it see *Works* I, p. 4.

References to Berkeley's works appear in the text. I refer to them by abbreviated titles, followed by dialogue, section, or entry numbers. For the *Three Dialogues* I also provide the page number in vol. II of the *Works*, and for *Alciphron* I provide both volume and page number. References to Locke's *Essay concerning Human Understanding*, edited by P. H. Nidditch, Oxford, 1975, also appear in the text; I use small-capital roman numerals for book numbers, lower-case roman numerals for chapter numbers, and arabic numerals for sections. (Thus *Essay* II xxiii I refers to Book One, chapter twenty-three, section one.) I follow a similar practice in quoting other works with parts and sub-parts: small-capital roman numerals pick out the largest divisions, lower-case roman numerals the next largest, and arabic numerals the next. Where there is likely to be confusion (as in Malebranche's *The Search after Truth*, where there are books, parts, chapters, and sometimes numbered sections), the citation is spelt out in full.

1
WORDS AND IDEAS

In the closing chapter of the *Essay* Locke divides all of science into three parts: the science of nature, the science of practice, and the science of signs (IV xxi). The science of nature, or natural philosophy, is concerned, he explains, with the constitutions, properties, and operations of both bodies and spirits (§ 2). The science of signs, or logic, is concerned with words and ideas. Ideas are defined, at this point at least, as the signs or representations of the things the mind considers (§ 4). Like most philosophers who taxonomize the sciences, Locke fails to say where his own book falls, but the subjects of Book III ('Of Words'), Book II ('Of Ideas'), and Book I ('Of Innate Notions') indicate that a great deal of it belongs to logic. In this book I try to show that Berkeley's most important writings belong there too. Berkeley offers an extended 'logical' argument, in Locke's sense of 'logical', for a 'natural-philosophical' conclusion, one which transforms the natural world from a system of bodies with powers and operations into a system of inert signs—a *text*—with no existence apart from the spirits who transmit and receive it.

Several of the most important and striking of the premisses in Berkeley's argument will be introduced in the next five chapters. One premiss turns on a difference between the ways in which Locke's two kinds of signs—words and ideas—represent or signify their objects. That difference is the subject of the present chapter.

1. *Two kinds of signs*

Consider the word *chair*. There is nothing special about the word that accounts for its ability to refer to chairs. *We* use the word, but speakers of other languages use other words, and if every speaker of English agreed to switch the roles of 'table' and 'chair' we would get along just fine, referring to tables when we used the word 'chair' and to chairs when we used the word 'table'. The relations between words and what they signify are arbitrary or *conventional*. This doesn't mean that at some time in the distant past people consciously and ceremonially agreed to use words in a certain way; but it means in part that we now have the power to alter the relations between words and the world by adopting new conventions, new associations of word and object.

Now consider a thought-experiment of which Berkeley was very fond.[1] Imagine someone alone in the world without language. She still has tables and chairs and mountains and rivers, but she lacks the words to refer to them. Can she think about them anyway? 'Of course she can,' runs the obvious reply. 'Thoughts, like words, have the capacity to refer to things, a capacity they do not owe to language.' But thoughts, unlike words, do not seem to be conventional. It is easy to imagine using the word 'table' to refer to a chair, but can we imagine using the *thought* of a table to refer to a chair? 'Call up the thought of a table but think of a chair instead' seems to be a contradiction, because to call up the thought of a table is, inevitably, to think of a table rather than a chair. A child may wonder what the word 'table' means, but it is impossible to wonder what the *thought* of a table means: if you don't already know the meaning of the thought, it is impossible to have it. Thoughts, it seems, are not conventionally appointed to their symbolic roles, but demand a certain interpretation by their very nature.

Locke calls thoughts 'ideas', and a great deal of what he says about them suggests that words depend on ideas for their ability to refer to things. According to Locke, the primary and immediate significations of words (apart from 'particles' such as *is* and *is not* and 'negative Names' such as *barrenness*) are ideas (*Essay* III ii 2; for the exceptions see III vi, II viii 5, and III i 4). Ideas in turn signify things. This double relation—of words to ideas and of ideas to things—establishes mediated or indirect relations between words and the world. In the case of some words at least Berkeley seems to accept this view. And he goes on to ask what it is about ideas that enables them to refer to things in such a direct and irresistible way:

Consider the different manners wherein words represent ideas, & ideas things. There is no similitude or resemblance betwixt words & the ideas that are marked by them. Any name may be used indifferently for the sign of any idea, or any number of ideas, it not being determin'd by any likeness to represent one more than another. But it is not so with ideas in respect of things, of which

---

[1] The device of the solitary man appears in the notebooks at entries 566, 607 ('the Solitary Man'), 648, and 727. It makes its way into the First Draft of the Introduction to the *Principles* (*Works* II, p. 141), but not into the published version.

they are suppos'd to be the copies & images. They are not thought to represent them any otherwise, than as they resemble them. (First Draft, *Works* II, p. 129.)

Ideas, it seems, are *images*: non-arbitrary or natural symbols, forced to represent what they resemble. Words on the other hand are arbitrary or conventional, and they refer to things only because they directly signify ideas. The link between words and ideas explains not only the capacity of language for reference (a capacity I will refer to as the *intentionality* of language) but also the possibility of communication. I am able to understand what you say because your words excite ideas in my mind which are very much like the ones that prompted you to speak.

Berkeley's case against materialism is, fundamentally, a case against the possibility of a certain thought or conception, and in Chapter 6 we will see how the difference between words and ideas contributes to his conclusion that we cannot think or conceive of matter. The present chapter is an attempt to clarify this difference. By the end of the chapter I hope to have shown that Berkeley does not *assume* that ideas are images but *concludes* it, as part of a deliberate attempt to explain how at least some of our thoughts succeed in referring to the world.

2. *Ideas as objects*

In his notebooks Berkeley instructs himself to apologize for his use of the word 'idea': 'Excuse to be made in the Introduction', reads entry 685, 'for the using the word Idea viz. because it has obtain'd.' Locke, who was partly responsible for the word's obtaining, had felt the need to apologize too:

Before I proceed on to what I have thought on this Subject [of human understanding], I must here in the Entrance beg pardon of my Reader, for the frequent use of the Word *Idea*, which he will find in the following Treatise. It being that Term, which, I think, serves best to stand for whatsoever is the Object of the Understanding when a Man thinks, I have used it to express whatever is meant by *Phantasm*, *Notion*, *Species*, or whatever it is, which the Mind can be employ'd about in thinking; and I could not avoid frequently using it. (*Essay* I i 8.)

According to this definition, which is echoed at II viii 8, an idea is not an act of thought but an *object*, an item the mind is 'employ'd about' in thinking. Locke does not always adhere to this characterization, as we will see in Chapter 2. But although Locke often strays from it, I believe that Berkeley does so only rarely. This accounts for some of the most important differences between the two philosophers. In the present section I hope to show that Berkeley's tendency to treat ideas as objects is a powerful one; in later chapters I will show how the tendency is expressed in his case for immaterialism. I think Berkeley's tendency to treat ideas as objects is not only powerful but dominant; it is, I think, virtually the only one governing his understanding of the word 'idea'. But proof of this will have to wait until Chapter 9.

Berkeley speaks of ideas as the objects of thought in many entries in the *Philosophical Commentaries*. The following entries are typical:

M   We see the Horse it self, the Church it self it being an Idea &   427
    nothing more

M   The Horse it self the Church it self as an Idea i:e object   427a
    immediate object of thought.

S   The grand Cause of perplexity & darkness in treating of the Will,   643
    is that we Imagine it to be an object of thought (to speak wth the
    vulgar), we think we may perceive, contemplate & view it like any
    of our Ideas whereas in truth 'tis no idea.

These entries are untroubled and definite, but learning to treat ideas as objects called for some adjustments in Berkeley's other views. One place where the strains of adjustment can be felt is in the following entry on the nature of the understanding:

*   the Understanding not distinct from particular percep-   614
    tions or Ideas.

Here Berkeley anticipates Hume's view of the self as a system or bundle of perceptions, and in doing so he suggests that an idea is an *act* of thought, a 'perception' rather than an object of perception. But he later had second thoughts about this entry: 'The Understanding taken for a faculty is not really distinct from ye Will', he says in a facing-page correction (614a). When we come to entry 808, where the unity of will and understanding is emphatically endorsed, we find the view of ideas as objects reasserted:

I. S.   Idea is ye object or Subject of thought; y^t I think on w^{t}ever it be, I   808
    call Idea. thought it self, or Thinking is no Idea tis an act i.e.
    Volition i.e. as contradistinguish'd to effects, the Will.

The word 'idea' is used to refer to perception or thought at one point in the Draft Introduction, where Berkeley speaks of the thoughts that 'ly hidden' in every man's mind, and can be disclosed to others only through writing or speech (*Works* II, p. 128). But in the *New Theory of Vision* the view of ideas as objects is firmly in control. A remark at the end of § 45 shows how distant Berkeley is from the view that had tempted him in the *Commentaries*. 'Note that when I speak of tangible ideas,' he writes in § 45, 'I take the word idea for any the immediate object of sense or understanding, in which large signification it is commonly used by the moderns.' What makes this cautionary note so revealing is that in the *Theory of Vision* Berkeley is deliberately avoiding the supposition that tangible ideas depend for their existence on the mind. Berkeley expects the readers of his essay on vision to think of tangible ideas as they think of ordinary objects. Looking back on the essay in § 44 of the *Principles* he writes,

That the proper objects of sight neither exist without the mind, nor are the images of external things, was shewn even in that treatise. Though throughout the same, *the contrary be supposed true of tangible objects* [emphasis mine]: not that to suppose that vulgar error, was necessary for establishing the notion therein laid down; but because it was beside my purpose to examine and refute it in a discourse concerning *vision*.

Here Berkeley is telling us that his theory of vision can be understood and accepted by someone who makes the mistake of supposing that tangible objects have an existence 'natural or real', distinct from their being perceived, an error 'strangely prevailing'—that is, *very much* prevailing—even among the vulgar (*Principles* 4).[2] He could hardly suggest this if he did not himself think of tangible ideas as objects, even though he secretly thinks of them as objects of a very different kind.

Berkeley continues to speak of ideas as objects in the *Principles*. 'It is evident to any one who takes a survey of the objects of human knowledge,' he writes in the opening sentence of Part I, 'that they are either ideas actually imprinted on the senses, or else such as are perceived by attending to the passions and operations of the mind, or lastly ideas formed by help of memory and imagination, either compounding, dividing, or barely representing those originally perceived in the aforesaid ways.' The mind that exercises 'divers operations' on these 'ideas or objects of knowledge', he explains in § 2, is 'a thing

---

[2] *Principles* 4 is sometimes read as suggesting that there is something *odd* about the prevalence of materialism, but *strangely* here means what it does at Introduction to the *Principles* 21 and on p. 172 of the First Dialogue. To let the obsolete meaning pass unnoticed is to miss an open confession of conflict with common sense.

entirely distinct from them'. Ideas, Berkeley insists, are one thing; the gaze of the mind's eye is another.

But what does it mean to say that ideas are the objects of thought? Uppermost in Berkeley's mind is an opposition between the objects of thought and the acts or operations directed towards them. When I am thinking of a tree in the park, the act or operation is my thinking of the tree. And the act of thinking, to borrow a traditional expression derived from Aristotle's *Categories*, can be *predicated* of me.[3] That is, it can truly be said that I am thinking of the tree. To borrow further pieces of traditional vocabulary, thinking of the tree is a *mode* or *attribute* of me. At *Principles* 49 Berkeley contrasts the way in which a mode or attribute is in me with the way in which an idea or quality is in me:

It may perhaps be objected, that if extension and figure exist only in the mind, it follows that the mind is extended and figured; since extension is a mode or attribute, which (to speak with the Schools) is predicated of the subject in which it exists. I answer, those qualities are in the mind only as they are perceived by it, that is, not by way of *mode* or *attribute*, but only by way of *idea*.

In Chapters 6, 7 and 9 I will discuss what it means for idea to exist 'only in the mind'. At this point in my exposition I do not want to say that an idea is a *mental* object, but only that it is an object. The content I have supplied for this claim is so far rather thin: ideas are objects distinct from (that is, not identical with) the acts or operations of the mind; they are not viewings or perceivings but objects viewed or perceived. I can, however, make two further points about the objects towards which the acts or operations of the mind are directed, and by considering an objection I can make an additional point about the acts or operations themselves.

The first point is that Berkeleyan ideas play a role in explaining why our mental acts and operations have the content that they do. The *content* of an act or operation is what is specified by the words following expressions such as 'George thinks that', 'George imagines that', or 'George decides that', in sentences such as 'George thinks that the horizon moon is large'. If ideas are going to explain the content of our mental acts and operations, even if only in part, then they must be distinct from (that is, not identical with) those acts and operations.

There is a sense of the expression 'object of thought' in which something can serve as such an object even if it does not exist. My

[3] Aristotle, *Categories* 2, p. 4, in J. L. Ackrill (trans.), *Aristotle's Categories and De Interpretatione*, Oxford, 1963.

second point is that a Berkeleyan idea is not an object of thought in this sense. It is not, in other words, an *intentional* object.[4] An idea is an entity, a real thing, and the relation between an idea and the mind is a genuine relation between two distinct items (see, for example, the Third Dialogue, pp. 230, 237, 249, and 260). An idea is an object of thought in a sense demanding that the object exists whenever it is true to say that a thought is directed towards it.

Third, in the First Dialogue Philonous argues at length against a distinction, invoked by Hylas, between a sensation and its object. As Philonous understands the distinction, in every perception there are 'two things . . . one an action of the mind, the other not' (*Works* II, p. 195). It might be objected that Philonous's dissatisfaction with the proposed distinction is evidence against my contention that Berkeley's ideas are distinct from the acts or operations of the mind. To see that this is not the case we need to look more closely at the relevant exchange.

Philonous's first step in attacking the distinction is to secure Hylas's agreement that the mind is active only when, by an act of will, it produces, changes, or puts an end to something (p. 196). Philonous then argues that because what we see and smell does not depend on our will, seeing and smelling (as opposed to looking or breathing) cannot properly be described as acts:

Since therefore you are in the very perception of light and colours altogether passive, what is become of that action you were speaking of, as an ingredient in every sensation? (p. 197.)

Philonous's question recalls the sentence that closed *Principles* 5 as it appeared in the 1710 edition: 'In truth the object and the sensation are the same thing, and cannot therefore be abstracted from each other.'

Hylas distinguishes between a sensation and its object because he

---

[4] On intentional objects see Roderick Chisholm, *Perceiving: A Philosophical Study*, Ithaca, 1957, pp. 168–73: G. E. M. Anscombe, 'The Intentionality of Sensation', pp. 3–20 in her *Metaphysics and the Philosophy of Mind*, Minneapolis, 1981; J. L. Mackie, 'What Is Really Wrong with Phenomenalism', *Proceedings of the British Academy* 55 (1969), 113–27, especially pp. 118–19, and 'Problems of Intentionality', pp. 102–16 in his *Logic and Knowledge*, Oxford, 1985; and, in a more historical setting, Phillip D. Cummins, 'Reid's Realism', *Journal of the History of Philosophy* 12 (1974), 317–40. When I say that Berkeleyan ideas are not intentional objects I do not mean to be denying that intentional objects play a role in explaining why Berkeley understands ideas as he does. For suggestions along these lines see Anscombe, p. 13, and Mackie, 'What Is Really Wrong with Phenomenalism', pp. 119–20. The possibility that Berkeleyan ideas are intentional objects is explored by Douglas Odegard, 'Berkeley and the Perception of Ideas', *Canadian Journal of Philosophy* 1 (1971), 155–71.

wants to make room for the belief that objects can exist without the mind. (He has already admitted that sensations cannot.) In response Philonous observes that 'if there was a perception without any act of the mind, it were possible such a perception should exist in an unthinking substance' (p. 196). Hylas agrees, but he denies that there can be such a perception. Now it seems to me that the burden of the subsequent argument is to show that there *can* be such a perception, a perception that is not (in at least one sense of the word) an *action*. Philonous concludes the argument with a series of three questions. The first question, quoted above, asks what has become of the action ingredient in every sensation. The implication of this rhetorical query is that Philonous has identified a kind of perception—'the very perception of light and colours'—that is 'altogether passive', the seeing rather than the looking (p. 197). Philonous then asks question two: 'And doth it not follow from your own concessions, that the perception of light and colours, including no action in it, may exist in an unperceiving substance?' (p. 197.) Now it does follow from Hylas's earlier concession—the concession being that if there were a perception without any act of mind, it would be possible for the perception to exist in an unthinking substance—that the perception of light and colours may be found even in an unperceiving thing. And because Hylas agrees, I think, that the answer to Philonous's third question—'is not this a plain contradiction?' (p. 197)—is also yes, he discards his distinction between a sensation and its object. But it is important to ask what Philonous himself makes of an argument which is, I think, *ad hominem*.[5]

Either Philonous agrees that the mind is passive in the perception of light and colours or he does not. Let us begin by supposing that he does. We know that he is far from believing that light and colour can be perceived by an unperceiving thing. He must therefore deny what Hylas concedes: he must insist that simply because a perception is inactive, it does not follow that it can exist in an unthinking or unperceiving thing. He must admit, that is, that there may be inactive things which are able to perceive. To say this is to suggest that perception is not an *action*—at least not if *action* is defined, as in the argument against Hylas, as something essentially voluntary or will-involving. But a belief in passive or inactive perception does not conflict with the distinction I have made between an act of the mind and

[5] The *ad hominem* character of the arguments in the First Dialogue has been neglected by most commentators. I will have more to say about it in Chap. 6.

the object towards which it is directed, because such an act is not necessarily voluntary. It can be an act in another sense, one that would be familiar to anyone acquainted with Aristotle or the scholastics: an actualization of a capacity possessed by the perceiving mind.[6]

Now let us suppose Philonous does not agree that the mind is altogether passive in the perception of light and colours. In that case he can avoid the conclusion that a perception can exist in an unperceiving thing only by insisting that there is a kind of action that is not will-involving. But once again, this would not conflict with the distinction between a mental act or operation and its objects. Hence either Philonous believes there are 'mental acts or operations' that are altogether passive, or he believes that mental acts are in some sense actions even though they are not voluntary. In either case he can acknowledge a distinction (once again, a non-identity) between my perceiving a tree and the tree I perceive. It is true that in the 1710 version of *Principles* 5, Berkeley writes that 'the object and the sensation are the same thing', but he may have eliminated this remark from the 1734 edition precisely because he came to accept the kind of view I have presented here. He continued to believe that the object cannot be abstracted from the sensation, but he may have realized that this could not be shown by saying that the object and the sensation are one and the same.

So far I have shown that Berkeley often *says* that ideas are objects of thought, and I have said as much as I am now prepared to say about what sort of thing those objects are. But it might be objected that Berkeley can be said to treat ideas as objects only if ideas function as

---

[6] In 'Berkeley and Descartes: Reflections on the Theory of Ideas', Peter K. Machamer and Robert G. Turnbull (eds.), *Studies in Perception*, Columbus, 1978, pp. 259–311, Wilfrid Sellars raises the possibility that a mental act is merely 'an *actualization* of a mental capacity' (p. 263). On this understanding of mental act, he says, 'the concept of a "passive act" would be a coherent one' (p. 264). He then observes that Descartes would have no objection to such a notion. But he later on suggests that Berkeley would: Berkeley rejects the act–object analysis, Sellars explains, and his reasoning turns 'on an equation of "act" with "deed" ' (p. 289). It is certainly true that Hylas lets the equation pass, but this is no reason for supposing that Philonous (or Berkeley) is committed to it. In several entries in the *Commentaries* Berkeley suggests that every perception—even the kind of perception at issue in the exchange between Hylas and Philonous—involves volition, and there is a remnant of this view at *Principles* 139. In entry 808, for example, he links the view that an idea is an object of thought with the suggestion that thinking is an act: 'Idea is ye object or Subject of thought: y^t I think on w'ever it be. I call Idea. thought it self, or Thinking is no idea tis an act i.e. Volition i.e. as contradistinguish'd to effects, the Will.' In *Principles* 142 Berkeley uses the word 'acts' in the Aristotelian or scholastic sense.

objects in his arguments. In his official pronouncements, after all, Locke portrays ideas as objects, yet I have already confessed that Locke often treats ideas as if they were something else. Couldn't the same be true of Berkeley? The answer is that it could, but nothing short of a complete survey of Berkeley's arguments will provide us with the evidence needed to decide the question. Further support for my interpretation will emerge as the book proceeds. I now ask the reader to follow my exposition in order to see where it leads; the question of the nature of ideas cannot be put to rest until the end of Chapter 9.

3. *Ideas as images*

Berkeley speaks freely of *ideas* 'imprinted on the senses' (*Principles* 33 and 90). 'Ideas of sense' may differ from ideas excited by the imagination in being more regular, vivid, and constant, and in being stronger, more orderly, and more coherent, 'yet still', he writes, 'they are *ideas*' (*Principles* 33). Yet at one point Berkeley recommends a more narrow employment of the term 'idea', one that is fully appropriate, he warns, only for ideas of imagination:

> The ideas imprinted on the senses by the Author of Nature are called *real things*: and those excited in the imagination being less regular, vivid and constant, are more properly terms *ideas*, or *images of things*, which they copy and represent. (*Principles* 33.)

His fussiness about 'idea', which does not last beyond the lines just quoted, has its source in the close link in meaning between *idea* and *image*, and in the implication (stronger in the case of *image*, despite their similarity in meaning) that an image corresponds to an original. At *Principles* 87 Berkeley warns that if colour, figure, motion, extension, and so on 'are looked on as notes or images, referred to *things* or *archetypes* existing without the mind, then are we involved all in *scepticism*', because on such a view we see 'only the appearances, and not the real qualities of things'. Only a representation can be an image. It follows that the only things fit to be called ideas in the strict sense are ideas of imagination.

An image owes its representational status to the fact that it *copies* or *resembles* its object or archetype. At *Principles* 33 Berkeley explains that ideas of imagination 'copy and represent' their archetypes, and in the Draft Introduction he observes that ideas, as opposed to words, 'are suppos'd to be the copies & images' of things. 'They are not thought to represent them any otherwise, than as they resemble them.' (*Works* II, p. 129.) This passage from the Draft Introduction might be discounted on the grounds that Berkeley is attributing the view to others. But the context of the passage makes it clear that the view is also Berkeley's own. The passage follows a paragraph ending with the claim that 'all the ends of language may be, & are, attain'd to without the help of any such faculty as abstraction' (*Works* II, p. 129). The references to what is generally 'suppos'd' or 'thought' are intended not to separate Berkeley from the claims the passage makes, but to secure consensus in his case against abstraction. Why, it might be asked, is there no passage corresponding to this one in the published version of the Introduction? I think there are two basic reasons. We know that Berkeley does not want to call attention to his immaterialist conclusion in the Introduction: I have 'omitted all mention of the non-existence of matter in the title-page, dedication, preface, and introduction, that so the notion might steal unawares on the reader, who possibly would never had meddled with a book that he had known contained such paradoxes' (*Works* VIII, p. 36). At the same time he does not want to encourage materialism. To refer to the distinction between ideas and things would be to do exactly that. Everything Berkeley says in the passage can, of course, be interpreted in a way consistent with his denial of matter (all we need to do is read 'idea' as an idea of imagination or memory, and 'thing' as an idea of sense), but at this point Berkeley cannot rely on the reader to assign words their proper interpretations. This is his first reason for discarding the passage. The second is that the passage fails to support his attack on abstraction. The point of the passage is that although the word 'man' is able to signify any man at all, the idea of man does not have the same latitude. The representative scope of an idea is limited by its physiognomy. A word, on the other hand, is 'featureless', and we can therefore assign to it as wide a scope as we please. From the standpoint of the published version of the Introduction, though, this is a very poor argument. The conclusion of the published version is that there *are* ideas of man in general, but they turn out to be ideas of particular men, put to a certain use. We can give an idea a wide representational scope, Berkeley argues, by ignoring its individuating features. The idea continues to represent only what it resembles, but because the resemblance is less specific the idea is capable of representing more. The physiognomy of an idea sets limits to its representational role, but the mind is free to adjust its role within those limits. The unpublished passage concludes with the observation that

the word Man may equally be put to signify any particular man I think of. But I cannot frame an idea of man, which shall equally represent & correspond to each particular of that sort of creatures that may possibly exist. (*Works* II, p. 129.)

By the time he came to publish Berkeley realized that he *could* frame such an idea of man. He does not give up his earlier view on the different manners in which words and ideas represent, but he realizes that the difference is not relevant to his attack on abstraction, at least not in the way he once thought. The passage is therefore eliminated, but not because Berkeley ceases to believe that representation involves resemblance. This is why he does not hesitate to appeal to the belief in arguing that passive ideas cannot represent active spirits.

The view Berkeley reports in the Draft Introduction is held by those who think that *all* ideas, even ideas of sense, are images or ideas in the narrow sense. Berkeley takes up this view at *Principles* 8, where he writes,

But say you, though the ideas themselves do not exist without the mind, yet there may be things like them whereof they are copies or resemblances, which things exist without the mind, in an unthinking substance. (See also the First Dialogue, p. 203.)

Although Berkeley takes this view to be gravely mistaken, he agrees that an image represents its archetype or original only because it copies or resembles it. The common core of the view he accepts and the view he rejects can be expressed as follows: representative ideas are images, objects that represent their archetypes only because they copy or resemble them. The view he opposes takes even ideas of sense to be images. Berkeley agrees that ideas of sense *would* be images if they were representations, but he believes that they are archetypes or originals. For Berkeley, ideas of sense remain ideas, but not in the narrow sense briefly delineated at *Principles* 33.

But what does it mean to say that ideas of sense remain ideas, and how do they differ from the ideas which represent them? We have already had a glimpse of Berkeley's answer. Ideas of sense are more regular, vivid, and constant—stronger, more orderly, and more coherent—than ideas of imagination. If we put aside the differences in regularity, constancy, order, and coherence—differences I will speak of as *extrinsic* or *external* because they arise only when ideas are united in a series—we are left with the *intrinsic* or *internal* characteristics of vivacity and strength. Features of both kinds are *phenomenological*, or fully available from the viewpoint of the perceiving subject, even though a fair chunk of time has to pass before the external features can be safely recognized. The intrinsic phenomenological differences between an idea of imagination and the corresponding idea of sense— the only differences between the two ideas taken in isolation—lie in their varying degrees of vivacity and strength. Ideas of imagination are images, then, and ideas of sense (when taken singly) are exactly like them, except for variations in vivacity and strength. Taken in series, ideas of sense are more regular, constant, orderly, and coherent, but such features cannot be ascribed to the ideas taken one by one.

We now know more about the kind of objects Berkeley takes his ideas to be. They divide into two groups. Ideas in the first group are images in the strictest sense. Each of us can produce examples by calling up images of colours or fruits. Ideas in the second group are, taken singly, just like the ideas in the first group, though they tend to be stronger and more vivid. Berkeley's ideas are therefore images, or objects that differ intrinsically from images only in vivacity and strength. This description of Berkeleyan ideas clarifies and to some extent supports my earlier contention that Berkeleyan ideas are not acts or operations of the mind, because mental acts cannot be straightforwardly described as if they vary in vivacity and strength, and it is not entirely natural to speak of one act or operation as the copy of another.[7]

It should be clear by now not only that Berkeley believes representative ideas are images, but that it is highly misleading to say that he *assumes* it. He is, to begin with, quite conscious of the belief: he states it several times; he appeals to it when he describes the different manner in which words and ideas represent their objects; and it figures prominently in his argument, to be reviewed in Chapter 9, that a passive idea cannot represent an active spirit. Moreover, once we recognize that he is conscious of it, there can be little doubt about the place he assigns to it. The belief provides his account of the

---

[7] These claims are, however, by no means void of sense. If ideas are acts or operations of the mind, Berkeley's claim that ideas of imagination resemble ideas of sense could be taken to mean that conceiving of a sensible thing is subjectively very much like sensing it. I discuss this possibility in Chap. 9.

intentionality or 'aboutness' of thought about the natural world. We are able to think about that world because our acts of thought are directed towards images of the objects in it. All thinking about things is representational, and the mechanism of representation is resemblance or similitude. It might be objected that if we are to be convinced that Berkeley does not *assume* that ideas are images, we ought to be shown that he considered several accounts of intentionality, and consciously preferred the imagistic one. I must admit that a patient and methodical comparison of competing hypotheses cannot be found in Berkeley's works. But as we look further into Berkeley's views on Locke's two kinds of signs, we will see that the absence of such a comparison does not tell against my view. Berkeley thinks there are severe constraints on any account of the intentionality of thought, and their effect is to render alternatives to the imagistic account unworthy of serious consideration.

4. *Representation and signification*

Berkeley sometimes uses 'represent' and its cognates (for example in the Draft Introduction, at *Principles* 1, and at *Principles* 8), but he speaks more often of signification, or of the relation between *sign* and *thing signified*. The relations of representation and signification are, he thinks, crucially. different. The relation of signification holds, for example, between 'the fire which I see' and 'the pain I suffer upon my approaching it' (*Principles* 65). The fire forewarns me of the pain, yet it does not represent the pain in anything like the way in which, according to Berkeley, an idea of imagination represents the corresponding idea of sense, or the way in which, according to the materialist, an idea of sense represents an unthinking substance without the mind. Representation and signification differ in two ways.

First, the relation of signification is arbitrary or conventional. Representation, on the other hand, is fixed by the nature of image and original; it is a natural relation, and it is beyond our power to alter or institute it. The relation of representation must be independent of convention because it is the relation that makes convention possible. We cannot decide to let one thing stand for another unless we are already able to think about them both.

In the seventeenth and eighteenth centuries, the relation between words and what they signify was widely taken to be the paradigm of arbitrary signification. Locke put the standard view as follows:[8]

Thus we may conceive how *Words* . . . come to be made use of by Men, as *the Signs of* their *Ideas*; not by any natural connexion, that there is between particular articulate Sounds and certain *Ideas*, . . . but by a voluntary Imposition, whereby such a Word is made arbitrarily the Mark of such an *Idea*. (*Essay* III ii 1.)

Berkeley's acceptance of what Locke says here is clearest in the works on vision, where the orthodox opinion that words are arbitrary signs is developed into the more unusual view that *any* system of arbitrary signs is in fact a language. In the *New Theory of Vision*, Berkeley sets out to show how 'we perceive by sight the distance, magnitude, and situation of objects' (§ 1). The treatment of distance sets the pattern for magnitude and situation. Berkeley begins by arguing briefly for what he takes to be the accepted view that distance, 'of itself and immediately, cannot be seen' (§ 2). Distance is seen mediately, or by virtue of something else. He goes beyond the accepted view in arguing that the idea or sensation by which distance is seen is not something with which distance has a natural or necessary connection. We judge the distance of an object by sensing the 'turn' or disposition of our eyes, by the confusion or fuzziness of the visual appearance, and by the strain we feel as we struggle to keep the object in focus. In all three cases the connection between distance and the idea by which we see it is 'habitual or customary' rather than natural or necessary (§ 17), and therefore judgements of distance based on information provided by the eyes are 'entirely the result of experience' (§ 20). Berkeley compares seeing the distance of an object to seeing shame by observing the blushing of a cheek (§ 23). Even more revealingly, he compares the case where sensing the turn of the eyes suggests an idea of distance to what happens when, 'upon hearing a certain sound, the idea is immediately suggested to the understanding which custom had united with it' (§ 17). Later on in the essay the analogy between these two relations is hardened into an identity:

---

[8] The many others who expressed such views include Descartes, *Dioptrics* IV (p. 89 in Paul J. Olscamp's trans., *Discourse on Method, Optics, Geometry, and Meteorology*, Indianapolis, 1965; p. 112 in vol. 6 of Charles Adam and Paul Tannery (eds.), *Œuvres de Descartes*, Paris, 1902); Géraud de Cordemoy, *A Philosophicall Discourse concerning Speech*, London, 1668, pp. 15–16; and Samuel Parker, *A Free and Impartial Censure of the Platonick Philosophie*, second edn., Oxford, 1667, p. 65, where Parker even suggests the experiment of 'imposing upon words contrary significations'.

Upon the whole, I think we may fairly conclude that the proper objects of vision constitute an universal language of the Author of nature, whereby we are instructed how to regulate our actions in order to attain those things that are necessary to the preservation and well-being of our bodies, as also to avoid whatever may be hurtful and destructive of them. It is by their information that we are principally guided in all the transactions and concerns of life. And the manner wherein they signify and mark unto us the objects which are at a distance is the same with that of languages and signs of human appointment, which do not suggest the things signified by any likeness or identity of nature, but only by an habitual connexion that experience has made us to observe between them. (*Theory of Vision* 147. See also *Principles* 44 and 66.)

Berkeley continues to insist on the identity in his later writings. In the *Theory of Vision Vindicated and Explained*, written more than twenty years after the essays it defends, he writes:

A great number of arbitrary signs, various and apposite, do constitute a language. If such arbitrary connexion be instituted by men, it is an artificial language; if by the Author of nature, it is a natural language. Infinitely various are the modifications of light and sound, whence they are each capable of supplying an endless variety of signs, and, accordingly, have been each employed to form languages; the one by the arbitrary appointment of mankind, the other by that of God Himself. A connexion established by the Author of nature, in the ordinary course of things, may surely be called natural; as that made by men will be named artificial. And yet this doth not hinder but the one may be as arbitrary as the other. And, in fact, there is no more likeness to exhibit, or necessity to infer, things tangible from the modifications of light, than there is in language to collect the meaning from the sound. (§ 40; see also another late work, *Alciphron* IV 10, *Works* III, p. 154.)

Here Berkeley both agrees with Locke that linguistic signification is arbitrary and goes beyond him in claiming that a system of arbitrary signs, various and apposite, *is* a language. Locke contrasts arbitrary connections with natural ones, but Berkeley, because of his interest in divinely instituted signs, cannot accept the Lockean contrast as it stands. Berkeley would certainly agree with Locke that if a natural connection flows from the nature of the items it connects, then not even divine signs can be called natural. But if a natural connection is, as Berkeley proposes, merely a dependable current in the course of nature, then the signs appointed by God are natural even though they are arbitrary or 'artificial'. They are artificial in the same sense as the parts and organs of plants or animals, which Berkeley describes at *Principles* 65 as 'machines', or 'artificial and regular combinations'.

They are the products of artifice or design. But the relation between an idea of imagination and its corresponding idea of sense is not even a matter of divine appointment. My recollection of a child's expression counts as a recollection of that expression only because the idea excited by my imagination resembles what I saw. Resemblance is a natural relation in Locke's sense, a relation that flows from the nature of the items related. Not even God can make an idea that in no way resembles the object into a representation of it. As Berkeley says in the Draft Introduction, ideas are 'determin'd by . . . likeness'—by something intrinsic, as opposed to something attached to them by convention—to play a certain representational role.

The second difference between representation and signification is that signs do not automatically impart conceptions of what they signify. Representations do. Forming an idea that resembles the colour I saw gives me a conception of the colour. Fire is a sign of pain but it cannot impart a conception of it. We cannot think of pain simply by recalling an idea of fire, unless past experience has forged an association between the idea of fire and an idea that resembles the pain.

The second difference can also be formulated by means of the word 'of'. In the *Philosophical Commentaries* Berkeley warns that the word is troublesome:

M   Of & thing causes of mistake   115

S   The referring Ideas to things wch are not Ideas, the using the   660
      Term, Idea of, is one great cause of mistake, as in other matters
      so also in this.

The problem, as entry 660 perhaps suggests, is not so much with the word 'of' as with the belief that even ideas of sense are representations of originals. In 657a, a precursor of Berkeley's warning about the word 'idea' in *Principles* 33, Berkeley writes,

M   properly speaking Idea is the picture of the Imagination's making
      this is ye likeness of & refer'd to the real Idea or (if you will) thing.

The word 'of' allows us to put the second difference as follows: an idea can be said to be an idea *of* a thing only if it represents it. It is not enough for the idea to signify it.

It might be objected that an idea that signifies something can impart a kind of conception of the thing it signifies, a conception that might be described as *relative*. But the contrast remains, since the signifying idea would not provide a conception of the thing as it is in itself. This means that the signifying idea could not be used to meet the challenge laid down by someone who questions our understanding of a particular word. This is not to say that in Berkeley's view such a challenge can *only* be met if we have at our disposal a representation of the thing. It is just that a representation gives us one way of meeting the challenge. No single signifier can do as much, because no single signifier carries with it a conception of the object it signifies.

According to Locke, '*Words in their primary or immediate Signification, stand for nothing, but the* Ideas *in the Mind of him that uses them*' (*Essay* III ii 2). Although he warns against saying that words stand for anything *other* than ideas (III ii 5), he often speaks as if words signify or stand for things themselves. At *Essay* III vi 1, for example, he writes that the common names of substances such as wax or gold are the 'signs of such complex *Ideas*, wherein several particular Substances do, or might agree, by virtue of which, they are capable to be comprehended in one common Conception, and be signified by one Name'. Here he begins by saying that the names of substances are signs of complex ideas (though as we know from II viii 8 by *ideas* he sometimes means qualities), yet he ends by saying that the particular *substances* are signified by the names. At III iv 2 he writes that the names of both simple ideas and substances are signs that '*intimate*' some real existence, 'from which was derived their original pattern'. The fact that words signify ideas in a way that is *primary* and *immediate*, when joined to the fact that they can also be said to signify qualities and things themselves, suggests that words signify qualities or things *by means of* the ideas that apparently intervene between them. Words signify ideas which represent things of qualities. Therefore words, in their *secondary* or *mediate* signification, stand for things.

I am doubtful that Locke actually accepted the picture just sketched.[9] But I suspect that it was attributed to him by Berkeley, and that Berkeley's opposition to the belief that all words signify ideas, an opposition which deepened as his career progressed, was at the same time a stand against what he took to be the Lockean picture.[10] Early in

---

[9] Useful accounts of Locke's views on meaning and signification include Norman Kretzmann, 'The Main Thesis of Locke's Semantic Theory', reprinted in Ian Tipton (ed.), *Locke on Human Understanding*, Oxford, 1977, pp. 123–40; E. J. Ashworth, 'Locke on Language', *Canadian Journal of Philosophy* 14 (1984), 45–73; and Charles Landesmann, 'Locke's Theory of Meaning', *Journal of the History of Philosophy* 14 (1976), 23–35.

[10] Berkeley never says explicitly that the picture is Locke's but he comes closest to doing so at Introduction 18. Berkeley asks how it is that words have contributed to the

his notebooks Berkeley accepts the view that all words signify ideas. At entry 378, for example, the proposition that every significant word stands for an idea appears at the top of a projected demonstration of the immaterialist principle. (The entry was later marked with a plus sign.) Soon after he begins to qualify the proposition, in ways Locke himself anticipates. At entry 661 he observes that particles (such as *is* and *not*) do not stand for ideas (a point Locke makes at *Essay* III vii), and writes on the facing page that 'particles stand for volitions & their concomitant Ideas'. This suggests a modified version of the proposition, according to which significant words stand for ideas or operations of the mind. But eventually even this is rejected. I will briefly indicate Berkeley's reasons here; several of them will be explored in more detail in later chapters.

First, in the Introduction to the *Principles* Berkeley argues against the view that 'every name hath, or ought to have, one only precise and settled signification' (§ 18; see also *Principles* 116). He argues that although a word such as *triangle* has a precise and settled *meaning*, embodied in its definition, it is not the case that it stands everywhere for the same idea.

Second, later on in the Introduction he observes that the 'communicating of ideas marked by words is not the chief and only end of language' (Introduction 20). Among its other ends are the raising of passion, the prompting of action, and the inculcation of dispositions. All these, he argues, can often be accomplished without the communicating of ideas. 'May we not, for example, be affected with the promise of a *good thing*, though we have not an idea of what it is?' And 'when a Schoolman tells me *Aristotle hath said it*, all I conceive he means by it, is to dispose me to embrace his opinion with the deference and submission which custom has annexed to that name. And this effect may be so instantly produced in the minds of those who are accustomed to resign their judgement to the authority of that philosopher, as it is impossible any idea either of his person, writings, or reputation should go before.' (Introduction 20. See also *Alciphron* VII 5.)

Third, the names of spirits and their acts and operations, Berkeley

---

mistaken belief in abstract ideas. After referring to the Essay (III vi 39 'and elsewhere') he points to the belief that every name 'hath, or ought to have, one only precise and settled signification'. He then writes that it is thought that 'it is by the *mediation* of these abstract ideas, that a general name comes to signify any particular thing' (emphasis mine).

argues in the *Principles* and later works, do not stand for ideas. We have *notions* of spirits and their acts and operations but no *ideas* of them, because active beings cannot be represented by ideas which, being inert and inactive, cannot resemble them. This exception to the principle that all words stand for ideas is more fully discussed in Chapter 9.

Fourth, because all relations include an act of the mind, the words that signify relations, like the words that signify spirits and their acts, do not signify ideas (*Principles* 142 and 89, in the 1734 edition only).

Fifth, in *Alciphron* VII Euphranor argues that even a word which can be said to signify an idea need not call up that idea on every occasion of its use, 'it being sufficient that we have it in our power to substitute things or ideas for their signs when there is occasion' (*Works* III p. 292; see also Introduction 19). Words, Euphranor suggests, are like counters used at card-tables as substitutes for money. Words no more need to recall the ideas they represent on every occasion of their use than counters need always to recall 'the distinct sum or value' that they represent (p. 291).

Finally, Euphranor goes on to argue that some words—*force* is his most important example—gain their meaning not by standing for ideas, but by the role they play in a system of propositions with practical applications.

Clearly Berkeley does not believe that all words signify ideas. And his opposition to the belief runs so deep that even the words that *do* signify ideas are not connected to things in the way the Lockean picture indicates. The Lockean picture suggests that a word stands for a thing only because it first stands for an idea that intervenes between them. But such a view, translated into Berkeley's scheme of things, would have the odd consequence that a word stands for a thing (that is, an idea of sense) only because it *first* stands for the idea of that thing (that is, for the idea of imagination which copies the thing and therefore represents it). If Berkeley believes that a word signifies an idea, and if we use the word *idea* in its strictest sense, then he cannot be said to believe that it signifies a thing *because* of the intervening idea. When he says that a word signifies an idea he can only mean that anyone who claims to understand the word—anyone who claims to have an understanding of whatever it is the word signifies—must be capable of imagining what it signifies. So Ian Hacking is wrong to call Berkeley an 'idea-ist', if an idea-ist believes that there is a class of objects—called 'ideas'—that intervene between the ego and the world.[11]

Berkeley proposes what amounts to a distinction between signs and representations. All ideas of sense are signs, despite the fact that they are not representations of patterns or originals. They are signs not of their 'archetypes', but of other ideas. This kind of *horizontal* signification, confined to the level of ideas, is compatible with Berkeley's claim that ideas of sense never signify *vertically*, or in a way that involves descent to a level of things different in kind from the ideas themselves. The difference between linguistic signification and imagistic representation plays a central role in Berkeley's case for immaterialism. But it also raises some awkward questions: how should we understand what is going on when a person thinks not of a particular thing (a feat he or she could presumably accomplish merely by calling up an idea that resembles the thing) but of a collection or kind? Do we think of human beings in general, for example, by calling up an idea? And if we do, is the idea a representation of everyone? How, if representation involves resemblance, could such an idea be possible? These questions raise the problem of abstraction, to which we now turn.

[11] *Why Does Language Matter to Philosophy?* Cambridge, 1975, p. 36.

2
ABSTRACT IDEAS

LOCKE, or rather Locke as Berkeley sees him, holds that words signify things by first signifying ideas. Ideas intervene between words and the world, and their intervention determines what it is in the world to which our words refer. The role of ideas is especially striking, Berkeley believes, in Locke's account of abstract or general thinking. According to that account as Berkeley portrays it, a general word signifies a kind, class, or collection of things because the idea intervening between the word and what it signifies is not the idea of a particular—an image resembling a single individual—but a distinctive kind of idea, one that is somehow abstract or general in its own right. Berkeley writes,

'Tis thought that every name hath, or ought to have, one only precise and settled signification, which inclines men to think there are certain *abstract*, *determinate ideas*, which constitute the true and only immediate signification of each general name. And that it is by the mediation of these abstract ideas, that a general name comes to signify any particular thing. (Introduction 18.)

Locke develops his account of *abstraction* in widely scattered portions of the *Essay*. His first attempt comes in a chapter charting the various operations of the mind:

The Mind makes the particular *Ideas*, received from particular Objects, to become general; which is done by considering them as they are in the Mind such Appearances, separate from all other Existences, and the circumstances of real Existence, as Time, Place, or any other concomitant *Ideas*. This is called *ABSTRACTION*, whereby *Ideas* taken from particular Beings, become general Representatives of all of the same kind; and their Names general Names, applicable to whatever exists conformable to such abstract *Ideas*. (II xi 9.)

There is a fuller discussion in Book III. Chapter 3 of that book is devoted to general terms. How, Locke asks, do general words come to be made? 'For since all things that exist are only particulars, how come we by general Terms, or where find we those general Natures they are supposed to stand for?' 'Words become general,' he answers, 'by being made the signs of general *Ideas*', and ideas become general by being separated from 'the circumstances of Time, and Place, and any other *Ideas*, that may determine them to this or that particular Existence. By this way of abstraction they are made capable of representing more Individuals than one; each of which, having in it a conformity to that abstract *Idea*, is (as we call it) of that sort.' (§ 6.)

He elaborates on the operation of abstraction or separation in the following section. Speaking of children whose first words are confined to individuals such as nurse and mother, Locke writes that

Afterwards, when time and a larger Acquaintance has made them observe, that there are a great many other Things in the World, that in some common agreements of Shape, and several other Qualities, resemble their Father and Mother, and those Persons they have been used to, they frame an *Idea*, which they find those many Particulars do partake in; and to that they give, with others, the name *Man*, for Example. And *thus they come to have a general Name*, and a general *Idea*. Wherein they make nothing new, but only leave out of the complex *Idea* they had of *Peter* and *James*, *Mary* and *Jane*, that which is peculiar to each, and retain only what is common to them all.

If we accept for the moment Berkeley's portrayal of Locke's view of word/world relations, it is not difficult to see why abstraction arouses Berkeley's suspicions. It is easy enough to understand the link between a word and the thing it signifies when the word is a proper name. The name 'George' refers to Berkeley because it is linked with an image which in turn resembles the man. But what about a general word—the common noun 'man', for example? It too refers to things in the world, and on the Lockean picture as Berkeley views it, it must therefore signify an idea or image. But what can the associated image be like? It cannot be the image of Berkeley or any other particular man, because those ideas have already been assigned the role of referring to particular men. If ideas alone are to account for the intentionality or 'aboutness' of language, as Berkeley takes Locke to suppose, then a word's signification must be fully determined by the associated idea. If we abandon this requirement, allowing one and the same idea to represent a particular man on some occasions and man in general on others, we introduce a looseness of fit between ideas and the world. But it was the promise of a tight fit that made ideas plausible candidates for explaining the aboutness of language in the first place. It therefore seems that the idea involved when we think of man in general must be an idea of a special sort, one which represents every man without representing any man in particular, or one man more than any other. But where can the idea come from? Ideas of particular men can be derived from experience directly. But because our experience is, as Locke admits, always of particular men and never of humanity itself, the idea of man in general must be the product of some kind of mental manufacturing.

The need for such mental activity is, in fact, already clear in the passages quoted from the *Essay*. Berkeley reports on the form of the alleged activity in § 9 of the Introduction to the *Principles*, a passage that borrows freely from *Essay* III iii 7:

For example, the mind having observed that Peter, James and John, resemble each other, in certain common agreements of shape and other qualities, leaves out of the complex or compounded idea it has of Peter, James, and any other particular man, that which is peculiar to each, retaining only what is common to all; and so makes an abstract idea wherein all the particulars equally partake, abstracting entirely from and cutting off all those circumstances and differences, which might determine it to any particular existence.

Here Berkeley describes the activity of abstracting or separating the quality of manhood from a collection of ideas of particular men. The product of the activity must, he thinks, be an image, but it will have to be an image of a very unusual kind. Because all men have both colour and shape, the image of man in general must also have colour and shape, yet it cannot have a *particular* colour and shape without endangering its role as the indifferent representative of all men. If the image, for example, were crooked and white, it would represent a crooked and white man rather than every man. Yet as Berkeley is quick to point out, any image with colour and shape must have a particular colour and shape—a fact he thinks each of us can verify by introspection. Try to imagine something with colour and shape but without any colour or shape in particular: 'The idea of man that I frame to my self,' Berkeley says of his own attempt, 'must be either of a white, or a black, or a tawny, a straight, or a crooked, a tall, or a low, or a middle-sized man.' (Introduction 10.) Because there can be no abstract images, he argues, there can be no abstract ideas.

A similar problem arises for general words that stand for specific qualities. Suppose for the sake of illustration that the word 'scarlet' designates a determinate shade of red. 'Scarlet' is still a 'common name', because it applies to many things, but it is associated, we will suppose, with an absolutely specific shade of colour. What image is linked with the word? It seems that it should be an image of scarlet and nothing else. For suppose it were an image of a scarlet shape. There would then be nothing *in the idea itself* that makes it an idea of scarlet rather than an idea of the shape. The signification of 'scarlet' would be indeterminate. The indeterminacy cannot be eliminated by saying that everything depends on what aspect of the idea we attend to, because according to the Lockean view as Berkeley develops it, the idea or image alone determines the content of our thought. We saw a moment ago that according to that view a single idea cannot represent Berkeley on some occasions and man in general on others, because if such variation were permitted—if the focus of thought could shift from Berkeley to all men even though the same idea remained in view—the idea alone would not determine the content of our thought. For the same reason a single idea cannot function as the idea of a colour on some occasions and the idea of a shape on others. It follows that the idea associated with 'scarlet' must be the idea of scarlet *by itself*, cut off from shape altogether. But a patch of scarlet of no shape whatsoever is as difficult to imagine as a general man.

Scarlet is unlike manhood in one significant respect: we do experience scarlet directly, even if in our experience it is always mixed with shape. Locke claims that although the qualities of the things that affect our senses are united and blended in the things themselves, the ideas produced by those qualities enter through the senses 'simple and unmixed' (*Essay* II ii 1). 'The simple *Ideas* . . . united in the same Subject'—even if they are intromitted by the same sense—'are as perfectly distinct, as those that come in by different Senses.' (§ 1.) But it does seem that if we want an idea of scarlet by itself, we cannot afford to be passive in our reception of ideas, any more than we can be passive in framing our idea of man. The idea of scarlet is always in fact joined to an idea of shape, and even if, early in life, some effort was required to bring the ideas together, surely now an effort is required to pry them apart.[1] Forming an abstract idea of scarlet may be an activity of precision or separation rather than assembly, but it is an activity none the less. Berkeley describes the alleged activity at Introduction 7:

It is agreed on all hands, that the qualities or modes of things do never really exist each of them apart by it self, and separated from all others, but are mixed, as it were, and blended together, several in the same object. But we are told, the mind being able to consider each quality singly, or abstracted from those other qualities with which it is united, does by that means frame to it self abstract ideas. For example, there is perceived by sight an object extended, coloured, and moved: this mixed or compound idea the mind resolving into its

[1] Despite what he says at II ii 1 Locke sometimes says that simple ideas of the same sense are necessarily connected. I discuss this below in sect. 2.

simple, constituent parts, and viewing each by it self, exclusive of the rest, does frame the abstract ideas of extension, colour and motion. Not that it is possible for colour or motion to exist without extension: but only that the mind can frame to it self by *abstraction* the idea of colour exclusive of extension, and of motion exclusive of both colour and extension.

Both varieties of abstraction—the derivation of a general quality such as manhood from ideas of particular men, and the isolation of a specific quality such as scarlet from ideas of scarlet squares, circles, and random blotches—can in fact be regarded as activities of precision or *separation*. In forming the idea of manhood, we separate the general quality of manhood from the individuating qualities of particular men. The quality of manhood is actually a complex of qualities, including both size and shape. If there is no respect in which all men are exactly alike, each of the qualities in the complex will be general rather than specific. In abstracting the quality of manhood we separate each of the constituent general qualities from the specific qualities falling under them. We form, in effect, a number of abstract general ideas, but we keep them together in a cluster, so that they are separated from specific qualities within their respective domains but not from one another. In the case of abstract ideas of specific qualities it is easier, perhaps, to see why the language of separation is appropriate. Specific qualities are like the transparencies which, when carefully overlaid, give us a complete view of the human anatomy. One transparency represents the bones, another the musculature, and a third the arteries and veins. To come up with a representation of one system we simply remove the transparencies depicting the others. In somewhat the same way we form an abstract idea of scarlet by lifting off the other qualities of the scarlet object. In a sense even general qualities—red in general, for example—are present in the things themselves, waiting to be removed, but redness seems to be more closely joined to the specific shades falling under it than a shade of colour is joined to shape.

However the two kinds of abstraction are described, Berkeley thinks that each one calls for an image it is beyond our capacity to form. Just as we are unable to form an image of a man without a particular size, shape, and colour, so we are unable to form an image of a colour without shape or extension:

+   Qu: How can all words be said to stand for ideas? The word Blue 494 stands for a Colour without any extension or abstract from extension. But we have not an idea of Colour without extension. we cannot imagine Colour without extension.

Few philosophers have been convinced by this argument. Perhaps Berkeley is right to insist that images cannot have the very high degree of indeterminacy demanded by the doctrine as he understands it.[2] But even if he is right about images, they say, his argument will miss the mark if abstractionists think of ideas in another way.[3] Others complain that even if we agree that ideas are images, Berkeley's reported failure to form an image of man in general or of colour without extension is a purely personal one, displaying the limits of his own mind but telling us nothing about the limits of the human mind itself.[4] Still others contend that highly abstract images are possible after all. If we are invited to imagine a man, they ask, must we always be able to specify the colour, size, or shape of the man we imagine? If we claim to have imagined our favourite colour, must we retract the claim, or confess to inattention, when we find ourselves unable to say just what shape the colour had? How can Berkeley be so confident that images cannot be indeterminate, when 'corporeal' images such as stick-drawings and clay models often are?

Yet all these complaints are less important than they seem: Berkeley's belief that ideas are images helps to explain his doubts about abstraction, but his main argument against it goes much deeper than anything we have seen so far, and it depends neither on his belief that abstract ideas must be images nor on his personal failure to bring them into introspective focus. The rest of this chapter is devoted to the presentation and analysis of this argument. Although I have been presenting abstraction as a problem for the abstractionists, abstraction —or the phenomenon of general thinking it is supposed to explain—is a problem for Berkeley himself, precisely because he conceives of ideas of imagination as images. If abstract or general thinking involves

[2] Joining Thomas Reid in this assessment are Geoffrey Warnock, *Berkeley*, Oxford, 1982, pp. 68–9; Jonathan Bennett, *Locke, Berkeley, Hume: Central Themes*, Oxford, 1971, p. 36; David Armstrong, ed.'s introduction to *Berkeley's Philosophical Writings*, New York and London, 1965, p. 28; J. L. Mackie, *Problems from Locke*, Oxford, 1976, pp. 115, 123–4; and J. O. Urmson, *Berkeley*, Oxford, 1982, p. 28. Foe Reid see *Essays on the Intellectual Powers of Man*, Essay V, chap. vi, p. 407 in vol. 1 of Sir William Hamilton (ed.), *The Works of Thomas Reid, D.D.*, 7th edn., Edinburgh, 1872.

[3] Those who say this include Mackie, p. 115, and Copleston, *A History of Philosophy*, vol. 5, Westminster, Md., 1959, pp. 216–17.

[4] For this complaint and some reactions to it see two pieces by Willis Doney: 'Is Berkeley's a Cartesian Mind?', in Colin M. Turbayne (ed.), *Berkeley: Critical and Interpretive Essays*, Minneapolis, 1982, pp. 273–82, and 'Berkeley's Argument against Abstract Ideas', *Midwest Studies in Philosophy* 8 (1983), 295–308; as well as Julius Weinberg, 'The Nominalism of Berkeley and Hume', in his *Abstraction, Relation, and Induction*, Madison, 1965, pp. 3–60, esp. pp. 13–24.

ideas, and if all ideas are either imprinted on the senses or excited by the mind, then the ideas involved in general thinking, whose occurrence Berkeley does not deny, must be among the latter. But if the ideas involved in general thinking are ideas of imagination, what is it that makes general thinking general? If an idea of imagination is a copy or likeness of a particular sensation, what is it about the idea that enables the thinker who focuses on it to range over universals, classes, or kinds? Berkeley's answers to these questions will emerge as our analysis proceeds.

1. *The argument*

Before turning to Berkeley's argument I want to take a closer look at the two kinds of abstraction he identifies. At Introduction 10 Berkeley denies that he can 'abstract one from another, or conceive separately, those qualities which it is impossible should exist so separated; or . . . frame a general notion by abstracting from particulars in the manner aforesaid. Which two last are the proper acceptations of *abstraction*.' Abstraction of the first kind is the separation of specific qualities—a determinate shade of red, for example—from qualities of other kinds (such as shape) with which they must occur. Berkeley, as we saw, describes the process at Introduction 7. 'It is agreed on all hands,' he observes, 'that the qualities or modes of things do never really exist each of them apart by it self, and separated from all others, but are mixed, as it were, and blended together, several in the same object.' But according to the abstractionists the mind can pry apart qualities which are inseparable in things themselves: 'we are told, the mind being able to consider each quality singly, or abstracted from those other qualities with which it is united, does by that means frame to it self abstract ideas.' Abstraction of this kind is what Thomas Reid later called abstraction 'strictly so called'.[5]

Abstraction of the second kind is a process of generalization. We have seen it discussed in Introduction 9, where Berkeley takes as an example the formation of the general idea of man. But it makes its first appearance in Introduction 8, where he writes that

The mind having observed that in the particular extensions perceived by sense,

---

[5] *Essays on the Intellectual Powers*, Essay v vi, pp. 394, 395, in vol. 1 of William Hamilton's edn.

there is something common and alike in all, and some other things peculiar, as this or that figure or magnitude, which distinguish them one from another; it considers apart or singles out by it self that which is common, making thereof a most abstract idea of extension, which is neither line, surface, nor solid, nor has any figure or magnitude but is an idea entirely prescinded from all these.

The idea of extension delineated here is 'most abstract' because it has been separated not only from qualities of other kinds with which it must occur, but also from specific or determinate qualities of its own kind. Like the general ideas of colour and motion, whose formation is described later in § 8, the general idea of extension is *doubly* abstract.

The second kind of abstraction is what Thomas Reid called *generalizing*.[6] Reid also recognized a third variety of abstraction: 'the combining into one whole a certain number of those attributes of which we have formed abstract notions, and giving a name to that combination' (p. 394). As we have seen, Berkeley describes this activity in Introduction 9, but he does not believe that it deserves to be ranked as a third kind of abstraction. In Berkeley's opinion it is just another example of what Reid calls generalizing, though the ideas it yields are ideas of 'compound beings'—what are ordinarily called *things*—as opposed to qualities or modes. It is therefore appropriate for Berkeley to open Introduction 9 by indicating that the process of abstraction described there has already been met with:

And as the mind frames to it self abstract ideas of qualities or modes, so does it, by the same precision or mental separation, attain abstract ideas of the more compounded beings, which include several coexistent qualities.

This is followed by a description of the formation of the general idea of man, and Berkeley then goes on to describe the formation of the ideas of animal and body. Berkeley is climbing the tree of Porphyry, moving from the narrowest categories of things (the species) to the wider ones (the genera). Locke had written that 'this whole *mystery* of *Genera* and *Species*, which make such a noise in the Schools, and are, with Justice, so little regarded out of them, is nothing else but abstract *Ideas*, more or less comprehensive, with names annexed to them.' (*Essay* III iii 9.) Berkeley recognizes that there is a distinction worth making between ideas of 'compounded beings'—ideas of genera and species, which were confined by the tradition to what are ordinarily called things— and the abstract ideas of qualities or modes (which can themselves, of

---

[6] Essay v, chap. vi, p. 394, vol. 1 of the *Works*. The next reference in this paragraph is to the same work.

course, be ranked according to their generality), but Berkeley thinks that the two kinds of ideas are abstract in the same way. They are ideas that prescind from whatever is peculiar to the individuals in some group, and they therefore embody only what is 'common and alike in all'.

Berkeley's main argument against abstraction applies to each of the two kinds of abstraction he identifies at Introduction 10, but it is especially clear when applied to the process Reid calls generalizing. Consider the abstract idea of a triangle in general. The idea calls for the mental separation of triangularity—the complex of qualities all triangles share—from the inessential qualities some triangles have and others lack. Triangularity itself is a *universal*, a property capable of existing (or being exemplified) in many different places at the same time. No one doubts that triangularity exists, or at any rate 'occurs', wherever triangles do. It is a separate question whether triangularity is capable of existing by itself. Berkeley's answer is an emphatic no. He claims that all 'things'—and by 'things' in this context he means all entities capable of independent existence—are 'in their own nature *particular*' (Introduction 15). In the First Dialogue he has his spokesman Philonous describe the maxim that '*every thing which exists, is particular*' as 'universally received' (*Works* II, p. 192), and there can be no doubt that when Philonous speaks, Berkeley is thinking of Locke— the only defender of abstraction identified by name in Berkeley's *Principles*—who denies the separate existence of universals several times in the *Essay*.[7]

Return now to the abstract idea of a triangle. To form the idea is to form an idea of triangularity and nothing else. On the view which Berkeley is opposing, the content of our thinking is determined by the idea that we confront in thought. On this assumption, however, we are apparently left with no way of distinguishing between *conceiving of nothing but triangularity* and *conceiving of the separate existence of triangularity*, because either content seems to call for the same idea. If so, it follows that in forming the idea of triangularity, we are conceiving of the separate existence of triangularity—conceiving, in other words, of the impossible. One of Berkeley's most deeply held beliefs is that

---

[7] See III iii 1 and 6. Emphatic pronouncements to this effect can also be found in *Remarks upon some of Mr. Norris's Books*, *The Works of John Locke*, London, 1823, vol. 10, pp. 250, 253, 257. The *Remarks* was written in 1693. On the nominalist background of the *Essay* see J. R. Milton, 'John Locke and the Nominalist Tradition', in Reinhard Brandt (ed.), *John Locke: Symposium Wolfenbüttel 1979*, Berlin, 1981, pp. 128–45.

conceivability and possibility coincide: a state of affairs is conceivable, he thinks, if and only if it is possible. He grants that we can abstract the smell of a rose from the flower itself, or the trunk of a human body from its limbs, but only because these things 'may really exist or be actually perceived asunder' (*Principles* 5). Abstraction in what regards as the strict sense—the mental separation of what cannot exist separately—is absolutely impossible: 'My conceiving or imagining power', he writes at *Principles* 5, 'does not extend beyond the possibility of real existence or perception.' Elsewhere he puts it this way:

It is, I think, a receiv'd axiom that an impossibility cannot be conceiv'd. For what created intelligence will pretend to conceive, that which God cannot cause to be? Now it is on all hands agreed, that nothing abstract or general can be made really to exist, whence it should seem to follow, that it cannot have so much as an ideal existence in the understanding. (First Draft of the Introduction, *Works* II, p. 125.)

Not even God, Berkeley thinks, can create an independently existing universal. And if it is beyond God's power, he asks, how can we hope to conceive of it, since God is certainly able to bring about anything a finite spirit is able to conceive. Berkeley's confidence on this last point is not hard to appreciate: if we can conceive of it God can conceive of it too, but then in view of his omnipotence—which Berkeley defines as the ability to 'indifferently produce every thing by a mere *fiat* or act of . . . will' (*Principles* 152)—what obstacle could there be to his bringing it about?

In two works of the 1730s—*Alciphron* (1732) and *A Defence of Free-thinking in Mathematics* (1735)—Berkeley's argument is presented in another form. The premiss that what is conceivable is possible is replaced by a pair of premisses which entail it: (1) what is conceivable is consistent; and (2) what is consistent is possible. In the *Defence* Berkeley writes,

I desire to know whether it is not possible for anything to exist which doth not include a contradiction: And if it is, whether we may not infer that what cannot possibly exist, the same doth include a contradiction: I further desire to know, whether the reader can frame a distinct idea of anything that includes a contradiction? For my part, I cannot, nor consequently of the above-mentioned triangle; though you (who it seems know better than myself what I can do) are pleased to assure me of the contrary. (§ 46.)

In *Alciphron* VII 6, in the first two editions only, the argument is presented as follows:

EUPHRANOR. Pray, Alciphron, which are those things you would call
absolutely impossible?

ALCIPHRON. Such as include a contradiction.

EUPHRANOR. Can you frame an idea of what includes a contradiction?

ALCIPHRON. I cannot.

EUPHRANOR. Consequently, whatever is absolutely impossible you cannot
form an idea of.

ALCIPHRON. This I grant.   (*Works* III, pp. 333–4.)

Berkeley added the distinctive premisses of the fuller version of the
argument to the second edition of the *Three Dialogues*.

PHILONOUS. I say in the first place, that I do not deny the existence of
material substance, merely because I have no notion of it, but because the
notion of it is inconsistent, or in other words, because it is repugnant there
should be a notion of it. Many things, for ought I know, may exist, whereof
neither I nor any other man hath or can have any idea or notion whatsoever.
But then those things must be possible, that is, nothing inconsistent must be
included in their definition.   (pp. 232–3.)

Philonous says that he cannot conceive of what is inconsistent (thereby
endorsing the premiss that what is conceivable is consistent), and he
identifies possibility with consistency (thereby endorsing the premiss
that what is consistent is possible). These premisses are also present,
though much less obvious, in the first edition of the *Dialogues*. The
premiss that what is consistent is possible (in the form of the equivalent
claim that what is impossible is inconsistent) is accepted by both Hylas
and Philonous in the following exchange at the end of the Second
Dialogue:

PHILONOUS. When is a thing shewn to be impossible?

HYLAS. When a repugnancy is demonstrated between the ideas comprehended
in its definition.   (p. 225.)

The premiss that what is conceivable is consistent is endorsed in the
following exchange, which begins when Philonous asks whether we
can frame an idea of figure abstracted from all other sensible qualities.

HYLAS. Let me think a little—I do not find that I can.

PHILONOUS. And can you think it possible, that should really exist in Nature,
which implies a repugnancy in its conception?

HYLAS. By no means.

PHILONOUS. Since therefore it is impossible even for the mind to disunite
the ideas of extension and motion from all other sensible qualities, doth it

not follow, that where the one exist, there necessarily the other exist
likewise?   (p. 194.)

Philonous's aim here is to convince Hylas that figure cannot be
separated from qualities such as colour because it cannot be separated
from them in thought. His argument calls for the premiss that what is
inconceivable is impossible, which is *not* one of the premisses in
Berkeley's case against abstraction. But in developing his argument
Philonous asserts an equivalence between conceivability and the
absence of repugnancy, and 'repugnancy' was a common eighteenth-
century synonym for 'contradiction'.[8] Philonous treats Hylas's failure
to separate figure from other sensible qualities as evidence that there is
a repugnancy implied by the separation. The very phrase 'a repugnancy
in its *conception*' indicates that as Philonous and Berkeley understand
them, inconsistency and inconceivability are at bottom the same. To
identify them is to accept the premiss that what is conceivable is
consistent.

Berkeley's argument against abstract ideas can be summarized as
follows. What an abstract idea purports to represent is impossible. But
what is impossible is inconsistent, and what is inconsistent cannot be
conceived. It follows that there can be no abstract ideas.

Although Berkeley's main argument against abstraction is clearest
when applied to the formation of general ideas, it applies in very much
the same way to ideas of specific qualities such as a determinate shade
of red. At Introduction 10 Berkeley admits that he is able 'to abstract in
one sense, as when I consider some particular parts or qualities
separated from others, with which though they are united in some
object, yet, it is possible they may really exist without them'. He then
issues the denial already quoted above: 'I deny that I can abstract one
from another, or conceive separately, those qualities which it is
impossible should exist so separated; or that I can frame a general
notion by abstracting from particulars in the manner aforesaid.' Here
Berkeley makes it clear that he has no objection to ideas of what is
genuinely possible. He speaks of 'those qualities which it is impossible
should exist so separated' not only to clarify his argument, but because
he realizes that it is perfectly possible for qualities joined in experience
to be disunited. A rose, for example, might lose its characteristic odour,
though its visible and tangible qualities remain the same. In general,
Berkeley thinks that the qualities detected by one sense can always be

----

[8] See the opening pp. of Chap. 4 below.

separated, both in the world and in thought, from the qualities detected by another.

Now the abstract idea of a determinate shade of red is, Berkeley thinks, an idea of quality separated from other qualities with which it must occur. It is what might be called an *incomplete* idea, because the single quality it represents is not a complete being able to exist on its own. In this respect it is similar to many of the ideas we allegedly arrive at by generalization: the abstract idea of triangularity, for example, fails to include the colour or tangible texture that must accompany extension or shape. The idea of triangularity is therefore incomplete in the same way as the idea of a determinate shade of red, even though it claims to represent a compounded being. Berkeley did not, it seems, take notice of this similarity. But in any case the incompleteness of the ideas of Introduction 7 makes them vulnerable to Berkeley's argument against abstraction. What an incomplete idea purports to represent is impossible. But what is impossible cannot be conceived. It follows that there can be no incomplete ideas.

Berkeley fails to notice a further similarity between incomplete and general ideas. He does not see that although the idea of a determinate shade of red is specific, it is general or universal in the sense required by his argument. Even absolutely determinate shades of colour can be shared by many things, and the separate existence of such a shade would therefore violate the maxim that every existing thing is a particular. It is curious that Berkeley does not make this observation himself, though it is noteworthy perhaps that in *Alciphron* and the *Defence of Free-thinking in Mathematics*, he says nothing about abstract ideas of specific qualities. Instead he concentrates entirely on 'general' ideas. Perhaps he came to realize that even an idea of a determinate shade of red is 'general' in the required sense. Whatever the reason for the change, there is no room for doubt that in the Introduction to the *Principles*, Berkeley's central objection to abstract ideas of determinate or specific qualities is that they claim to represent what cannot possibly exist. In view of his commitment to the belief that anything impossible is contradictory or repugnant, he should therefore be prepared to say that the separate existence of a determinate shade of red is no less repugnant than the separate existence of triangularity or manhood.

Berkeley's objection to abstract ideas is the same, then, whether the ideas are general or specific. If we had the power to frame an idea of either kind, we would have the power to conceive of a being it is beyond even the power of God to create. Abstraction was associated by many of its defenders with the imperfection of the human mind. According to Locke, for example, abstract ideas are 'marks of our Imperfection' (*Essay* IV vii 9). God, we can presume, has no need of them at all, because his infinite mind is able to survey an entire range of particulars at once. Though the power of abstraction places man above the brutes (II xi 10–11), the need for it places him below God. Abstraction is the comparatively imperfect way in which a limited mind conceives of a very large class. John Norris agrees with Locke that abstraction is 'occasion'd by the Infirmity of the Understanding', and that a 'perfect intelligence' has no need of it.[9] Berkeley's complaint is that the defenders of abstraction have inadvertently assigned to the human mind a power that goes beyond the power of God. Abstraction is rejected because God's power cannot be superseded, because the limits of the divine mind coincide with the limits of the world.

2. *Objections and replies*

'What right does Berkeley have,' it might be asked, 'to say that God cannot create the entities which abstract ideas allegedly represent? If God is really omnipotent he should be able to do so, but if he is, then the entities are possible after all and Berkeley's argument collapses.' The reply to this objection turns on Berkeley's understanding of impossibility. When Berkeley calls something impossible, he means that it is contradictory or inconsistent. A thing is shown to be impossible, Hylas tells Philonous, 'when a repugnancy is demonstrated between the ideas comprehended in its definition' (p. 225). Those things which are absolutely impossible, Alciphron tells Euphranor, are 'such as include a contradiction' (*Alciphron* VII 6, in the first two editions only, *Works* III, p. 334). The fact that Berkeley attributes these views to representatives of positions he opposes means not that he does not accept them himself, but that he takes them to be widely held. The Berkeleyan arguments made by Philonous and Euphranor will be all the more effective if they turn on premises volunteered by Hylas and Alciphron.

An example of an inconsistent or contradictory state of affairs is the

---

[9] *An Essay towards the Theory of the Idea or Intelligible World*, London, 1701–4, vol. 2, p. 176. The same sentiment is expressed by Suarez, *On the Various Kinds of Distinctions*, trans. Cyrus Vollert, Milwaukee, 1947, p. 21: 'The divine intellect never makes a mental distinction.'

existence of a four-sided triangle. Because a triangle is three-sided by definition, the suggestion that a triangle might be a triangle and four-sided at one and the same time is inconsistent, and because it is inconsistent, not even God can bring a four-sided triangle into being. If God creates a triangle, then by definition he creates a figure with three sides, and if he creates a figure with four sides, then by the same definition he creates something other than a triangle. Berkeley thinks that the entities represented by abstract ideas are, like four-sided triangles or married bachelors, inconsistent. He therefore concludes that even God is powerless to create them. It is not as if God can conceive of the entities, but finds himself frustrated when he attempts to give what he conceives a wordly form. It is 'impossible even for an infinite mind to reconcile contradictions' (*Principles* 129). The apparent limit on God's power is therefore no limit at all. An omnipotent being is not a being who can do anything at all, but a being who can do anything that can be done.

The defence I have just provided succeeds only if the separate existence of the entities in question really is contradictory or inconsistent. Can Berkeley prove that it is? We can see the magnitude of the problem he faces if we look more closely at the notion of a married bachelor. It is easy to show that the notion is inconsistent because the notion of a bachelor is itself complex. We can analyse *being a bachelor* into *being a man who is unmarried*, and because to call a man unmarried is to deny that he is married, 'married bachelor' is a clear contradiction. But the idea of triangularity is different. It is derived from ideas of particular triangles, just as the idea of man in general is derived from ideas of particular men, and Berkeley's account of such derivation at Introduction 9 suggests that the idea of triangularity is *part* of every idea of a particular triangle.[10] Yet the idea of any particular triangle must be consistent (otherwise the triangle would not exist), and if it is, how can we come up with an inconsistent idea simply by removing or abstracting a certain part of it? The abstract idea of scarlet presents the same problem, since framing the idea is simply a matter of removing the ideas in its company. The possibility of contradiction or inconsistency seems to depend on opposition between elements in a complex ('repugnancy', as Hylas puts it, between ideas comprehended in a definition), and if the opposition is not there in the complex to begin with, it hardly seems possible to introduce it by simplification. This is one of the deepest problems in Berkeley's

[10] At *Essay* III 9 Locke speaks of more general ideas as parts of the less general ideas ranged beneath them.

philosophy. On the one hand, he wants to understand necessity and possibility objectively. He does not want to claim that something is impossible to be nothing more than a report of the failure of some mind or other to conceive of it. He identifies impossibility with inconsistency because he wants the claim to tell us that *no one*—not even God—can conceive of it. On the other hand, Berkeley's objective test of inconsistency—the analysis of complex notions into their constituent parts and the subsequent search for oppositions—does not allow him to prove that everything he wants to call impossible really is. We will be looking more deeply into this problem in the two chapters that follow.

It would be a mistake to conclude that the problem we have identified robs Berkeley's argument of all its force. This is because it was taken for granted by Berkeley's contemporaries that abstraction involves the separation in thought of things that are inseparable in the world. John Norris writes for example that 'Where things are really separate or distinct, then considering them apart is not *Abstraction*, but only a mere divided Consideration.'[11] He observes that 'Abstraction is, as it were, the drawing of a thing away from it self.' (Compare these remarks to *Principles* 5, where Berkeley gives the same analysis of the proper meaning of abstraction, and says that he might as easily 'divide a thing from it self' as abstract the being of a thing from its being perceived.) Isaac Watts, whose *Logick* of 1725 is a compendium of entrenched distinctions, calls attention to the difference between *negative* abstraction, which occurs when 'we consider one Thing separate from another, which may also exist without it', and *precisive* abstraction, which occurs when 'we consider those Things apart which cannot really exist apart; as when we consider a *Mode* without considering its *Substance* and *Subject*, or *one essential Mode* without another'.[12] Even if Berkeley's argument fails to show that abstract ideas are absolutely impossible, then, it can succeed as an *ad hominem* argument against the defenders of abstraction; *ad hominem* not in the sense that it attacks a position by insulting the person who takes it up, but in the sense that it attacks the position of a concrete opponent, whose other commitments may rule the position out.

Locke himself accepts every one of the explicit premises in

---

[11] *An Essay towards the Theory of the Ideal or Intelligible World*, vol. 2, p. 174. The following remark appears on the same page.

[12] *Logick, Or, The Right Use of Reason in the Enquiry after Truth*, London, 1725, p. 200. Watts's distinction can be traced as far back as St Thomas Aquinas, *Summa Theologiae* Ia. 85, 1, p. 53 in *Summa Theologiae*, vol. 12 (Ia 84–9), New York, 1968, and Suarez, *On the Various Kinds of Distinctions*, p. 19.

Berkeley's case against abstraction: abstract ideas represent the impossible; what is impossible is inconsistent; and what is inconsistent cannot be conceived. We have already taken note of Locke's claim in the *Essay* that 'all things that exist are only particulars' (III iii 6). In *An Examination of P. Malebranche's Opinion* he strengthens this by adding that its truth is necessary: 'Whatever exists is particular,' he writes, 'it cannot be otherwise.'[12] At *Essay* III x 33 he says that

> if I put in my *Ideas* of mixed Modes or Relations, any inconsistent *Ideas* together, I fill my Head also with *Chimæras*; since such *Ideas*, if well examined, cannot so much as exist in the Mind, much less any real Being, be ever denominated from them.

Berkeley cites this remark in § 125 of *A New Theory of Vision*, and though it concerns only mixed modes and relations, Berkeley rightly takes it to commit Locke to the inconceivability of inconsistent ideas. Locke does not state the remaining premiss in an unrestricted form, but he does say at *Essay* IV iii 6 that his reason for supposing matter may think is that 'I see no contradiction in it'. What is consistent, then, must be possible. Locke admits that the general idea of a triangle is 'something imperfect, that cannot exist' (IV vii 9), which is his way of saying that the object of the idea cannot be realized.[14] From this, Berkeley thinks, Locke should have concluded that the idea cannot be formed. We can conceive of something that cannot exist only if the impossible item is consistent, or, supposing it is inconsistent, if we are able to conceive of it anyway. Locke, however, denies both possibilities.

Locke also agrees with Berkeley that certain specific qualities are necessarily connected. 'Some few of the primary Qualities have a necessary dependence, and visible connexion one with another,' he writes at *Essay* IV iii 14, 'as Figure necessarily presupposes Extension'. At II xiii 11 he writes,

> 'Tis true, Solidity cannot exist without Extension, neither can Scarlet-Colour exist without Extension; but this hinders not, but that they are distinct *Ideas*. Many *Ideas* require others as necessary to their Existence or Conception, which are yet very distinct *Ideas*. Motion can neither be, nor be conceived without Space; yet Motion is not Space, nor Space Motion.

Discerning the necessary connections among simple ideas is, in fact, one of the prerequisites of fruitful inquiry.

---

[13] § 45, p. 241 in *The Works of John Locke*, vol. 9.
[14] Berkeley reads Locke's admission as I do here. See *A Defence of Free-thinking in Mathematics* 45.

'Tis not easie for the Mind to put off those confused Notions and Prejudices it has imbibed from Custom, Inadvertency, and common Conversation: it requires pains and assiduity to examine its *Ideas*, till it resolves them into those clear and distinct simple ones, out of which they are compounded; and to see which, amongst its simple ones, have or have not a necessary connexion and dependence one upon another: Till a Man doth this in the primary and original Notions of Things, he builds upon floating and uncertain Principles, •
and will often find himself at a loss. (ii xiii 27.)

Locke, then, accepts every explicit premiss in Berkeley's argument against abstraction. But the argument depends for its success on a suppressed premiss which Locke can and does disown.

Locke can escape Berkeley's argument by making a simple distinction. 'It is true that I cannot conceive of the separate existence of triangularity,' he might say, 'but why suppose that I conceive of any such thing when I form the abstract idea of a triangle? There is a difference between conceiving of nothing but triangularity, and conceiving of its separate existence; while the latter is impossible for the very reason you suggest, only the former is required by my doctrine of abstraction.' Locke will be able to take advantage of this defence if he conceives of abstraction as selective attention. 'When I conceive of nothing but triangularity,' he can say, 'the only ideas before my mind are perfectly ordinary ideas of particular triangles. They have all the complexity characteristic of particular ideas, but I ignore all that and focus on triangularity—the one quality they have in common.' To conceive of abstraction as selective attention or partial consideration is to deny what I call the *content assumption*—the assumption that the content of thought is determined by its object. On the view I am now suggesting might be Locke's, we may be thinking of a particular triangle or of triangularity in general while confronting one and the same idea, *depending on how much of the idea we attend to.* The content assumption is essential to Berkeley's argument, because only on that assumption can he move from the claim that we cannot conceive of the separate existence of triangularity (a claim entailed by those premisses in the argument Locke himself accepts) to the conclusion that we cannot frame the abstract idea of a triangle. If he denies the content assumption, Locke has no obligation to account for the abstract character of our thinking by pointing to a strangely abbreviated object of thought. He can grant that it is impossible to form an idea which, due to its internal features, represents nothing but triangularity, but he can add that this in no way detracts from our ability to attend selectively to our ideas. The burden would then be on Berkeley to prove that the distinction between conceiving of nothing but triangularity and conceiving of its separate existence cannot be maintained. But it is a distinction Berkeley accepts himself: 'We may consider Peter so far forth as man, or so far forth as animal,' he writes, '. . . inasmuch as all that is perceived is not considered'—that is, inasmuch as all that an idea contains is not attended to (Introduction 16, in the second edition only). Berkeley even appeals to our capacity for selective attention to explain how a geometrical proof involving the diagram of a particular triangle can nevertheless apply to any triangle whatsoever. He explains that the individuating features of the triangle are not 'concerned in the demonstration'. 'And here it must be acknowledged', he adds, 'that a man may consider a figure merely as a triangular. . . . So far he may abstract' (Introduction 16, in the second edition only).

Several scholars have argued that Locke conceives of abstraction as selective attention.[15] The decisive text is *Essay* II xiii 13, where Locke argues that body and extension are two distinct ideas. The two ideas are distinct, he maintains, because the parts of body are separable but the parts of space or pure extension are not, even in thought. 'For I demand of any one, to remove any part of [space] from another, with which it is continued, even so much as in Thought.' 'To divide and separate actually,' he continues,

is, as I think, by removing the parts one from another, to make two Superficies, where before there was a Continuity: And to divide mentally, is to make in the Mind two Superficies, where before there was a Continuity, and consider them as removed one from the other; which can only be done in things considered by the Mind, as capable of being separated; and by separation, of acquiring new distinct Superficies, which they then have not, but are capable of: But neither of these ways of Separation, whether real or mental, is, as I think, compatible to pure *Space*.

In spite of this, Locke believes, we can 'consider so much of such a *Space*, as is answerable or commensurate to a Foot, without considering the rest; which is indeed a partial Consideration, but not so much as mental Separation, or Division'. Partial consideration and

---

[15] A recent example is Mackie, *Problems from Locke*, pp. 107–12. See also Michael Ayers, 'Locke's Doctrine of Abstraction: Some Aspects of its Historical and Philosophical Significance', in Brandt (ed.), *John Locke*, pp. 5–24, and C. C. W. Taylor, 'Berkeley's Theory of Abstract Ideas', *The Philosophical Quarterly* 28 (1978), 97–115, esp. pp. 99–105.

mental separation are wholly different: 'A Man may consider Light in the Sun, without its Heat; or Mobility in Body without its Extension, without thinking of their separation. One is only a partial Consideration, terminating in one alone; and the other is a Consideration of both, as existing separately.'

Locke does not connect these remarks with his discussions of abstraction, where the vocabulary of separation or division is at least as prominent as the vocabulary of consideration. At II xi 9, for example, we are told that abstract ideas are 'precise, naked Appearances in the Mind', which we hold there 'without *considering*, how, whence or with what others they came there' (emphasis mine). But five pages later at II xii 1, abstraction is defined as 'separating [ideas] from all other *Ideas* that accompany them in their real existence'. Which way of speaking represents his real view? We know from his discussion of the inseparability of the parts of space that Locke, like Berkeley, is unwilling to allow mental separation where he refuses to allow actual separation. He is committed to this, of course, by his views on the relations among conceivability, possibility, and consistency, and he seems to accept the need for it in other places, for example at *Essay* II xiii 21, where he maintains that there is no necessary connection between space and solidity because we can conceive of the first without the second. In view of his belief that everything that exists is particular, then, it would be unwise for him to regard abstraction as mental separation or division. Locke needs the distinction between mental separation (which entails the possibility of actual separation) and partial consideration (which does not) in order to harmonize his account of abstraction with his metaphysical presuppositions. We therefore have no choice but to suppose that at II xii 1, where he resorts to the language of separation, Locke is speaking loosely or metaphorically. We should suppose, that is, that he denies the content assumption.

We have seen that Berkeley denies the content assumption, but he attributes it to Locke. How can Berkeley make the attribution so confidently? The answer lies, I think, in Locke's use of the word 'idea'. Locke sometimes writes as if ideas determine the content of thought, but when he does, he is not thinking of ideas as the objects of thought—as entities we confront in the way we confront images and pains—but as the acts of thought themselves.[16] On this interpretation

---

[16] For a study of Locke's views on the nature of ideas see John Yolton, 'Locke and Malebranche: Two Concepts of Ideas', pp. 208–24 in Brandt (ed.), *John Locke*, as well as

of 'idea', the claim that ideas determine the content of thought is true, but trivially so. Ideas, on this interpretation, do not *explain* the content of thought. At other times Locke writes as if ideas are objects, but then he tends *not* to suppose that they determine content. Berkeley is much more definite in his understanding of ideas: he thinks of them as a kind of object. So definite is his understanding that he cannot help but suppose it is Locke's understanding too. The result is that when Locke writes as if ideas determine content, Berkeley takes him to be saying that the objects of thought determine content, and the possibility that Locke conceives of abstraction as selective attention never occurs to him. Berkeley then treats selective attention and the accompanying denial of the content assumption as his own philosophical discoveries, though they may well have been made (admittedly in less clear a form) by Locke himself. Berkeley's anti-abstractionist argument fails, then, even as an *ad hominem* case against Locke.

Berkeley's discovery of selective attention complicates and enriches his belief that representation involves resemblance. A general idea of man—the idea of a particular man which is transformed by the mind into a representative of every man—resembles the men it represents, but it does not resemble them in every detail. In a letter to Samuel Molyneux, Berkeley says that an idea can represent a thing even when it resembles it 'very rudely', and does 'not in each Circumstance accurately correspond with it' (8 December 1709; *Works* VIII, p. 25). But resemblance remains a necessary condition of representation even if the resemblance between idea and object can vary in exactness. And Berkeley's general ideas, unlike the abstract general ideas he takes to be defended by Locke, are exact copies of particular men, or copies as exact as their diminished vivacity allows. '*Universality*,' Berkeley explains at Introduction 15, consists 'not . . . in the absolute, positive nature or conception of any thing, but in the relation it bears to the particulars signified or represented by it: by virtue whereof it is that things, names, or notions, being in their own nature *particular*, are rendered *universal*.' The particular idea I consider in the course of a demonstration 'doth equally stand for and represent all rectilinear triangles whatsoever, and is in that sense *universal*' (Introduction 15),

Yolton's *Perceptual Acquaintance from Descartes to Reid*, Minneapolis, 1984, pp. 88–104. Yolton's more recent views are discussed by Michael Ayers in 'Are Locke's "Ideas" Images, Intentional Objects or Natural Signs?', *The Locke Newsletter* 17 (1986), 3–36. See also Yolton's earlier book *Locke and the Compass of Human Understanding*, Cambridge, 1970, pp. 118–37, and the essays by Douglas Greenlee, Gunnar Aspelin, and H. E. Matthews in I. C. Tipton (ed.), *Locke on Human Understanding*, Oxford, 1977.

but in its own nature it is nothing but a particular idea of sense or imagination.[17]

Berkeley's emphasis on selective attention or partial consideration lends support to my earlier contention that he thinks of ideas as objects of thought and distinguishes them from the acts of mind that focus on them. A single idea—a single object of thought—can be the focus of different acts, and the content of those acts will be determined jointly by the intrinsic nature of the object and the character of the act.

I said earlier that Berkeley's argument fails, even as an *ad hominem* one against Locke, because Locke does not accept the content assumption. Other commentators have made a similar point about Berkeley's imagism: the anti-abstractionist argument depends on the assumption that ideas are images, they say, and because this assumption needn't be made by the abstractionists themselves, the argument fails.[18] This criticism is, I think, misguided, and in the following section I try to explain why.

3. *Abstract ideas as images*

In this section I will assume agreement on the premises in the argument against abstraction that Berkeley states explicitly: first, all things are necessarily particular, and some qualities are necessarily connected with others (for example, motion with extension, colour with shape); second, anything impossible involves a contradiction or 'repugnancy'; and third, contradictions or repugnancies cannot be conceived. (My presentation will actually depend not on the second and third propositions but on a proposition they together entail: nothing impossible can be conceived.) We have already seen that Berkeley's argument succeeds against anyone who accepts these premises and at the same time believes that abstract ideas are images, provided he or she also accepts the content assumption. This is because anyone who meets all of these conditions is left with no way of distinguishing between *conceiving of nothing but triangularity or manhood* (which the abstractionist wants to allow) and *conceiving of the separate*

---

[17] Berkeley's account of general thinking is developed further at Introduction 18. Taylor provides a useful evaluation of the account in 'Berkeley's Theory of Abstract Ideas', esp. pp. 111–15.

[18] George Pitcher gives a powerful defence of this view in *Berkeley*, London, 1977, pp. 62–90.

existence of triangularity or manhood (which anyone who accepts the three premisses is committed to deny). The argument does not succeed against someone who believes that general ideas are images but denies the content assumption. Berkeley fits this description himself, and he is safe from the implications of his own argument because he interprets abstraction as selective attention. The mind can attend selectively to images as well as it can to anything else. Hence the belief that abstract or general ideas are images does not entail the impossibility of abstract or general ideas, even for those who accept every explicit premiss in Berkeley's argument.

The question before us is whether the argument succeeds *only* against those who believe that abstract ideas are images. Imagine an abstractionist who accepts the content assumption and thinks of ideas as the objects of thought, though he or she does not believe that these objects are images. I will not say exactly what these objects are taken to be; I share David Armstrong's view that if abstractionists take ideas to be objects and yet do not take them to be images, it is hard to tell what sort of object they have in mind.[19] If the abstractionist we are imagining accepts the explicit premisses in Berkeley's argument, he or she is committed to the conclusion that we are unable to conceive of the separate existence of universals or of qualities, such as determinate shades of colour, necessarily connected with others. In order to defend the possibility of abstraction he or she must therefore say that we can conceive of such objects abstractly without conceiving of their separate existence. The difficulty is this: so long as he or she accepts the content assumption, there is no apparent way of distinguishing between partial consideration and what Locke calls 'mental separation'. Because the hypothetical abstractionist accepts the content assumption, any difference between *conceiving of triangularity apart from particular triangles* and *conceiving of the separate existence of triangularity* can only depend on differences in the corresponding objects of thought. But it is not obvious what difference in the objects could account for the difference in content. Berkeley's argument therefore presents an explanatory challenge to anyone who accepts the content assumption, whether or not he or she believes that ideas are images.

It might be objected that if the argument has nothing more to offer than an explanatory challenge, then it is not the success that Berkeley makes it out to be. The argument fails to establish the 'impossibility of

---

[19] Ed.'s introd. to *Berkeley's Philosophical Writings*, p. 28.

abstract ideas' (Introduction 21). But this is equally true of the argument when it is made against someone who *identifies* ideas with images, not only because the identification is compatible with denying the content assumption, but also because the argument does not close out the possibility of distinguishing between an image that represents triangularity 'apart' and an image that represents its separate existence. The argument simply points out that no way of making the distinction has so far been provided. The complaint that Berkeley's argument depends on the belief that ideas are images, then, is misleading in two ways. First, it suggests that the argument succeeds against anyone who accepts the belief, a suggestion which is false, since such a person might (like Berkeley) deny the content assumption. Second, it suggests that the argument owes whatever strength it has to the belief. But even if it fails to prove that abstract ideas are impossible, Berkeley's argument confronts the defenders of abstraction with an explanatory task, one which is of far greater magnitude for some of those who do not identify ideas with images (for those, that is, who make the content assumption) than it is for some of those who do.

Not every abstractionist will be disturbed by Berkeley's explanatory challenge. One way to deny the content assumption is to deny that ideas are entities at all. An abstractionist who makes this denial will not suppose that ideas account (even in part) for the content of thought. He or she will regard ideas as either acts of thought (modifications of the mind) or intentional objects, and what he or she says about ideas will then be a *description* of what passes in our minds, rather than an explanation of it. In the hands of such a natural historian of the mind the claim that we can form 'abstract ideas' will amount to nothing more than a recognition of the fact that we sometimes think in abstract or general terms. At times our thoughts are confined to the particular or concrete, he or she will say, but at other times they rise to the general or abstract. The 'doctrine of abstract ideas' will merely record this fact and make no effort to explain it. Reid, who depending on the context thinks of ideas as either acts of the mind or intentional objects (which he calls 'things barely conceived'), is an example of an abstractionist who sacrifices explanation.[20] He recognizes the existence of abstract thinking—of what he calls 'general conceptions'—but he does not try to explain it. 'As to the manner how we conceive universals', he writes, 'I confess my ignorance' (p. 407). We can no more explain how we

[20] All quotations in this paragraph are from *Essays* V vi in vol. 1 of the Hamilton edn. of Reid's *Works*.

think abstractly than we can explain how we hear, see, and remember. 'In all our original faculties, the fabric and manner of operation is, I apprehend, beyond our comprehension, and perhaps is perfectly understood by him only who made them.' (pp. 407–8.) But it would be rash, he warns, thinking no doubt of Berkeley, to deny 'a fact of which we are conscious' merely because we do not know how it is brought about (p. 408).

4. *Abstract ideas as objects*

Berkeley's explanatory challenge cannot disturb an abstractionist who does not aim at explanation. I indicated earlier that Locke sometimes speaks of ideas as acts of thought or modifications of the mind. In these passages Locke's ideas, like Reid's, do not play an explanatory role. But it is noteworthy that this way of speaking is not found in Locke's discussions of abstraction. There he speaks of ideas as entities with an explanatory role. His doctrine of selective attention or partial consideration portrays ideas as objects we confront. We attend to various aspects of them, but the ideas themselves are there before the mind in their full particularity, explaining why we are thinking in general terms about men as opposed to horses. It is therefore fair to say that Locke's rejection of the content assumption is not as radical or complete as the rejection found in Reid. Although he rejects the content assumption, Locke sometimes thinks of an idea as an existing object of thought. It is, of course, misleading to call an idea 'abstract' merely because it is partially considered: there is no inherent difference between an idea we confront when we think of manhood and the idea we confront when we think of some particular man. The word 'abstract', instead of modifying the object, should modify the act. Berkeley's belief that Locke accepts the content assumption must have been encouraged by the fact that Locke speaks of 'abstract ideas' and describes them as 'precise, naked Appearances' (II xi 9). If a philosopher speaks of ideas as objects—as Locke does in his discussions of abstraction, even when he is denying the content assumption—and if he speaks of those ideas as if they are somehow special—as Locke does when he describes certain ideas as 'abstract', 'naked', or 'precise'—it is not hard to see how even the most careful reader might suppose that he accepts the content assumption.

We have seen how an interest in explanation might discourage someone who denies the assumption from coming to the more extreme conclusion that thought about sensible things does not require an existing object. Selective attention allows for play in the representative scope of an idea, but there is an outer limit on the scope of the idea which is set by its physiognomy. In Berkeley we find an account of abstract thinking consistent with his account of intentionality. But it might still be asked why, if the object of thought does not determine content, we need to have an object at all. Berkeley does not ever ask this question, but he comes closest to doing so in *Alciphron*. In the Seventh Dialogue Alciphron presents Euphranor with an argument that Christian faith is impossible. The argument rests on the general assumption that every form of assent—religous faith as well as scientific acceptance—has an idea as its object. If there is no idea annexed to a term, Alciphron insists that 'it can be neither the subject of a rational dispute, nor the object of real faith' (*Works* III, p. 290). 'There can be no assent where there are no ideas: and where there is no assent there can be no faith: and what cannot be, that no man is obliged to do. This is as clear as anything in Euclid!' (p. 291.) Because the word *grace*, 'the main point in the Christian dispensation' (p. 289), does not stand for an idea, Alciphron concludes that faith is neither possible nor obligatory.

Euphranor's response is to barrage Alciphron with instances of meaningful words that do not stand for ideas: *myself, will, memory, love, hate, number*, and *force*. He gives *force* the most attention, because it allows him to argue that if Alciphron were right about Christian faith, his argument would threaten the scientific convictions that fortify his opposition to religion. We have no distinct idea of force, Euphranor argues, but this is no obstacle to holding beliefs about it:

There are very evident propositions or theorems relating to force, which contain useful truths. . . . Doth not the doctrine of the composition and resolution of forces depend upon it, and, in consequence thereof, numberless rules and theorems directing men how to act, and explaining phenomena throughout the Mechanics and mathematical philosophy? And if, by considering this doctrine of force, men arrive at the knowledge of many inventions in Mechanics, and are taught to frame engines, by means of which things difficult and otherwise impossible may be performed; and if the same doctrine which is so beneficial here below serveth also as a key to discover the nature of the celestial motions; shall we deny that it is of use, either in practice or speculation, because we have no distinct idea of force? (pp. 295–6.)

Euphranor concludes that for all Alciphron has said, grace 'may ... be an object of our faith, and influence our life and actions'.

In Chapter 1 we saw that even in the *Principles* Berkeley had identified two broad groups of words that do not stand for ideas: words designating spirits or their acts and operations, and words expressing relations. The word *grace* should probably be treated as a word designating an act or operation of God. The detailed account of the meaningfulness of *force* is intended less as an analogy to the way in which grace acquires its meaning than as a reminder to Alciphron of how much will be lost if he insists on saying that all significant words stand for ideas. But the discussion of *force* is important because it goes beyond anything said in the *Principles*. The kind of force that is at stake—*physical* force—is not a property of spirit, and the word expressing it is not relational but substantive. Euphranor's account of the meaningfulness of force shows that even a word whose linguistic role gives every indication that it stands for an idea acquires its meaning in another way. When we 'think about force' there is no distinct object before our mind that represents force. But this does not show that Berkeley came to the conclusion that thinking about things does not require an existing object. Thinking about force does not require an existing object that represents force, but it does require existing objects representing the sensible things whose behaviour the word *force* helps to describe. (These objects, as Berkeley repeatedly emphasizes, need not be thought of at every step in our reasoning.) Thought about sensible things calls for distinct objects that represent those things, but not every word that is *apparently* or *nominally* substantive actually stands for such an object.

In this chapter I have shown that Berkeley's case against abstraction does not rest on his belief that ideas are images. Instead of drawing attention to his imagism, a proper understanding of Berkeley's central argument calls attention to another belief which should guide the interpretation of his imagism: his belief that the content assumption is mistaken. Berkeley believes ideas are images because he sees no other way of securing the intentionality of thought regarding sensible things. Yet the images we contemplate do not determine what we think, because the mind is free to ignore selected features. A proper understanding of Berkeley's argument also exhibits his commitment to an objective interpretation of the modal notions, an interpretation that pivots on the notion of a contradiction or 'repugnancy'. In the following two chapters we will take a closer look at that commitment.

Appendix: Does Berkeley blunder in reading Locke?

I have argued that Berkeley is wrong to assign the content assumption to Locke. But is it true that he blunders in reading Locke's description of the general idea of a triangle, as many commentators have alleged?[21]

For example, Does it not require some pains and skill to form the *general Idea* of a *Triangle*, (which is yet none of the most abstract, comprehensive, and difficult,) for it must be neither Oblique, nor Rectangle, neither Equilateral, Equicrural, nor Scalenon; but all and none of these at once. In effect, it is something imperfect, that cannot exist; an *Idea* wherein some parts of several different and inconsistent *Ideas* are put together. (*Essay* IV vii 9.)

In quoting Locke, Berkeley underlines the words 'all and none' and 'inconsistent'. He refers back to the description in the closing lines of Introduction 13:

What more easy than for any one to look a little into his own thoughts, and there try whether he has, or can attain to have, an idea that shall correspond with the description that is here given of the general idea of a triangle, which is, *neither oblique, nor rectangle, equilateral, equicrural, nor scalenon, but all and none of these at once?*

How does Berkeley read Locke's description? The question is not what Berkeley concludes about the idea, but what he thinks Locke intends to say about it. There are two basic possibilities. On the one hand, Berkeley may read the description in the way it is natural to read his own descriptions of abstract ideas at Introduction 8 and 9. These descriptions suggest that abstract ideas acquire their generality by a sacrifice of detail. The abstract idea of man, for example, includes colour, but no particular colour, and stature, but no particular stature. On the other hand, the description might be read as saying that generality is acquired by an accretion of detail which yields an idea of overwhelming richness. The usual view is that Berkeley reads the description in this second, ungenerous, way. According to R. I. Aaron, for example, Berkeley takes Locke to be saying that 'the general idea of a triangle is a complex idea containing within itself contradictory simple ideas, an idea, therefore, which is both absurd and impossible' (p. 195). 'Why', Aaron asks, 'should we attribute so absurd a view to a

---

[21] This is the view taken by R. I. Aaron, *John Locke*, 3rd edn., Oxford, 1971, pp. 195–6. Aaron is followed by E. J. Craig, 'Berkeley's Attack on Abstract Ideas,' *Philosophical Review* 77 (1968), 425–37. It is also accepted by Julius Weinberg in an essay to which I am otherwise very much indebted: 'The Nominalism of Berkeley and Hume', p. 14.

great thinker?' (p. 196.) He goes on to present what he takes to be the correct reading of Locke's description:

Surely all Locke wishes to say is that the general idea of a triangle—whatever it be—stands for the oblique, the rectangle, the equilateral, the equicrural, and the scalenon triangles, without being any one of them in particular. (p. 196.)

Aaron reads Locke's description in the way it is natural to read Berkeley's own descriptions at Introduction 8 and 9. But Aaron attributes a very different reading to Berkeley, a reading so insensitive he is forced to characterize Berkeley as a 'young enthusiast' whose eagerness to refute Locke disrupted his interpretive faculties (p. 196).

Aaron presents two lines of evidence for his attribution. First, he points to published passages, such as Introduction 13, where Berkeley emphasizes Locke's inconsistency. But in view of Berkeley's case against abstraction such an emphasis is just what we should expect, no matter how Berkeley interprets this particular description. It cannot be evidence that Berkeley reads Locke as Aaron says. Second, Aaron quotes notebook entries in which Berkeley assigns some special importance to Locke's description:

I. . . . abstract general ideas. These include a contradiction in 561 their nature v. Locke Lib. 4.S.9.c.7.

I. & c. Mem: to bring the killing blow at the last v.g. in the matter of Abstraction to bring Lockes general triangle at the last.

These entries do not show we must accept Aaron's view. They merely express Berkeley's recognition of the rhetorical advantage Locke's description offers him. When he says that the general idea of a triangle is both equilateral and not equilateral, Locke plays into his critic's hands. Berkeley knows that Locke does not *mean* that the general idea of a triangle is both equilateral and not, just as he knows that no one who describes the general idea of colour means to say that it is both red and blue. But the opportunity to take advantage of Locke is irresistible. There is nothing vicious in this. Berkeley has an argument that Locke must say what he seems to say, and he has reason to believe that Locke accepts each of the argument's premisses. Berkeley is convinced, of course, that the general idea of a triangle is inconsistent, but that does not mean he thinks Locke affirms the inconsistency.

My interpretation is confirmed by the fact that when he quotes Locke, Berkeley does not suggest that he is introducing a new kind of abstract idea.[22] At Introduction 10, before he quotes Locke's description, Berkeley refers to the 'two . . . proper acceptations of *abstraction*', which are introduced in §§ 7–9. In § 13 he says he quotes Locke's description in order 'to give the reader a yet clearer view of the nature of abstract ideas'. And his inability to see a new kind of abstract idea in Locke's description is not confined to the Introduction. In the first two editions of *Alciphron* VII 5, for example, Alciphron gives the following account of abstraction:

But the mind, excluding out of its ideas all these peculiar properties and distinctions, frameth the general abstract idea of a triangle, which is neither equilateral, equicrural, nor scalenum, neither obtusangular, acutangular nor rectangular, but all and none of these at once. *The same* may be said of the general abstract idea of colour, which is something distinct from and exclusive of blue, red, green, yellow, and every other particular colour, including only that general essence in which they all agree. (*Works* III, p. 332; emphasis mine.)

Here Alciphron is unable to see a difference between a close paraphrase of Locke's description and description very much like the ones Berkeley gives at Introduction 8 and 9. In *A Defence of Free-thinking in Mathematics* Berkeley speaks in the same way. In § 45 he writes,

Mr. Locke acknowledgeth it doth require pains and skill to form his general idea of a triangle. He further expressly saith it must be neither oblique nor rectangular, neither equilateral nor scalenum; but all and none of these at once.

He then says two sections later that

It is Mr. Locke's opinion that every general name stands for a general *abstract* idea, which prescinds from the species or individuals comprehended under it. Thus, for example, according to him, the general name *colour* stands for an idea which is neither blue, red, green, nor any other particular colour, but somewhat distinct and abstracted from them all. . . . Let the reader judge . . . whether he can distinctly frame such an idea of colour which shall prescind from all the species thereof, or of a triangle which shall answer Mr. Locke's account, prescinding and abstracting from all the particular sorts of triangles, in the manner aforesaid.

In this passage Berkeley does not take Locke's 'but all and none of

---

[22] Craig argues that Berkeley attacks three separate targets. In 'Berkeley on Abstract Ideas', *Archiv für Geschichte der Philosophie* 65 (1983), 63–80, I try to show that Craig is mistaken. See esp. pp. 63–73.

these at once' literally. He takes it to be Locke's way of saying the sort of thing he himself says at Introduction 8, that a general idea of colour, for example, corresponds to every colour and represents no one colour in particular. There is no reason to suppose that in the *Principles* he does not read Locke's description in the same way. When he ridicules the description or fastens on Locke's use of the word 'inconsistent' it is not because he thinks Locke acknowledges the inconsistency, but because he has an argument that Locke must acknowledge it.

3
SIMPLE IDEAS

LOCKE makes a distinction between simple and complex ideas. Simple ideas, he writes, contain 'nothing but *one uniform Appearance*, or Conception in the mind, and [are] not distinguishable into different *Ideas*' (*Essay* II ii 1). The first examples he gives are the coldness and hardness of a piece of ice, the smell and whiteness of a lily, the taste of sugar, and the smell of a rose. Simple ideas are furnished only by experience; it is beyond the mind's power to '*invent or frame*' a new one (II ii 2). But once it is supplied with simple ideas the mind has the power 'to repeat, compare, and unite them even to an almost infinite variety' (§ 2). The ideas produced by repetition, comparison, and unification are *complex*.[1]

Hume also divides ideas of perceptions into simple and complex. He writes that

simple perceptions or impressions and ideas are such as admit of no distinction nor separation. The complex are the contrary to these, and may be distinguished into parts. Tho' a particular colour, taste, and smell are qualities all united together in this apple, 'tis easy to perceive they are not the same, but are at least distinguishable from each other.[2]

According to Hume all our thoughts and ideas, no matter how 'compounded or sublime', resolve into simple ideas copied from simple impressions.[3]

Berkeley seems to be making a distinction along the lines of Locke's or Hume's in § 1 of the *Principles*:

It is evident to any one who takes a survey of the objects of human knowledge, that they are either ideas actually imprinted on the senses, or else such as are

[1] For a valuable discussion of Locke's distinction between simple and complex ideas see R. S. Woolhouse, *Locke's Philosophy of Science and Knowledge*, Oxford, 1971, pp. 33–58. See also Michael Ayers, 'Locke's Logical Atomism', *Proceedings of the British Academy* 67 (1981), 209–25.

[2] *A Treatise of Human Nature*, ed. by L. A. Selby-Bigge and P. H. Nidditch, 2nd edn., Oxford, 1978, I i 1, p. 2.

[3] *An Enquiry concerning Human Understanding*, ed. by L. A. Selby-Bigge and P. H. Nidditch, 3rd edn., Oxford, 1975, § 2, p. 19.

perceived by attending to the passions and operations of the mind, or lastly ideas formed by help of memory and imagination, either compounding, dividing, or barely representing those originally perceived in the aforesaid ways. By sight I have the ideas of light and colours with their several degrees and variations. By touch I perceive, for example, hard and soft, heat and cold, motion and resistance, and of all these more and less either as to quantity or degree. Smelling furnishes me with odours; the palate with tastes, and hearing conveys sounds to the mind in all their variety of tone and composition. And as several of these are observed to accompany each other, they come to be marked by one name, and so to be reputed as one thing. Thus, for example, a certain colour, taste, smell, figure and consistence having been observed to go together, are accounted one distinct thing, signified by the name *apple*. Other collections of ideas constitute a stone, a tree, a book, and the like sensible things; which, as they are pleasing or disagreeable, excite the passions of love, hatred, joy, grief, and so forth.

Here we seem to have the main ingredient of the passages from Locke and Hume: a contrast between ideas originally perceived and the 'collections' made of them by the 'compounding' mind. But one crucial ingredient is missing: Berkeley never says that the ideas collected together by the mind are simple. In this chapter I will document Berkeley's little-known rejection of what he took to be the Lockean distinction between simple and complex ideas, and I will explore some of the dramatic consequences of that rejection.

The distinction between simple and complex ideas is used and endorsed in several entries in Berkeley's notebooks. These entries are outnumbered, however, by expressions of doubt, all of them results of arguments to the effect that convincing examples of simple ideas just cannot be found. All of Locke's examples fail, Berkeley argues; some fail because they turn out not to be simple, others because they turn out not to be distinct ideas. In Berkeley's published works the distinction is decisively rejected in the *Principles*. Berkeley's repudiation of the distinction has been stressed by A. A. Luce, but nearly everyone else has failed to notice it, partly because the *Principles* deals with simple ideas under a different name—they are called *abstract*—and partly because Berkeley, like Locke and Hume, wants to distinguish between ideas given in sense (or faithfully copied by the reproducing imagination) and ideas constructed or composed by the mind.[4]

---

[4] Luce calls attention in several places to Berkeley's repudiation of the distinction. See *Berkeley and Malebranche*, London, 1934, p. 72; his remarks in the diplomatic edn. of the *Commentaries*, London, 1944, pp. 331–2; his notes on the *Commentaries* in the Luce

Berkeley believes that the mind can frame or invent new ideas by blending and dividing the ideas of sense, but he does not believe that any idea deserves to be called *simple*.[5]

1. *The search for a simple idea*

In his notebooks Berkeley not only works out his views but provides himself with rhetorical and compositional advice. In entry 378, for example, he gives a list of the arguments he will present 'shorter & more separate' in the *Principles*. Here he is prepared not only to distinguish between simple and complex ideas, but to assign the distinction a leading role in his argument for immaterialism, as in the following six-step proof that nothing like an idea can exist in an unperceiving thing:

10   the bare passive reception or having of ideas is call'd perception

11   Whatever has in it an idea, tho it be never so passive, tho it exert no manner of act about it, yet it must perceive. 10

12   all ideas either are simple ideas, or made up of simple ideas.

+13   that thing wch is like unto another thing must agree wth it in one or more simple ideas.

14   whatever is like a simple idea must either be another simple idea of the

+   same sort or contain a simple idea of the same sort. 13.

15   nothing like an idea can be in an unperceiving thing. 11.14.

Yet earlier in the same notebook he had expressed considerable uneasiness about the examples of simple ideas furnished by others:

+   Simple ideas include no parts nor relations, hardly separated &   134
considered in themselves, not yet rightly singl'd by any Authour.
instance in power, red extension etc

and Jessop edn. of the works (e.g. *Works* I, p. 109) and in the George H. Thomas edn. of the *Commentaries*, Alliance, Ohio, 1976, particularly pp. 137–8; and *The Dialectic of Immaterialism*, London, 1963, p. 61. Luce comments on the connection between simplicity and abstraction. Among more recent commentators Stuart C. Brown is the only one to have done so; see 'Berkeley on the Unity of the Self' in *Reason and Reality*, Royal Institute of Philosophy Lectures, vol. 5, London, 1972, esp. pp. 78–82 and 86.

[5] At Introduction to the *Principles* 22, Berkeley writes that nothing more than 'attentive perception' is required in order to see 'what ideas are included in any compound idea'. He does not however say that the ideas included in a compound idea are simple. In this respect Introduction 22 differs from the corresponding passage in the Draft Introduction (*Works* II, p. 143). Berkeley's decision to remove the word 'simple' lends some support to what I say in this chapter.

Locke is one of the authors Berkeley has in mind here. In the *Essay* Locke gives each of the ideas Berkeley mentions as an example of a simple idea: colours (red among them) at *Essay* II ii 2 and iii 1; power at II vii 8; and extension at II v. In various entries in the notebooks Berkeley gives reasons for distrusting each of the three.

His remarks on power and extension are rather brief. In each case he finds that the allegedly simple idea includes parts or relations incompatible with simplicity. 'Power no simple Idea', he writes at entry 493, 'it means nothing but the Relation between Cause & Effect.' Extension includes 'length, breadth & solidity being three severall ideas' (105). Extension, like motion, time, and number, also includes succession. Succession 'seems to be a simple idea', but no idea that contains it can be (167).

Berkeley's case against the simplicity of colours is more interesting. It rests on the claim that there are only two ways in which a simple idea can resemble another: either the two ideas are intromitted by the same sense, or they are connected with the same third idea:

<blockquote>
×   One idea may be like another idea tho' they Contain no common   484
    simple idea. thus the simple idea red is in some sense like the
+   simple idea blue. tis liker it than sweet or shrill. But then those
    ideas wch are so said to be alike agree both in their connexion with
    another simple idea viz. extension & in their being receiv'd by one
    & ye same sense.[6]
</blockquote>

Strictly speaking, then, it is not true that one thing that resembles another 'must agree wth it in one or more simple ideas'. Even simple ideas can resemble one another provided the resemblance has nothing to do with their internal make-up:

<blockquote>
+   No one abstract simple idea like another two simple ideas may be   496
    connected with one & the same 3d simple idea, or be intromitted by
    one & the same sense. But consider'd in themselves they can have
    nothing common & consequently no likeness.
</blockquote>

Two simple ideas can be alike only if the resemblance between them is external rather than internal. 'Consider'd in themselves' they can have nothing in common.

The condition Berkeley imposes on resemblance among simple ideas derives, at least in part, from his reading of Locke's *Essay*. At III iv

---

[6] In a facing-page entry Berkeley writes that he does not 'altogether approve' of this entry (484a). But in view of what he says in the entries I quote below, it appears that he did not disapprove of entry 484 because of what it says about resemblance.

16 Locke observes that there is nothing to subtract from a simple idea that will make it agree with another. 'There is nothing can be left out of the *Idea* of White and Red, to make them agree in one common appearance, and so have one general name; as *Rationality* being left out of the complex *Idea* of *Man*, makes it agree with Brute, in the more general *Idea* and name of *Animal*.' Here Locke is responding to the fact that colour is a determinable rather than a genus. What separates one colour from another is not some difference which can be grasped independently of the notion of colour—a difference which then 'attaches' to colour-in-general as rationality attaches to the *genus* animal—but something graspable only by those familiar with colours themselves. Locke's conclusion is that when we collect several colours together under the name 'colour', 'it signifies no more, but such *Ideas*, as are produced in the Mind only by the Sight, and have entrance only through the Eyes'. The general word, in other words, 'denotes only the way they get into the Mind'. Berkeley probably believes that being intromitted by the same sense and being linked with the same idea amount to the same thing, because unlike Locke he believes there is no idea common to two or more senses.

It seems, however, that two shades of red have more in common than their intromission by sight and their connection with visible extension. They are both shades of red, and this resemblance, unlike the others, is internal. This means that if Berkeley wants to hold on to the claim that simple ideas can have no internal similarities, he must deny that ideas of colour are simple. And the denial in fact comes at entry 551:

M+ W^t I say is Demonstration, perfect Demonstration. Whenever men have fix'd & determin'd Ideas annex'd to their words they can hardly be mistaken. Stick but to my Definition of Likeness & tis a Demonstration y^t Colours are not simple Ideas. All Reds being like etc. So also in other things. This to be heartily insisted on.

What is true for red is true for 'other things' because the argument against red's simplicity turns on nothing more than the fact that shades of colour have degrees. As Berkeley writes at entry 526,

+ Locke says the modes of simple Ideas besides extension & number are counted by degrees. I deny there are any modes or degrees of simple Ideas. W^t He terms such are complex Ideas as I have prov'd in Green.

The mention of what 'I have prov'd in Green' is a reference to entry

503, where Berkeley presents an argument against the simplicity of
green very much like his argument against the simplicity of red:

+   There is in green 2 foundations of 2 relations of likeness to blew & yellow.
     therefore Green is compounded.

Green resembles both blue and yellow. Or, to make the point in a form
more suitable for the use to which Berkeley puts it, green is like each in
a way neither is like the other. All three are intromitted by sight, and all
three connected with extension. Hence green cannot be simple if blue
and yellow are. We can derive an even stronger conclusion if we add
the premiss that all three have an equal claim to be considered simple.
If all three ideas have an equal claim and at least one of them is
complex, then all three must be complex.

   Although colours, extension, and power all fail as examples of
simple ideas, there may be other ideas that pass the test. Among the
more promising candidates are the simpler things Berkeley points to in
some of his attacks on Locke's examples. Perhaps length, breadth, and
succession are simple ideas, even if the extension composed of them is
not. Berkeley never objects to the simplicity of length, breadth, or
extension, but he does object to the notion that they are simple *ideas*. A
simple idea, as Locke explains when he introduces the term, is '*one
uniform Appearance*, or Conception in the mind' (*Essay* II ii 1), an item
with the ability to stand before the mind on its own. Length, breadth,
and succession are according to Berkeley all incapable of this.
'Succession a simple idea,' he writes in entry 53 of the notebooks,
which is marked with a plus sign, and he refers himself to 'Lock cap.
7'—to *Essay* II vii ('*Of simple* Ideas *of both Sensation and Reflection*'),
where in § 9 Locke gives succession as an example of an idea conveyed
to the mind by both inner and outer sense. Like other entries in the
Commentaries, 53 is probably a report of a Lockean view rather than an
endorsement of it. In any case Berkeley later comments on the entry on
the facing page: 'Succession is an abstract *ie*. an unconceivable idea.'
(53a.) Length is discussed in entries 21, 85, 254, 342, 483, and 722; in
each one Berkeley denies that length can be conceived without
breadth, and his attitude towards breadth without length, which he
does not consider, would not doubt have been equally hostile. A typical
entry about length without breadth is 365a, which will be useful to us
later on because, like Berkeley's afterthought about the idea of
succession at 53a, it establishes a connection between simplicity and
abstraction:

* Extension without breadth i.e. invisible, intangible length is not conceivable
✕ tis a mistake we are led into by the Doctrine of Abstraction.

To sum up, Berkeley's arguments against Locke's examples of simple ideas aim to show that a given idea is not a simple (as in the case of power, extension, red, and green), or that a given simple is not an idea (as in the case of succession and length). It follows that Locke's examples of simple ideas are either complex ideas, or elements or aspects of ideas. Berkeley's arguments in the first kind of case depend on the belief that a genuinely simple idea cannot, considered in itself, resemble another simple idea. His arguments in the second kind of case depend on the belief that a genuine idea can fill the mind, or stand before it apart from any other. The belief is forcefully expressed at *Principles* 116: 'we are apt to think', Berkeley writes, that 'every noun substantive stands for a distinct idea, that may be separated from all others.'[7] Berkeley deplores the tendency to suppose that every word stands for a distinct idea, but this is in part because he believes that anything worth calling an idea is 'distinct', an object whose presence in the mind does not depend on the presence of other ideas.

Berkeley has one last argument against the simplicity of colour, and it is worth examining even though it will play no role in my later argument. The arguments we have looked at so far have all been phenomenological: they turn on features of ideas which are apparent to the contemplating mind. The remaining argument is physical or causal, and was inspired by Berkeley's reading of Newton's *Opticks*:

> A various or mixt cause must necessarily produce a various or mixt   562
> effect. This demonstrable from the Definition of a Cause. wch way
> of Demonstrating must be frequently made use of in my Treatise &
> to that end Definitions often præmis'd. Hence 'tis evident that
> according to Newton's Doctrines Colours cannot be simple ideas.

In the *Opticks* Newton calls light *simple* when its rays—'*its least Parts, and those as well Successive in the same lines, as Contemporary in several lines*' (I i Def. 1)—all have the same 'refrangibility', or disposition to be '*turned out of their Way*', when passing from one transparent medium to another (I i Def. 2).[8] Light composed of rays of varying degrees of refrangibility is *compound* (I i Def. 7). The colours of simple or 'homogeneal' light are called simple or homogeneal, while the colours of compound or 'heterogeneal' light are compound or heterogeneal (I i

---

[7] The same view is put forward in *Alciphron* VII 5, *Works* III, p. 293.

[8] Isaac Newton, *Opticks*, New York, 1952. Refs. to the *Opticks* are supplied in the body of the text.

Def. 8). If we assume that all bodies reflect heterogeneal light, it follows from these definitions that the colours of bodies are all compound. Berkeley makes the required assumption at entry 151:

+   We have not pure, simple ideas of blue, red or any other colour   151
    (except perhaps black) because all bodies reflect heterogeneal light.

Yet it does not follow that *ideas* of colour are complex. The argument stands in need of a premiss connecting the complexity of colour (which Newton regards as a property of light) to the complexity of ideas. This is apparently where the 'Definition of a Cause' comes into play. Berkeley's strategy at 562 is to argue that because the light or colour that causes our ideas is complex, our ideas must be complex as well. 'A mixt cause will produce a mixt Effect', he writes at entry 504 (marked with a plus sign) 'therefore Colours are all compounded that we see.' It is impossible to say just what definition of 'cause' Berkeley has in mind at 562, but he is probably thinking of entry 461:

+   The simple idea call'd Power seems obscure or rather none at all.   461
    but onely the relation 'twixt cause & Effect. W^n I ask whether A can
    move B. if A be an intelligent thing. I mean no more than whether
    the volition of A that B move be attended with the motion of B, if A
    be be senseless whether the impulse of A against B be follow'd by y^e
    motion of B.

Berkeley's argument can now be reconstructed as follows. We know that the causes of our ideas of colour are compound or mixed. And we know from the definition of *cause* that a cause always has its characteristic effect; the fact that it occurs along with other events should not inhibit its operation. It follows that the effect of a compound or mixed cause will always be compound or mixed. Therefore ideas of the colour of bodies are always complex and never simple.

Berkeley's Newtonian argument is open to two decisive objections. The first is that the definition of *cause* is defective, or if correct then not properly applied. Perhaps a *total* cause always has the same characteristic effect—other circumstances being powerless to interfere due to its totality—but a single event in a constellation of events need not. The constellation may bring about an event which no constituent can bring about on its own, an event which is not in any sense a mix or blend of the characteristic effects of its constituents. The second objection is that even if the argument shows the ideas of colour are compound in one sense, it remains possible that they present 'one uniform appearance' to the mind, as Locke's definition of simplicity requires.

An idea can be *phenomenologically* simple—and therefore simple in the sense intended by Locke and Berkeley—even though it has a complex cause. The difference between causal and phenomenological complexity can be illustrated by what Berkeley refers to as 'Newton's two sorts of Green', a topic he reminds himself to consider at entry 505. The colour green, according to Newton, is associated with two different kinds of light. 'Mix'd green' is what we would produce if we mixed blue and yellow light together. If we send mixed green light through a prism we will find both blue and yellow light emerging on the other side. But just as there can be 'pure' or homogeneal light of blue or yellow—blue or yellow light that resists being fractured into separate bands of colour when it passes through a prism—there can be pure or homogeneal light of green. As Newton says of orange,

A Mixture of homogeneal red and yellow compounds an Orange, like in appearance of Colour to that orange which in the series of unmixed prismatick Colours lies between them; but the Light of one orange is homogeneal as to its Refrangibility, and that of the other is heterogeneal, and the Colour of the one, if viewed through a Prism, remains unchanged, that of the other is changed and resolved into its component Colours red and yellow. (I ii Prop. iv Theor. iii.)

Now if, as Newton says, the two sorts of orange are 'like in appearance', and if the distinction between simple and complex ideas is a phenomenological one, then we cannot appeal to the complexity of the cause of an idea of colour in order to establish that the idea is complex. Newton's example shows that an idea's cause can be changed from simple to complex and back again, even though the phenomenological character of the idea remains the same. Berkeley's reminder to consider Newton's two sorts of green may be a recognition that it presents a problem for his argument.

Given Berkeley's failure to find an example of a simple idea either in Notebook B or in the early part of Notebook A, the second notebook to be filled, it is not surprising that he says relatively little about simple and complex ideas in the rest of the later notebook. At entry 570, though, he still has plans to discuss the distinction in print:

+ Mem: to observe (w^n you talk of the division of Ideas into simple & complex) that there may be another cause of the Undefinableness of certain Ideas besides that which Locke gives viz. the want of Names.

An even later entry entertains the possibility that there are two kinds of complexity:

+ N.B. Simple Ideas viz. Colours are not devoid of all sort of 664
Composition. tho it must be granted they are not made up of
distinguishable Ideas. yet there is another sort of composition. Men
are wont to call those things compounded in which we do not
actually discover the component ingredients. Bodies are said to be
compounded of Chymical Principles wch nevertheless come not
into view till after the dissolution of the Bodies. & wch were not
could not be discerned in the Bodies whilst remaining entire.

'Complexation of Ideas twofold.' he writes at 721, 'y^s refers to colours being complex ideas.'

The last two entries quoted do not take back what Berkeley establishes in earlier entries. It is true that 664 describes colours as simple ideas, but this is no more than a way of speaking. Entry 664 suggests that no matter how the distinction between simple and complex ideas is understood, it must be legitimate to call ideas of colour 'simple'. But this does not mean they are devoid of *all* composition. There is a kind of composition or complexity that can be found even in the paradigms of 'simplicity'. Berkeley does not say what the difference between the two kinds of 'complexation' is, but it is not hard to see what he has in mind. The idea of an apple is *decomposably* complex. It can be separated into individually conceivable parts—its colour, smell, visual appearance, and texture. The idea of scarlet is not complex in this sense, for although it has 'parts' or 'aspects' they cannot be separately conceived. They come to our attention only when we ask what scarlet resembles. We then discover that scarlet can be placed in two distinct resemblance-classes—in the class of colours, but also in the class of reds. The idea of scarlet is not decomposably complex, but it *is* complex. Berkeley, though, does not develop his views on 'indecomposable' complexity. Like most of his entries about simple and complex ideas, 664 and 721 are marked with a plus sign, and they are not followed up in later entries.

Our survey of Berkeley's notebooks reveals that he once planned to use the distinction between simple and complex ideas in his argument for immaterialism. He searched unsuccessfully for an example of a simple idea, and the numerous plus signs and facing-page corrections show that he eventually lost faith in the distinction. Before I document Berkeley's published *rejection* of the existence of simple ideas, I want to return to the argument, projected at *Commentaries* 378, where the distinction between simple and complex ideas receives its most emphatic endorsement.

The relevant items within entry 378, quoted above on p. 55, are numbered 10 to 15. The conclusion of the argument (item 15) reads, 'nothing like an idea can be in an unperceiving thing'. The intention is to show that no idea can *represent* an unperceiving thing because no idea can resemble such a thing. According to the notations that accompany nearly every line, item 15 depends jointly on items 14 ('whatever is like a simple idea must either be another simple idea of the same sort or contain a simple idea of the same sort') and 11 ('Whatever has in it an idea, tho it be never so passive, tho it exert no manner of act about it, yet it must perceive'). In offering item 14 Berkeley appeals to item 13: 'that thing wch is like unto another thing must agree wth it in one or more simple ideas.' The argument as developed so far can be summarized as follows:

1. Two things can be alike only if they agree in at least one simple idea.
2. But x can resemble y in a simple idea only if x is a simple idea or contains a simple idea.
3. An unperceiving thing (as understood by the materialists) is neither an idea nor the sort of thing able to contain an idea.
4. Therefore an unperceiving thing cannot be like an idea.

Now that is the role of item 12, which holds that 'all ideas either are simple ideas, or made up of simple ideas'?

The line is there, I think, because Berkeley sees that it is needed to reply to the following objection, which might be made on behalf of the materialist: 'I agree with Locke that simple ideas are the materials of all our knowledge (*Essay* II ii 1), and that they somehow set the limits of our thought (*Essay* II vii 10). But it follows from the argument just given that we have no idea of an unperceiving thing or external object only if unreasonably severe restrictions are placed on our ability to use simple ideas in forming new ones. If our methods of construction are inventive enough, isn't it possible for us to come up with an idea that can represent the kind of thing no simple idea can? Strictly speaking, the argument shows only that we have no *simple* idea of an unperceiving thing, not that we have no idea of such a thing at all.' Unless Berkeley is able to rule out the kind of inventiveness the objector is imagining, he will have no right to conclude that we can have no idea of an unperceiving thing. He therefore needs the distinction between simple and complex ideas to ensure that our imaginations are of suitably limited power. If every idea is either a simple idea or a cluster of simple ideas, then no idea, no matter how complex, can represent a thing which cannot be represented, even if only in part, by a simple one. Clustering simple ideas together does not make possible the representation of a new *kind* of thing, but only the representation *in one thing* of properties or features which can already be represented separately. As Berkeley puts it at entry 280,

M   . . . Complex thoughts or ideas are onely an assemblage of simple ideas and can be the image or like unto nothing but another assemblage of simple ideas. &c

Berkeley's proof needs line 12, then, to protect it against a possible objection. If Berkeley lets the imagination run free, he will lose his argument that we can have no idea of an 'unperceiving thing', even if the materialist grants (as does Locke) that simple ideas are in some sense the materials of all our thought.

In the end the argument of entry 378 was of no importance to Berkeley. Even in the notebooks it is followed by a second argument for the same conclusion, in which the distinction between simple and complex ideas plays no role.[9] And the first argument does not in fact require that the simple ideas of which it speaks actually satisfy the requirements for simplicity laid down elsewhere in the notebooks. Berkeley may once have thought that he needed Lockean simple ideas to defend an immaterialist argument against a possible objection, but in fact he needed no more than the indecomposably complex 'simples' of entries 664 and 721, and in view of his other argument for the same conclusion, he did not need even them.

We have already glimpsed several entries—53a, 365a, and 496— where Berkeley associates simplicity with abstraction. The association is most explicit at entry 139: 'Preliminary discourse', he writes, referring apparently to the projected Introduction to the *Principles*, 'about singling & abstracting simple ideas.' this entry is marked with a plus sign, and the published version of the Introduction seems to be about abstract ideas instead of simple ones. But the concern with simple ideas, despite the change in vocabulary, survives.

[9] See items 16 to 19, which are described by Berkeley as 'another demonstration of the same thing'.

2. *Simplicity and abstraction*

At *Essay* II xiii 24 Locke dismisses 'those Men, who take the measure and possibility of all Being, only from their narrow and gross Imaginations'. It is not possible, he writes at *Essay* II ii 3, for anyone '*to imagine* any other *Qualities* in Bodies, howsoever constituted, whereby they can be taken notice of, besides Sounds, Tastes, Smells, visible and tangible Qualities', not because qualities beyond these cannot exist, but because God has given us only five senses: 'Had Mankind been made with but four Senses, the Qualities then, which are the Object of the Fifth Sense, had been as far from our Notice, Imagination, and Conception, as now any *belonging to a Sixth, Seventh, or Eighth Sense*, can possibly be: which, whether yet some other Creatures, in some other Parts of this vast, and stupendious Universe, may not have, will be a great Presumption to deny.' Berkeley too admits that 'there may be, for aught that I know, innumerable sorts of ideas or sensations, as different from one another, and from all that I have perceived, as colours are from sounds.' (*Principles* 81.) This admission does not threaten Berkeley's argument against abstraction because the argument, as I showed in Chapter 2, does not rest on the assumption that abstract ideas are images, or on the similar assumption that abstraction is the work of the imagination, strictly so called. Berkeley is aware of the distinction between imagination and pure intellect, and his main objection to abstraction is not that we cannot *imagine* what an abstract idea represents (though this is an objection on which he would insist), but that no operation of the mind can frame an idea that can justly be called abstract. Alciphron is rebuked in just these terms when he accuses Euphranor of ignoring the difference between pure intellect and imagination. 'Abstract general ideas', Alciphron explains, 'I take to be the object of pure intellect, which may conceive them although they cannot perhaps be imagined.' (*Works* III, p. 334.) Euphranor replies that he cannot 'by *any* faculty, whether of intellect or imagination, conceive or frame an idea of that which is impossible and includes a contradiction' (emphasis mine). Philonous replies in the same way to a similar objection by Hylas:

Since I cannot frame abstract ideas at all, it is plain, I cannot frame them by the help of *pure intellect*, whatsoever faculty you understand by those words. (pp. 193–4.)[10]

In this section I hope to show that Berkeley's claim that we cannot frame abstract ideas is, in part, a claim that we cannot frame Lockean simple ideas. I want to begin by turning to § 7 of the Introduction to the *Principles*, a passage cited by Monroe Beardsley in support of his contention that Berkeley is an 'atomistic sensationalist' who believes that the mind takes in qualitative atoms of experience which it is then free to reorganize in any way it pleases.[11]

It is agreed on all hands, that the qualities or modes of things do never really exist each of them apart by it self, and separated from all others, but are mixed, as it were, and blended together, several in the same object. But we are told, the mind being able to consider each quality singly, or abstracted from those other qualities with which it is united, does by that means frame to it self abstract ideas. For example, there is perceived by sight an object extended, coloured, and moved: this mixed or compound idea the mind resolving into its simple, constituent parts, and viewing each by it self, exclusive of the rest, does frame the abstract ideas of extension, colour, and motion. Not that it is possible for colour or motion to exist without extension: but only that the mind can frame to it self by *abstraction* the idea of colour exclusive of extension, and of motion exclusive of both colour and extension.(§ 7.)

Berkeley has just informed us in § 6 that he intends to devote the Introduction to unravelling what he later calls 'that fine and subtle net of *abstract ideas*' (§ 22). The doctrine of abstract ideas has had 'a chief part in rendering speculation intricate and perplexed, and . . . occasioned innumerable errors and difficulties in almost all parts of knowledge' (§ 6), and Berkeley clearly hopes to avoid it. It is therefore unwise to attribute a view to Berkeley on the basis of a passage in which he sets up a target. It is relatively safe to ascribe to him anything he claims to be 'agreed on all hands', but it would be rash to suppose that he takes the ideas of extension, colour, and motion to be the 'simple, constituent parts' of the complex idea of an object, atoms to the object's molecule.

---

[10] Philonous goes on to say that the objects of pure intellect are spiritual, and that sensible things 'are only to be perceived by sense, or represented by the imagination'. For Berkeley's earliest reaction to the suggestion that pure intellect can form abstract ideas see *Works* VIII, pp. 49–50.

[11] Monroe Beardsley, 'Berkeley on "Abstract Ideas"', reprinted in C. B. Martin and D. M. Armstrong (eds.), *Locke and Berkeley*, Notre Dame, 1968, pp. 409–25. He refers to the present passage on p. 416. His reading of the passage is also disputed by Brown, 'Berkeley on the Unity of the Self', p. 79.

Introduction 7 is in fact reminiscent of the following passage from Locke's *Essay*:

Though the Qualities that affect our Senses, are, in the things themselves, so united and blended, that there is no separation, no distance between them; yet 'tis plain, the *Ideas* they produce in the Mind, enter by the Senses simple and unmixed. For though the Sight and Touch often take in from the same Object, at the same time, different *Ideas*; as a Man sees at once Motion and Colour; the Hand feels Softness and Warmth in the same piece of Wax: Yet the simple *Ideas* thus united in the same Subject, are as perfectly distinct, as those that come in by different Senses.(II ii 1.)

The points of correspondence between the passages from the *Principles* and the *Essay* strongly suggest that Berkeley identifies the abstract ideas he describes in § 7 with the simple ideas Locke describes at II ii 1. I can imagine two reasons why one might hesitate to accept this suggestion, but neither is finally convincing.

The first reason for doubt is that the simple ideas of *Essay* II ii 1 seem to be determinate or specific. They represent the determinate motion, colour, or warmth of a particular individual. The extension, colour, and motion of Introduction 7, on the other hand, may well be general or determinable. 'The abstract ideas of extension, colour, and motion' *could* be determinate or specific, but for all the passage says about them they may be otherwise.

But when § 7 is read in its intended setting it clearly emerges that the ideas described there are absolutely specific. The evidence for this reading was actually presented at scattered locations in the previous chapter, and here it needs only to be brought together. Berkeley introduces abstract 'general' ideas at Introduction 8:

Again, the mind having observed that in the particular extensions perceived by sense, there is something common and alike in all, and some other things peculiar, as this or that figure or magnitude, which distinguish them one from another; it considers apart or singles out by it self that which is common, making thereof a most abstract idea of extension, which is neither line, surface, nor solid, nor has any figure or magnitude but is an idea entirely prescinded from all these.

We discover here that the ideas of § 7, which serve as the input for the process described in § 8, are 'particular' ideas, distinguished from one another by certain 'peculiarities'. By the end of § 8 we have witnessed the formation of a 'most abstract idea', or what I suggested in the previous chapter might be called a *doubly* abstract idea, because it is the product of two distinct abstractive feats, one separating a determinate or specific quality from the qualities of other kinds with which it must occur, the other separating a determinable or general quality from the determinate or specific qualities of its own kind. The distinction between the ideas of §§ 7 and 8 is preserved in § 9, where Berkeley's description of the formation of abstract ideas of 'the more compounded beings' refers back to the generalizing described in § 8, and it is reinforced in § 10, where Berkeley writes that he can neither 'abstract one from another, or conceive separately, those qualities which it is impossible should exist so separated'—a reference back to § 7—nor 'frame a general notion by abstracting from particulars in the manner aforesaid'—a reference back to §§ 8 and 9. 'Which two last', he adds, 'are the proper acceptations of *abstraction*.'

The second reason for hesitating to accept the suggestion that Berkeley identifies one kind of abstract idea with Lockean simple ideas is that the ideas of Introduction 7 are *achievements*—products of the mind's activity—while the ideas of *Essay* II i are described as if they were *givens*, ideas laid before the mind asking only to be taken up. Locke's simple ideas enter 'by the Senses simple and unmixed'. The ideas of Introduction 7, on the other hand, are the products of energetic precision or separation.

This difference between the ideas of § 7 and *Essay* II ii i would be an obstacle to acceptance of what the points of correspondence suggest only if there were reason to believe that in the present context Berkeley attaches significance to the difference between givens and achievements. But he in fact has little interest in the difference, and his lack of interest is perfectly appropriate. It is natural to read the Introduction to the *Principles* as a contribution to what might be called the psychology of idea-formation. Berkeley seems to be interested in the activities or operations which stock the mind with ideas. When the Introduction is read against this background Berkeley will be seen as a psychologist who denies the possibility of a *process* called abstraction. Readers may even be tempted to compare his attack on abstraction to Descartes's defence of innate ideas.[12] But it seems to me that this is the wrong

---

[12] This is the reaction of H. M. Bracken in *Berkeley*, London, 1974. 'Abstract ideas', Bracken writes on p. 45, 'are abstracted ideas.' This motto blurs the distinction I go on to draw between epistemological and metaphysical issues. Berkeley opposes abstract ideas but it does not follow from this—whatever might be said for it on other grounds—that he is interested in what Bracken calls 'a non-abstractionist source for concepts' (p. 45). (It is undeniable, of course, that Berkeley seeks a *non-sensory* source for certain concepts.)

approach. Berkeley's Introduction is not primarily epistemological but metaphysical. The moving parts of his argument are not epistemological considerations but metaphysical ones. His objection to abstract ideas is not that there is something wrong with the *process* of abstraction (and so he does not object, as Ralph Cudworth had done, that we must already possess the idea to be abstracted in order to know which features to consider and which ones to ignore), but that there is something wrong with the *product*. It purports to represent what cannot possibly exist.

The range of positions on the topic of abstraction is in fact much wider than most commentators on Berkeley have realized. There is first of all the disagreement between those who believe in abstract ideas and those who do not. Locke belongs with the believers, as do Malebranche and Norris, even though they do not agree with Locke that such ideas are drawn from experience by abstraction. When Berkeley makes Philonous accuse Malebranche of building on 'the most abstract general ideas' he does not mean that Malebranche holds a Lockean theory of their genesis, but that he builds on ideas—such as the idea of intelligible extension, or the idea of 'being without restriction' which Malebranche identifies with the idea of God— which purport to represent what cannot possibly exist (Second Dialogue, p. 214). There are, in other words, both 'empiricist' and 'rationalist' versions of the doctrine of abstract ideas; only the first includes a belief in abstraction from experience, the proponents of the second preferring instead to make abstract ideas innate (Descartes) or to place them in the mind of God (Malebranche, Norris), who then vouchsafes glimpses to us. Berkeley's argument applies with equal force to each, even though his language—adapted as it is to the case of Locke, and to the schoolmen who share Locke's view that *nihil est in intellectu quod non prius fuit in sensu* (quoted from *Philosophical Commentaries* 779)—more readily suggests the anti-empiricist application. The fact that the simple ideas of *Essay* II ii 1 are givens rather than accomplishments is therefore no obstacle to my view that the ideas of Introduction 7 are meant to be Lockean simple ideas.

My interpretation is supported by an association between simplicity and abstraction that runs through several of Berkeley's most important works. At *Principles* 13, for example, he discusses the idea of unity, which 'some will have to be a simple or uncompounded idea, accompanying all other ideas into the mind'. Berkeley inspects his mind and claims he can find no such idea; 'to say no more,' he concludes, 'it is an *abstract idea*'. At *Principles* 98 he recounts his attempts 'to frame a simple idea of *time*, abstracted from the succession of ideas in my mind, which flows uniformly, and is participated by all beings'. The attempts, he reports, left him 'lost and embrangled in inextricable difficulties'. Time is nothing, he concludes, once it is 'abstracted from the succession of ideas in our minds'.

In the Seventh Dialogue of *Alciphron*, Euphranor and Alciphron speak of the idea of number as both 'simple' and 'abstract'.

EUPHRANOR. Do but try now whether you can frame an idea of number in abstract, exclusive of all signs, words, and things numbered. I profess for my own part I cannot.

ALCIPHRON. Can it be so hard a matter to form a simple idea of number, the object of a most evident demonstrable science? Hold, let me see if I can't abstract the idea of number from the numerical names and characters, and all particular numerable things.—Upon which Alciphron paused a while, and then said, To confess the truth I do not find that I can.

EUPHRANOR. But, though it seems neither you nor I can form distinct simple ideas of number, we can nevertheless make a very proper and significant use of numeral names. They direct us in the disposition and management of our affairs, and are of such necessary use that we should not know how to do without them. And yet, if other men's faculties may be judged of by mine, to attain a precise simple abstract idea of number is as difficult as to comprehend any mystery in religion.   (VII 5, *Works* III, p. 293.)

Simplicity and abstraction are even associated by Locke himself, and in a way that renders plausible Berkeley's view that Locke's simple ideas are abstract. *Essay* III viii is devoted to the distinction between abstract and concrete names. Abstract names are what Locke (employing 'the Language of Grammarians') calls *substantives*; examples are 'whiteness' and 'sweetness'. Concrete names are *adjectives*, such as 'white' and 'sweet'. At III viii 2 Locke lays stress on the claim that 'our *simple Ideas have all abstract, as well as concrete Names*', and abstract names or words, he tells us in the preceding section, are '*Names of abstract Ideas*'. Despite *Essay* II ii 1, which is definite in its suggestion that simple ideas are somehow given, there is, overall, a good deal of ambiguity in Locke's views on the origins of simple ideas. He often claims that the mind has to work to distinguish them. In *Essay* II xi, for example, Locke takes up the operation or faculty of *discerning*, which he defines first as the faculty of 'distinguishing between the several *Ideas*' possessed by the mind, and later as the faculty by which we perceive 'two *Ideas* to be the same, or different' (both definitions appear in § 1). He discusses at length in §§ 2 and 3 the contribution this faculty makes to clear thinking. The discussion suggests that although simple ideas may enter the mind unmixed, some effort is required to *see* them as unmixed, and this suggestion makes it plausible to say that on Locke's view, the mind has to act in order to perceive simple ideas as separate and distinct. Locke's discussion of discerning is followed by a discussion of comparing (§§ 4 and 5) and then, after three sections on *composition*, by three sections on *abstraction*. Perhaps this chapter suggested to Berkeley the arrangement of Introduction 7–9, where a discussion of our alleged capacity to separate the qualities of things is followed by a discussion of our ability to compare them and notice their similarity, and then to form abstract general ideas of what they have in common. In any event, the evidence is overwhelming that Berkeley takes Locke's simple ideas to be illegitimately abstract, whether or not he believes that Locke himself takes them to be abstract ideas.

I can locate only one passage in his published writings where Berkeley makes constructive use of the notion of a simple idea. The notion figures in one of Philonous's attempts to convince Hylas that qualities immediately perceived cannot exist without the mind. Philonous argues that these qualities are inseparable from pleasure and pain, and since pleasure and pain cannot exist without the mind, he concludes that the qualities we immediately perceive must likewise depend for their existence on the mind. The argument is developed at greatest length in the case of heat, which increased beyond a certain threshold becomes pain. The intense heat and the pain are inseparable, Philonous suggests, because they are one and the same. 'Hold, Philonous,' Hylas objects, 'I fear I was out in yielding intense heat to be a pain. It should seem rather, that pain is something distinct from heat, and the consequence or effect of it.' (First Dialogue, p. 176.) Philonous then uses the notion of a simple sensation or idea to lead Hylas away from the proposed distinction:

PHILONOUS. Upon putting your hand near the fire, do you perceive one simple uniform sensation, or two distinct sensations?

HYLAS. But one simple sensation.

PHILONOUS. Is not the heat immediately perceived?

HYLAS. It is.

PHILONOUS. And the pain?

HYLAS. True.

PHILONOUS. Seeing therefore they are both immediately perceived at the same time, and the fire affects you only with one simple, or uncompounded idea, it follows that this same simple idea is both the intense heat immediately perceived, and the pain; and consequently, that the intense heat immediately perceived, is nothing distinct from a particular sort of pain. HYLAS. It seems so.

In this exchange Philonous certainly accepts the view that the idea or sensation of heat-plus-pain is in some way simple. But the passage is not a retraction of complaints elsewhere voiced against Lockean simple ideas. The sensation of heat-plus-pain is neither simple in the sense at work in Berkeley's notebooks nor abstract in the way described at Introduction 7. The sensation falls into two resemblance-classes, one by virtue of its resemblance to heat too moderate to be painful, the other by virtue of its resemblance to painful cold or pressure. Philonous does not deny that he can *consider* heat apart from pain or pain apart from heat. He denies only that the two features or aspects make two ideas, that we might be able to have a 'vehement sensation . . . without pain, or pleasure' or 'an idea of sensible pain or pleasure in general, abstracted from every particular idea of heat, cold tastes, smells' (pp. 176–7). Locke counts both heat and pain as simple ideas (heat, an idea of touch, at *Essay* II iii 1, and pain, an idea of both sensation and reflection, at II vii 1).[13] There is, then, a complexity or articulation to the sensation of heat-plus-pain, but such complexity is internal and ineliminable, and it is only the *elements* or *components* of the sensation that would be simple ideas in Locke's sense. Yet in another sense the idea of heat-plus-pain is simple, because a distinct idea of either component would be illegitimately abstract: it is as simple as it can be. Philonous might therefore have put his point in a way that recalls the passages from the *Principles* and *Alciphron*. He might have said that we have no distinct, simple idea of heat or pain, instead of saying that the idea of heat-plus-pain is simple in the sense of being atomic or unbreakable.

In this section I have argued that Berkeley's denial of abstract ideas is, in part, a denial of what he takes to be Lockean simple ideas. There is evidence for my interpretation in almost all of his main works. We have seen that, in the notebooks, Berkeley dismisses simple ideas as abstract. In the *Principles* the distinction between simple and complex ideas drops out of sight, but the attack on abstraction remains, and

---

[13] Locke even discusses the painfulness of intense heat (II vii 4).

Berkeley carefully arranges its targets so that simple ideas are among them. In the *Principles* and *Alciphron* the ideas of unity, time, and number are labelled 'abstract' because they are, as it were , too simple: they contain too little to stand before the mind on their own. The idea of heat-plus-pain is classified as simple in the *Dialogues*, but only as a way of saying that if we try to decompose the idea into the separate aspects it so closely combines, we will find our way blocked. As for Locke's examples of simple ideas, we find extension, colour, and motion under attack at Introduction 7 because they cannot be separately conceived. Unity is attacked at *Principles* 13 for the same reason. In *Principles* 10 Berkeley argues that 'extension, figure, and motion, abstracted from all other qualities, are inconceivable', although he does not mention that Locke regards all three ideas as simple. Berkeley makes the same point in his notebooks (for example in entry 362), though once again no connection is drawn with the topic of simple ideas. Given all this I think the evidence is overwhelming that in rejecting abstract ideas, Berkeley consciously rejected the existence of simple ideas, whether defined by his own criteria for simplicity, or by the examples provided in the *Essay*.

3. *Consequences*

What is the significance of Berkeley's rejection of simple ideas? I will briefly sketch two consequences here. Chapter 4 will be devoted to a third.

Berkeley's rejection of simple ideas shows, first, that it is wrong to classify Berkeley as an atomistic sensationalist. Beardsley writes,[14]

When . . . ideas first appear to the mind they come through various senses, by various channels; they are distinct and *several*, for they are observed severally to go together, and they may be 'apprehended by divers senses, or by the same sense at different times, or in different circumstances' [Third Dialogue, *Works* II, p. 245]. Then they are 'united into one thing by the mind' [p. 246]. It is the mind which gives them a substantial unity, and a name, and the mind is led to do this, not by any intrinsic relation among the ideas, but by extrinsic spatial and temporal relations; men, says Berkeley, select those collections of ideas which are 'observed, however, to have some connexion in nature, either with respect to coexistence or succession; all which they refer to one name, and consider as one thing' [p. 245].

[14] 'Berkeley on "Abstract ideas"', pp. 413–14.

Beardsley suggests that in Berkeley's view *all* relations among distinct ideas are extrinsic or external. But Berkeley's rejection of simple ideas is a recognition that distinct ideas are often internally related, and that ideas have a structure which is not (or at any rate not typically) imposed by the mind. Berkeleyan ideas are not pieced together by the mind from scratch, but enter the mind already structured, held together by connections which no mind creates and no mind can sever. The idea of colour, for example, cannot occur apart from some idea of figure or shape, and no idea of figure or shape can occur apart from an idea of extension. An idea of colour apart from figure or figure apart from extension would be an example of a Lockean simple idea, and such ideas are illegitimately abstract. There is therefore no cause for Beardsley's concern that Berkeley's attack on abstract ideas is not wholly consistent with his account of perception. It is true that Berkeley follows Locke in distinguishing between the ideas given in sensation and the ideas excited by the mind itself, and that he describes the imagination as a faculty of 'compounding, dividing, or barely representing' ideas of the first kind. But there is no evidence that Berkeley supposes that an idea can be resolved into qualitative atoms—distinct ideas of a single qualitative aspect—and then reassembled in any way that we please. Although there is considerable freedom allotted to the mind, and although that freedom can appropriately be described in terms of composition and division, there are qualities, such as intense heat and pain on the one hand, or colour and figure on the other, which the mind cannot separate. Berkeley's rejection of simple ideas is an affirmation of the internal and inescapable structure of the perceived world.

A second consequence of Berkeley's rejection of simple ideas is a validation of the contrast drawn in Chapter 2 between the Lockean and Berkeleyan conceptions of *idea*. Berkeley's refusal to call unity a simple idea is a direct expression of his view that an idea is an object, an entity able to stand before the mind on its own. Locke is willing to call unity a simple idea because he often intends what he says about ideas to be a way of identifying the *content* of thought, rather than its object. If I am considering or attending to the unity of a thing, Locke is prepared to say that I have a simple idea of unity. He is prepared, in other words, to apply the word 'idea' to something Berkeley would regard as a mere *aspect* or *feature* of an idea. It should be clear from the passages quoted in § 2 of Chapter 2 that Locke never intended his simple ideas to satisfy the requirements Berkeley lays down in the notebooks. We have already seen how important it is, in Locke's view, to discern the necessary connections among simple ideas (*Essay* II xiii 27). Unlike Berkeley, Locke thinks that 'distinct ideas' can be necessarily connected. Both solidity and scarlet are necessarily connected with extension, but this 'hinders not . . . that they are distinct *Ideas*' (II xiii 11). 'Many *Ideas*', he adds, 'require others as necessary to their Existence or Conception, which are yet very distinct *Ideas*. Motion can neither be, nor be conceived without Space; yet Motion is not Space, nor Space Motion.' The idea of motion is distinct from the idea of space because *thinking of space* and *thinking of motion* are different acts with different contents. The idea of space and the idea of motion are different contents even if it is true that whenever we conceive of motion we confront an object that is inevitably spatial. Berkeley acknowledges that motion and space are different contents— we can consider either one, he would agree, without considering the other—but he denies that they are distinct ideas. Contrary to what Locke affirms at II xiii 11, Berkeley thinks that a distinct idea cannot depend on another for its existence or conception. If Berkeley intends his attack on simple ideas as an attack on Locke, then, we must conclude that the attack is misdirected. But at the same time it is understandable, if only because Locke maintains at one point that the simple ideas of one sense are 'as perfectly distinct, as those that come in by different Senses' (II ii 1). Since one sense might be lost while the others are retained, there are no necessary connections across the senses. But in that case Locke seems to be saying that there are no necessary connections among ideas of a single sense. We know that Locke does not intend this (the passage can be read instead as a claim that any two simple ideas, even when they are ideas of the same sense, are distinct *contents*), but it is not hard to see how even a careful reader of the *Essay* might come to a different conclusion.

A final consequence of our discoveries in this chapter has to do with Berkeley's belief in the inescapable structure of the perceived world. Berkeley's rejection of simple ideas has important implications for his views on the nature of necessity. The rejection clarifies those views, but at the same time heightens a difficulty, one of the deepest in Berkeley's own philosophy and one of the deepest in philosophy since his time. This difficulty is the subject of the following chapter.

4

NECESSITY

Asked by Philonous when a thing is shown to be impossible, Hylas answers as most of Berkeley's contemporaries would have answered: a thing is shown to be impossible, he says, 'when a repugnancy is demonstrated between the ideas comprehended in its definition' (*Works* II, p. 225). The identification of impossibility with repugnancy or contradiction was a commonplace of seventeenth and eighteenth century philosophical writing. Locke's reason for supposing matter may think was that he saw no contradiction in it, and in the course of defending his supposition he tells Stillingfleet that anything is possible provided it 'involves no contradiction'.[1] In Malebranche's *Dialogues on Metaphysics* Theodore proclaims that it is beyond the power of God to 'do what is impossible or what contains a manifest contradiction'.[2] John Toland sums up the prevailing view with the observation that '*Contradiction* . . . is a Synonym for Impossibility',[3] and claims to the same effect can be found in the *Port-Royal Logic* and in works by Ralph Cudworth, Samuel Clarke, and Berkeley's friend Samuel Johnson.[4]

The identification of impossibility with repugnancy, which carried with it an identification of possibility with non-repugnancy or consistency, was assisted by the theistic context in which the modal

---

[1] 'Mr. Locke's Reply to the Right Reverend the Lord Bishop of Worcester's Answer to His Second Letter', in *The Works of John Locke*, London, 1823, vol. 4, p. 483: 'For I only say, that it is possible, i.e. involves no contradiction, that God, the omnipotent immaterial spirit, should, if he pleases, give to some parcels of matter, disposed as he thinks fit, a power of thinking and moving.'

[2] Nicolas Malebranche, *Dialogues on Metaphysics* VII, trans. by Willis Doney New York, 1980, p. 153: 'God cannot do what is impossible or what contains a manifest contradiction. He cannot will what cannot be conceived.'

[3] *Christianity Not Mysterious*, 2nd edn., London, 1696, p. 40. See also pp. 39 and 170.

[4] For the *Port-Royal Logic* see the translation by John Ozell, *Logic: Or, the Art of Thinking*, London, 1973, pt. IV, chap. 7, p. 403. For Cudworth see *The True Intellectual System of the Universe*, London, 1678, pp. 647 ('whatsoever is *Possible*, that is, whatsoever is *Conceivable*, and implies no manner of *Contradiction*'), 650, 651, and 719. For Clarke see *A Discourse Concerning the Being and Attributes of God*, 6th edn., London, 1725, pp. 16 ('a plain Impossibility or Implying a Contradiction'), 71 ('Contradiction, (which is the alone real Impossibility,)'), 79. For Johnson see *Elementa Philosophica*, Philadelphia, 1752, 'Noetica', pp. 26, 28.

notions—possibility, impossibility, and necessity—then had their place. Possible things or states of affairs were viewed as those that God had the power to realize, impossible things or states of affairs as those that not even God could bring about. It was also assumed that an omnipotent God could bring about anything of which he could conceive, and that he could conceive of anything that did not involve a contradiction. It followed that a thing or state of affairs is possible if and only if it involves no contradiction or repugnancy.[5]

When philosophers of the period spoke of impossibilities and repugnancies it was not altogether clear what kind of item—thing or fact, notion or conception, term or proposition—they had in mind, but some rough generalizations can be ventured. The modal notions themselves were generally applied to things or states of affairs. To say a thing is possible (or impossible, or necessary) was to say that it could obtain (or couldn't obtain, or couldn't fail to obtain). Things or facts could also be described as contradictory or repugnant, but it could also be said that their *existence* or their *obtaining* was contradictory or repugnant, that the *notion* or *conception* of such a thing was contradictory or repugnant, that the *propositions* saying that the things exist or that the facts obtain were contradictory or repugnant, or that these propositions (or the things and states of affairs themselves) 'involved' or 'implied' a contradiction or repugnancy. In general the notion of contradiction or repugnancy was more closely associated with linguistic or conceptual items than were the modal notions, largely because contradiction and repugnancy were technical terms in logic. It might be said, for example, that a thing is impossible if its non-existence implies a contradiction, and this would probably be understood to mean that a thing is impossible if the thing (or the proposition asserting its existence) implies a proposition which is contradictory.

Logic texts spoke of contradictory terms as well as contradictory propositions. According to the *Port-Royal Logic*, two propositions are

---

[5] For passages illustrating this context see Cudworth, *True Intellectual System*, p. 719; Toland, *Christianity Not Mysterious*, p. 39; Clarke, *Discourse*, p. 70 ('That infinite Power reaches to all *Possible* things; but cannot be said to extend to the working any thing which implies a *Contradiction*'); 'Mr. Leibnitz's Fifth Paper', p. 81 in H. G. Alexander (ed.), *The Leibniz–Clarke Correspondence*, Manchester, 1956: 'God can produce every thing that is possible, or whatever does not imply a contradiction'; Henry More, *An Antidote against Atheism*, Book I, chap. vii, § 4 in Flora MacKinnon (ed.) *Philosophical Writings of Henry More*, New York, 1925: 'For *Omnipotency* signifies a power that can effect any thing that implies no contradiction to be effected' (p. 19); and the passages from Locke and Malebranche quoted in nn. 1 and 2.

contradictory when they differ both in quantity (that is, in whether the subject term applies to all or some members of a class) and in quality (that is, in whether the proposition is affirmative or negative).[6] This standard definition was enshrined in general dictionaries such as John Harris's *Lexicon Technicum:*[7]

CONTRADICTORY *Propositions*, in Logick, are either such as consist of an Universal and Particular, of which one Affirms, and the other Denies, as thus; *All Right lined Triangles have the sum of their Angles equal to two Right ones; Some Right lined Triangles have not the sum of their Angles equal to two Right ones*, or else they are both Singular and Particular, one Affirming, the other Denying the same Thing, as *the Circle is Squarable, the Circle is not Squarable.*

Arnauld and Nicole say that *terms* are contradictories 'which consist in a Term, and the simple Negation of that Term—*seeing, not seeing*'. Contradictory terms are used, they explain, in such a way that one denies the other. Contradictory terms have this property, they say, 'that in rejecting one we establish the other.'[8] In view of the strong linguistic or logical associations of contradiction and repugnancy it is perhaps misleading to say that the philosophers of the period tended to *identify* impossibility with repugnancy. It would be more accurate to say that they *understood* the modal notions *in terms* of repugnancy: a thing is *impossible* if its definition involves or implies contradictory terms, *possible* if its definition does not involve or imply contradictory terms, and *necessary* if its non-existence involves or implies a contradiction. A state of affairs is *impossible* if the proposition asserting that it obtains involves or implies a contradiction, *possible* if the proposition does not involve or imply a contradiction, and *necessary* if the negation of the proposition involves or implies a contradiction. From a twentieth-century point of view there are difficulties in these formulations, but these difficulties will not interfere with the interpretation of seventeenth and eighteenth century texts and concerns. From now on, when I speak of the identification of impossibility with repugnancy, it is the view encapsulated in these more cumbersome formulas that I will have in mind.

The modal notions raise two important problems. The first

[6] *Logic: Or, the Art of Thinking*, pt. II, chap. iv, p. 132. This definition was standard in logic textbooks and handbooks used in Britain in the late 17th and early 18th centuries. See e.g. *Monitio Logica: Or, An Abstract and Translation of Burgersdicius His Logick*, London, 1697, pp. 93, 129.

[7] London, 1704.

[8] *Logic: Or, the Art of Thinking*, pt. III, chap. xviii, pp. 305–6.

concerns the nature of modality. What are possibility, impossibility, and necessity? Just what is it, in other words, that gives a thing or state of affairs its modal status? If these questions had been raised in these terms in the seventeenth or early eighteenth century, it would have been demanded that the modal notions turn out to be *objective*. Whether a thing is possible or impossible would not be permitted to vary from knower to knower or from time to time. The identification of impossibility with repugnancy seems to meet this condition, because repugnancy seems to be an objective matter. Either a proposition is repugnant or it is not, and if it is repugnant for one person at one time then it is repugnant for anyone at any time. But success with the first problem only makes the second, epistemological, problem more acute: how do we *know* when a proposition is possible, impossible, or necessary? How can we be confident of a judgement with a scope as wide as that of modal judgements, embracing all persons, places, and times? Once again the identification of impossibility with repugnancy provides an answer. The identification removes the mystery from our knowledge of modality because once the identification is accepted, knowing what is possible or necessary is simply a matter of mastering the terms and syncategorematic apparatus on which contradiction or repugnancy depends. The mechanism of repugnancy is laid bare by logic, and if the modal notions are analysed in terms of the notion of repugnancy then our knowledge of modality, if it isn't explained entirely, is at any rate reduced to our knowledge of the logic of the language that we speak.

Berkeley's contemporaries were aware of the gap between taking a proposition or state of affairs to be contradictory or repugnant and its actually being so. This awareness accounts for Locke's caution in announcing the possibility that matter may think. For all we know, he says, it is possible that we are systems of matter, because we see no contradiction in it. But it might nevertheless be impossible, and if it is then there is, in Locke's view, a contradiction in it, even if we are too dim-witted to see it. But despite their awareness of the gap, Berkeley's contemporaries for the most part ignored the problem to which it leads. How reliable are our judgements of contradictoriness, and if the modal notions are to be understood in terms of contradictoriness, how reliable are our judgements of possibility, impossibility, and necessity? In his *Essay concerning the Use of Reason*, for example, Anthony Collins raises this problem only to put it aside as one which, if taken too seriously, would stifle enquiry altogether. The distinction between a real and seeming contradiction, he says, 'is manifestly of no use when apply'd to the Understanding, but only to teach us to examine with Care and Caution'. He concludes that 'while things appear repugnant, we must judge them repugnant, if we will ever make any judgment at all'.[9] John Toland also claimed that 'a *seeming* Contradiction is to us as much as a *real* one'.[10] One mark of a great philosopher is that he allows himself to be engaged by problems which others dismiss. In this chapter I will suggest that Berkeley eventually abandoned the distinction between simple and complex ideas because he was dissatisfied with the account of modality he took it to imply.

1. *Simple and complex ideas*

In this chapter I want to develop what I have already said about Berkeley's views on possibility and necessity by defending the following hypothesis: Berkeley was attracted to the distinction between simple and complex ideas because he saw it as a way of understanding or analysing the modal notions, and he eventually rejected the distinction largely because he came to see that it failed in the role he had envisaged for it. Because there is no text in which Berkeley openly confesses to this, or even a text which can be explained only by supposing it is true, my hypothesis cannot be proven. What I have to offer in its defence is the unification and illumination the hypothesis provides for a good deal of what goes on in Berkeley's notebooks. The hypothesis will also supply a useful background against which we can view the claims of impossibility, necessity, and repugnancy in Berkeley's published works.

I want to begin by asking what might be done with the kind of distinction between simple and complex ideas contemplated by Berkeley in the notebooks. It will be recalled that Berkeley places two conditions on genuinely simple ideas, apart from the requirement that they be 'distinct', or able to stand before the mind in isolation. First, a genuinely simple idea must not be necessarily connected with any other simple idea. The existence of a simple idea, in other words, cannot entail or imply the existence of any other. Second, if two genuinely simple ideas are, despite their diversity, alike, Berkeley

---

[9] *An Essay concerning the Use of Reason in Propositions The Evidence whereof depends upon Human Testimony* 2nd edn., London, 1709, pp. 32 (first passage), 33 (second passage).

[10] *Christianity Not Mysterious*, p. 35.

stipulates that they can only be alike in ways that are external or extrinsic. They may be intromitted by the same sense, or connected with the same kind of ideas, but they canot be alike considered in themselves. Even if they are connected with the same kind of ideas the connections cannot, of course, be necessary. If they were, that would violate the first condition.

Although there can be no necessary connections between simple ideas or internal resemblances among them, such connections or resemblances would be possible if one of the terms were a *complex* idea, an idea created by blending simple ideas together. The word 'blending' can be misleading; as Berkeley understands the process of blending or composition, it is really one of *definition*. We create a complex idea by defining the associated expression. The complex idea then 'includes' the simple ideas of which the definition speaks. Because it is merely a process of definition the creation of complex ideas does nothing to alter the course of our experience. How I choose to collect ideas will not affect the ideas of sense I receive, though the patterns formed by ideas of sense will naturally influence the definitions I choose to make. Once complex ideas have been created there will be necessary connections with complex ideas as terms. If, for example, a complex idea includes a particular simple idea in its definition then the two ideas will be necessarily connected: the existence of the complex idea (that is, the occurrence of an idea or object corresponding to the definition) will entail the existence of the simple one. Furthermore, two complex ideas will be internally alike whenever they share a common element, and every complex idea will resemble, internally, the simple ideas of which it is composed.[11]

The effect of a successful distinction between simple and complex idea would thus be to rule out two kinds of necessary truth at the level

[11] A moment ago I spoke of the *existence of a complex idea*, a notion that can be interpreted in at least two ways. When a complex idea is created by an act of definition, the only entity thereby brought into existence is an idea of imagination. If, for example, the word apple is defined in terms of 'a certain colour, taste, smell, figure and consistence' (*Principles* 1), the act of definition will carry with it an idea of imagination of five constituents, each of them an abstract idea as described in Introduction 7 or 8. Once the word apple has been defined it will be possible for the newly-created idea of imagination to be *instantiated*: ideas of sense can now occur in patterns that will count as *instances* of the complex idea of apple, even though the ideas of sense (taken by themselves) are as loose and separate as they were before the definition had been contemplated. The *existence of a complex idea* can refer either to the existence of the idea of imagination created by the act of definition (an idea which, once created, might be brought into view on other occasions), or to the occurrence of a pattern of sensations which instantiates the idea defined.

of simple ideas: truths asserting necessary connections, and truths asserting internal resemblances. Such truths would, however, be available one level up, at the level of complex ideas. If y is, by definition, part of the complex which is x, then x cannot be conceived apart from y. And if y is, again by definition, part of both x and z, then x and z are internally alike. But as Berkeley observes at *Commentaries* 760, 'Complex Ideas are the Creatures of the Mind.' Although it would be necessarily true that x is y or that x and z are alike, x and z would be our own creations, and the necessary truths in which they figure would merely record our determination to collect ideas together in a certain way. These truths would be *formal* or *definitional*, consequences of the ways in which our complex ideas had been assembled or defined. They would also be *analytic* in a sense close to Kant's: their truth could be discovered by analysing or dissecting the complex ideas that they involve. To deny such a truth would be to take away what its subject already posits.

The distinction as I have deployed it would not of course render *all* necessary truths formal or analytic. Like Kant's own definition of analyticity, which is confined to judgements of subject–predicate form, the distinction does not even begin to deal with certain judgements which are, pre-analytically at any rate, necessarily true. I nevertheless believe that at one time Berkeley saw the distinction as a way of unlocking the secret of *all* modality. The important point here is not so much that he wanted to understand modality in terms of this particular distinction, but that he wanted to understand it in a way that would make modality something formal or definitional, a consequence of our linguistic or conceptual activity rather than a reflection of something built into the course of experience itself. He came to see that this attempt failed, yet he never really decided whether the failure proved that modality is not, after all, a formal matter, or proved instead that the machinery he had relied on to expose its formal character was insufficient for the task. As a first step in defence of this hypothesis, I want to turn to the notebook entries on demonstration. Demonstration is closely related to the topic of contradiction or repugnancy, because a truth capable of demonstration was universally regarded as a truth whose denial is contradictory.

2. *Demonstration, necessity, and certainty*

The main theme of Berkeley's notebook entries on demonstration is that demonstration is a verbal matter, a drawing out of the consequences of our definitions.

| Mo | The reason why we can demonstrate so well about signs is that | 732 |
| × | they are perfectly arbitrary & in our power, made at pleasure. | |

Mo	Let any Man shew me a Demonstration not verbal that does	734
×	not depend either on some false principle or at best on some	
×	principle of Nature which is ye effect of God's will and we	
	know not how soon it may be changed.	

| Mo.× | Reasoning there may be about things or Ideas Actions but | 804 |
| N | Demonstration can be only Verbal. I question, no matter etc | |

The notebooks also show that at one time Berkeley planned to demonstrate the truth of immaterialism.

| + | Newton begs his Principle, † I demonstrate mine | 407 |

	I shall Demonstrate all my Doctrines. The Nature of Demonstra-	586
	tion to be set forth & insisted on in the Introduction. In that I must	
	needs differ from Locke forasmuch as he makes all Demonstration	
	to be about abstract Ideas wch I say we have not nor can have.	

We have already seen one attempt at demonstration in entry 378. Note that in 586 Berkeley says that he will demonstrate *all* his doctrines, and that he will pave the way for the demonstrations by setting forth (in a projected Introduction) the nature of demonstration itself. The same plan for the Introduction is laid at entry 212: '+ Mem: Introduction to contain the design of the whole the nature & manner of demonstrating &c.' In a later entry these bold plans are cancelled:

I	I must not pretend to promise much of Demonstration, I must	858
	cancell all passages that look like that sort of Pride, that raising of	
	Expectation in my Readers.	

In spite of this entry the first edition of the *Principles* did contain promises of demonstration, though they were promises it was very easy to overlook. In the Preface, after saying that he will make no apology for the '*novelty and singularity*' of his conclusions, Berkeley writes that:

He must surely be either very weak, or very little acquainted with the sciences, who shall reject a truth, that is capable of demonstration, for no other reason but because it's newly known and contrary to the prejudices of mankind.

In § 7 he offers what he describes as a 'demonstration' of the view that 'there is not any other substance than *spirit*', and in § 61 he claims that his conclusions are established '*a priori*, with the utmost evidence and rigor of demonstration'. But in spite of these claims made in 1710 entry 858 does reflect his considered view of the demonstrability of immaterialism. In the 1734 edition of the *Principles* the Preface is withdrawn; § 7 speaks not of 'demonstration' but, much more weakly, of 'proof', which in the eighteenth century generally signified a non-demonstrative argument; and § 61 says that Berkeley's arguments enjoy not the rigour of demonstration but only 'the utmost evidence'.[12]

Although he was unable to demonstrate the truth of immaterialism Berkeley continued to believe in its necessity. Because he never questioned the widespread conviction that a necessary truth is one that can be demonstrated, his failure to demonstrate his principle left him with a choice, one he never finally resolved. On the one hand, he could have decided that the immaterialist principle was not after all a demonstrable truth. On the other hand, he could have decided that the mechanisms of demonstration he had at his disposal were somehow insufficient to demonstrate everything that could be demonstrated. Either choice is consistent with the view of demonstration explored in the notebooks—the view that demonstration is an unfolding of the definitions of meanings of words—and each is consistent with the closely related view that necessary truths are those whose denial is contradictory. We have already seen evidence of Berkeley's attachment to these views in Hylas's claim that a thing is shown to be impossible when a repugnancy is demonstrated 'between the ideas comprehended in its definition'. I now hope to show that the notebook view of demonstration is also at work in the *Principles*, and that it survives even in passages added in 1734, when, as we have seen, Berkeley finally brings the text of the *Principles* into line with his youthful injunction not to promise much in the way of demonstration. The depth and persistence of Berkeley's commitment to the notebook view will lend support to my account of his interest in the distinction between simple and complex ideas. A study of the Introduction will also give me an opportunity to look more closely at the way in which the mind attends selectively to ideas.

At Introduction 16 Berkeley explains how a geometrical demonstration is able to support a universal conclusion:

---

[12] On proof v. demonstration see David Hume, *Treatise of Human Nature*, Bk. I, pt. III, sect. xi, p. 124, and *Enquiry concerning Human Understanding*, sect. vi, p. 56. The background of these passages is presented by M. Jamie Ferreira in *Scepticism and Reasonable Doubt*, Oxford, 1986, pp. 1–61.

Though the idea I have in view whilst I make the demonstration, be, for instance, that of an isosceles rectangular triangle, whose sides are of a determinate length, I may nevertheless be certain it extends to all other rectilinear triangles, of what sort or bigness soever. And that, because neither the right angle, nor the equality, nor determinate length of the sides, are at all concerned in the demonstration. It is true, the diagram I have in view includes all these particulars, but then there is not the least mention made of them in the proof of the proposition.

This passage is usually read to imply that diagrams are *essential* to geometrical proofs. But the final sentence says just the opposite: when I work through the proof I may have in view an idea or diagram that includes certain particulars, but 'not the least mention' is made of those particulars in the proof itself. This means that the idea or diagram cannot be part of the proof, for if it were, its inclusion of certain features would certainly constitute 'mention' of them. Berkeley's point at Introduction 16, it seems to me, is precisely that a demonstration does *not* involve an idea or diagram. Demonstration depends instead on *definitions*, as Berkeley explains in a letter to Samuel Molyneux, written six months before the passage just quoted was published:

It appears to Me That in Geometricall Reasonings We do not make any Discovery by contemplating the Ideas of the Lines whose Properties are investigated. For example, In order to discover the Method of drawing Tangents to a Parabola, 'tis true a Figure is drawn on paper & so suggested to your Fancy, but no Matter whether it be of a Parabolic Line or no, the Demonstration proceeds as well tho it be an Hyperbole or the Portion of an Ellipsis, provided that I have regard to the Equation expressing the nature of a Parabola . . . it being this Equation of the nature of the Curve thus expressed and not the Idea of it that leads to the Solution. (*Works* VIII, p. 27.)

The proof, Berkeley tells Molyneux, depends on 'the Equation expressing the Nature of the Parabola'—not on the accompanying idea or diagram, but on the definition of 'parabola'. If, as I am suggesting, he is making a similar point at Introduction 16, then the words which close Introduction 18 make perfect sense:

'Tis one thing for to keep a name constantly to the same definition, and another to make it stand everywhere for the same idea: the one is necessary, the other useless and impracticable.

Constancy of definition is required because it is the definition that the demonstration unfolds. Constancy of idea is unnecessary because the idea is simply irrelevant. Demonstration can proceed without ideas, or at least 'without other Ideas than the Words & their standing for one idea, i.e. their being to be used indifferently' (*Commentaries* 730a).[13]

This reading of the Introduction to the *Principles* has not been proposed before because it seems to go against some lines added to Introduction 16 in 1734:

And here it must be acknowledged that a man may consider a figure merely as triangular, without attending to the particular qualities of the angles, or relations of the sides. So far he may abstract: but this will never prove, that he can frame an abstract general inconsistent idea of a triangle. In like manner we may consider Peter so far forth as man, or so far forth as animal, without framing the forementioned abstract idea, either of man or of animal, in as much as all that is perceived is not considered.

These lines are intended to accommodate selective attention, and they do suggest that when we work through a demonstration we have an idea in view, some of whose features we attend to and some of whose features we ignore. 'All that is perceived is not considered', Berkeley writes, and this certainly suggests that the geometer contemplates an object even if the object does not determine the content of his or her thought. But a closer look at the notion of selective attention—which has so far remained unanalysed—will reveal that this is not the only reading of the added lines, and when the lines are placed against the background of the notebooks and the letter to Molyneux it will be apparent, I think, that it is not the best reading.

The doctrine of selective attention can be understood in two very different ways. On what might be called the *contemplation* interpretation of the doctrine, the mind manages to think abstractly or in general terms by making a purely intellectual adjustment. The mind fixes its gaze on certain features of the object before it and pays no attention to the other features that remain. But on what might be called the *activity* version of the doctrine, the mind manages to think abstractly by engaging in an activity other than purely intellectual concentration on the features of a presented object. One such activity might be conversation. I might consider Peter 'so far forth as man' by participating in a conversation about Peter—a medical conversation, perhaps—in which Peter's manhood is the only thing about him that

---

[13] It is worth observing how odd it would be odd for Berkeley to contend that visible diagrams are essential to demonstrations. He believes, after all, that the proper object of geometry is *tangible* extension, and he often stresses that tangible and visible extension have nothing at all in common.

matters. Another such activity might be *demonstration*. I might consider a figure merely as triangular by exploring the consequences of the definition of *triangle*, even though the idea I have in view (the diagram or image I contemplate) is of a triangle whose angles and sides have particular proportions. It seems to me that *both* versions of the doctrine of selective attention have a hold on Berkeley. At times—when he writes, for example, that all that is perceived is not considered—what he has in mind, I think, is the contemplation interpretation. But in his remarks on demonstration it is the activity interpretation to which he is giving a voice. This is what we should expect in view of the notebook entries and the letter to Molyneux. And it is the most natural reading of Philonous' account of abstract thinking in the First Dialogue:

I acknowledge, Hylas, it is not difficult to form general propositions and reasonings about those qualities, without mentioning any other; and in this sense to consider or treat of them abstractedly. But how doth it follow that because I can produce the word *motion* by itself, I can form the idea of it in my mind exclusive of body? Or because theorems may be made of extension and figures, without any mention of *great* or *small*, or any other sensible mode or quality; that therefore it is possible such an abstract idea of extension, without any particular size or figure, or sensible quality, should be distinctly formed, and apprehended by the mind? Mathematicians treat of quantity, without regarding what other sensible qualities it is attended with, as being altogether indifferent to their demonstrations. But when laying aside the words, they contemplate the bare ideas, I believe you will find, they are not the pure abstracted ideas of extension. (*Works* II, p. 193.)

Here Philonous tells us that when mathematicians lay aside words and contemplate 'the bare ideas'—when they lay aside the definitions that are their real concern and turn back to the corresponding objects—they realize that the objects have sensible qualities their definitions ignore. As Berkeley writes at entry 750 in the *Commentaries*,

× Words (by them meaning all sorts of signs) are so necessary that instead of being (w^n duly us'd or in their own Nature) prejudicial to the Advancement of knowledge, or an hindrance to knowledge that wth out them there could in Mathematiques themselves be no demonstration.

It might be thought that the activity interpretation of the doctrine of selective attention amounts to a purely behaviouristic account of abstract thinking, according to which thinking in abstract terms is simply a matter of making patterned marks or sounds. This is by no means the case. The activity interpretation specifies that *on a particular occasion*, a person can think in general terms by manipulating sounds or marks. Yet it may still be the case that what allows us to say that the person *understands* what he or she is doing—what guarantees that he or she is not just manipulating sounds or marks—is that he or she has had an idea of a triangle, or, perhaps, even that he or she has attended to the triangularity of that idea in the way described by the contemplation interpretation. The power to contemplate the idea of a triangle while considering nothing but its triangularity would then be a necessary condition of considering nothing but triangularity when working through a demonstration, even though the act of demonstration narrowly taken (from the time the axioms are recorded to the time the theorem to be proved is reached) may involve only the manipulation of signs.

I believe that Berkeley would give the contemplation interpretation priority over the activity interpretation in something like the way I have described. It is true, though, that there are resources in Berkeley's writing that would permit a more thoroughly behaviouristic treatment. Berkeley could say that what is required for understanding is not the vision of an object a mere machine is denied, but an engagement with the world—an engagement involving both sense-perception and action—of which a device whose only output consists of other signs is simply incapable. If sense-perception and action were then analysed behaviouristically, this account could then be extended into a fully behaviouristic account of abstract thinking. But it would be a misrepresentation to say that Berkeley gives such an account, even in passages where the dependence of understanding on practice is particularly emphasized.

That Berkeley takes contemplation to be basic is suggested by several passages in the Introduction. At Introduction 19 we are told it is unnecessary for names that stand for ideas to excite those ideas on every occasion of their use. In reading and discoursing, Berkeley explains, names are used for the most part as letters are in algebra, 'in which though a particular quantity be marked by each letter, yet to proceed right it is not requisite that in every step each letter suggest to your thoughts, that particular quantity it was appointed to stand for'. The claim that stimulating the idea is not necessary at *every* step is obviously meant to leave room for insisting that those who understand the discourse must have had the idea in mind at *some* time.[14] Berkeley

---

[14] See similar passages at *Alciphron* VII 5 and 7 (pp. 331, 335 in vol. 3 of the *Works*) in the 1st and 2nd edns.

does not say that understanding the discourse is possible only for those who have attended to the abstract features with which the discourse is concerned. But he clearly suggests it in passages such as the following, which concludes his initial attempt to account for the universality of demonstration:

When I demonstrate any proposition concerning triangles, it is to be supposed that I have in view the universal idea of a triangle; which ought not to be understood as if I could frame an idea of a triangle which was neither equilateral nor scalenon nor equicrural. But only that the particular triangle I consider, whether of this or that sort it matters not, doth equally stand for and represent all rectilinear triangles whatsoever, and is in that sense *universal*. All which seems very plain and not to include any difficulty in it. (Introduction 15.)

In this passage Berkeley insists on the presence of an idea, and although he does not say that the mind must concentrate on its triangularity (ignoring, let us say, its equal sides), it is scarcely credible that he would insist on the idea if the idea did not link up in some important way with the activity of proof. Yet he refrains from saying that the idea is an essential part of the demonstration. On the view I am proposing, idea and proof are linked because the comprehending mind must at some point attend to the features of the idea picked out by the definition on which the demonstration turns. The demonstration narrowly considered does not depend on such partial consideration, but the attribution of understanding to the mind of the demonstrator does.

My discussion of Berkeley's published comments on demonstration was prompted by the observation that Berkeley never explicitly decided whether the immaterialist principle, which he was unable to demonstrate, was not after all demonstrable, or whether the mechanisms of demonstration at his disposal were simply insufficient to demonstrate everything that could be demonstrated. I am now prepared to state and defend a hypothesis which is preliminary to the main hypothesis it is the purpose of this chapter to establish. According to the preliminary hypothesis, Berkeley explored the distinction between simple and complex ideas because he saw its potential as a device for displaying the formal or verbal character of both contradiction and demonstration. When it is placed in the context of the eighteenth-century association between the notion of necessity on the one hand, and the notions of contradiction and demonstration on the other, this preliminary hypothesis leads to the main one: Berkeley explored the distinction between simple and complex ideas because he saw it as a device for displaying or clarifying the formal or verbal character of necessary truth, and he lost faith in the distinction because he realized that it could not play the role he had envisaged for it. He found nothing to take its place, and his views on modality were left suspended between a number of alternatives, though it is far from clear that the alternatives were clearly delineated by Berkeley himself.

We have seen that according to Berkeley's notebooks, demonstration must be 'only verbal' (entry 804). In other entries, which I will discuss at greater length in a moment, Berkeley characterized certain truths of demonstration as 'only' or 'meerly' *nominal* (793, 739). All these entries were composed against the background of Locke's discussion of trifling propositions at *Essay* IV viii. At entry 771 of the notebooks Berkeley calls attention to this chapter:

×Mo   Locke of Trifling Propositions. Mem: well to observe & con over that
       chapter.

In *Essay* IV viii Locke isolates two types of trifling propositions: first, '*All purely identical Propositions*' (§ 2), such as *body is body* (Locke's own example at § 3); and second, propositions in which '*a part of the complex* Idea *is predicated of the Name of the whole*; a part of the Definition of the Word defined' (§ 4). Propositions of either type are according to Locke '*only* verbal' (§ 13), or 'barely about the signification of Sounds' (§ 12). Locke explains what it means to call a proposition 'only verbal' in chapter v of Book IV. There he defines truth as '*the joining or separating of Signs, as the Things signified by them, do agree or disagree with one another*' (§ 2). The joining or separating of signs is a proposition, and because there are two kinds of signs—ideas and words—there are two kinds of propositions: *mental* propositions, which join or separate ideas without the use of words; and *verbal* propositions, which join or separate words. The distinction between the two kinds of propositions complicates Locke's definition of truth:

When *Ideas* are so put together, or separated in the Mind, as they, or the Things they stand for do agree, or not, that is, as I may call it, *mental Truth*. But *Truth of Words* is something more, and that is the affirming or denying of Words one of another, as the *Ideas* they stand for agree or disagree. (IV v 6.)

Truth of words is 'something more' because it presupposes mental truth or 'truth of ideas': if I say that all *S* are *P* the verbal proposition I create is true only if the corresponding mental proposition is also true.

Locke goes on to distinguish two kinds of truth of words: 'Either *purely Verbal*, and trifling, . . . *or Real* and instructive' (§ 6). Locke explains that the difference between the two varieties of verbal truth is that in the first case, 'Terms are joined according to the agreement or disagreement of the *Ideas* they stand for, without regarding whether our Ideas are such, as really have, or are capable of having an Existence in Nature' (IV v 8).

When it is placed alongside remarks made elsewhere in the *Essay*, Locke's taxonomy of the kinds of truth is liable to be confusing. One of the themes of *Essay* IV iv, for example, is that we have real knowledge—knowledge whose object is real truth (see IV v 6)—when our ideas answer their archetypes. But when ideas serve as their own archetypes, as they do in the case of mixed modes, knowledge and the truth which is its object will be real even when we do not consider whether the modes in question really exist in nature. Many truths about mixed modes will, in fact, be trifling, a circumstance that casts doubt on Locke's apparent assumption at IV v 6 that the class of real truths and the class of instructive truths will always coincide. Another difficulty is Locke's claim at *Essay* IV viii 12 that certain 'barely verbal propositions' (which are, as *Essay* IV v 8 seems to suggest, the same as *purely* verbal propositions) are propositions 'barely about the signification of Sounds'. If even purely verbal truths are a species of verbal truth, and if every verbal truth presupposes the corresonding mental one, then how can any purely verbal truth be about sounds or words alone?

Locke is actually working to articulate several different distinctions in the passages we have reviewed. One distinction he is seeking to make—the distinction of particular importance to Berkeley—is a distinction between propositions which depend for their truth only on the way in which words are defined (propositions which might be described as being 'barely about the signification of Sounds') and propositions which depend for their truth on something else. It is fair to say that propositions of the former kind are *purely verbal*. Locke has trouble isolating these truths by means of the labels 'verbal' or 'purely verbal' because he is committed to the view that all verbal truth depends on mental truth. It seems that a proposition cannot be 'barely about the signification of Sounds' if its truth-conditions involve the agreement or disagreement of ideas. But there is in fact no difficulty. To say that a proposition depends for its truth on the way in which words are defined is just to say that it depends for its truth on the way in which complex ideas are composed by the mind. As Locke himself indicates at *Essay* IV viii 4, to predicate part of the complex idea of the name of the whole is to predicate 'a part of the Definition of the word defined'. The characteristic property of the verbal truths Locke calls *trifling* is that their truth depends only on the mind's determination to use signs in a certain way, and because such determination can be understood equally well as an act of definition or as a process of idea-formation, these truths can be 'barely about the signification of Sounds' even though, like other verbal truths, they rest on mental propositions.

I said earlier that Berkeley's notebook entries on demonstration were composed against the background of Locke's discussion of trifling propositions. When Berkeley says that the truths of demonstration are verbal or nominal he means that they are purely verbal in the sense just identified, that they are what Locke calls *trifling* propositions. This lends support to my preliminary hypothesis because Locke characterizes trifling propositions in terms of the distinction between simple and complex ideas.

We can see that Berkeley views the truths of demonstration as trifling if we consider some of the ways in which he differs from Locke. Locke himself denies that all demonstrable truths are trifling. He writes at *Essay* IV viii 8, in a remark foreshadowing Kant's characterization of synthetic a priori judgement, that 'we can know the Truth, and so may be *certain* in Propositions, which affirm something of another, which is a necessary consequence of its precise complex *Idea*, but not contained in it.'[15] The example he goes on to provide is mathematical:

As that *the external Angle of all Triangles, is bigger than either of the opposite internal Angles*; which relation of the outward Angle, to either of the opposite internal Angles, making no part of the complex *Idea*, signified by the name Triangle, this is a real truth, and conveys with it instructive *real Knowledge*.

Berkeley responds to these passages in several notebook entries suggesting that apparently instructive certainties can in fact be reduced to trifling and uninstructive truths of inclusion. In entry 676 Berkeley identifies three sorts of truth: natural, mathematical, and moral. In the next entry he writes,

Mo   Agreement of relation onely where Numbers do obtain. of Coexistence

---

[15] Kant's characterization comes in the *Critique of Pure Reason*, trans. Norman Kemp Smith, London, 1929, p. 49: 'A predicate, not contained in this concept, nevertheless belongs to it.'

×   in nature, of signification or Including or thinking by Including in Morality.

In this entry Berkeley is making use of two categories identified by Locke, as well as proposing a new one of his own. Locke had said (*Essay* IV i) that all agreement or disagreement of ideas can be reduced to four heads: identity or diversity (*white is white*, or *white is not red*); relation (*two triangles upon equal basis, between two parallels, are equal*); coexistence or noncoexistence (*gold is fixed*, where fixedness is understood not to be included in the complex idea of gold; see IV i 6) and real existence (*God is*). In entry 677 Berkeley adds knowledge 'of signification or Including' to the second and third Lockean categories. Locke places mathematical knowledge under the second of his four headings, and his claim that morality is capable of demonstration—a claim typically made by comparing morality to mathematics (see IV iii 18 and IV xii 8)—indicates that he would place moral knowledge there as well. Locke writes,

The *Relation* of other *Modes* may certainly be perceived, as well as those of Number and Extension: and I cannot see, why they should not also be capable of Demonstration, if due Methods were thought on to examine, or pursue their Agreement or Disagreement. *Where there is no Property, there is no Injustice*, is a Proposition as certain as any Demonstration in *Euclid*. . . . (IV iii 18.)

As Berkeley observes in entry 691, 'Locke's instances of Demonstration in Morality are according to his own Rule trifling Propositions.' But Berkeley also commits himself to the more extreme conclusion that all truths of relation are trifling or uninstructive. In entry 739 he claims that knowledge of relation is 'meerly Nominal'. (As noted above, at *Essay* IV v 8 Locke uses 'barely nominal' as an apparent substitute for 'purely verbal'.) The entry reads:

N   Knowledge or certainty or perception of agreement of ideas as to
Mo   Identity & diversity & real existence Vanisheth of relation becometh
×   meerly Nominal of Coexistence remaineth. Locke thought in this later our knowledge was little or nothing whereas in this onely real knowledge seemeth to be found.

In entry 853 Berkeley writes,

Mo   Three sorts of usefull knowledge, that of coexistence to be treated of in
N   our Principles of Natural Philosophy, that of Relation in Mathematiques,
×   that of definition, or inclusion, or Words (wch perhaps differs not from that of Relation) in Morality.

In entry 853 Berkeley makes it clear that moral knowledge is nominal or trifling. But he also observes that knowledge of definition or inclusion 'differs not' from knowledge of relation. It is clear, I think, that Berkeley's intention is not to propose that knowledge of definition or inclusion is a special case of knowledge of relation, but that knowledge of relation is instead a special case of knowledge of inclusion, in terms of which it must be understood. If I am right, then Berkeley is saying in effect that the most conspicuous examples of truths of demonstration can be reduced to truths of inclusion. Both mathematical and moral science are reduced to systems of trifling propositions, the uninstructive character of which can be revealed by means of the distinction between simple and complex ideas. Locke himself had said that all relations terminate in simple ideas (II xxviii 18, II xxv 9), and in the context of the notebook entries on the reduction of relation to inclusion the stringent conditions Berkeley places on simple ideas fall into place. There can be no internal similarities among simple ideas because all relations—resemblance included—must be understood in terms of inclusion, or in terms of the identities on which truths of inclusion rest. If distinct ideas are alike they must include a common element; the only relation permitted among the ultimate constituents is the relation of sameness or identity.

The discussion of the last few pages can now be brought to bear on my preliminary hypothesis. I have suggested that Berkeley's notebook entries on demonstration and truth were informed by Locke's discussions of these topics in the *Essay*, and that Berkeley's claim that the truths of demonstration are only verbal must be understood as the claim that they are, in Locke's language, trifling. According to the notebooks they are propositions which depend for their truth on nothing more than the way in which words are defined. Against the background of his reading of the *Essay*, Berkeley's interest in the distinction between simple and complex ideas, and the surprisingly strict conditions he places on simplicity, now seem comprehensible. In the notebooks Berkeley is experimenting with the possibility that the notion of demonstrable truth—and with it the closely related notion of contradiction—can be analysed in terms of the distinction between simple and complex ideas. A truth is demonstrable (and its denial a contradiction) if and only if it is a trifling proposition of one of the two kinds identified by Locke. My preliminary hypothesis ties together the various notebook entries on demonstration and truth and makes sense of Berkeley's preoccupation with the corresponding chapters in

Locke's *Essay*, to which those entries are plainly indebted. The reading of the notebooks it permits lends significant support to my preliminary hypothesis.

Further support is provided by the notebook entries on certainty. Berkeley's views on certainty developed in an interesting way. Unlike Locke, who insisted that all verbal propositions depend for their truth on underlying mental propositions, Berkeley was unwilling to say that there are mental propositions corresponding to the verbal propositions he calls trifling.

Mo   Homo est Homo etc comes at last to Petrus est Petrus etc Now if   728
these identical Propositions are sought after in the Mind they
will not be found. there are no identical mental Propositions tis
all about sounds & terms.

This leads Berkeley to conclude that

Mo   Hence we see the Doctrine of Certainty by Ideas & proving by   729
intermediate Ideas comes to Nothing.

The doctrine 'comes to Nothing' because all of the propositions involved in demonstration—not just identical propositions—are 'about sounds & terms'. Demonstration or proof does not involve mental propositions at all:

Mo   We may have certainty & knowledge without ideas ∧   730

Mo   ∧ i.e. without other Ideas than the Words & their standing for   730a
one idea i.e. their being to be used indifferently.

In the next entry in the series Berkeley moves from the claim that we can have certainty and knowledge without ideas to the claim that we *cannot* have it *with* them:

*   It seems to me that we have no certainty about Ideas but onely   731
Mo   about words. tis improper to say I am certain I see, I feel etc.
there are no Mental propositions form'd answering to these
Words & in simple perception tis allowed by all there is no
affirmation or negation & consequently no certainty.

This series of entries is followed by Berkeley's explanation of how we can demonstrate 'so well about signs', where by *signs* he clearly means words: signs, he explains, are 'perfectly arbitrary & in our power, made at pleasure' (732).

Now in entry 731 Berkeley is thinking only of the kind of certainty found in mathematics and, if Locke is correct, in morals. He has the same kind of certainty in mind in the following entry from earlier in the notebooks, which is, however, marked with a plus sign:

+ Metaphisiques as capable of Certainty as Ethiques but not so   239
    capable to be demonstrated in a Geometrical way because men
    see clearer & have not so many prejudices in Ethiques.

Locke himself had recognized at least one other kind of certainty: our certainty of the real existence of an object at the moment we are sensing it, which he called *sensitive knowledge* (IV xi 3; IV ii 14). After composing 731 Berkeley realized that he too wanted to recognize a kind of certainty that mathematics cannot be expected to provide. On the *verso* page he added the following correction to 731:

*   this seems wrong certainty real certainty is of sensible Ideas pro hic &
    nunc. I may be certain without affirmation or negation.

Berkeley realizes that he does not want to confine certainty to the demonstrative sciences. But if we put what might be called sensible certainty aside, confining our attention to the demonstrative certainty that is the topic of entries 728 to 731, it seems clear that Berkeley seriously considered the possibility that all certainty is verbal in a very strong sense: it does not depend on ideas, 'other than the Words & their standing for one idea'. These entries support my claim that Berkeley experimented with the idea that demonstrative truths are trifling.[16]

With the exception of entry 239, the entries we have just been studying are concerned entirely with ethics or mathematics and make no mention of philosophical or metaphysical propositions. But in three entries in the earlier Notebook B, entry 239 among them, Berkeley classifies metaphysics, mathematics, and morals as demonstrable sciences, just as his early boast that he would demonstrate immaterialism would lead us to expect. In entry 162 for example, Berkeley explains that mathematics has an advantage over both metaphysics and morality because the definitions on which mathematics turns are of words not already known to the learner. Because 'words in Metaphysiques & Morality [are] mostly known to all', he observes, 'the definitions of them may chance to be controverted'. In the next entry he claims that the 'dry strigose rigid way' of proof in mathematics will not be enough in metaphysics or ethics, where there are 'anticipated opinions' to be encountered and turned aside. In mathematics, he explains, straight-

---

[16] There is more on the verbal character of demonstration in entries 767–8.

forward demonstration is enough to secure a proposition, but in the other two sciences 'a man must not onely demonstrate the truth, he must also vindicate it against scruples & establish'd opinions wch contradict it', an eloquent statement of the need to vindicate immaterialism against objections that led to sections 38–84 of the *Principles* and gave the *Three Dialogues* its form.

The notebook entries on demonstration and certainty strongly suggest that Berkeley, at least for a time, treated the distinction between simple and complex ideas as a device for laying bare the formal or verbal character of contradiction and demonstration. Because the notions of contradiction and demonstration were so closely linked with that of necessity, the same evidence strongly supports the first part of my main hypothesis, the claim that Berkeley saw the distinction between simple and complex ideas as a device for uncovering the formal or verbal character of necessary truth. The second part of my main hypothesis is that Berkeley rejected the distinction because he saw that it was not adequate to the task he had set for it. I offer this part of my hypothesis as the best explanation of Berkeley's final attitude toward the distinction. Berkeley renounced the distinction because it did not meet certain demands, and these demands fall into place if we suppose that Berkeley turned to the distinction in an attempt to understand the nature of necessary truth.

One final theme deserves emphasis. It follows from the notebook view of demonstration that demonstrable truths are trifling or uninstructive. But this should make Berkeley uneasy about claiming to demonstrate his immaterialist principle. If his conclusion were demonstrable it would be 'purely verbal', 'entirely nominal', or 'trifling'. But the knowledge it conveys is real. What Berkeley therefore emphasizes in the *Principles* is not the demonstrability of his conclusion, but the importance of attending to ideas and putting words aside. 'Since therefore words are so apt to impose on the understanding, whatever ideas I consider, I shall endeavour to take them bare and naked into my view, keeping out of my thoughts, so far as I am able, those names which long and constant use hath so strictly united with them.' (Introduction 21.) He entreats his reader

to make my words the occasion of his own thinking, and endeavour to attain the same train of thoughts in reading, that I had in writing them. By this means it will be easy for him to discover the truth or falsity of what I say. He will be out of all danger of being deceived by my words, and I do not see how he can be led into error by considering his own naked, undisguised ideas. (Introduction 25.)

Coming to Berkeley's conclusions, according to *Principles* 22, 'is but looking into your own thoughts'.

3. *An anachronistic hypothesis?*

Before turning to the consequences of my hypothesis I want to acknowledge an interesting objection to it. I have been saying that Berkeley identifies possibility with consistency—that he understands the former in terms of the latter—and this raises a certain difficulty. On the one hand I want to say that according to Berkeley (and most of his contemporaries) possibility and consistency are one and the same. On the other hand I want Berkeley to view the notion of consistency as one that can be used to illuminate the notion of possibility. But if the two notions really are one and the same, how can such illumination reasonably be sought? What makes this question troubling is that it would not be implausible to maintain that in philosophical writing of the seventeenth and early eighteenth centuries the notions of *possibility* and *consistency* really are interchangeable. How, it might be asked, can I be sure that Berkeley *feels a difference* between the two, one that allows him to appeal to one in an attempt to understand the other?

These questions can be made more pointed if we return for a moment to Locke. Locke, as I have indicated, identifies possibility—a metaphysical or modal notion—with consistency, which I have been treating as a formal notion. But does Locke really have a formal conception of consistency? *We* do, but perhaps it is anachronistic to attribute the same kind of understanding to Locke. If we turn to the text of the *Essay* we find that Locke is on the whole indifferent to the formal character of consistency. He speaks freely of necessary connections and unavoidable repugnancies in places where he would apparently refuse to speak of demonstration or purely verbal certainty. Besides the passages already cited in this chapter and the last, consider the following passage from *Essay* IV iii 15, which follows Locke's observation that there are few visibly necessary connections among ideas:

As to incompatibility or repugnancy to co-existence, we may know, that any Subject can have of each sort of primary Qualities, but one particular at once, *v.g.* each particular Extension, Figure, number of Parts, Motion, excludes all other of each kind. The like also is certain of all sensible *Ideas* peculiar to each Sense; for whatever of each kind is present in any Subject, excludes all other of that sort; *v.g.* no one Subject can have two Smells, or two Colours, at the same time.

Locke speaks here of repugnancies, or exclusions known with certainty, but it is evident that he regards them as real instructive certainties, rather than purely identical truths of identity and inclusion. Hylas, to turn now to Berkeley, does indeed say that a thing is shown to be impossible 'when a repugnancy is demonstrated between the ideas comprehended in its definition' but can we safely say that Hylas (or Berkeley) has a formal conception of the repugnancies that a demonstration might disclose? Berkeley refers to *Essay* IV iii 15 at entry 534:

P   Any subject can have of each sort of primary Qualities but one particular at once. Lib. 4.c. 3 S 15 Locke.

No doubt Hylas would think we had 'demonstrated a repugnancy' if we managed to reduce an idea to both *red all over* and *green all over*. But red and green are not *formally* inconsistent, at least not as they stand. Perhaps what Locke and Berkeley take to be a 'repugnancy' with the power to clinch a *reductio* is nothing more than a clear case of an impossibility: formal contradictions would be examples, but so would the mutual exclusion of 'disparates' such as red and green.

It must be granted that neither Locke nor Berkeley had a conception of repugnancy that would qualify as formal by twentieth-century standards. Their approach to colour-incompatibility, for example, differs markedly from that of Wittgenstein, who gave a formal account of modality but adhered to a rigid standard of formality, and hence refused to accept the opposition between red and green as something ultimate.[17] But despite the fact that Berkeley's conception of repugnancy is not formal by our standards it was, I am convinced, formal by his own. Words such as 'repugnancy' and 'contradiction' had strong formal affiliations, due primarily to their appearance in textbooks of logic, and Berkeley's notebooks show that he took these affiliations seriously. The exchange between Hylas and Philonous shows that he took the identification of impossibility in terms of contradiction to be informative.

[17] See *Tractatus Logico-Philosophicus*, trans. by D. F. Pears and B. F. McGuinness, London, 1961, Prop. 6.3751, and 'Some Remarks on Logical Form', in *Knowledge, Experience and Realism*, Aristotelian Society Supplementary Vol. 9 (1929), 162–71.

In my opinion, the identification was quite generally taken to be informative, but most writers who made the identification—and found it to some extent helpful or clarifying—were not inclined to inquire more deeply into it. Berkeley was. He had, as we will see in Chapter 6, a significant stake in understanding the mechanism responsible for necessary truth and falsehood, though he was unable in the end to come up with a satisfying portrayal of it.

Although the notions of contradiction and repugnancy are interchangeable in many seventeenth and eighteenth century contexts, then, it is simply too crude to describe them as synonyms. It is not anachronistic to suggest that Berkeley felt a difference between them, a difference that allowed him to appeal to one in an attempt to understand the other. The same difference had already been felt and the same appeal already made, in fact, by Hobbes. In the first part of his *De Corpore*, Hobbes writes,[18]

A *necessary* proposition is when nothing can at any time be conceived or feigned, whereof the subject is the name, but the predicate also is the name of the same thing. . . . In every *necessary* proposition, the predicate is either equivalent to the subject, as in this, *man is a rational living creature*; or part of an equivalent name, as in this, *man is a living creature.*

Hobbes's view of necessary truth was, of course, an unusual one, but his formal conception of contradiction or repugnancy was quite orthodox.

4. *Berkeley's response*

How, after his failure to depict the underlying nature of modality, did Berkeley view the identification of possibility with consistency? There were two responses available: he might have concluded that the modal notions were not formal after all, which would have allowed him to retain the identification only if he ceased to take the notion of a contradiction to be a genuinely formal one; or, clinging to the formal conception of modality, he might have concluded that the distinction between simple and complex ideas is too blunt an instrument to

---

[18] *Elements of Philosophy, Concerning Body*, 'Computation or Logic', chap. 3, sect. 10, pp. 37–8 in William Molesworth (ed.), *The English Works of Thomas Hobbes*, vol. 1, London, 1839. The views of Hobbes and Berkeley are briefly discussed in W. and M. Kneale, *The Development of Logic*, Oxford, 1962, p. 312. Locke experimented with similar views in early drafts of the *Essay*.

provide a complete account of contradiction or repugnancy. Although we cannot be sure of Berkeley's choice, it is likely that he tended toward the second response, which is more conservative and perhaps more reasonable. Berkeley is always most confident in making accusations of contradiction or repugnancy when he is faced with a formal contradiction. Hylas calls it a contradiction 'to see a thing which is at the same time unseen' (*Works* II p. 200), and 'is it not as great a contradiction,' Philonous asks, 'to talk of *conceiving* a thing which is *unconceived*?' Hylas is later caught 'in a plain contradiction' when he asserts that there is no imperfection in God, that God suffers pain, and that to suffer pain is an imperfection (p. 240). Philonous maintains that it is a contradiction for an idea to exist in an unperceiving thing because an idea, by definition, is a thing which is perceived (p. 233). It is likewise a contradiction for a finite quantity or extension to consist of an infinite number of parts (*Principles* 124). These texts do not prove that Berkeley made the second response; he might have responded in the first way and remained more confident of formal contradictions only because they were clear or 'plain' instances of a non-formal kind of repugnancy. But he viewed them, I think, as contradictions or repugnancies in the strict sense, to which other repugnancies less clear or plain could, had we accurate knowledge of the formal mechanisms of our language, be reduced.

My hypothesis has two important consequences for the interpretation of Berkeley. In Chapter 2 I argued that Berkeley's case against abstract ideas turns on a view of possibility and necessity according to which they are objective, the same for all persons in all places at all times.[19] In this chapter we have seen how deep Berkeley's commitment to the objectivity of modality in fact was. In Chapter 3 I showed that Berkeley recognized necessary truths that are not the work of the mind. In rejecting the reduction of necessary truth to one kind of formal truth, Berkeley moved toward a recognition of connections and repugnancies which are grounded in the nature of ideas or things themselves, apart from the mind's activity. My hypothesis therefore heightens the conflict between Berkeley's demand for an objective test of possibility and impossibility—a demand which edges him towards a formal conception of modality—and his rejection of the distinction between

---

[19] Berkeley's commitment to objectivity is forcefully expressed by Euphranor in *Alciphron* VI, p. 229 in *Works* III. He admits that his eyes are naturally weak, and then observes that 'since it is possible it may be with my understanding as it is with my eyes, I dare not pronounce a thing to be nonsense because I do not understand it'.

simple and complex ideas, which takes him at least one step towards the conclusion that a formal conception of modality may not in the end be tenable.

The second consequence of my hypothesis is that it provides us with a new way of reading Berkeley's claims regarding what is possible and what is not. At *Principles* 10, to consider one such claim, Berkeley writes that 'it is not in my power to frame an idea of a body extended and moved, but I must withal give it some colour or other sensible quality. . . . In short, extension, figure, and motion, abstracted from all other qualities, are inconceivable.' This remark and others like it no longer have to be taken to express either a psychologistic conception of possibility or a naïve reliance on imagistic tests of it. The discoveries of this chapter and the two previous ones—Berkeley's insistence on the objectivity of necessity, his willingness to consider an account of the modal notions that makes them formal, and his recognition that such an account fails because of connections among ideas that seem to be independent of the activity of the mind—allow us to read such remarks as intuitions of an objective impossibility which may be formal in character. At *Principles* 81 Berkeley says that 'For anyone to pretend to a notion of entity or existence, *abstracted* from *spirit* and *idea*, from perceiving and being perceived, is, I suspect, a downright repugnancy and trifling with words.' Here Berkeley is, I think, reporting an intuition of objective impossibility, rather than inferring a modal conclusion from a premiss about what he is able to imagine or conceive. And this is the reading I will give such claims in later chapters.

5. *Conclusion*

I have described my main contention in this chapter as a *hypothesis* because there is no passage in the notebooks where Berkeley *says* that the distinction between simple and complex ideas enables us to clarify the modal notions, or to depict the inner workings of demonstration. My view is supported instead by a network of facts which it accounts for or illuminates, partly by presenting the facts as a network, rather than as a haphazard collection of isolated circumstances. The hypothesis accounts for the very strong conditions Berkeley imposes on simple ideas. It permits us to connect Berkeley's belief that complex ideas are creatures of the mind (*Commentaries* 760) with his view that we owe our success in demonstrating about words to the fact that they are 'perfectly arbitrary & in our power, made at pleasure' (732). To create a complex idea out of simple ideas is to assign an 'arbitrary' meaning to a word, 'arbitrary' because there are no necessary connections among simple ideas which dictate the manner in which we should bring the ideas together. Taken as a whole the notebooks show a deep interest in, and temporary commitment to, a very strict distinction between simple and complex ideas. They also show a deep interest in the topic of demonstration, and in the modal status and certainty of philosophical and other kinds of claims. Given the rich connections between Berkeley's understanding of simple and complex ideas and the topics of modality and demonstration, as well as his commitment—evident throughout his career—to the identification of possibility with consistency, it is hardly credible that Berkeley did not at least *consider* the prospects of explicating modality and demonstration in terms of the distinction between simple and complex ideas. And if he did consider them, the text of the notebooks supplies powerful evidence that he was aware of the difficulties such a project presents. Berkeley experimented with a more radically formal conception of modality than one finds in the published writings of Locke or Malebranche. But in the end he deemed the experiment a failure.

5

CAUSE AND EFFECT

IN this chapter I explain why Berkeley believes that only spirits can be causes. Berkeley holds that anything other than a spirit is causally inert, a passive thing unable to serve as a locus of causal responsibility. This conclusion can be reached by means of Berkeley's immaterialism: if only substances can be active—a premiss widely shared among Berkeley's predecessors and contemporaries—and if spirits are the only substances—a corollary of immaterialism drawn at *Principles* 7— it follows that any entity other than a spirit is causally inert. (Berkeley presents an argument along these lines at *Principles* 26.) But in this chapter, as in the previous four, I will limit myself to arguments that do not depend on immaterialism. Berkeley's deepest reasons for restricting causal power to spirits are independent of immaterialism; in Chapter 6 we will see how these reasons contribute to Berkeley's conclusion that matter does not exist.

It is difficult to read Berkeley on the topic of cause and effect without thinking of Malebranche and Hume. Malebranche believed that there must be a necessary connection between cause and effect, and he therefore concluded that true causal power is the exclusive privilege of an omnipotent God, whose will inevitably realizes its object. Hume saw no need for an intrinsic connection between cause and effect—his definitions of cause, at least on the side of the object, demand nothing more than constant conjunction—and he was therefore free to say that, a priori, anything can be the cause of anything. Berkeley seems to be caught in between, not exactly standing—because that suggests he has found a position to occupy— but suspended, the victim of opposing attractions. He is pulled towards Malebranche by his belief that spirits other than God can be causes, even though he thinks that the precise extent of their power can be measured only by their experience of constant conjunction. Had Berkeley given in completely to one of these pulls it would have been understandable. But his resistance to both, it might be thought, cannot be so easily comprehended, at least not without having him make what many take to be a serious mistake, later exposed by Hume.

The mistake was to think that he could find in finite spirits the causal power he could not find in nature. Beginning with the Malebranchean view that causation calls for something more than mere conjunction ('*efficacy, agency, power, force, energy, necessity, connexion, productive quality*'[1]—whatever it was that Hume was unable to find), Berkeley denied that natural events were causes because he could not locate that something extra. He was headed, it seems, towards a Malebranchean conclusion, having begun with the premiss that Hume was later to deny. But instead of seeing what Hume was clear-headed or courageous enough to see, Berkeley found agency, power, force, or energy in the operations of his own mind. He managed to see nothing but constant conjunction in the external world, it might be said, but he could not tell that nothing more was to be found even within his own soul.

Many commentators have remarked on the injustice of viewing Berkeley as a transitional figure in a continuous development of British philosophy from Locke to Hume.[2] One commentator, classifying him as a continental metaphysician, has moved Berkeley out of the empiricist tradition altogether.[3] It is tempting to use Berkeley's views on cause and effect to place him in a new triumvirate: not Locke–Berkeley–Hume but Malebranche–Berkeley–Hume. In each triumvirate Berkeley occupies the middle position, and in each he is guilty of the same unhappy moderation. In the empiricist triumvirate he is the one who realized that a Humean argument worked against material substance, but failed to see that the same kind of argument works equally well against spiritual substance. In the new triumvirate he realizes once again that a Humean argument tells against some belief about the natural world, but fails to see that it works just as well against the counterpart belief about the spiritual world. In each case what is demanded of Berkeley is consistency. As a member of the empiricist triumvirate he is asked to decide whether to say that qualities need a substratum in which to inhere, or to deny the existence of a substratum which experience cannot disclose. As a member of the new triumvirate

[1] David Hume, *A Treatise of Human Nature*, 2nd edn., Oxford, 1978, I iii 14, p. 157.

[2] For an early and influential statement of this view see A. A. Luce, *Berkeley and Malebranche*, London, 1934. Some of Berkeley's earliest readers detected the influence of Malebranche; see *Works* VIII, p. 41.

[3] This is the most dramatic feature of the realignment of schools or traditions proposed by Louis Loeb in *From Descartes to Hume*, Ithaca, 1981. H. M. Bracken argues on different grounds that Berkeley is best understood as a Cartesian; see his *Berkeley*, London, 1974.

he is asked to decide whether to insist on a force or connection between cause and effect, or to settle for constant conjunction, the only thing sensation or reflection can reveal. In each case, Berkeley faces a choice between experience and a metaphysical demand.

This chapter is divided into three sections. In the first I present Berkeley's account of the causal relation. There I show that Berkeley does not make a mistake Hume was later to expose, though he does take something for granted which readers of Hume tend to regard more sceptically. The second section examines the notion of necessary connection. Berkeley had trouble deciding whether cause and effect are necessarily connected: in several passages he indicates that they are, but in another passage he denies it. I argue that Berkeley glimpsed at least some of the reasons why he could not rely on the notion of necessary connection in defending his account of causation. In the final section I show how Berkeley makes his way between occasionalism—the view that natural events and human volitions are not true causes but mere occasions when God's standing volitions take effect—and the view that causation (on the side of the object) is nothing but constant conjunction.

1. Berkeley on the causal relation

The belief that Berkeley makes a mistake Hume was later to expose is independent of the view that he belongs in the new triumvirate. The belief originated with John Stuart Mill, who praised Berkeley for anticipating Hume's observation that natural events have no real power or efficiency, but criticized him for concluding, on the basis of what Mill called 'our daily experience', that volitions do.[4] 'True it is', Mill writes,

that all we can observe of physical phenomena is their constancies of co-existence, succession, and similitude. Berkeley had the merit of clearly discerning this fundamental truth, and handing down to his successors the true conception of that which alone the study of physical nature can consist in. He saw that the causation we think we see in nature is but uniformity of sequence.

'Let us be thankful to Berkeley', he continues, 'for the half of the truth

---

[4] All quotations from Mill are from 'Berkeley's Life and Writings', in Mill's *Collected Works*, vol. 11, ed. J. M. Robson, Toronto, 1978, p. 462.

which he saw, though the remainder was hidden from him by that mist of natural prejudice from which he had cleared so many other mental phenomena.' Hume was first to see all the way through the mist:

No one, before Hume, ventured to think that this supposed experience of efficient causation by volitions is as mere an illusion as any of those which Berkeley exploded, and that what we really know of the power of our own volitions is only that certain facts . . .·immediately follow them.

Berkeley saw that 'no physical phenomenon . . . can be an efficient cause', Mill concludes, but mistakenly supposed that 'our daily experience proves to us that minds, by their volitions, can be, and are'.

Mill's diagnosis has been accepted by several commentators, and his assumption that Berkeley counts finite spirits as causes on phenomen-ological grounds is widely shared.[5] I do not want to deny that the causal power of spirits is, according to Berkeley, a phenomenological or empirical fact. But I do want to deny what Mill and others infer from this, that the power Berkeley finds within himself is a power Hume looks for and fails to find.

Berkeley's only sustained account of the causal relation appears in his notebooks. It is a rough account, but it helps to clarify and systematize what he says about cause and effect in his published works, and there is no reason to suppose that he later came to question it. The account first appears at entry 499:

S   What means Cause as distinguish'd from Occasion? nothing but a Being wch wills w^n the Effect follows the volition.

Entry 699 speaks of power instead of cause but the account it provides is the same:

S   There is a difference betwixt Power & Volition. There may be volition without Power. But there can be no Power without Volition, Power implyeth volition & at the same time a Connotation of the Effects following the Volition.

One reason this account is rough is that Berkeley never specifies what *kind* of thing a cause is supposed to be; 699 is silent on the matter, and 499 tells us only that a cause is 'a Being'. In his published works Berkeley generally speaks of causes using words that stand for what we

[5] See John Passmore, *Hume's Intentions*, 3rd edn., London, 1980, p. 87; J. O. Urmson, *Berkeley*, Oxford, 1982, pp. 61 and 49–50; and John Immerwahr, 'Berkeley's Causal Thesis', *New Scholasticism* 48 (1974), 153–70, esp. pp. 160–1.

would call *things* (for example, 'fire', 'water', and 'spirit' at *Principles* 51), but at other times he uses more complex expressions, such as 'that motion or collision of the ambient bodies' (*Principles* 65), which designate what we would call *events*. In the end I think it makes little difference whether Berkeley's account is refined in one of these directions rather than the other, since the events he mentions are always events involving things, and the obvious intention of the two entries is that a thing can be a cause on a particular occasion only if some event occurs in it. It will be convenient to restate the account so that both events and things can be causes. An *event* will count as a cause if and only if (a) it is followed by another event (its effect); and (b) the first event is a volition. A *thing* will count as a cause on a particular occasion if and only if there is an event in the thing, occurring on that occasion, which satisfies conditions (a) and (b). The notion of an event's *being in* a thing is a difficult one to explicate, but I have in mind something akin to the notion of being in or inherence that Aristotle makes use of in the *Categories*: the exemplification of an attribute at a time.[6] Examples of events are the motion of a billiard ball, the expansion of a gas, and the volition of a deliberating soul or spirit.[7]

A second rough spot in the account is that we are not told exactly what it means for one event to follow another. Is it enough for the effect to follow the cause on one occasion, or must events of the same type as the effect *regularly* follow events of the same type as the cause? Our two entries perhaps suggest the former, as does 461.[8]

+ W^n I ask whether A can move B. if A be an intelligent thing. I mean no more than whether the volition of A that B move be attended with the

---

[6] For more on the notion of an event see Jaegwon Kim, 'Causation, Nomic Subsumption, and the Concept of Event', *Journal of Philosophy* 70 (1973), 217–36, esp. pp. 222–6.

[7] In a letter to Johnson, Berkeley (perhaps without intending to) suggests a useful distinction. He writes that 'a proper active efficient cause I can conceive none but Spirit; nor any action, strictly speaking, but where there is will' (*Works*, p. 280). This remark embodies a distinction between a *cause* (a spirit or will) and an *action* (an event for which a spirit or will is immediately responsible). But in his use of the word 'cause' Berkeley does not generally honour this distinction, perhaps because it is so natural to call an action a cause.

[8] The earliest entry expressing Berkeley's account of causation is 107, which like 461 is marked with a plus sign: 'Strange impotence of men. Man without God. Wretcheder than a stone or tree, he having onely the power to be miserable by his unperformed wills, these having no power at all'. Before God delegates what Berkeley in this entry calls 'power'—before God associates cause and effect—a finite spirit is impotent, wretcheder than a stone or tree, though no more deficient in power, because unlike them it is able to will and to see that its willing is pointless.

motion of B, if A be be senseless whether the impulse of A against B be follow'd by ye motion of B.

The most reasonable explanation of the presence of the plus sign is that Berkeley eventually decided that a senseless thing cannot impart motion. But the account of what it is for A to move B when A is intelligent matches the account given in 499 and 699. And entry 461 seems to require only that a particular volition be 'attended' with the motion of B on a particular occasion.[9]

In his published works, however, Berkeley explains ordinary attributions of causal power as responses to regularities or uniformities. At *Principles* 32 he observes that the uniform working of nature,

which so evidently displays the goodness and wisdom of that governing spirit whose will constitutes the Laws of Nature, is so far from leading our thoughts to him, that it rather sends them a wandering after second causes. For when we perceive certain ideas of sense *constantly followed by other ideas* [emphasis mine], and we know this is not of our doing, we forthwith attribute power and agency to the ideas themselves, and make one the cause of another. . . .

In continuing the passage Berkeley employs some of the vocabulary of 461 in a way that suggests he was likely to have had *regular* association in mind even there:

Thus, for example, having observed that when we perceive by sight a certain round luminous figure, we at the same time perceive by touch the idea or sensation called *heat*, we do from thence conclude the sun to be the cause of heat. And in like manner perceiving the motion and collision of bodies to be *attended* [my emphasis] with sound, we are inclined to think the latter an effect of the former.

This passage suggests that regular association is a component of the cause and effect relation; ordinary people, struck by regularity, mistakenly infer that natural events are causes. The mistake has its source in an appreciation of part (and only part) of what it means to be a cause. Looking back at the notebooks from the vantage point of the *Principles*, even entries 499 and 699 can be read without distortion as if they speak of event-types as opposed to particular occurrences. I will therefore restate Berkeley's account of what it is for an event to be a cause as follows: an event will count as a cause if and only if (a) it is followed by another event (its effect); (b) events of the first type are

---

[9] I am grateful to Ian Tipton for forcing me to come to grips with this reading of the entry.

regularly followed by events of the second type; and (c) the first event is a volition. As before, a thing will count as a cause on a particular occasion if and only if there is an event in the thing, occurring on that occasion, which qualifies as a cause.

There is a passage later in the *Principles* that may count against the restatement just proposed. At *Principles* 69 Berkeley asks what is meant by *occasion* and gives the following answer:

So far as I can gather from the common use of language, that word signifies, either the agent which produces any effect, or else something that is observed to accompany, or go before it, in the ordinary course of things.

An occasion, in other words, is either a cause or a constant accompaniment. But are we meant to assume that a cause is *something more* than a constant accompaniment, or that a cause can produce an effect on a given occasion even if events of the same type are not always followed by events like the effect? The passage raises the possibility that regular association plays no role in Berkeley's account of true causation, all the weight being borne by clauses (a) and (c) ((a) and (b) in my first restatement). But it seems to me that this is very unlikely; Berkeley probably thinks it goes without saying that effects follow their causes 'in the ordinary course of things'. This is clearly implied by *Principles* 64, where Berkeley writes that 'ideas are not any how and at random produced, there being a certain order and connexion between them, *like to that of cause and effect*' (emphasis mine).

There is a third rough spot in Berkeley's account. In its present form the account requires that events of one type be followed by events of another. Is it enough for the two types to be linked *for a time*, or must their association hold for ever? And if it must hold for ever, is it also required that every *possible* event of the first type be followed by an event of the second, so that counterfactuals such as 'that bread would have nourished him had he eaten it' hold true? Berkeley does not deal with these questions directly, but it seems that perpetual association is *not* required. Berkeley believes, after all, that for all we know God could change the laws of nature:

By a diligent observation of the phenomena within our view, we may discover the general laws of Nature, and from them deduce the other phenomena, I do not say *demonstrate*; for all deductions of that kind depend on a supposition that the Author of Nature always operates uniformly, and in a constant observance of those rules we take for principles: which we cannot evidently know.   (*Principles* 107.)

In the first edition the closing words are 'which we cannot *certainly* know' (emphasis mine).

Berkeley's main point in § 107 is that we cannot know that God always operates according to the laws we take for principles. Yet he also says we cannot know that God operates uniformly, and the reason, I take it, is that it is within God's power to operate a different way. If the power of finite causes is, as Philonous says, 'ultimately . . . derived from God' (Third Dialogue, p. 237), then cause and effect associations that hold for a time might one day be cancelled and replaced. But if God's decrees change, Berkeley's retrospective reaction would not be that there have never been causes (not then, because the old associations have been cancelled; not now, because the new associations are new), but that events which were causes once are causes no longer.[10]

Note, however, that for as long as God's decrees remain the same, cause and effect will be associated not just in fact, but in such a way that if the cause occurs the effect *must* occur.[11] God is an omnipotent spirit, a being who 'can indifferently produce everything by a mere *fiat* or act of his will' (*Principles* 152). What God wills to happen *has* to happen. If my volition is the kind of event which, according to one of God's decrees, is to be followed by the movement of a limb, then my limb will have to move if I direct it to. There is a connection between my volition and its effect which might be described as necessary, even though the association between them need not be perpetual. This is because the necessary connection is *hypothetically* necessary, necessary only on the condition that God's decrees remain the same. Cause-and-effect associations support counterfactuals, then, but these counterfactuals rest for their truth on the same condition.

Our beliefs about what has to happen or would happen were certain possibilities fulfilled need not, of course, be true. Leaving God aside, our only evidence for cause and effect association is *observed* association. The association which is one component of cause and effect is *manifested* in experience, but the conjunctions disclosed by any actual course of experience, no matter how rich, fall far short of cause and effect itself. Berkeley believes that observed association is adequate

[10] Berkeley's belief in miracles may force him to say that God *has not* operated uniformly. See *Principles* 63, where it is, unfortunately, not entirely clear whether miracles go against the laws of nature or against the observed regularities we *take* to be laws.

[11] God could have unchanging decrees that call for different associations at different times, but I will put this complication aside.

evidence for causal association, and he would presumably say that the evidence becomes stronger as the observed associations grow in number and variety.

The following account of what it is to be a finite cause summarizes the discussion of the last few pages. An event counts as a cause if and only if

(a) it is followed by another event (its effect);
(b) supposing only that God's decrees remain the same, an event of the first type must be followed by an event of the second type; and
(c) the first event is a volition.

Once again, a thing counts as a cause on a particular occasion if and only if there is an event in the thing, occurring on that occasion, which satisfies the three conditions.

I am now in a position to show that in counting finite spirits as causes Berkeley does not make a mistake Hume was later to expose. Berkeley's belief that he is a cause rests on two facts: the phenomenological fact that he is capable of volition, and the observed fact that his volitions are reliably followed by events of certain kinds.[12] These facts are safe from Humean criticism. They do not involve the perception of a necessary connection between the volition and its effect, or of an 'energy' or 'power' internal to the cause. There is certainly an 'activity' internal to the cause, but this activity is volitional, and taken by itself it implies no power over items, natural or spiritual, distinct from the volition itself. Hume explicitly acknowledges the existence of such activity. In the Appendix to the *Treatise*, for example, he considers the suggestion that we feel 'an energy, or power' in our own minds.[13] The will, he objects,

has no more a discoverable connexion with its effects, than any material cause has with its proper effect. So far from perceiving the connexion betwixt an act of volition, and a motion of the body; 'tis allow'd that no effect is more inexplicable from the powers and essence of thought and matter. Nor is the

---

[12] Both George Pitcher (in *Berkeley*, London, 1977, pp. 185–6) and Urmson (*Berkeley*, pp. 60–1) deny that Berkeley treats volitions as objects of direct awareness. He reserves such treatment, they say, for ideas. I have tried to state my criticism of Mill's interpretation so that it applies even if Pitcher and Urmson are correct. As I understand the notion of a 'phenomenological fact', volitional activity can count as such a fact even if volitions are not objects of observation. The important point is that both Hume and Berkeley take it to be apparent that we will, and they agree that we are aware that certain events follow our volitions 'straightway'.

[13] Both this quotation and the next come from pp. 632–3.

empire of the will over our mind more intelligible. The effect is there distinguishable and separable from the cause, and cou'd not be foreseen without the experience of their constant conjunction. We have command over our mind to a certain degree, but beyond *that* lose all empire over it: And 'tis evidently impossible to fix any precise bounds to our authority, where we consult not experience. In short, the actions of the mind are, in this respect, the same with those of matter. We perceive only their constant conjunction; nor can we ever reason beyond it. No internal impression has an apparent energy, more than external objects have.

Hume affirms here the existence of 'actions of the mind'. What he denies is that we perceive any connection between these actions and their effects, or any power or energy within the actions that allows us to reason beyond them. We remain, as he says in the first *Enquiry*, 'every moment conscious' that 'the motion of our body follows upon the command of the will'.[14] It is this consciousness of the association of two items, each phenomenologically accessible, on which Berkeley insists.

We should examine some of the passages in which he is thought to insist on more. At *Principles* 28, Berkeley claims to find in his own will the activity or power he is unable to find in his ideas:

I find I can excite ideas in my mind at pleasure, and vary and shift the scene as oft as I think fit. It is no more than willing, and straightway this or that idea arises in my fancy: and by the same power it is obliterated, and makes way for another. This making an unmaking of ideas doth very properly denominate the mind active. Thus much is certain, and grounded on experience: but when we talk of unthinking agents, or of exciting ideas exclusive of volition, we only amuse our selves with words.

All that Berkeley claims to observe or 'find' is an act of will, followed by an idea that 'arises straightway'. He does not claim to observe anything Hume claims not to observe. In § 25 of *De Motu*, Berkeley again appeals to experience to establish the efficacy of spirit, though he concentrates this time on its dominion over the body:

Besides corporeal things there is the other class, *viz*. thinking things, and that there is in them the power of moving bodies we have learned by personal experience, since our mind at will can stir and stay the movements of our limbs, whatever be the ultimate explanation of the fact. This is certain that

---

[14] *Enquiry concerning Human Understanding*, 3rd edn., Oxford, 1975, VII i, p. 65. There are numerous passages to the same effect throughout section VII of the first *Enquiry*. See also the *Treatise*, II iii 1, p. 399.

bodies are moved at the will of the mind, and accordingly the mind can be called, correctly enough, a principle of motion, a particular and subordinate principle indeed, and one which itself depends on the first and universal principle.

Once again, there is no reason to suppose that Berkeley is claiming to find power in any sense in which Hume denies it can be found. If to observe power is, on Berkeley's view, to be conscious of a volition's being reliably followed by a particular kind of event, then the power he observes within himself is a power Hume also claims to observe.

My defence of Berkeley against Mill's criticism may seem to save him from one difficulty only to land him in another. For by what right does he *define* causation so that only willing spirits are capable of it? Ian Tipton notes that 'The definition is very useful given Berkeley's purposes'—'indeed', he adds, 'suspiciously useful.'[15] John Immerwahr grants that Berkeley is free to define causation as he pleases, but points out that the view that ideas lack causal power then becomes a 'trivial outcome' of the definition.[16] The worry shared by Tipton and Immerwahr is a significant source of the appeal of Mill's interpretation. When Berkeley infers from a 'bare observation of our ideas' (*Principles* 25) that they lack causal power, it seems that he cannot simply be reporting that ideas are not volitions. That would make his argument too easy. So it is natural to suppose that he is making what we vaguely classify as a 'Humean' point. But this makes it hard not to say that when he goes on to affirm the power and activity of the self he must be *denying* a Humean point. We have arrived at Mill's interpretation.[17]

I have called Berkeley's view of what it is to be a cause an *account*. I do not think it is intended as an analysis of the *meaning* of the word 'cause', because Berkeley does not think it is a *contradiction* to deny condition (c). His argument in the *Principles* that ideas cannot be

---

[15] *Berkeley: The Philosophy of Immaterialism*, London, 1974, p. 307.

[16] 'Berkeley's Causal Thesis', p. 168.

[17] There is another, more deeply philosophical source of the appeal of Mill's interpretation. Hume is sometimes credited with the observation that mental activity— as opposed to the perceptions in which it terminates—cannot be disclosed by introspection. It is a short step from this to the conclusion that he denies what Berkeley affirms. But we must ask ourselves what this observation is supposed to mean. If it means that volitions cannot be objects of observation, a strong case can be made for crediting Berkeley with the same insight (see e.g. Pitcher, *Berkeley*, pp. 185–6, and Urmson, *Berkeley*, pp. 60–1). If it means that volitional activity is not a phenomenological fact in any sense, then it is doubtful that Hume makes the observation. It might be said that his remarks on personal identity commit him to it, but it is one thing to say that he ought to make an observation, and another thing to say that he does. It is not, in any case, the point Mill praises Hume for making and faults Berkeley for missing.

causes seems to involve more than the realization that they are not volitions. It seems to be an argument that they lack a kind of activity of which volition is perhaps just one example.

A closer look at *Principles* 25 will reveal that Berkeley does more than report that ideas are not volitions. He begins the section by claiming that our ideas are 'visibly inactive, there is nothing of power or agency included in them', and for proof he appeals to the naked observation of what passes in our minds:

Since they and every part of them exist only in the mind, it follows that there is nothing in them but what is perceived. But whoever shall attend to his ideas, whether of sense or reflexion, will not perceive in them any power or activity; there is therefore no such thing contained in them. A little attention will discover to us that the very being of an idea implies passiveness and inertness in it, insomuch that it is impossible for any idea to do any thing, or, strictly speaking, to be the cause of any thing: neither can it be the resemblance or pattern of any active being.

Here Berkeley is responding not just to the absence of volition but to an absence less obvious, the absence of what he terms *power* or *activity*. It is an absence of something that would resemble a volition in permitting us to say that the item is involved in a change it does not suffer but *originates*. The argument of the first part of the section is thoroughly phenomenological: Berkeley states that there is nothing in our ideas but what is perceived, thereby establishing the exclusive relevance of a certain kind of phenomenological consideration, and he then observes that power or activity is not perceived in our ideas. What is not perceived is, at least in part, something that would enable us to know that the idea (or something in which the idea exists) is *originating* the changes we observe. Nothing in our perception intimates an *agent* of change as oppose to a passive *subject* of change. We cannot be certain whether a change in our ideas is a change they suffer or a change for which they are responsible. Ideas are immediately perceived, and any agency they exhibit must therefore be immediately perceived as well. But to perceive agency immediately is to be *certain* that the item observed is bringing change about, and this is an assurance ideas cannot provide.

The rest of *Principles* 25 may be a restatement of the phenomological argument, but the point there may also be conceptual. The 'very being of an idea' to which Berkeley draws our attention may be a characterization of *what it is to be an idea*; this is a plausible reading in view of Berkeley's claim that the very being of an idea *implies* passivity and inertness. Berkeley concludes *Principles* 2 with one such characterization: 'the existence of an idea', he writes, 'consists in being perceived', and according to § 6, the 'being' of an idea is to be perceived or known. If this means that an idea *depends* on being perceived, in something like the way in which a mode or quality depends on the substance in which it inheres, then Berkeley may have a conceptual argument for the conclusion he reaches in § 25. If an idea depends for its existence on its being perceived, and if there is nothing in an idea that is not perceived, then it is plausible to conclude that every *feature* of an idea depends on its being perceived. Now suppose that an idea could be active. There would then be events among ideas of which ideas themselves were the cause. Because nothing in our ideas goes unperceived, the mind would have to perceive the new features these events bring about. But this would leave us with a causal relation between ideas and the mind that seems to run in the wrong direction. We have said that the features of ideas depend for their existence on being perceived. But if ideas are active, what the mind perceives will depend to some extent on the features ideas possess, features which cannot exist apart from the support the mind provides for them. But can a causal relation in one direction be plausibly combined with ontological dependence in the reverse direction?

Whether or not he is making the conceptual argument, in his phenomenological argument Berkeley records not only the absence of volition but also the absence of activity. When in § 28 he finds that he can excite ideas in his mind at pleasure, shifting the scene as often as he thinks fit, he is *aware* that he is active—his belief in his own activity is, as he explains, 'grounded on experience'—but his activity is not *perceived*, because it does not present itself as an object. The manner in which volitions present themselves is difficult to clarify, but the phenomenological difference between volitions and sensations is undeniable. Our awareness of our own activity is immediate (Third Dialogue, p. 232).

Although Berkeley does not say it is a contradiction to suppose that there are forms of activity other than volition, he does say he is unable to conceive of any. Philonous says he has no notion of any action distinct from volition (p. 239), and Berkeley tells Johnson that 'A proper active efficient cause I can conceive none but Spirit; nor any action, strictly speaking, but where there is Will.' (*Works* II, p. 280.) Condition (c) is therefore included in Berkeley's account of causation, even though a weaker condition—one requiring activity *simpliciter*—is all that is implied by the meaning of the word 'cause'.

Tipton and Immerwahr ask for a justification of condition (c). At *Commentaries* 850 Berkeley anticipates their demand:

N.S. I say there are no Causes (properly speaking) but Spiritual, nothing active but Spirit. Say you, this is only Verbal, tis only annexing a new sort of signification to the word Cause, & why may not others as well retain the old one, & call one Idea the Cause of another wch always follows it.

He continues,

I answer, if you do so, I shall drive you into many absurditys. I say you cannot avoid running into opinions you'll be glad to disown if you stick firmly to that signification of the Word Cause.

Though the absurdities are never specified, later entries suggest that they have something to do with distinguishing causes from occasions:

N. We must carefully distinguish betwixt two sorts of Causes Physical   855
    & Spirituall;

N. Those may more properly be called occasions yet (to comply) we   856
    may term them Causes. but then we must mean Causes y^t do
    nothing.

I want to construct, out of Berkeleyan materials, a defence of Berkeley's account of causation, and of condition (c) in particular, but it will first be necessary to take a closer look at the notion of necessary connection.

2. *Necessary connection*

In the seventeenth and eighteenth centuries a necessary connection was taken to be a connection flowing from the nature of the things connected. Berkeley's commitment to his common understanding is voiced in *Principles* 43, where he writes that in his earlier essay on vision,

it is shewn that *distance* or outness is neither immediately of it self perceived by sight, nor yet apprehended or judged of by lines and angles, or anything that hath a necessary connexion with it: but that it is only suggested to our thoughts, by certain visible ideas and sensations attending vision, which in their own nature have no manner of similitude or relation, either with distance, or things placed at a distance.

Here 'necessary connection' is equated with a kind of 'similitude or relation' which arises out of the 'natures' of things. Because the relation is rooted in natures alone, anyone acquainted with those natures will be able to infer the relation a priori. Berkeley draws this consequence at *Theory of Vision Vindicated* 42. He writes, 'We infer causes from effects, effects from causes, and properties one from another, where the connection is necessary.'

The same understanding of necessary connection informs a rich passage spanning § § 39–40 of the *Theory of Vision Vindicated*. Berkeley closes § 39 by contrasting arbitrary connections with necessary ones. 'Where there is no . . . relation of similitude or causality, nor any necessary connexion whatsoever, two things, by their mere coexistence, or two ideas, merely by being perceived together, may suggest or signify one the other, their connexion being all the while arbitrary.' He then turns in § 40 to the word 'natural', which was usually opposed to the arbitrary and—as *Principles* 43 itself suggests—affiliated with the necessary:

A great number of arbitrary signs, various and apposite, do constitute a language. If such arbitrary connexion be instituted by men, it is an artificial language; if by the Author of nature, it is a natural language. Infinitely various are the modifications of light and sound, whence they are each capable of supplying an endless variety of signs, and, accordingly, have been each employed to form languages; the one by the arbitrary appointment of mankind, the other by that of God Himself. A connexion established by the Author of nature, in the ordinary course of things, may surely be called natural; as that made by men will be named artificial. And yet this doth not hinder but the one may be as arbitrary as the other. And, in fact, there is no more likeness to exhibit, or necessity to infer, things tangible from the modifications of light, than there is in language to collect the meaning from the sound. But, such as the connexion is of the various tones and articulations of voice with several meanings, the same is it between the various modes of light and their respective correlates; or, in other words, between the ideas of sight and touch.

If a natural connection is merely an aspect of what Berkeley elsewhere calls 'the *course of Nature*' (*Principles* 141), then a connection can be natural and arbitrary at the same time. A connection is necessary or non-arbitrary only if it carries along with it a 'necessity to infer', an opportunity for a priori inference. The inferential opportunity will vary with the connection. There is, for example, a necessary connection between an object's distance and the size of the angle formed by the optic axes as they converge on the object. 'There appears', Berkeley writes, 'a very necessary connexion between an obtuse angle and near distance, and an acute angle and farther distance.' (*Theory of Vision* 5.) The connection, he continues, 'does not in the least depend upon experience'—that is, we do not depend on experience for our knowledge of it. It 'may be evidently known by any one before he had experienced it, that the nearer the concurrence of the optic axes, the greater the angle, and the remoter their concurrence is, the lesser will be the angle comprehended by them'. In this case the inference is from property (the size of an angle) to property (the distance of the object). But the inferential opportunity provided by a necessary connection can also be existential. If, for example, there were a necessary connection between the existence of our ideas and the existence of external bodies, then the existence of bodies could be inferred 'by reason' (*Principles* 18). But even the 'patrons of matter' do not pretend that there is such a 'necessary connexion' (*Principles* 18). Dreams and frenzies prove that 'we might be affected with all the ideas we have now, though no bodies existed without, resembling them.' Necessary connections provide inferential opportunities of different kinds, but in every case the inference they offer is a priori. Experience may be required to acquaint us with the natures of the items connected, but no further experience is required in order for us to make the associated inference.

Berkeley's understanding of necessary connection can be summarized as follows: a necessary connection is a relation which flows from the nature of its terms, and thereby provides an inferential opportunity. The connection may invite us to infer the possession of one property from the possession of another, or the existence of an object from the existence of another. This list of opportunities is not necessarily exhaustive: a necessary connection could perhaps take us from a change in one object to the existence of another, or from the action of one object to a change in another. In every case, however, the inference is a priori, as secure as the deductions of geometry. Experience may sometimes be required to acquaint us with the nature of the things connected, but no further experience—no trial or experimentation—will be required to support the inferential step.

Although Berkeley's conception of necessary connection is both traditional and definite, his application of the notion is not altogether clear. In § § 39 and 42 of the *Theory of Vision Vindicated* he seems to accept the view that cause-and-effect relations are necessary connections. One thing or idea may signify another, he writes in the earlier section, even though 'there is no . . . relation of similitude or causality, nor any necessary connexion whatsoever' between them. The 'whatsoever' would be out of place if similitude and causality were not examples of necessary connection. In § 42 he explains that we infer 'causes from effects, effects from causes, and properties one from another, where the connection is necessary'. It is conceivable that the closing words apply only to the inference of property from property, but even if this is Berkeley's intention—an intention that would have been more plainly realized were the closing words placed immediately after the word 'and'—the most natural reading of the sentence would then be that we infer causes from effects and effects from causes, where the connection is always necessary, and properties one from another, where the connection is necessary only some of the time.

The real difficulty with these passages is that finite causes fall far short of Berkeley's criteria for necessary connection. I said earlier that the connection between a volition and its upshot might be described as necessary, because once God's volitions are settled, the upshot cannot fail to follow. But the hypothetical character of this connection—its dependence on divine volitions that go beyond those required for my creation, or for the constitution of my *nature*—disqualifies it as a necessary connection in Berkeley's sense. God might have created me as a willing being but left me 'strangely impotent', a possibility entertained in entry 107 of the notebooks. My *nature* would be intact, as the nature of Boylean matter would be intact had God refrained from endowing it with motion, but I would have 'onely the power to be miserable by [my] unperformed wills, these having no power at all'.[18] This is why I can learn only by *experience* what my will is able to accomplish. Seen from some perspective outside me—or even from my own, provided I put aside the familiarity with my own causal powers that can make them seem inevitable—the connection between my volitions and their upshots should appear *arbitrary*, as that word is understood at *Theory of Vision Vindicated* 42. God's will, of course, is necessarily connected with its effects, but finite wills are not. So

---

[18] God, Berkeley thinks, could not have created me without a will. My will may not exhaust my nature, but it is certainly essential to it. In a stimulating paper, A. C. Lloyd argues that according to Berkeley, my will exhausts my nature. See 'The Self in Berkeley's Philosophy', in John Foster and Howard Robinson (eds.), *Essays on Berkeley: A Tercentennial Celebration*, Oxford, 1985, pp. 187–209.

causation, it seems, cannot in every case be a kind of necessary connection.

Although it seems to run counter to his understanding of necessary connection, Berkeley's tendency to treat causation as a kind of necessary connection is not confined to the *Theory of Vision Vindicated*.[19] It manifests itself even in the *Principles*, where Berkeley responds to an imaginary interlocutor who wonders what purpose is served by the parts of plants and animals, if all such parts, being nothing but ideas, 'have nothing powerful or operative in them, nor have any necessary connexion with the effects ascribed to them' (§ 60). And the tendency is forcefully encouraged by two large contrasts drawn by Berkeley in numerous passages. The first is a contrast between arbitrary and necessary connections (*Theory of Vision* 147 and *Alciphron* IV 7–9, *Theory of Vision Vindicated* 39–40). The second is a contrast between the bearing of an event on the object ordinarily viewed as its effect—a bearing Berkeley interprets as one of arbitrary signification—and the bearing of a genuine cause on its effect. It is hard to resist supposing that in Berkeley's view these contrasts fall into line: if the relation of sign and signified is arbitrary, as Berkeley consistently holds, and if arbitrary connections are characterized by opposing them to connections that are necessary, then if the relation of sign and signified is contrasted with that between cause and effect, the causal relation must presumably be necessary.

At *Theory of Vision Vindicated* 30, however, Berkeley actually seems to *deny* that cause and effect are necessarily connected:

As to what you advance, that our ideas have a *necessary* connexion with such cause, it seems to me *gratis dictum*: no reason is produced for this assertion; and I cannot assent to it without a reason. The ideas or effects I grant are evidently perceived: but the cause, you say, is utterly unknown. How, therefore, can you tell whether such unknown cause acts arbitrarily or necessarily? I see the effects or appearances: and I know that effects must have a cause: but I neither see nor know that their connexion with that cause is necessary. Whatever there may be, I am sure I see no such necessary connexion, nor, consequently, can demonstrate by means thereof from ideas of one sense to those of another.

The severity of the conflict we have discovered can be reduced

---

[19] I put aside passages in which Berkeley makes positive use of the notion of necessary connection, apparently identifying it with causation. See *Alciphron* I 16 (*Works* III, p. 64) and *Passive Obedience* 11 (*Works* VI, p. 22). In both cases the context indicates that the notion carries none of the weight it does in the works on vision.

somewhat by attending to the context of the various passages I have cited. In many passages where Berkeley speaks of cause and effect as a necessary connection he is, as in *Principles* 60, giving voice to an interlocutor, real or imagined. The view that causation is a kind of necessary connection was, as the writings of Hume attest, widely held. The most problematic of the passages I have quoted are those from the *Theory of Vision Vindicated*, because there Berkeley seems to be speaking on his own behalf. Yet the whole of that work is a reply to an attack on the *Theory of Vision*. The attack came in a letter to the author of *Alciphron*, and Berkeley's reply is subtitled, 'In answer to an anonymous Writer'. The author of the letter shares the usual view that necessary connections license a priori or demonstrative inferences (see *Works* I, p. 279). He supposes as well that cause and effect are necessarily connected. Perhaps Berkeley speaks as if the connection is necessary, then, only to meet the interlocutor on his own ground. The presence of § 30, where the interlocutor's assumption is apparently denied, is strong evidence that contrary remarks elsewhere should not be taken to reflect Berkeley's own view.

I will look more closely at § 30 in a moment. I want first to observe that these remarks about the context do not altogether eliminate the conflict, because the pair of contrasts that lie behind it—the first between the arbitrary and the necessary, the second between signification and causation—are central to Berkeley's mostly deeply held beliefs. The instability to which they lead is evidence that they are simply too crude for Berkeley's purposes. Berkeley does not want the contrasts to fall into line because he needs a special place for causation. Causation cannot be a necessary connection—the stock understanding of necessary connection will not allow it—but it cannot be merely arbitrary, because it is different from the relation of sign and signified, the paradigm of arbitrary connection, and different from it in something *like* the way in which a necessary connection is different. This brings us up against Berkeley's need to defend his account of causation. The relation between cause and effect has to be stronger or tighter than the relation of sign and signified, and yet the only way in which the former goes beyond the latter lies in condition (c). Condition (c) cannot make the connection as strong or as tight as a necessary one; it can do nothing to eliminate the fact that the connection as specified in condition (b) is *hypothetically* necessary, and therefore not necessary in Berkeley's sense. How, then, can condition (c) strengthen the relation or make it more intimate? How can Berkeley say it is misleading to classify the volitions of finite spirits with the inert signs in God's language of nature?

We may now return to § 30 of the *Theory of Vision Vindicated*. The passage is a response to the following suggestion, made by the anonymous critic in the closing paragraph of his letter:

Though our ideas of magnitude and distance in one sense are intirely different from our ideas of magnitude and distance in another, yet we may justly argue from one to the other, as they have one common cause without, of which, as without, we cannot possibly have the faintest idea. The ideas I have of distance and magnitude by feeling [i.e., by touch] are widely different from the ideas I have of them by seeing; but that something without which is the cause of all the variety of the ideas within, in one sense, is the cause also of the variety in the other; and, as they have a necessary connexion with it, we very justly demonstrate from our ideas of feelings of the same object what will be our ideas in seeing. And though to talk of seeing by tangible angles and lines be, I agree with you, direct nonsense, yet to demonstrate from angles and lines in feeling to the ideas in seeing that arise from the same common object, is very good sense, and so *vice versa*. (*Works* I, pp. 278–9.)

The correspondent exaggerates when he describes the ideas of diverse senses as 'intirely' different. The exaggeration threatens his own proposal, which rests on the assumption that the ideas of sight and touch are somehow alike. What he calls their 'variety' is, I take it, something structural or geometrical, though this variety will exist in a qualitiative dimension that varies 'widely' from sense to sense. Structural or geometrical similarities, manifestations of a common cause, permit us to argue from certain features of one object to the corresponding features of another. The correspondent takes this common cause to be a body. Berkeley believes just as firmly that there is 'something without which is the cause of all the variety of the ideas within', and the question he asks—'How . . . can you tell whether such unknown cause acts arbitrarily or necessarily?'—points to an important difference between his cause and that of the correspondent. His question also tells us how he is interpreting the notion of necessary connection. Berkeley denies that there is a necessary connection between the cause and our sensations of sight and touch because God acts arbitrarily or freely in causing our ideas. We cannot infer the structural features of a visible idea from the structural features of a tangible one—the discontinuities in the look of Molyneux's cube, for example, from the discontinuities in its feel—because whatever 'variety' or multiplicity an idea exemplifies is the result of God's free choice. Molyneux's cube might have felt like a cube but looked like a sphere.[20]

Here it is helpful to pay close attention to the ontology of the causal relation, and to the distinction, made earlier on Berkeley's behalf, between *things* and *events* as causes. According to Berkeley there is no necessary connection between God and his effects, because God is a free agent. His *nature* does not dictate what he brings about. But a recognition of this does not preclude believing in a necessary connection between God's *will* and its effects, or, to make the important shift in ontology more explicit, between God's *volitions* and their upshots. It is odd, perhaps, to speak of the *nature* of an event. Yet the notion of necessary connection is flexible enough, I think, to permit belief in a necessary connection with an event of some kind as its first term. God's nature is such that the objects of his volitions unavoidably come to pass. Once we know God has willed that there be light we can conclude without delay that there will be. The *nature* of a volition, if it makes sense to speak of it at all, cannot be understood apart from the spirit whose volition it is. And if a volition is God's—if its being God's is part of its very identity—then there is a relation, flowing from its very nature, between that volition and its upshot, a relation that gives rise to a 'necessity to infer' the occurrence of the effect.

Malebranche understood necessary connection in the way I have described. He refused to treat God as a cause whose effects emanate directly from his nature, as he believed Spinoza had done.[21] In an attempt to preserve God's providence and freedom, Malebranche insisted that God's effects are caused by his *will*.[22] Even if God's will is

[20] This is, of course, too simple. For some of the complications see H. P. Grice, 'Some Remarks About the Senses', in R. J. Butler (ed.), *Analytical Philosophy*, New York, 1962, pp. 135–53; Judith Jarvis Thomson, 'Molyneux's Problem', *Journal of Philosophy* 71 (1974), 637–50; and Gareth Evans, 'Molyneux's Question', pp. 364–99 in his *Collected Papers*, Oxford, 1985.

[21] For a criticism of Spinoza as a reviver of the ancient impiety that the world is a 'necessary emanation of the Deity' see the *Dialogues on Metaphysics* IX, pp. 199 and 201 in Willis Doney's trans., New York, 1980.

[22] See *The Search after Truth*, trans. Thomas M. Lennon and Paul J. Olscamp, Columbus, 1980, Bk. IV, chap. xi, § 3, p. 319, and 'Elucidation Ten' (trans. Lennon in the same vol.), p. 627, where Malebranche says that God knows of the existence of things not through his ideas or essence, but through his will. Theodore makes the same point in *Dialogues on Metaphysics* I, p. 29 in Doney's translation. See also Charles J. McCracken, *Malebranche and British Philosophy*, Oxford, 1983, p. 99: 'The necessary connection . . . is between God's *will* and the events he wills, not between God's *nature* and those events. God has *freely* chosen to create this world and its laws.' None the less Malebranche's God, like the God of Leibniz, acts according to his nature (*Dialogues* VIII

in turn determined by his nature—an admission Malebranche appears to make, and one which brings him face to face with difficulties made familiar by Leibniz—divine effects do not flow from God's nature or essence directly. Yet God can still be described as a cause, notwithstanding Malebranche's definition of a true cause as 'one such that the mind perceives a necessary connection between it and its effects'. Strictly speaking the necessary connection holds between God's *volitions* and their effects, but because they are *God's* volitions, their content specified by his understanding, their efficacy is under-written by his omnipotence. We can therefore say there is a necessary connection between God and his effects, though we must bear in mind that it is the connection between God's will and what occurs, rather than the connection between God's nature and what occurs, which Malebranche is most concerned to emphasize.

What our discussion of § 30 and its context has shown is that the notion of necessary connection is flexible enough to permit a free agent to count as a cause, even if a cause and its effect must be necessarily connected. But the agent's freedom influences the inferential op-portunity the necessary connection provides. Berkeley's anonymous correspondent hopes for a connection that will allow him to anticipate at least the structural features of a tangible idea, given only the structural features of a visible one. But if the cause is not a body, its images flowing ineluctably from the structure they manifest, but instead a freely acting God, who arbitrarily annexes ideas in one modality to those in another, the opportunity the correspondent seeks will not be found. There is a necessary connection between Berkeley's God and his effects, but the connection does not license the a priori inference for which the correspondent hopes.

What I have said so far does not enable Berkeley to say that *every* cause is necessarily connected with its effects, because the volitions of finite spirits are not connected with their effects in the same that way God's are. Finite spirits are not omnipotent, and even if an omnipotent God has delegated power to them, it is not a consequence of the *nature* of a finite spirit that its volitions lead unfailingly to their upshots. Malebranche shows us that the notion of necessary connection can be adapted to the case of a free being, but the success of that adaptation seems to depend on that being's absolute power. In the case of finite

and IX). 'He cannot', in fact, 'choose and take the lesser course' (*Dialogues* IX, p. 215 in Doney).

spirits, causal connections hold only by virtue of divine acts of delegation. Our freedom may be no obstacle to our status as causes, but our being less than divine apparently is. Even if the movement of my limbs cannot help but follow the appropriate volitions, the connection does not depend on *me*, or my nature, but on something so distant it seems to exaggerate our intimacy even to describe it as a power God has superadded to me.

The difficulties Berkeley would face if he said that finite spirits are necessarily connected with their effects can be more sharply drawn if we turn for a moment to Locke, who speaks often in the *Essay* of necessary connections between bodies and their effects. Like Berkeley, Locke thinks of necessary connection as a relation which, when 'visible', 'conceivable', or 'discoverable', supports the kind of inference found in geometry. If we aspire to make natural philosophy a science, as geometry already is, then according to Locke we aspire not to a knowledge of the mere conjunction of properties, but to a knowledge of a kind of coexistence which he is prepared to identify with necessary connection. Locke's pessimism about the prospects for genuine knowledge of nature—his low estimate of the likelihood that 'natural philosophy' will ever become a science (*Essay* IV xii 10)—has its source in his belief that the real essences of bodies—the internal constitutions from which their manifest properties flow—are hidden from us. If we had greater powers of discernment—if we had, for example, 'Microscopical Eyes' (II xxiii 12)—we could infer the power of resisting loss upon heating from the internal constitution of gold, just as we now infer the properties of a triangle from its 'internal constitution', which is known to us because it is we who decide what a triangle is to be.

Despite its modest estimate of what we can hope to know, there are some serious problems confronting this conception of a body's relation to its properties and powers, problems serious enough, in the opinion of some, to call Locke's commitment to the conception into question.[23] The issue of interpretation cannot be pursued here, but some of the

[23] The literature on this topic includes Margaret Wilson, 'Superadded Properties: The Limits of Mechanism in Locke', *American Philosophical Quarterly* 16 (1979), 143–50; M. R. Ayers, 'Mechanism, Superaddition, and the Proof of God's Existence in Locke's Essay', *Philosophical Review* 90 (1981), 210–51; Wilson, 'Superadded Properties: A Reply to M. R. Ayers', *Philosophical Review* 91 (1982), 247–52; and Edwin McCann, 'Lockean Mechanism', pp. 209–31, and J. R. Milton, 'Lockean Mechanism: A Comment', pp. 233–9, in A. J. Holland (ed.), *Philosophy, Its History and Historiography*, Dordrecht, 1985.

difficulties deserve to be briefly mentioned. The first is what might be called the problem of retainership.[24] It is misleading to speak as if the fixedness of gold depends only on the internal constitution of the metal. The essence of gold is obviously *relevant* to its fixedness, but so is the essence of fire. In general it seems that we must have insight into the real essences of several bodies in order to infer a power or effect which we, in an understandable attempt to simplify, attribute to a single one. Locke develops this point himself at *Essay* IV vi 11, where he observes that 'Things, however absolute and entire they seem in themselves, are but Retainers to other parts of Nature, for that which they are most taken notice of by us.' Yet despite this acknowledgement Locke continues to speak as if the properties of a natural substance can be seen to flow from its internal constitution taken in isolation, so that God or an angel no more needs to consult the essences of other things than we need to consult the essence of a circle when we are demonstrating truths about a triangle.

A second problem is introduced in passages where Locke seems to assign some of the powers of bodies to God's arbitrary will, rather than to the internal constitutions of things themselves. He writes at *Essay* IV iii 29 that

the coherence and continuity of the parts of Matter; the production of Sensation in us of Colours and Sounds, *etc.* by impulse and motion; nay, the original Rules and Communication of Motion being such, wherein we can discover no natural connexion with any *Ideas* we have, we cannot but ascribe them to the arbitrary Will and good Pleasure of the Wise Architect.

Locke blames our failure here on two things: our ignorance of internal constitutions, and our ignorance of the manner in which observable qualities flow from them (IV vi 10). At IV iii 12 the second deficiency is said to be more 'incurable' than the first; mere sensory enhancement would not be enough to alleviate it. Michael Ayers has persuasively argued that a commitment to mechanism—which he defines as the view that 'the laws of physics can be explained, in principle if not by us, by being deduced from the attributes possessed essentially by all bodies *qua* bodies'—is wholly consistent with Locke's recognition that the powers and properties of bodies have no discoverable or even conceivable connection with the *acknowledged* properties of matter.[25]

[24] There are discussions of this problem in John Yolton, *John Locke, An Introduction,* Oxford, 1985, pp. 115–16, and Peter Alexander, *Ideas, Qualities and Corpuscles: Locke and Boyle on the External World,* Cambridge, 1985, pp. 179–82.
[25] 'Mechanism, Superaddition, and the Proof of God's Existence', p. 210.

Ayers suggests that Locke is not a dogmatic Boylean about the nature of matter but an agnostic more akin to Gassendi, whose pessimistic appraisal of the scope of our insight into necessary connection is compatible with a confidence that at the deepest level—a level that may forever be closed to our view—properties and powers do in fact flow from the nature of matter itself. The merits of his suggestion aside, Ayers is certainly right to see a tension between the belief that an effect is necessarily connected to its bodily cause and the belief in divine annexation. Even if the connection between a body and its supposed effect is invariable (so that the connection becomes one aspect of what Berkeley called the course of nature), and even if the connection is consistent with the nature of the substance to which the power is annexed, the connection between the body and its effect cannot be natural in the sense at work at *Essay* IV iii 29. The connection is neither natural nor necessary because its abrogation does not run counter to the nature of the substance.

The third problem is actually a special case of the second. Locke believes that impulse is 'the only way which we can conceive Bodies operate in' (II viii 11). This means that a body's power, as far as we can understand it, resides in its capacity to move adjoining bodies. Now as Locke makes clear at *Essay* IV iii 29, the laws of motion have no natural connection with body as we understand it, and as a result they can only be ascribed to the arbitrary will of God. Locke could there be implying that sensory insight into the nature of matter would, if it penetrated deeply enough, make the laws of motion perspicuous to us. Yet it is hard to imagine how sensory penetration could yield that kind of understanding. Sensory enhancement, even if it acquaints us with the motions of a body's ultimate parts, could not remedy the defect to which Locke points in the following passage from *Essay* II xxiii 28:

In the communication of Motion by impulse, wherein as much Motion is lost to one Body, as is got to the other, which is the ordinariest case, we can have no other conception, but of the passing of Motion out of one Body into another; which, I think, is as obscure and unconceivable, as how our Minds move or stop our Bodies by Thought; which we every moment find they do.

It is difficult to see how sensory enhancement, by itself, could make the communication of motion by impulse intelligible. It seems that God could have decreed that motion be gained or lost rather than conserved, and it is hard to see how bodies themselves could bear the mark of one divine decree as opposed to another. Ayers might reply by suggesting that Locke's agnosticism may extend more deeply than many of his readers have imagined, so deep that Locke feels no obligation to explain how a deeper insight into the nature of things could cure the defects in our understanding. Our limited comprehension of the nature of body may limit our ability even to understand how our comprehension might be improved. As before, the important point for our purposes is that divine annexation seems to be incompatible with necessary connection. Bodies cannot be necessarily connected to their effects if those effects are annexed to them by the arbitrary appointment of the deity.

Our survey of Malebranche and Locke suggests that Berkeley should not speak as if there is a necessary connection between a finite cause and its effects. As soon as he admits that the power of finite causes comes to them by delegation or superaddition, he is in no position to respect the understanding of necessary connection he inherits from Malebranche and Locke, requiring as it does that the abrogation of a genuinely necessary connection be inconsistent with the nature of the items it connects. Yet Berkeley is powerfully tempted to speak as if there is such a connection. He is tempted because he sees that causal connection is more than arbitrary. The dichotomy between the arbitrary and the natural or necessary is too crude for Berkeley's purposes, but his allegiance to it edges him toward the conclusion that cause and effect are necessarily connected. What Berkeley needs is a non-arbitrary connection which is not natural or necessary in the sense at work in Locke and Malebranche. He needs a connection that will allow for the *understanding* of an effect even if it would not allow for its a priori anticipation. This is just another way of describing his need to steer a middle course between Malebranche's occasionalism and Hume's latitudinarianism. Malebranche and Hume are alike in seeing no non-arbitrary alternative to strict necessity; Berkeley has to show that they are missing something.

3. *The account defended*

A defence of Berkeley's account of causation calls for two things: a defence of the joint sufficiency of (a), (b), and (c), in order to separate his view from Malebranche's; and a defence of the need for condition (c), in order to separate his view from Hume's. It is not my aim in this section to prove that Berkeley's account of causation is correct. But I do hope to show that the course Berkeley charts between Malebranche and Hume is not without its attractions.

Berkeley links causation with intelligibility: for Berkeley, to specify its cause is to render an event intelligible. It is partly for this reason that he rejects the view that material things cause our ideas: even if we suppose that such things exist, the materialists themselves admit that they do not understand how matter can act upon the mind. If the interaction of matter and mind is unintelligible, the materialist hypothesis cannot even begin to explain why our ideas take the form they do (*Principles* 19). According to the defence I will provide for Berkeley, in order for an event or substance to qualify as a cause of a given event it is both necessary and sufficient that it help to render its occurrence intelligible. I will argue on Berkeleyan grounds that a substance need not be omnipotent in order to play this role, but that the qualifications for being a cause should not be relaxed as far as Hume would like—so far that putting experience aside, anything could be the cause of anything.

Suppose we know that God has willed our limbs to move whenever a certain volition takes place. This knowledge helps us to understand the movement because an arrangement decreed by an omnipotent God must actually take effect, and Berkeley believes that we would find the movement even more perspicuous if we knew the end served by the arrangement. To explain an event, Berkeley writes at *Siris* 231, is 'to assign its proper efficient and final cause'. When it comes to the laws of nature, efficiency and finality coalesce: the being who has the power to enforce the laws is the being who frames the ends which those laws serve. 'It should seem to become philosophers,' Berkeley writes at *Principles* 107, 'to employ their thoughts (contrary to what some hold) about the final causes of things.' Nature exhibits a *degree* of intelligibility when we see its laws or constitutive arrangements as the decrees of an omnipotent God; but when we move beneath the surface and ask for an explanation of the laws themselves, Berkeley is convinced that the intelligibility of our view can be enhanced.

My defence of Berkeley against Malebranche begins with the assumption that the ends framed by human wills resemble God's in their capacity to confer intelligibility. Just as knowledge of God's ends confers intelligibility on the laws that govern nature, knowledge of our own ends confers intelligibility on our movements. This is not to say, of course, that God plays no role in accounting for them. As we saw above, the intelligibility of our movements is enhanced by an understanding of the ends served by the regularities under which they fall. But if God can confer intelligibility by means of his ends, *we* can confer intelligibility by means of ours. We better understand why a bodily movement occurs when we learn why, from the viewpoint of the human agent, a decision was made to undertake it.

It is likely to be objected that even if we accept what might be called Berkeley's teleological requirement—his requirement that an event be explained by providing a final cause or end—human ends are quite superfluous. Divine ends do all of the work, it might be maintained, because God knows both what we will intend, and how our bodies will respond to our intentions. Even if some of our volitions or bodily motions are unintended by God, they are certainly foreseen by him, and if in spite of them he chooses to create us, these events can be explained as the price he is prepared to pay for the sake of achieving other things. Berkeley does not, of course, reply to this objection, because he does not explicitly endorse the view to which it is addressed. But a passage in *Alciphron* suggests a line of response. In the Seventh Dialogue Alciphron presents two arguments against the freedom of the will. The second argument turns on 'the prescience of God':

That which is certainly foreknown will certainly be. And what is certain is necessary. And necessary actions cannot be the effect of free-will. Thus you have this fundamental point of our free-thinking philosophy. (*Alciphron* IV 17, *Works* III, p. 312.)

Euphranor replies in the following section:

In the first place, I observe you take that for granted which I cannot grant, when you assert whatever is certain the same to be necessary. To me, certain and necessary seem very different, there being nothing in the former notion that implies constraint, nor consequently which may not consist with a man's being accountable for his actions. If it is foreseen that such an action shall be done, may it not also be foreseen that it shall be an effect of human choice and liberty? (IV 18, pp. 313–14.)

Euphranor attempts in a familiar way to reconcile predictability with free agency: my actions can be my actions—events initiated by me rather than by something external—even if their occurrence is certain. They simply need to be unconstrained. Berkeley's criteria for constraint are probably the ordinary ones, familiar from other attempts to reconcile predictability with free agency: I am a free agent as long as I am neither in prison nor in chains. The challenge of the present objection is that divine foreknowledge, or divine creation carried out in the light of that knowledge, presents as great a threat to agency as constraint does. Berkeley's reply is that the objection confuses predictability ('certainty') with necessity. It is true that the objector is willing to do more than subsume my action beneath a regularity; he or she is willing to account for those regularities by appealing to the will of God, and to account for particular events as events chosen (at least as unintended side-effects) by that same will, who could have chosen otherwise. But Berkeley believes that we will improve our understanding of an action if we place it within the structure of a human agent's motives. In Berkeley's view God's decision to create free agents is a decision to create beings whose motives can make precisely this kind of contribution to the understanding of events. As long as I can be said to be active, then Berkeley thinks that I can also be said to be free. It may in fact be helpful to think of Berkeley's problem as one occasioned more by activity than by freedom. The problem is understanding how genuinely active creatures can exist under the governance of an omnipotent being. Berkeley's solution is that their active nature is a matter of being able to play a certain explanatory role, a role they can play even if God is the source of all power. In the *Dialogues on Metaphysics* Malebranche has Aristes remark that 'Nothing is more sacred than power. Nothing is more divine.'[26] Berkeley differs from Aristes in thinking that power or efficacy is not the only thing to be considered when assigning causal responsibility. Final causation is at least as fundamental as efficient causation—so fundamental that even a feeble human spirit, whose efficacy is derived from God, can nonetheless count as a cause. Because all power is originally held by God, Berkeley counts him as the ultimate cause, but this does not make him the only cause.[27]

These last remarks may raise another objection. It seems that in creating finite spirits, Berkeley's God must endow them with some kind of active principle, even if it is something as modest as an

---

[26] *Dialogues* VII, p. 165.

[27] In its emphasis on the special connection between a volition and its upshot, my defence resembles Jonathan Bennett's conjecture that Berkeley's account of causation has its source in his belief that 'a genuinely causal connexion must enable us to predict non-inductively a state of affairs', and that 'the only such connexion we know of is that between a decision ("volition") and the subsequent action of a "spirit" ' (*Locke, Berkeley, Hume: Central Themes*, Oxford, 1971, p. 203). On my view, what impresses Berkeley is not that the connection permits a non-inductive prediction—I think he realizes that it does so only in the case of God—but that it makes the upshot intelligible.

unarticulated impulse toward the good. Education and environment may then work together to transform this impulse into an organized motivational system, one that will equip the spirit for action. But is the assignment of such an original principle an offence against Berkeley's high standard of intelligibility? Can a finite spirit have even the power to will? The only defence I am able to provide is *ad hominem*: Malebranche must himself assume that God has the power to will, and God's omnipotence does not help to make its possession intelligible. It is difficult to conceive of an omnipotent being as anything other than a spirit who 'can indifferently produce everything by a mere *fiat* or act of his will' (*Principles* 152). An omnipotent but unthinking piece of matter might be able to shove aside everything with which it came into contact, but its incapacity for design would deprive it of fitting opportunities for the display of its power, and it should deprive us, I think, of the assurance that it even makes sense to say that it has such power. Our very conception of omnipotence rests, in other words, on a *prior* conception of a spirit as an active being, a being that sets itself ends. Unless the notion of such a being were already available, the notion of omnipotence would be beyond our reach. From Berkeley's viewpoint, then, even Malebranche takes a kind of occurrence for granted: the occurrence of an act of will. Because the notion of such an occurrence is analytically prior to the notion of omnipotence, the threat to the intelligibility of finite volitions is as yet no greater than the threat to the intelligibility of divine volitions.[28]

Malebranche, however, presents a challenging puzzle for any view according to which God delegates power to finite spirits. 'Let us suppose that God wills to produce the opposite of what some minds will', he writes. 'One could not say in this case that God would communicate His power to them, since they could do nothing they willed to do. Nevertheless, the wills of these minds would be the natural causes of the effects produced. Such bodies would be moved to the right only because these minds willed them moved to the left; and the volitions of these minds would determine the will of God to act, as our willing to move the parts of our bodies determines the first cause to move them. Thus, all the volitions of minds are only occasional

---

[28] Malebranche would, of course, deny this. Even if he acknowledged the analytical priority of volition, he would deny that it is enough to make finite volitions intelligible. For some of the problems facing his own account of finite volitions see McCracken, *Malebranche*, pp. 105–10, and Thomas Lennon's 'Philosophical Commentary', pp. 762–73 in the Lennon and Olscamp trans. of the *Search after Truth*.

causes.'[29] Malebranche's objection, adapted to Berkeley's account of
finite causation, is that a finite spirit can meet the three conditions the
account lays down and yet be unable to do anything it wills to do. If
God inverts his decrees so that my will is frustrated and mocked at
every turn, my volitions none the less remain volitions (so that I
continue to satisfy condition (c)), and they are (from the time of the
inversion on) constantly conjoined with their new upshots (so that I
satisfy conditions (a) and (b)). And yet not only is it the case that I am
unable to do anything I will to do, it seems wrong to say that my
volitions confer intelligibility on my movements. If Berkeley agrees that
it is wrong then he must enrich his account of causation. It is not
enough for the cause to be a volition; the volition must be related in the
appropriate way to its upshot. It will not be easy for Berkeley to spell
out what it is for the relation to be appropriate, and if he takes this
course he will have to answer a vexing question: If we don't impart
intelligibility under inversion, why do we in the normal case? The
heroic alternative of insisting that we *do* confer intelligibility even
under inversion seems, however, an even worse course to take. It is
true that a spirit under inversion could not do anything it wills to do,
Berkeley might say, but it could still be causally responsible for events
in the natural world, and its motives, against the background of God's
newly inverted decrees, could continue to help us see why a given
event occurs. But the particular *content* of our volitions would no longer
help to illuminate what we do. It is perhaps worth noting, however,
how difficult it would be for a finite spirit anything like ourselves to
maintain its sanity—perhaps even to maintain its ability to will—under
inversion. If God cannot possibly be fooled—if he reads our real
intentions even when we try to get our way by mentally rehearsing false
intentions—it is probable that our ability to form intentions would
eventually be lost.

Berkeley's reply to Malebranche is that causes need not be
omnipotent. The volitional activity of finite spirits is enough, once God
has made the apropriate decrees, to establish them as causes. Against
Hume Berkeley has to argue that anything less is not enough—or,
more specifically, that mere constant conjunction is not enough.

Lying behind Hume's belief that constant conjunction or regularity
is enough is a repudiation of the ideal of intelligibility. In Hume's view
all that a final cause can explain is a volition or decision, and it is

---

[29] *The Search after Truth*, Bk. VI, pt. ii, chap. 3, p. 450 in Lennon and Olscamp.
Berkeley is in no position to rule out the possibility of inversion; see *Principles* 107.

capable of this only because final causes are represented in beliefs and desires, which enter into regularities under which our volitions or decisions can be subsumed. A volition or decision can in turn be used to explain an action, but only by virtue of a further regularity in which the volition or decision is the first term and the action the second. The disagreement with Berkeley runs so deep that I can do little more than point it out. Berkeley seeks a kind of understanding that goes beyond subsumption under a regularity. Human ends seem to him to provide it. Because unthinking things have no ends, Berkeley thinks, they can make no contribution to the intelligibility of events. By reducing causation (at least on its objective side) to constant conjunction, Hume loses the contrast between causes and occasions emphasized at *Commentaries* 855-6.

It has not been my intention to argue in this chapter that Berkeley's account of causation is sound. I have instead tried to show why Berkeley believes there is middle ground between Malebranche and Hume, though I confess that part of explaining why Berkeley believes it consists in showing that it is not entirely implausible. Much of Berkeley's philosophy is an attempt to employ some fact about spirits which he takes to be well understood—the fact that their motives can rationalize their decisions, or the fact that ideas are in the mind by virtue of being perceived—to illuminate a fact about the natural world which he takes to be poorly understood. The categories all of us use in thinking about spirits are stretched by Berkeley to cover everything. Although the view I have attributed to Berkeley is by no means free of difficulties, it enables us to see, for example, how he can reconcile his belief that we move our own limbs with his insistence that God is the cause of all ideas of sense (and thereby, it seems, of all real movement).[30] If our contribution to bodily movement is one of intelligibility rather than underived power, we can be the partial cause as well. If in certain respects my account goes beyond what Berkeley actually says, I think it is none the less faithful to his deepest intentions, and that it brings out very clearly the deep difference between Berkeley and Hume, compared to which the difference between Berkeley and Malebranche is a matter of detail. Hume

---

[30] The difficulty of reconciling these two beliefs has been pointed out by a number of commentators: Pitcher, 'Berkeley on the Mind's Activity', *American Philosophical Quarterly* 18 (1981), 221-7; Tipton, *Berkeley*, p. 311; Bracken, *Berkeley*, London, 1974, p. 117; Olscamp, *The Moral Philosophy of George Berkeley*, The Hague, 1970, p. 101; and Ayers, 'Perception and Action', in *Knowledge and Necessity*, Royal Institute of Philosophy Lectures, vol. 3, London, 1970, pp. 91-106, esp. pp. 95-6.

explicitly denies there is an *objective* difference between a cause and an occasion.[31] When Berkeley distinguishes between them he makes an appeal not to necessary connection but to the more fundamental, if less clear, notion of intelligibility. Their disagreement brings out what is, it seems to me, most significant in Hume's treatment of causation: not his denial of necessary connection, but his belief that considerations of intelligibility have nothing to do with what counts as a cause.

---

[31] See the *Treatise*, I iii 14, p. 171.

6

IMMATERIALISM

There is a peculiar character in the metaphysical writings of Berkeley which is to be found no where else. . . . His writings show that he had thought with the utmost intensity on almost every subject, yet he has the same careless freedom of manner as if he had never thought at all. He is never entangled in the labyrinth of his own thoughts, and the buoyancy of his spirit surmounts every objection with a singular felicity, as if his mind had wings.

William Hazlitt, 'On Locke's Essay on the Human Understanding'

BERKELEY'S immaterialist arguments are numerous, confident, and simply stated. They justify Hazlitt's feeling that Berkeley enjoys a kind of higher felicity: the arguments entangle *us*, but Berkeley himself is never entangled. In this chapter I propose to examine Berkeley's most important arguments for immaterialism, taking note of the role played by Berkeley's views on intentionality, necessity, and intelligibility, but looking too at other notions, some related and some not. My aim throughout is to make Berkeley's arguments look as deep and as entangling as I think they are, but I hope I do not fail to convey Berkeley's own sense of their simplicity, of their common movement toward a conclusion of liberating clarity.

1. The argument of *Principles* 4

In *Principles* 4, and once again on the closing page of the *Three Dialogues*, Berkeley presents an immaterialist argument of astonishing brevity. The opinion that houses, mountains, and rivers 'have an existence natural or real, distinct from their being perceived by the understanding' is 'strangely prevailing amongst men', Berkeley admits in *Principles* 4. 'But with how great an assurance and acquiescence soever this principle may be entertained in the world', he says, it involves a 'manifest contradiction':

For what are the forementioned objects but the things we perceive by sense, and what do we perceive besides our own ideas or sensations; and is it not plainly repugnant that any one of these or any combination of them should exist unperceived?

When Philonous presents the argument he stresses its consistency with common sense:

> I do not pretend to be a setter-up of *new notions*. My endeavours tend only to unite and place in a clearer light that truth, which was before shared between the vulgar and the philosophers: the former being of opinion, that *those things they immediately perceive are the real things*; and the latter, that *the things immediately perceived, are ideas which exist only in the mind*. Which two notions put together, do in effect constitute the substance of what I advance.   (p. 262.)

The argument is simple: We perceive houses, mountains, and rivers (the 'real things' of Philonous's peroration). But we perceive nothing but our own ideas or sensations, which exist only in the mind. Therefore houses, mountains, and rivers—real things of all kinds— are ideas or sensations, which cannot exist unperceived.

The premisses of this argument, particularly the second, will occupy us for some time. But the initial cause for concern is structural: the argument appears to turn on an ambiguity in the notion of perception. Let us grant for the moment that ideas or sensations are all that we *immediately* perceive. Even so, it might be objected, perhaps real things are perceived in another manner. Perhaps we perceive them *mediately* or *indirectly*, in virtue of perceiving the ideas that represent them. If there are two kinds of perception, then things and ideas need not be one and the same, even though both are perceived.

Berkeley is vividly aware of this objection, though the first seven sections of the *Principles* give little sign of this. In § 8 he argues that if things are assumed to have an existence 'without the mind', there is nothing that can make ideas their representatives. In order for the immediate perception of ideas to count as mediate perception of things, there must be something about ideas that enables them to reach beyond themselves; the relation of representation, Berkeley believes, cannot be ungrounded or brute. But there is no relation that can give ideas the needed reach. Ideas can represent nothing but other ideas, and if the mind immediately perceives nothing but ideas, it cannot perceive something else by perceiving them.

Berkeley believes that representation can only be a matter of resemblance. In confining his attention to resemblance he ignores the relation of cause and effect, which is a plausible candidate in view of the use made of it by Locke, who took ideas of secondary qualities to be ideas 'of' things, even though he denied that they resemble anything in things themselves. Berkeley is actually equipped to argue that cause and effect is incapable of grounding the representation relation, but before examining the arguments he might have given against cause and effect I want to look at the arguments he does in fact offer against resemblance. And it is best to begin by asking why resemblance is the only candidate he took seriously.

Berkeley believes that perception always permits the formation of what might be described as an *absolute* conception of what is perceived. Unlike a merely *relative* conception, which exhibits an object in terms of its relation to something else, an absolute conception exhibits an object as it is in itself, in one or more of its aspects. Now suppose that we immediately perceive an object x. Can we perceive y by virtue of the fact that y is the cause of x? For two related reasons the Berkeleyan answer is no. First, if we conceive of y purely as the cause of x, our conception of y will be relative. Second, if we conceive of y purely as the cause of x, we will owe our conception of y to the active employment of our reason. It will not be a conception we owe to the *perception* of y, because Berkeley takes perception to be a passive operation: it takes place without the assistance of reason. The two reasons are related because Berkeley is unable to see how a faculty such as reason can bring us to anything but a relative conception of an object. In forming conceptions reason plays a role very much like the role it plays in deriving conclusions from premises: it does not originate conceptions, but puts them together out of materials already at hand.

This line of reasoning may suggest that the only way of arriving at an absolute conception of an object is by allowing it to impress itself upon us. Only then can perception be passive enough for the object to disclose itself. This is close to the position Berkeley eventually arrives at, but he is willing to take resemblance seriously because it seems to offer a compromise—a way of perceiving something indirectly which exhibits the object as it really is. An absolute conception of the direct object of perception apparently provides a route to an absolute conception of any object it resembles. And conceiving of the indirect object will not, it seems, call for active exertion on our part: an aspect of the indirect object will simply show itself. It is fair to object, of course, that this will give us no more than a conception of the *aspect*. In order to conceive of the *object*, it might be said, we must believe at the very least that it exists, and that the aspect revealed belongs to it. It might even be argued that beliefs such as these are among the operations of reason, and that indirect perception as Berkeley understands it was therefore doomed from the very outset: passive perception could never yield an absolute conception of an indirect object. For various reasons Berkeley is prepared to put such points aside. He is willing to take resemblance seriously because it holds out the hope that we can grasp an object even though we do not confront it directly, because it is faithfully mirrored in our ideas.

Yet even resemblance fails in the end, because only an idea can be like an idea:

> But say you, though the ideas themselves do not exist without the mind, yet there may be things like them whereof they are copies or resemblances, which things exist without the mind, in an unthinking substance. I answer, an idea can be like nothing but an idea; a colour or figure can be like nothing but another colour or figure. If we look but ever so little into our own thoughts, we shall find it impossible for us to conceive a likeness except only between our ideas. Again, I ask whether those supposed originals or external things, of which our ideas are the pictures or representations, be themselves perceivable or no? If they are, then they are ideas, and we have gained our point; but if you say they are not, I appeal to anyone whether it be sense, to assert a colour is like something which is invisible; hard or soft, like something which is intangible; and so of the rest (*Principles* 8.)

The point is repeated by Philonous in the First Dialogue:

PHILONOUS. Ideas then are sensible, and their archetypes or originals insensible.

HYLAS. Right.

PHILONOUS. But how can that which is sensible be like that which is insensible? Can a real thing in itself *invisible* be like a *colour*, or a real thing which is not *audible*, be like a *sound*? In a word, can any thing be like a sensation or idea, but another sensation or idea?

HYLAS. I must own, I think not.

PHILONOUS. Is it possible there should be any doubt in the point? Do you not perfectly know your own ideas?

HYLAS. I know them perfectly; since what I do not perceive or know, can be no part of my idea.

PHILONOUS. Consider therefore, and examine them, and then tell me if there be any thing in them which can exist without the mind: or if you can conceive any thing like them existing without the mind.

HYLAS. Upon inquiry, I find it is impossible for me to conceive or understand how any thing but an idea can be like an idea.   (p. 206.)

If resemblance is the only relation capable of securing representation, and if an idea can be like nothing but another idea, it follows that the argument of *Principles* 4 does not equivocate. If real things are perceived they must be perceived immediately, because they cannot be perceived by means of ideas. But should we accept Berkeley's view that only an idea can be like an idea?

There are two broad ways in which this view—Berkeley's *likeness principle*—can be defended. The first is metaphysical: because resemblance is the sharing of a feature, metaphysical argument might be used to show that ideas and things cannot be alike because their natures do not permit them to possess a feature in common. Phillip D. Cummins has offered a metaphysical argument for the likeness principle, but I do not think that it explains why Berkeley embraced it.[1] I will examine Cummins's argument in a moment. My own view is that an epistemological defence of the principle is more faithful to Berkeley's intentions: through a consideration of the conditions that must be met if it is to be known (or reasonably believed) that two things are alike, an epistemological defence of the likeness principle arrives at the conclusion that ideas and things cannot in fact be alike.

Cummins does not explicitly offer his argument as an explanation of why Berkeley accepts the likeness principle. But he does say that the likeness principle is 'a shorthand formulation' of the following three claims:[2]

A, all qualities which are determinates of the same determinable have the same ontological status; *B*, a necessary condition of resemblance between two entities is that they are or possess qualities which are determinates of the same determinable; *C*, none of the qualities we immediately perceive (hereafter termed 'sensible qualities') can occur unperceived.

A and *B*, which Cummins takes to be 'relatively non-controversial' (pp. 355 and 362), together entail that a necessary condition of resemblance between two entities is that they are or possess qualities of the same ontological status. *C*, which Cummins takes to be 'highly controversial'—so controversial he labels it 'Berkeley's idealistic premiss' (p. 363)—assigns an ontological status to the qualities we immediately perceive: they are *ideas*, or entities which cannot occur unperceived. It follows that a necessary condition of resemblance

---

[1] The argument appears in 'Berkeley's Likeness Principle', reprinted in C. B. Martin and David M. Armstrong (eds.), *Locke and Berkeley*, Notre Dame, 1968, pp. 353–63.
[2] Ibid., p. 356. Subsequent references are included in the text.

between two entities, one of which we immediately perceive, is that the second entity either possesses a quality which cannot occur unperceived, or is identical with a quality which cannot occur unperceived. If we assume that an entity cannot differ in ontological status from the qualities it possesses—if we assume, as Berkeley certainly seems to, that material substance, because it is unthinking, cannot have or possess a quality which is unable to exist apart from a thinking thing (p. 361)—we can conclude that 'only an idea can be like an idea', that only an entity which cannot occur unperceived can resemble a sensible quality.

Cummins's argument is designed to make no mention of ideas (see p. 355). It takes us from the claim that what is immediately perceived is mind-dependent to the broader claim that what *resembles* what is immediately perceived is mind-dependent. Now there is some evidence in the First Dialogue for the suggestion that Berkeley came to the likeness principle by such a route. When Hylas is brought to the conclusion that 'there is no extension or figure in an object' (First Dialogue, p. 189) he is understandably hesitant. He is afraid that 'odd consequences' will follow from his concession. In the first and second editions of the *Dialogues* Philonous scoffs at Hylas's squeamishness: 'Odd, say you? After the concessions already made, I hope you will stick at nothing for its oddness.' In the third edition, however, Philonous makes an interesting attempt to soften the impression of oddness. The attempt is interesting because it calls for the premature introduction of the topic of likeness, which does not receive extended treatment until pp. 205–6:

But on the other hand should it not seem very odd, if the general reasoning which includes all other sensible qualities did not also include extension? If it be allowed that no idea nor any thing like an idea can exist in an unperceiving substance, then surely it follows, that no figure or mode of extension, which we can either perceive or imagine, or have any idea of, can be really inherent in matter. (pp. 189–90.)

Here Philonous moves without comment from the claim that sensible qualities cannot exist in an unperceiving substance to the broader claim that anything *like* a sensible quality cannot exist in an unperceiving substance. Berkeley's apparent belief that the more narrow claim entitles him to make the broader one gives us some reason to suppose that Cummins's argument explains his allegiance to the likeness principle.

In Cummins's reconstruction the movement from the narrow to the broad claim is brought about by *A* and *B*: anything that resembles an object must have (if it is not identical with) a quality which is a determinate of the same determinable as some quality of the object (claim *B*, adjusted to fit the case at hand); and the ontological status of the two qualities must therefore be the same (claim *A*). Despite Cummins's belief that they are relatively non-controversial, I do not find *A* and *B* compelling. Why should it be the case that two *instances* of a given quality must have the same ontological status? Austin questions a very similar principle in *Sense and Sensibilia*:[3]

One may well wish at least to ask for the credentials of a curious general principle . . . to the effect that, if two things are not 'generally the same', the same 'in nature', then they can't be alike, or even very nearly alike. If it were true, Ayer says, that from time to time we perceived things of two different kinds, then 'we should expect' them to be qualitatively different. But why on earth should we?

I do not mean to suggest that Cummins's principles are false, but if Berkeley's acceptance of the likeness principle puzzles us, I suspect that *A* and *B* are themselves too puzzling to explain it.[4] There is, however, a more serious obstacle to the explanation we are considering. In my restatement of Cummins's argument I introduced an additional premiss: if an entity possesses qualities which cannot exist unperceived, then the entity itself cannot exist unperceived. It seems to me that the premiss is required if the argument for the likeness principle is to be valid. Without the additional premiss the argument has to stop with the claim that an external object, if it is to resemble an object of immediate perception, must have a quality which cannot exist unperceived. Cummins points out that in Berkeley's view the very existence of such an object is a contradiction, but an additional premiss is required to make the grounds for this explicit. Berkeley treats the external object as a substance, and like Descartes he supposes that if a substance has a quality, then no other substance apart from God is required to support the existence of the quality. It follows that if the substance in question is material (and therefore unthinking), it cannot have a quality which depends for its existence on being perceived.

Now it seems to me that the additional premiss is not only essential

---

[3] Oxford, 1962, p. 50.

[4] Cummins points out that *A* and *B* are 'virtually axiomatic' for Berkeley (p. 355), but the same might be said of the likeness principle itself.

to the argument even if we accept *A* and *B*, but capable of taking us from *C* to the likeness principle all by itself, provided we bear in mind what it means for an external object to have a quality. If an external object is to resemble an object of immediate perception they must have a quality in common. The external object must therefore have a quality which cannot exist unperceived. But it cannot have such a quality, because the added premiss tells us that if it did, it would not be an external object, but would depend for its existence on being perceived. Hence no external object can be like an idea.[5]

The argument from *A*, *B*, and *C* to the likeness principle may be invalid, however, even if we supply the additional premiss. The argument assumes that every instance of a quality—every instance of a determinate of some determinable—must have the same ontological status. Or, to put the point another way, the argument assumes that the ontological status of a determinate quality is fixed by the status of the determinable quality under which it falls. But even if it is true that the instances we immediately perceive cannot exist unperceived, why should it be the case that other instances—instances which we do not perceive immediately—cannot exist unperceived? The question points to an ambiguity in Cummins's claim *C*, 'none of the qualities we immediately perceive can occur unperceived.' Does it mean that none of the *instances* or *occurrences* we immediately perceive can exist unperceived, or does it mean that no instance or occurrence of a quality, *some instance or occurrence of which* we immediately perceive, can occur unperceived? Cummins no doubt takes claim *C* in the second way, and on this understanding the argument is no longer open to the objection just made. On such an understanding, claim *C* is hardly distinguishable from the likeness principle: applied to the case of colour, for example, this reading of claim *C* tells us that no immediately perceived instance of a colour-quality can exist unperceived, and that no instance of the same quality—no instance that matches the first-mentioned instance in colour—can exist unperceived. In fact the claim goes even further, because it is not confined to instances that perfectly match the instance we perceive. Every instance of a determinate colour-quality is at the same time an instance of the

---

[5] This conclusion does not have the apparent generality of the likeness principle, which says that *nothing* but an idea can be like an idea, but that generality is, I think, more apparent than real. Although Berkeley speaks in general terms he means to exclude something in particular: material substance, or an unthinking support of qualities.

determinable *colour*. If *C* is understood in Cummins's way and then applied to determinables as well as to determinates, it tells us that no instance of a colour can occur unperceived if any instance of any colour is an object of immediate perception. It tells us, that is, that no instance of a quality can occur unperceived if any instance of that quality is an object of immediate perception. But this is just another way of saying that only an idea can be like an idea.

It seems to me that Berkeley takes claim *C* in the first way, and that Cummins's metaphysical argument therefore fails as an explanation of why Berkeley embraces the likeness principle. Apart from the passage added to the third edition of the *Dialogues* and discussed above, Berkeley consistently separates the truth of *C* from that of the likeness principle. In the First Dialogue, where he undertakes to establish *C*, Berkeley seems to recognize that his arguments are enough to establish *C* only on the first of the two readings, and he appeals to the likeness principle later in the dialogue precisely to overcome this limitation. These facts suggest that Berkeley does not read *C* as Cummins does.

To sum up my discussion of Cummins's argument: it depends on a suppressed premiss, according to which an unperceiving substance cannot have or possess a quality which cannot exist unperceived; and yet it fails to establish the likeness principle even when the missing premiss is supplied, because Berkeley does not read claim *C* as Cummins does. Hence I do not think it can explain why Berkeley embraces the likeness principle.[6]

An epistemological argument for the likeness principle is fully

---

[6] In 'Perceptual Relativity and Ideas in the Mind', *Philosophy and Phenomenological Research* 24 (1963–4), 202–14, Cummins presents another metaphysical argument in favour of the likeness principle. According to the argument, a modification of the mind can have nothing in common with a modification of matter, because the principal attributes of mind and matter—thought and extension—are wholly distinct. Since the modifications of a substance are nothing more than modifications of its principal attribute—nothing more, that is, than the ways in which that attribute exists—the modifications of mind and matter must be entirely different. See 'Perceptual Relativity', p. 210. As Cummins himself points out, the argument assumes that ideas are modifications of the mind. Cummins thinks that the success of the argument in explaining his allegiance to the likeness principle is evidence that Berkeley treats ideas as modifications. Because I think that Berkeleyan ideas are objects, I do not think this markedly Cartesian argument should be attributed to Berkeley. Cummins defends the view that Berkeleyan ideas are modifications in 'Berkeley's Ideas of Sense', *Nous* 9 (1975), 55–72. For a discussion of the sources and influence of the argument see both 'Perceptual Relativity' and Richard A. Watson, *The Downfall of Cartesianism, 1673–1712*, The Hague, 1966.

presented in the *Philosophical Commentaries*. Berkeley argues in entry 378 that only an idea can be like an idea because two things cannot be said to be alike unless they have been compared, and only an idea can be compared to an idea:[7]

16 Two things cannot be said to be alike or unlike till they have been compar'd

17 Comparing is the viewing two ideas together, & marking w^t they agree in & w^t they disagree in.

18 The mind can compare nothing but its' own ideas. 17.

19 Nothing like an idea can be in an ūperceiving thing. 11. 16. 18.

Line 11, to which Berkeley appeals in justifying line 19, plays roughly the role of the premiss which, I argued, should be added to Cummins's second argument for the likeness principle: 'Whatever has in it an idea,' the line reads, 'tho it be never so passive, tho it exert no manner of act about it, yet it must perceive.'

The argument of entry 378 does not appear in Berkeley's published works, but in § 8 of the *Principles* Berkeley alludes to it: 'If we look but ever so little into our thoughts,' he writes, 'we shall find it impossible for us to conceive a likeness except only between our ideas.' The allusion is followed by his only published defence of the likeness principle (which is repeated in the First Dialogue on p. 206):

Again, I ask whether those supposed originals or external things, of which our ideas are the pictures or representations, be themselves perceivable or no? If they are, then they are ideas, and we have gained our point; but if you say they are not, I appeal to anyone whether it be sense, to assert a colour is like something which is invisible; hard or soft, like something which is intangible; and so of the rest. (*Principles* 8).

This disappointing passage seems to ignore the distinction between direct and indirect perception. When Berkeley asks whether external things or originals are perceivable, he needs to have *one* sense of 'perceivable' in mind. If he does not, anyone who distinguishes between direct and indirect perception will be able to wriggle free. As the argument stands the defender of the distinction can reply that objects are *mediately* perceivable, and at the same time deny that this means they are ideas. He or she can even deny that external things or originals are invisible. They may not be *directly* perceivable by sight, he or she can say, but they can be seen by perceiving the ideas that represent them.

---

[7] Pieces of the argument also appear in entries 46, 47, 50, and 51.

At this point the argument of entry 378 comes to Berkeley's rescue. The argument is *verificationist* because it rests on the belief that if it is impossible to find out that two things are alike, they cannot be said to be alike. Any genuine state of affairs is such that we can, at least in principle, verify that it obtains. The defender of the distinction between direct and indirect perception might object that two things can be alike even if we are unable to find that out. 'The argument may force me to acknowledge that the resemblance between idea and object is something which can never be known,' he or she might say, 'but it cannot force me to conclude that such resemblance is impossible. Although an external object cannot enter into a comparison directly, perhaps it can enter into it *indirectly*, in something like the way it can be seen or touched.' In this case, however, Berkeley has a reply. It seems that any genuine attempt at comparison must have as a possible outcome the judgement that the things compared are not alike. But there is no chance that comparing an idea to an external object will issue in the judgement that they differ, because the object is perceived only because we perceive the other party to the comparison. Comparing idea and thing by perceiving them both is like comparing the colour of a table to the colour of its top when the table is seen only because we see the table-top.

But even if we grant that two things cannot be said to be alike unless we are able to tell that they are, it does not seem to be the case that similarity can be detected only by perceiving things and weighing their differences. The verificationist argument invites us to take a point of view toward the question of resemblance or likeness that might be described as *subjective*. Berkeley's preoccupation with comparison suggests the existence of a viewpoint from which judgements of likeness are made, and in which a standard of likeness is consciously embodied. The obvious alternative to perceptual comparison is an inference to the best explanation. But any such inference will presumably assign a causal role to the external object, and we will soon see that Berkeley has an argument against this. It is no use retreating to the more modest view that the hypothesis follows from an observed regularity when taken together with some acknowledged fact. Observed regularities can lend support to the hypothesis only if they tell us about the behaviour of external things, and Berkeley's opponent has no right to suppose that they do.

I conclude that the epistemological argument of *Commentaries* 378 is not implausible, and that it explains Berkeley's acceptance of the likeness principle. The argument does not appear in Berkeley's published works but *Principles* 8 alludes to it, and it is fully presented in the notebooks. It is more firmly grounded in the texts than Cummins's metaphysical argument, which is not set out in any of Berkeley's writings.

Earlier in this section I tried to explain why Berkeley treats resemblance as the only serious candidate for securing the relation of representation. The very wording of *Principles* 8 and 9 shows how powerful a hold resemblance had on Berkeley's thinking about representation. The natural objection to the argument of *Principles* 1–7 is that for all that has been said, there may be things outside the mind which our ideas represent. But when Berkeley gives voice to this concern in § 8 he chooses the language of resemblance: they may be things, the interlocutor suggests, whereof ideas are the 'copies or resemblances'. As the section progresses Berkeley continues to regard ideas as 'pictures or representation' of 'those supposed originals or external things'. In § 9, where he introduces the distinction between primary and secondary qualities, he again selects the language of resemblance over the more neutral language of representation. Ideas of primary qualities are characterized as 'patterns or images of things', whereas ideas of secondary qualities are not 'resemblances of any thing' without the mind. Locke himself had said that 'the *Ideas, produced* in us *by* these *Secondary Qualities, have no resemblance* of them at all', and that 'there is nothing like our *Ideas*, existing in the Bodies themselves' (II viii 15), yet Locke believed that even these ideas refer beyond themselves to structural features of the objects that produce them. I think Berkeley realizes that in Locke's opinion, ideas of secondary qualities do not impart conceptions of bodies as they are in themselves. To describe such an idea as a representation would, he thinks, make even Locke uneasy.

In the *Principles*, Berkeley first touches on the topic of causation in §§ 18–20, where he argues that 'if there were external bodies, it is impossible we should ever come to know it' (§ 20), and he returns to it in §§ 25–7, where he asks how ideas are caused. Although these sections are not intended as part of his attack on the distinction between direct and indirect perception, his argument that ideas cannot be caused by material things shows that causal relations cannot account for our ability to think of such things. As we know from Chapter 5, Berkeley demands that causes render their effects intelligible. If we do not understand how an alleged cause produces its effect, we have no right to speak of it as a cause at all. Berkeley argues in § 19 that

> though we give the materialists their external bodies, they by their own confession are never the nearer knowing how our ideas are produced: since they own themselves unable to comprehend in what manner body can act upon spirit, or how it is possible it should imprint any idea in the mind. Hence it is evident the production of ideas or sensations in our minds, can be no reason why we should suppose matter or corporeal substances, since that is acknowledged to remain equally inexplicable with, or without this supposition.

Berkeley's official defence of the argument of *Principles* 4 rests on the account of intentionality discussed in Chapter 1. But his account of causation strengthens that defence by showing that cause and effect is as useless to the materialist as resemblance is.

2. *Immediate perception*

Now that we have seen how Berkeley protects the argument of *Principles* 4 from the charge of equivocation, we are ready to examine its premisses. I will not be looking very closely at premiss one, which says that we perceive real things. I will take the truth of this premiss for granted, though later on I will ask how the immediate perception of things is related to the immediate perception of ideas such as colour and shape. The second premiss—'we perceive only our own ideas or sensations, which exist only in the mind'—is much more interesting. Its defence in the *Principles* is rather cursory—I take it up in section 4 below—but Philonous gives a vigorous defence of the premiss in the First Dialogue. This defence is the topic of the following section, which takes the form of a commentary on the First Dialogue; in the present section I try to explain what immediate perception is.

Berkeley's characterizations of immediate perception fall into two main families. Characterizations of the first kind separate immediate perception from operations traditionally assigned to faculties other than sense, such as reason, imagination, or memory. Immediate perception is first of all perception without *inference*, which is the work of reason. It is also perception without *suggestion*, which is the work of imagination or memory. It follows that 'those things alone are actually and strictly perceived by any sense, which would have been perceived, in case that same sense had then been first conferred on us.' (First Dialogue, p. 204.) Immediate perception is perception that would have taken place even if past experience had not inculcated habits of perception. In perception by suggestion 'the immediate perception of ideas by one sense suggests to the mind others perhaps belonging to another sense, which are wont to be connected with them.' (First Dialogue, p. 204.) Berkeley does not explain how to distinguish between inference and suggestion, but I think he would insist that inference, unlike suggestion, is both *conscious* and *active*.[8] To say that inference is conscious is to say that the inferring mind is aware not only of the idea inferred but of some principle by which the transition is made. To say that inference is active is to say that the mind's grasp of this principle plays a role in explaining the step taken by the mind. A third difference between inference and suggestion, less important than the others in the present context, is that an object perceived by suggestion must at one time have been immediately perceived.[9]

According to the characterizations of immediate perception in Berkeley's second family, no object intervenes between the mind and the object it immediately perceives. Berkeley takes immediate perception in this sense to be equivalent to immediate perception in the first sense. We can see why he does this if we ask how the notion of an intervening object is supposed to be understood. Here is how Philonous introduces the notion in the First Dialogue:

Pardon me, Hylas, if I am desirous clearly to apprehend your notions, since this may much shorten our inquiry. Suffer me then to ask you this farther question. Are those things only perceived by the sense which are perceived immediately? Or may those things properly be said to be *sensible*, which are perceived mediately, or not without the intervention of others? (p. 174. See also *Theory of Vision* 64.)

The subsequent exchange shows clearly that both Hylas and Philonous take perception without intervention to be the same as perception without inference. In the end Hylas offers the following answer to Philonous's questions:

---

[8] Berkeley distinguishes between inference and suggestion at *Theory of Vision Vindicated* 42: 'To perceive is one thing, to judge another. So likewise, *to be suggested is one thing*, and *to be inferred another* [emphasis mine]. Things are suggested and perceived by sense. We make judgments and inferences by the understanding.' In 'The Concept of Immediate Perception in Berkeley's Immaterialism', Georges Dicker argues that Berkeley does not clearly distinguish between conscious inference and unconscious association. See Colin M. Turbayne (ed.), *Berkeley: Critical and Interpretive Essays*, Minneapolis, 1982, pp. 48–66, esp. pp. 48–56 and n. 12 on p. 65.

[9] A philosopher who allows for unconscious inference will take the difference between inference and suggestion to be less dramatic than Berkeley does.

To prevent any more questions of this kind, I tell you once for all, that by *sensible things* I mean those only which are perceived by sense, and that in truth the senses perceive nothing which they do not perceive immediately: for they make no inferences. The deducing therefore of causes or occasions from effects and appearances, which alone are perceived by sense, entirely relates to reason. (pp. 174–5.)

The two characterizations of immediate perception come to the same thing because intervention is understood not spatially, but in terms of perception itself. To perceive one object through the intervention of another is to be perceive the first in virtue of perceiving the second. One object is perceived without inference or suggestion. The other is perceived or known only because it is inferred from (or suggested by) the first.

I have followed Berkeley in speaking of perception as the perception of *objects*. Berkeley tends to focus his attention on thoughts about perception that take the form '*S* perceives *o*': 'by touch I perceive . . . hard and soft, heat and cold, motion and resistance' (*Principles* 1): 'the table I write on, I say, exists, that is, I see and feel it; and if I were out of my study I should say it existed, meaning thereby that if I was in my study I might perceive it' (*Principles* 3); 'what are the forementioned objects but the things we perceive by sense' (*Principles* 4). How, it might be asked, can Berkeley draw a distinction when the items that figure in inference are *sentential* or *propositional* rather than thing-like? It would make perfect sense to distinguish between the inferred and the uninferred in perception if Berkeley were concerned with thoughts that take the form '*S* perceives that *p*', but if the objects of perception do not have propositional structure, it might be urged, the distinction cannot be maintained.[10]

Part of the answer to this objection is that suggestion, unlike inference, does not call for an object which is propositional rather than thing-like. But the more important point is that Berkeley has a tendency to fuse perceiving an object with perceiving either than an object is present, or that one's conscious awareness is of a certain kind. I do not mean to say that Berkeley fuses the *concept* of perceiving an object with that of perceiving that the object is present. He does not. Like many of his predecessors and contemporaries, Berkeley holds that immediate perception is an operation of the unaided senses, and

---

[10] See David Armstrong, 'Immediate Perception', pp. 119–24 in *The Nature of the Mind and Other Essays*, Ithaca, 1981, and *A Materialist Theory of the Mind*, London, 1968, pp. 233–4.

he follows tradition in opposing the senses to the faculties of judgement and belief. But he nevertheless believes that immediate perception, *as it occurs in us*, always carries belief along with it. It may not be a conceptual truth that perception involves belief, but for Berkeley it is an *anthropological* truth, a truth about perception in its human form. This permits him to move freely from one account of the distinction between immediate and mediate perception to another: from *perception with or without inference*, which apparently calls for a propositional object, to *perception with or without an intervening object*, which does not.

Some recent writers on perception have employed a notion of immediate or direct perception which in some respects resembles Berkeley's. They distinguish between immediate and mediate perception by appealing to what one of them calls 'the *in virtue of* relation'.[11]

We commonly see things in virtue of seeing *other* things: I see the aircraft flying overhead in virtue of seeing its underside (and the airplane is not identical with its underside); I see the table I am writing on in virtue of seeing its top; I first see England on the cross-channel ferry in virtue of seeing the white cliffs of Dover.[12]

Generalizing somewhat from the particular accounts these writers give, one object (*n*) is perceived in virtue of perceiving another object (*o*) only if perceiving *o* accounts for the perception of *n*. There is room for disagreement over the form the account must take. Berkeley believes that *n* can be perceived in virtue of perceiving *o* only if the presence of *n* is inferred from or suggested by the sensuous awareness of *o*.

Berkeley assigns a number of important characteristics to immediate perception, several of which we have already touched on. The following list deals only with the perception of qualities; the immediate perception of objects, which differs from that of qualities in several significant respects, will be taken up later on.

First, immediate perception is *passive*. It does not depend on the perceiver's will (First Dialogue, pp. 196–7); nor does it involve inference, or the active exercise of reason.

Second, immediate perception is *self-contained* in a way that perception by inference and perception by suggestion are not.

[11] Frank Jackson, *Perception: A Representative Theory*, Cambridge, 1977, p. 15. Moreland Perkins, in *Sensing the World*, Indianapolis, 1983, also uses the '*in virtue of*' locution. See e.g. p. 12.

[12] Jackson, *Perception*, p. 19. See also Perkins, *Sensing the World*, pp. 14–17.

Perception by inference calls for the collaboration of reason. The senses alone cannot issue in it. Perception by suggestion depends on past experience and its embodiment in memory or habit. Berkeley captures the last point by specifying that the objects of immediate perception 'would have been perceived, in case the same sense had then been first conferred on us' (First Dialogue, p. 204). Of course even if suggestion were an innate function Berkeley would refuse to say that the objects suggested were immediately perceived. The main point is that associative tendencies, whether inculcated by experience or implanted in our nature, involve more than the operation of our senses.

Third, immediate perception is *infallible*. It is a 'manifest contradiction' to suppose that we should err in respect of what we perceive 'immediately and at present' (Third Dialogue, p. 238). That is, if we believe that an object of immediate perception has a certain property then it does in fact have that property. Furthermore, immediate perception is *transparent*: there is nothing in an object of immediate perception but what is perceived (*Principles* 25). If an object of immediate perception has a certain property then it perceptually appears to the attentive mind as if it does. In fact we *know* that the object has the property; as Hylas and Philonous join in saying at the end of the First Dialogue, we know our ideas perfectly (p. 206).

Fourth, immediate perception implies the existence of the object perceived. 'Every thing that is seen, felt, heard, or any way perceived by the senses, is on the principles I embrace, a real being.' (Third Dialogue, p. 260.) 'I see this *cherry*, I feel it, I taste it: and I am sure *nothing* cannot be seen, felt, or tasted: it is therefore *real*.' (Third Dialogue, p. 249.) 'Let me be represented as one who trusts his senses, who thinks he knows the things he sees and feels, and entertains no doubts, of their existence'. (Third Dialogue, p. 237.) 'That a thing should be really perceived by my senses, and at the same time not really exist, is to me a plain contradiction'. (Third Dialogue, p. 230.)

Finally, immediate perception is a form of *conscious* or *sensuous awareness*, which Berkeley describes as a form of *knowledge*. The being of bodies, Berkeley writes at *Principles* 6, 'is to be perceived *or known*' (*Principles* 6, emphasis mine). Hylas likewise agrees with Philonous that 'what I do not perceive or know, cannot be part of my idea' (First Dialogue, p. 206; see also p. 202). It is therefore misleading of George Pitcher to suggest that immediate perception, as Berkeley construes it, is analogous to what Fred Dretske calls *non-epistemic seeing*.[13] Immediate perception is, at the very least, a form of non-propositional awareness, and as it occurs in human beings belief tends to follow in its train. In Berkeleyan seeing there is, characteristically, epistemic or doxastic involvement.

Near the beginning of the First Dialogue Philonous provides a list of the qualities that are immediately perceived:

> This point then is agreed between us, that *sensible things are those only which are immediately perceived by sense.* You will farther inform me, whether we immediately perceive by sight any thing beside light, and colours, and figures: or by hearing, any thing but sounds: by the palate, any thing besides tastes: by the smell, beside odours: or by the touch, more than tangible qualities. (p. 175.)

Hylas agrees that if the qualities listed are taken away, nothing sensible remains. This list will be important in the following section, where we will examine Berkeley's case for saying that colours, figures, sounds and other qualities exist only in the mind. For the moment I want to concentrate on something the list does not include. The opening section of Part I of the *Principles* begins with a similar list:

> By sight I have the ideas of light and colours with their several degrees and variations. By touch I perceive, for example, hard and soft, heat and cold, motion and resistance, and of all these more and less either as to quantity or degree. Smelling furnishes me with odours; the palate with tastes, and hearing conveys sounds to the mind in all their variety of tone and composition.

But as the section continues the list goes beyond the one provided by Philonous:

> And as several of these are observed to accompany each other, they come to be marked by one name, and so to be reputed as one thing. Thus, for example, a certain colour, taste, smell, figure and consistence having been observed to go together, are accounted one distinct thing, signified by the name *apple*. Other collections of ideas constitute a stone, a tree, a book, and the like sensible things.

It is obviously Berkeley's view that the qualities listed both in the First Dialogue and in the opening section of the *Principles* are objects of immediate perception. It is plausible to suggest that they are perceived

---

[13] For Pitcher's suggestion see *Berkeley*, London, 1977, p. 9. On non-epistemic seeing see G. J. Warnock (who calls it 'simple seeing'), 'Seeing', reprinted in Robert J. Swartz (ed.), *Perceiving, Sensing, and Knowing*, New York, 1965, pp. 49–67, and Dretske, *Seeing and Knowing*, London, 1969, chap. 2.

without inference or suggestion, and a case can be made for saying that they possess the five characteristics listed above. But what about apples, stones, trees, and books? Does Berkeley believe that these too are immediately perceived? In a provocative paper George Pitcher answers no.[14]

Pitcher's paper is a response to Michael Ayers and George Pappas, who hold that Berkeley accepts the following principle:[15]

1. In normal sense perception, one immediately perceives so-called physical objects—i.e., things like apples, trees, etc.

Pitcher, who acknowledges the plausibility of the attribution, presents several passages where Berkeley endorses (1), among them *Principles* 95 and p. 230 in the Third Dialogue. The first passage is worth presenting:

Take away this *material substance* . . . and mean by *body* what every plain ordinary person means by that word, to wit, that which is immediately seen and felt, which is only a combination of sensible qualities, or ideas: and then their most unanswerable objections come to nothing. (Quoted by Pitcher on p. 99.)

But Pitcher goes on to produce passages where Berkeley (he claims) denies (1). Rather than accuse Berkeley of a contradiction, Pitcher proposes that Berkeley is speaking strictly when he denies (1), and speaking loosely ('with the vulgar') when he affirms it. 'As understood by ordinary unlearned people', he writes, the principle is in Berkeley's opinion 'doubtless false' (p. 104). But when taken to express a 'suitable, but philosophically unsound' notion of sense perception—a notion Pitcher identifies with *mediate* perception—it is true (p. 105).

The most compelling feature of Pitcher's case is the presence of such phrases as 'in truth and strictness' and 'in strict philosophical truth' in the alleged denials of (1). As Pitcher observes, these phrases 'ought to serve as signals that Berkeley is stating what he takes to be the actual, literal truth about sense perception' (p. 105). They should therefore be given priority over the affirmations of (1), and if the distinction between philosophical and popular speech allows us to give

---

[14] 'Berkeley and the Perception of Objects', *Journal of the History of Philosophy* 24 (1986), 99–105.

[15] Ibid., p. 99. Pitcher attributes two related principles to Ayers and Pappas but I will not discuss those further principles here. For Ayers see p. xiv of his Introduction to George Berkeley, *Philosophical Works*, London, 1975. For Pappas see 'Berkeley, Perception, and Common Sense', in Turbayne (ed.), *Berkeley*, pp. 3–21, esp. p. 6 and n. 9 on p. 21. Pappas's views are further developed in 'Berkeley and Immediate Perception', in Ernest Sosa (ed.), *Essays on the Philosophy of George Berkeley*, Dordrecht, 1987.

priority to the denials without burdening Berkeley with a contradiction, so much the better. But I am not convinced by Pitcher's argument, partly because it deals with too selective a range of texts, and partly because it neglects an interesting feature of the texts on which it concentrates. This feature suggests an alternative interpretation which is, I think, superior to Pitcher's, though his argument does raise some awkward questions for the interpretation of immediate perception I have so far defended in this chapter.

Here are the kernels of the alleged denials of (1) quoted by Pitcher on p. 100 of his paper:

(a) In truth and strictness, nothing can be *heard* but *sound*: and the coach is then not properly perceived by sense, but suggested from experience.
                              (First Dialogue, p. 204, emphasis mine.)

(b) ALCIPHRON. Do we not, strictly speaking, perceive by sight such things as trees, houses, men, rivers, and the like?
    EUPHRANOR. We do, indeed, perceive or apprehend those things by the faculty of sight. But will it follow from thence that they are the proper and immediate objects of sight?
                              (*Alciphron*, Fourth Dialogue, *Works* III, p. 154.)

(c) ALCIPHRON. I see, therefore, in strict philosophical truth, that rock only in the same sense that I may be said to hear it, when the word *rock* is pronounced.
    EUPHRANOR. In the very same.
                              (*Alciphron*, Fourth Dialogue, *Works*, III, p. 155.)

Pitcher does not comment on the occurrence of the words 'proper' and 'properly' in (a) and (b), nor does he notice the occurrence of 'proper' in the conclusion of the stretch of dialogue from which he extracts (c):

ALCIPHRON. And if we also consider that it is the same throughout the whole world, and not, like other languages, differing in different places, it will not seem unaccountable that men should mistake the connexion between the proper objects of sight and the things signified by them to be found in necessary relations or likeness; or, that they should even take them for the same things. (p. 156.)

It seems to me that the occurrence of these words is crucially important. In (a), (b), and (c), where Berkeley or his representative speaks in truth and strictness, he is speaking not about the immediate objects of perception in general, but about the *proper* and immediate objects of the various senses in particular. The objects he is talking about in (a) to (c) are the ideas characteristic of the various senses. He is not talking about the objects these ideas compose when they are blended together, objects which are not the *proper* and immediate objects of any sense but which can, none the less, be immediately perceived. To put the point another way, there is an ambiguity in Berkeley's notion of an object. An object can be what *Principles* 25 calls 'an idea or object of thought', or it can be the kind of object that comes into being when, as *Principles* 3 and 38 explain, objects of the first kind are blended together. There is a related ambiguity in the notion of immediate perception. Both a sound and a coach are immediately perceived, but only sound is the *proper* and immediate object of a sense. The coach is not the proper and immediate object of *any* sense, though it is an immediate object of sight, touch, and hearing.

Pitcher is correct when he writes that the passages where Berkeley indicates he is speaking strictly present what he takes to be 'the true philosophical notion of sense perception' (p. 105). But it does not follow that these passages are meant as denials of (1). The passages quoted by Pitcher speak of the *proper* and immediate objects of our senses—of the objects properly and immediately perceived by sight, touch, and hearing—and as such they state the *deepest* truth (or, if you like, the *philosophical* truth) about sense perception. But this does not mean that (1) cannot also be true, *literally* true.

On the interpretation I have proposed the senses have their *common* immediate objects as well as their proper immediate objects. This allows Berkeley to say that ordinary people are in large part right about sense perception. Ordinary physical objects are immediately perceived; they are not, as materialist philosophers suppose, perceived by means of images or representations that intervene between object and perceiver.

My interpretation is supported by passages where Berkeley seems to commit himself to the truth—the *literal* truth—of (1). Pitcher does not discuss the following passage from the Third Dialogue, where Philonous gives every sign that he is speaking strictly when he says that we immediately perceive such things as apples and trees.

PHILONOUS. I do not pretend to be a setter-up of *new notions*. My endeavours tend only to unite and place in a clearer light that truth, which was before shared between the vulgar and the philosophers: the former being of opinion, that *those things they immediately perceive are the real things*; and the latter, that *the things immediately perceived, are ideas which exist only in the mind.* Which two notions put together, do in effect constitute the substance of what I advance.   (Third Dialogue, p. 262.)

(See also the First Dialogue, p. 195, where Philonous explicitly includes 'combinations of ideas' among the immediate objects of the senses.) Philonous speaks of a *truth* formerly shared (that is, distributed) between the vulgar and the philosophers and finally united in immaterialism, a truth which constitutes the *substance* of what he advances. Modifiers such as 'strictly speaking' do not appear here, but this does not detract from the claim of the passage to state the literal truth as Berkeley sees it. The same is true of *Principles* 4, where Berkeley uses the claim that we perceive houses, mountains, and rivers in one of his main arguments for immaterialism. If in Berkeley's opinion it is not literally true that we immediately perceive such things as apples and trees, then presumably it is not literally true that we perceive them by sense at all, since he insists, in passages where he can only be speaking strictly, that the only kind of sense-perception is immediate perception:

PHILONOUS. And do we perceive any thing by sense, which we do not perceive immediately?

HYLAS. How often must I be obliged to repeat the same thing? I tell you, we do not.   (First Dialogue, p. 183.)

PHILONOUS. How! is there any thing perceived by sense, which is not immediately perceived?   (First Dialogue, p. 203.)

PHILONOUS. Whatever we perceive, is perceived either immediately or mediately: by sense, or by reason and reflexion.   (First Dialogue, p. 205.)

I conclude that Berkeley does not contradict himself. A distinction must be made in order to eliminate the appearance of contradiction, but it is not the distinction between speaking strictly and speaking loosely. It is a distinction between the immediate objects proper to a single sense and the immediate objects common to two or more senses.

Pitcher's paper does, however, raise a challenge to the account of immediate perception I have so far defended in this chapter. Apples and stones seem to diverge from my account of the objects of such perception in at least three ways. First, it seems that perceiving apples and other congeries of ideas is, at least in part, a matter of perceiving the ideas that enter into them. But why is it that the immediate perception of a constituent counts as the immediate perception of the congeries itself? It seems that suggestion or inference *must* be involved, and that the perception of the congeries must therefore be mediate. The congeries is, after all, perceived in virtue of perceiving some constituent, and if we hope to avoid the conclusion that someone with no experience of coaches immediately perceives one merely by hearing a sound, we must admit that perceiving the coach must include a movement of the mind from the constituent idea to some other object, either the congeries itself or some of the ideas that belong to it.

The first point can be sharpened if we recall my earlier claim that to perceive an object is, characteristically and perhaps unavoidably, to perceive that it is present. In a number of passages, among them *Principles* 3, Berkeley suggests that claims about the existence of objects such as tables and rivers tell us not only about the ideas we happen to have at the moment, but also about the ideas we *will* have, or *would* have under certain circumstances. As Jonathan Bennett writes, 'My belief that "I hear a coach" is answerable to facts about what I shall or should experience under different conditions.'[16] But if perceiving that an object is present involves *knowing* that it is present, anyone who hears a coach must know what at least some of those facts are. But those facts can only be known by inference or suggestion, by what Bennett describes as a 'disciplined appeal' to the ways in which our experiences have been joined together in the past (p. 143). Hence the perception of things differs from that of qualities in a second way.

Third, the immediate perception of an apple or a coach need not be transparent. If I hear the coach but do not see it I will not know its colour, and relying on past experience may not be enough to cure my ignorance. The immediate perception of an apple will not be infallible either. Suppose that I perceive the apple in virtue of tasting it. I might see it at the same time, but due to poor light my idea of its colour might be off. Even my past experience may not be enough to allow me to correct my judgement. As Berkeley himself admits, 'We do not know by sense . . . the true extension or colour of the object.' (*Principles* 15.)

These discrepancies call into question Berkeley's belief that the perception of objects can be immediate. But I see two ways in which the belief can be defended.

First, we can propose that the perception of objects, in so far as it goes beyond the perception of qualities, is *non-epistemic*. To perceive an object immediately, on this view, is to perceive immediately a quality that belongs to it. Nothing further is required: no expectations

---

[16] *Locke, Berkeley, Hume*, Oxford, 1971, p. 142. See also p. 143.

regarding other qualities in the congeries, no beliefs about the object, no linguistic dispositions involving the name of the object. It is not implausible to suggest that someone utterly ignorant of coaches can perceive one if he or she hears nothing but the ringing of its bells; this would be an instance of non-epistemic hearing, akin to the simple seeing or non-epistemic seeing of Warnock and Dretske. There are significant differences between the immediate perception of objects, so understood, and the immediate perception of the qualities that enter into them. The immediate perception of objects will be neither infallible nor transparent, and it will not be a form of knowledge. But it will be passive, it will involve neither inference nor suggestion, and it will not depend on the perception of an intervening object wholly distinct from the object perceived. It can therefore be described as a form of immediate perception. It will fail to be infallible and transparent without being fallible or opaque. The question of its infallibility or transparency will simply not arise. On this suggestion it follows that in order to know that an object exists it isn't enough to have one or even a few ideas of sense. 'When I see, and feel, and taste, in sundry certain manners, I am sure the cherry *exists*, or is real', Philonous explains in the Third Dialogue (p. 249). Only when I perceive 'in sundry certain manners' can I be sure I am perceiving a real thing.

The immediate perception of things can be defended even if we retain the view that perception is a form of knowledge. All of the discrepancies listed above would remain, but the immediacy of the perception of objects might be defended on the ground that although suggestion or inference plays a role, it is triggered by an idea which is a *component* of the object, rather than by an idea wholly distinct from the object. Notice that even if the perception of the coach is a form of knowledge, one can perceive the coach without being able to use a word that plays the role of 'coach'. It is enough to have the expectations of which Bennett speaks. These are expectations regarding other components of the congeries; these components will be perceived by inference or suggesion, but the component that triggers the expectations will be perceived immediately. Hence the congeries contains elements of which some are perceived in one way and some are perceived in another. Its intermediate status provides at least an opening for those inclined to say it is immediately perceived.

I think the first defence listed is more compelling, though it may have less textual warrant: Berkeley's characterization of perceiving as a form of knowing seems to be unqualified. It is possible, though, that in offering such characterizations he has in mind not propositional knowledge but something more like knowledge by acquaintance. Even knowledge by acquaintance or sensuous awareness can serve as a basis for inference, provided it carries a belief along with it.

3. *A commentary on the First Dialogue*

In the *Three Dialogues* there is a double movement. On the one hand there is an argument or contest between Hylas and Philonous, as each strives to show that the other is the greater sceptic or enemy of common sense. On the other hand there is a continuous argument developed by Philonous on behalf of Berkeley, an argument which can be extracted from the dialogue by a reader who carefully separates the assumptions Philonous makes for the sake of defeating Hylas from the premisses and inferences to which he has a lasting commitment. The First Dialogue contributes to the continuous argument in at least two ways: it supplies the premiss that we immediately perceive only our own ideas, and, by portraying Hylas as a sceptical enemy of common sense, it answers an objection that had been made to immaterialism as it was presented in the *Principles*.[17]

Hylas begins the First Dialogue by putting forward a standard of reality. The standard specifies that in order to count as *real*, sensible things must have 'a real absolute being, distinct from, and without any relation to their being perceived' (p. 175). Sugar, fire, and water, he thinks, all meet this standard. So do their sensible qualities. The arguments Philonous presents in order to dislodge this standard prove two things at once: first, that sensible qualities exist only in the mind; and second, that Hylas's standard of reality forces him to conclude that sensible qualities are unreal, that sugar is not sweet, that nothing has the qualities it seems to have.

Philonous himself accepts the arguments that sensible qualities are ideas, but he does not agree that sensible qualities are therefore unreal, or that sugar is not sweet and fire is not hot. He is free to do this because he does not share Hylas's standard of reality. It takes Hylas some time to appreciate this fact. At the beginning of the Second Dialogue, for example, where Hylas comes face to face with his

[17] See *Works* VIII, pp. 36–7.

sceptical misery, he tries to take comfort in the company of Philonous: 'My comfort is, you are as much a *sceptic* as I am.' (p. 211.) To his shock Philonous denies it:

I deny that I agreed with you in those notions that led to scepticism. You indeed said, the reality of sensible things consisted in an *absolute existence* out of the minds of spirits, or distinct from their being perceived. And pursuant to this notion of reality, you are obliged to deny sensible things any real existence: that is, according to your own definition, you profess yourself a *sceptic*. But I neither said nor thought the reality of sensible things was to be defined after that manner. To me it is evident, for the reasons you allow of, that sensible things cannot exist otherwise than in a mind or spirit. Whence I conclude, not that they have no real existence, but that seeing they depend not on my thought, and have an existence distinct from being perceived by me, *there must be some other mind wherein they exist.* (pp. 211–12, Second Dialogue.)

Philonous returns to the point again and again: the arguments that sensible qualities exist only in the mind are perfectly sound. The trouble lies in the standard of reality which Hylas thinks these qualities must satisfy:

PHILONOUS. I cannot for my life help thinking that snow is white, and fire hot. You indeed, who by *snow* and *fire* mean certain external, unperceived, unperceiving substances, are in the right to deny whiteness or heat, to be affections inherent in them. But I, who understand by those words the things I see and feel, am obliged to think like other folks.
(Third Dialogue, p. 230.)

PHILONOUS. Can you produce so much as one argument against the reality of corporeal things, or in behalf of that avowed utter ignorance of their natures, which doth not suppose their reality to consist in an external absolute existence? Upon this supposition indeed, the objections from the change of colours in a pigeon's neck, or the appearances of a broken oar in water, must be allowed to have weight. But those and the like objections vanish, if we do not maintain the being of absolute external originals, but place the reality of things in ideas, fleeting indeed, and changeable; however not changed at random, but according to the fixed order of Nature. For herein consists that constancy and truth of things, which secures all the concerns of life, and distinguishes that which is *real* from the irregular visions of the fancy.   (Third Dialogue, p. 258.)

Throughout the First Dialogue there are indications that in Berkeley's view Philonous's arguments do more work against Hylas than they do when taken by themselves. In their sceptical import the arguments are thoroughly *ad hominem*: they lead to sceptical conclusions only against the background of a standard of reality it is Philonous's intention to subvert.[18] Because of this Philonous often insinuates those conclusions instead of stating them: 'How could this be,' he asks on p. 180, 'if the taste were something really inherent in the food?' In other places he reminds Hylas that the sceptical conclusions turn on his concessions. 'I think it may evidently be concluded from your own concessions, that all the colours we see with our naked eyes, are only apparent as those on the clouds.' (p. 184.) At the end Hylas is told that he has been convinced 'out of [his] own mouth' (p. 207), and when he is invited in the Second Dialogue to review the earlier arguments Philonous asks him to identify 'any mistakes in your concessions, or fallacies in my reasonings from them' (p. 208). Philonous distances himself from the sceptical conclusions in other ways as well. When the oddness of saying there is no extension in objects causes Hylas to hesitate, Philonous underlines the oddness and at the same time encourages Hylas to go on: 'Odd, say you? After the concessions already made, I hope you will stick at nothing for its oddness.' (p. 189.) 'Your judgment will soon be determined,' he is told just a few lines above, 'if you will venture to think as freely concerning this quality, as you have done concerning the rest. Was it not admitted as a good argument, that neither heat nor cold was in the water, because it seemed warm to one hand, and cold to the other?' The injunction to think freely may be no more than a demand to follow the argument where it leads. Yet the use of the word 'freely' is jarring, and it cannot help but recall the Preface to the *Dialogues*, where Berkeley contrasts his own '*close and methodical*' manner of reasoning with '*that loose, rambling way, not altogether improperly termed* free-thinking, *by certain libertines in thought, who can no more endure the restraints of* logic, *than those of* religion, *or* government' (p. 168).

The First Dialogue is complex and carefully crafted, and before I present and assess its main argumentative strategies I would like to give the reader a sense of its overall structure. The following outline omits many details, and it covers only the first two-thirds of the Dialogue, the part directly relevant to the premiss that sensible qualities exist only in the mind.

[18] Luce and Jessop both call attention to the *ad hominem* character of the arguments of the First Dialogue: for Jessop see *Works* II, p. 192; for Luce see 'Berkeley and the Living Thing', *Hermathena* 123 (1977), 19–25, esp. pp. 19–21. Konrad Marc-Wogau raises the point only to dismiss it; see 'The Argument from Illusion and Berkeley's Idealism', reprinted in Martin and Armstrong, p. 345. For a more balanced discussion see Tipton, *Berkeley: The Philosophy of Immaterialism*, London, 1974, pp. 237–8.

pp. 171–5: *Preliminary.* Hylas and Philonous agree to accept that opinion which 'upon examination shall appear most agreeable to common sense, and remote from scepticism' (p. 172). The sceptic is someone who 'denies the reality of sensible things, or professes the greatest ignorance of them' (p. 173). Sensible things are defined as those things we perceive immediately by sense. Although Philonous will eventually commit himself to saying that such things as apples and stones are immediately perceived, the first list he gives includes only qualities: light, colours, figures, sounds, tastes, odour, and tangible qualities (p. 175). The ensuing discussion is strictly limited to immediate perception, a restriction Philonous reinforces many times as the dialogue proceeds.

pp. 175–9: *Two argumentative strategies.*

Strategy 1 (*the pain/pleasure strategy*, pp. 175–8): Heat and cold cannot exist without the mind (and cannot be real, if Hylas's standard of reality is the proper one) because they are, at least in extreme degrees, pleasures and pains, which cannot exist unperceived.

Strategy 2 (*the relativity strategy*, pp. 178–9): Heat and cold cannot exist without the mind (and cannot be real, if Hylas's standard of reality is the proper one) because the sensations of heat and cold occasioned by water, for example, change as we change, even though the water itself remains the same. Philonous also compares the heat occasioned by a piece of coal to the pain occasioned by the prick of a pin. 'Since therefore you neither judge the sensation itself occasioned by the pin, nor any thing like it to be in the pin; you should not, conformably to what you have now granted, judge the sensation occasioned by the fire, or any thing like it, to be in the fire.' (p. 179.)[19]

pp. 179–81: *The strategies are applied to taste and smell.*

pp. 181–3: *Sound is considered*, though the discussion does not follow the earlier pattern. It pivots instead on Hylas's view that sound is a 'vibrative or undulatory motion in the air' (p. 182). Philonous fastens on the apparent implication that sound 'may possibly be *seen* or *felt*, but never *heard*' (p. 182).

---

[19] This was a familiar argument, used for example by Descartes, Locke, and the authors of the *Port-Royal Logic*. See the Sixth Meditation, p. 57 in John Cottingham, Robert Stoothoff, and Dugald Murdoch (trans.), *The Philosophical Writings of Descartes*, Cambridge, 1984, vol. 2, and *Principles* I 68, p. 217 in vol. 1; *Essay* II viii 16; and *Logic: Or, The Art of Thinking* I ix, pp. 74–5 in the Ozell trans.

pp. 183–94: *Hylas distinguishes between secondary qualities* such as colour, taste, and sound, *and primary qualities* such as extension, figure, solidity, gravity, motion, and rest. Although secondary qualities have no existence without the mind, he contends, the primary qualities really exist in bodies (p. 188). Philonous brings the relativity strategy to bear on extension, figure, motion, and solidity (to p. 191). He argues that the ideas of extension and motion cannot be abstracted from all ideas of the qualities termed secondary, not even by pure intellect.

pp. 194–7: *Hylas ventures a distinction between sensations and their objects,* but it is found unavailing. This passage was examined in Chapter 1.

I now turn to the argumentative strategies themselves. The pain/ pleasure strategy is elaborated most fully in the case of heat. The argument runs as follows:

1. There is no reason why we should attribute real existence to some degrees of heat and deny it to others.
2. We can attribute real existence to a quality only if its existence is distinct from, and without any relation to, its being perceived. (This is Hylas's criterion of real existence. Part of what Philonous hopes to show is that this criterion leads to scepticism.)
3. The most vehement and intense degree of heat is a very great pain.
4. A pain cannot exist without the mind.
5. Hence from (3) and (4)) the most vehement and intense degree of heat cannot exist without the mind.
6. Hence (from (5) and (2)) the most vehement and intense degree of heat has no real existence.
7. Hence (from (6) and (1)) heat has no real being. A flame (supposing that it satisfies Hylas's standard of reality) has no heat in it. It is not really hot.

The argument closely resembles one that Hobbes presents in *Human Nature:*[20]

So likewise the *heat* we feel from the fire is manifestly in *us*, and is quite *different* from the heat which is in the *fire*: for *our* heat is *pleasure* or *pain*, according as it is *great* or *moderate*; but in the *coal* there is no such thing. . . . As in vision, so also in conceptions that arise from *other* senses, the subject of their inherence is not in the object, but in the sentient.

---

[20] Sir William Molesworth (ed.), *The English Works of Thomas Hobbes*, vol. 4, p. 8.

Hobbes distinguishes between *the heat in us* and *the heat in the fire*, and Hylas advocates a similar distinction between qualities 'as perceived by us' and the same qualities 'as existing in the external objects' (p. 180). Both Hobbes and Hylas hope to avoid saying that there is no heat in the fire or sweetness in the sugar. Philonous's response at first seems to be a just one: he points out that whatever qualities Hylas pretends to have discovered in the fire or the sugar, they are 'nothing to the purpose' because they are not immediately perceived. But in fact this is quite unfair. 'Tell me then once more,' Philonous demands, 'do you acknowledge that heat and cold, sweetness and bitterness (meaning those qualities which are perceived by the senses) do not exist without the mind?' (p. 180). Hylas meekly replies,

I see it is to no purpose to hold out, so I give up the cause as to those mentioned qualities. Though I profess it sounds oddly, to say that sugar is not sweet. (p. 180.)

Hylas wants to avoid the conclusion of the heat/pain argument, and the distinction he offers is not irrelevant because it gives him the right to call for an adjustment in that conclusion: it should say that there is no *sensible* heat in the flame, not that there is no heat in the flame at all. Philonous's failure to see the need for the adjustment is disappointing, even if it is mitigated by the tendency of those who defend the distinction made by Hylas and Hobbes to treat 'heat' and 'sweet' as names for the qualities *as perceived*.[21] Philonous himself, of course, is really committed only to the core of the argument—propositions (3) through (5).

Hylas is more stubborn in pressing a different objection. He claims

---

[21] Arnauld and Nicole observe that in common use 'heat' signifies 'both the Sensation we have, and a Quality we imagine in the Fire exactly like what we feel'. To avoid the ambiguity they recommend applying 'heat' to the sensation, 'giving to the Cause of this Sensation either a Name wholly different, as *Ardor*, or *Burning*, or the same Name, with some Addition, that may determine it, and distinguish it from Heat taken from Sensation, as to say *Virtual Heat*' (*Logic: Or, The Art of Thinking* I xiii, p. 100 in the Ozell trans.). Thomas Reid also observes that *heat* and *cold* have two significations. He explains that Locke and 'other modern philosophers' use such words to designate sensations. Had they 'given the name . . . to the cause, as they ought to have done, they must then have affirmed, with the vulgar, that colour is a quality of bodies; and that there is neither colour nor anything like it, in the mind' (*An Inquiry into the Human Mind* VI v, p. 140 in vol. I of Sir William Hamilton's edn. of Reid's *Works*, 7th edn., London, 1872). As it is, the simplest man of common sense 'justly laughs at the philosopher who denies that there is any heat in the fire' (*Inquiry* v i, p. 119 in vol. I of Hamilton). Peter Alexander also argues that Locke uses words such as 'heat' and 'colour' to designate sensations. See 'The Names of Secondary Qualities', *Proceedings of the Aristotelian Society* 77 (1976), 207–20.

that the argument gives us no reason to deny that inferior degrees of heat, too gentle to be pains, are outside the mind (p. 177). Philonous replies that moderate degrees of heat are pleasures. At first Hylas agrees but a moment later he corrects himself. Warmth, he proposes, is an *indolence*, a privation of pleasure and pain (p. 178). Philonous chooses not to press the point, and although premiss (1) retains much of its initial plausibility it does seem that Hylas has found a weak spot.

Philonous then shifts to the relativity strategy. At first he seems to be proceeding in the old way: he encourages Hylas to argue that intense degrees of cold do not exist outside the mind, but allows him to add that that milder degrees perhaps do. He then asks Hylas to imagine a bucket of water that feels cold to one hand and warm to another. The bucket was a stock device, employed among others by Malebranche and Locke, but in view of its relevance to moderate degrees of heat and cold it is ingeniously placed.[22] The following summary includes paraphrases of several of Philonous's speeches on pp. 178–9:

1. Suppose one of your hands is hot, and the other cold, and they are both at once put into the same vessel of water, in an intermediate state. Then the water will seem cold to one hand and warm to the other. (pp. 178–9.)

2. Bodies occasioning moderate degrees of heat or cold must be concluded to have moderate degrees of heat and cold in them. (Hylas makes this concession on p. 178.)

3. (from 1 and 2) Both heat and cold must exist in the lukewarm water.

4. But this is absurd. (p. 178, Philonous speaking: 'Is it not an absurdity to think that the same thing should be at the same time both cold and warm?')

5. Hence we must reject 2.

Strictly speaking all that (5) allows us to say is that both heat and cold cannot be in the water. This means that (2) cannot stand in its present form, but we need not go to the length of saying that moderate degrees of heat and cold are *never* outside the mind. There is, however, every reason to treat the heat and cold we perceive when our hands are in the water as if they were on a par, and if it is not the case that *both* are in the water, parity demands that neither is. The fact that intense degrees of heat and cold have been shown to exist only in the mind

[22] Hobbes and Bayle are among the other writers who use the bucket to make a point about the objects of perception.

fortifies the case for this conclusion, but nothing Philonous says actually entails it.

Later in the dialogue Philonous applies the relativity strategy to colour:

1. If colours were real properties inherent in external bodies, they could admit of no alteration without some change wrought in the very bodies themselves (p. 185, close paraphrase).
2. The use of optical instruments, variations in the eye, in distance, and in lighting—all these cause changes in the colours we perceive, without any alteration in the bodies themselves (pp. 185–6).
3. Therefore (from (1) and (2)) it is not the case that 'the same colours which we see, exist in external bodies' (p. 184).

Like the one before it, this argument may tempt us to suppose it proves more than it does. The most it permits us to conclude is that a body cannot have more than one of the sensible colours it occasions. (I will assume for the sake of simplicity that the colours in question are supposed to be all over the objects, and that it is just as absurd for a body to be both red and green as it is for a body to be both warm and cold.) Philonous seems to recognize this limitation, and he attemts to overcome it by asking Hylas how one colour could justifiably be singled out as the true colour of the object:

Now tell me, whether you are still of opinion, that every body hath its true real colour inhering in it; and if you think it hath, I would fain know farther from you, what certain distance and position of the object, what peculiar texture and formation of the eye, what degree or kind of light is necessary for ascertaining that true colour, and distinguishing it from apparent ones. (p. 186.)

Once again it is a matter of parity: unless there is a reason for favouring one colour over others, we should conclude that none is in the object. Hylas pronounces himself 'entirely satisfied', but he is not yet ready to concede that sensible colours exist only in the mind. He says instead that colour 'is altogether in the light' (p. 186), but when light as he conceives it proves to be a corporeal substance external to the mind—a fluid mixture of agitated particles—he admits that it cannot contain colour as immediately perceived, though nothing Philonous says or does forces this admission on him. With that taken care of he is prepared to accept Philonous's claim that colours, 'taken for the immediate objects of sight, cannot agree to any but a perceiving substance' (p. 187). Given his standard of reality it follows, as

Philonous is quick to emphasize, that '*the red and blue which we see are not real colours*' (p. 187).

A final instance of the relativity strategy is applied to extension or size, though at the end Philonous also mentions figure.

PHILONOUS. Again, have you not acknowledged that no real inherent property of any object can be changed, without some change in the thing itself?

HYLAS. I have.

PHILONOUS. But as we approach to or recede from an object, the visible extension varies, being at one distance ten or an hundred times greater than at another. Doth it not therefore follow from hence likewise, that it is not really inherent in the object? . . .

PHILONOUS. Was it not admitted as a good argument, that neither heat nor cold was in the water, because it seemed warm to one hand, and cold to the other?

HYLAS. It was.

PHILONOUS. Is it not the very same reasoning to conclude, there is no extension or figure in an object, because to one eye it shall seem little, smooth, and round, when at the same time it appears to the other, great, uneven, and angular?

HYLAS. The very same. But doth this latter fact ever happen?

PHILONOUS. You may at any time make the experiment, by looking with one eye bare, and with the other through a microscope.   (p. 189.)

I have already made several criticisms of Philonous's argumentative strategies. In the case of the first I echoed Hylas's observation that it cannot be applied to the moderate sensations—the intermediate qualities Hylas calls indolences. Berkeley is aware of this objection and he may regard it as sound, but the pain/pleasure strategy is built around a core he doubtlessly accepts. His attitude towards the relativity strategy is more difficult to discern. I have argued that the strategy falls short of showing that there is no heat, colour or extension in outward objects. This is because it does not rule out the possibility that one of the many qualities an object appears to have can be singled out as the true one. Philonous tries to guard against this by asking how the true quality will be identified, but the difficulty of identifying the quality does not prove that it is not there. Philonous says,

Since all sensible qualities, as size, figure, colour, &c. that is, our ideas are continually changing upon every alteration in the distance, medium, or instruments of sensation; how can any determinate material objects be properly represented or painted forth by several distinct things, each of which is so different from and unlike the rest? Or if you say it resembles some one only of our ideas, how shall we be able to distinguish the true copy from all the false ones?   (pp. 205–6.)

As our ideas are perpetually varied, without any change in the supposed real things, it necessarily follows they cannot all be true copies of them: or if some are, and others are not, it is impossible to distinguish the former from the latter.   (Third Dialogue, *Works* ii, p. 246.)

(See also the Third Dialogue, pp. 238, 245 and 258, and the passage from the First Dialogue, p. 186, quoted above on p. 168.) Clearly Berkeley is aware of my criticism, but it is hard to say how convincing he finds Philonous's reply. This is partly because the relativity arguments do not contain a core, clearly acceptable to Philonous, which can be extracted whole. Aggravating the difficulty is a section of the *Principles* where Berkeley calls the relativity strategy into question.

At *Principles* 14 Berkeley argues that the relativity strategy works as well for primary qualities as it does for heat, cold, and taste:[23]

I shall farther add, that after the same manner, as modern philosophers prove certain sensible qualities to have no existence in matter, or without the mind, the same thing may be likewise proved of all other sensible qualities whatsoever. Thus, for instance, it is said that heat and cold are affections only of the mind, and not at all patterns of real beings, existing in the corporeal substances which excite them, for that the same body which appears cold to one hand, seems warm to another. Now why may we not as well argue that figure and extension are not patterns or resemblances of qualities existing in matter, because to the same eye at different stations, or eyes of a different texture at the same station, they appear various, and cannot therefore be the images of any thing settled and determinate without the mind? Again, it is proved that sweetness is not really in the sapid thing, because the thing remaining unaltered the sweetness is changed into bitter, as in case of a fever or otherwise vitiated palate. Is it not as reasonable to say, that motion is not without the mind, since if the succession of ideas in the mind become swifter, the motion, it is acknowledged, shall appear slower without any alteration in any external object.

In the next section Berkeley repeats his main point, but then observes

---

[23] Berkeley may have borrowed this point from Bayle. See Richard Popkin, 'Berkeley and Pyrrhonism', *Review of Metaphysics* 5 (1951–2), 223–46, and Pierre Bayle, *Historical and Critical Dictionary: Selections*, trans. by Richard Popkin, Indianapolis, 1965, pp. 364–5 ('Zeno of Elea', Note G). The argument's history is sketched in Watson, *The Downfall of Cartesianism*, and in Charles J. McCracken, 'Stages on a Cartesian Road to Immaterialism', *Journal of the History of Philosophy* 24 (1986), 19–40.

that the argument does not prove as much as the modern philosophers suppose:[24]

In short, let anyone consider those arguments, which are thought manifestly to prove that colours and tastes exist only in the mind, and he shall find they may with equal force, be brought to prove the same thing of extension, figure, and motion. Though it must be confessed this method of arguing doth not so much prove that there is no extension or colour in an outward object, as that we do not know by sense which is the true extension or colour of the object. But the arguments foregoing plainly shew it to be impossible that any colour or extension at all, or other sensible quality whatsoever, should exist in an unthinking subject without the mind, or in truth, that there should be any such thing as an outward object.

The 'arguments foregoing' are the arguments of *Principles* 1–8, not the relativity arguments that have just been found wanting.[25] Berkeley's main argument against the distinction between primary and secondary qualities comes in *Principles* 9, and it is, as he makes plain, nothing more than a reminder of 'what we have already shewn' (§ 9).

What does Berkeley mean when he says that the arguments prove only 'that we do not know by sense which is the true extension or colour of the object', and what are the implications of his remark for the interpretation of the First Dialogue?[26] We can begin by noticing that Philonous's arguments differ from the one presented in *Principles* 14. The aim of the argument presented in the *Principles* is to show that there is nothing like colour or extension in things themselves. There it is taken for granted that the qualities we immediately perceive exist only in the mind; the question is whether these qualities or ideas are the images of outward originals. In the First Dialogue, on the other hand, Philonous sets out to establish what the argument in *Principles* 14 takes for granted. But whether this makes a difference depends on how Berkeley's cautionary observation at *Principles* 15 is interpreted.

---

[24] He may also be making this observation in entry 265 of the *Commentaries*. The 'first arguings' he refers to there may include entry 20: 'Primary ideas prov'd not to exist in matter, after the same manner y^t secondary qualities are prov^d not to exist therein.'

[25] See Stroud, 'Berkeley *v.* Locke on Primary Qualities', *Philosophy* 55 (1980), pp. 156–7, and Jessop, *Works* II, p. 44.

[26] There are a number of suggestive passages where Berkeley's predecessors come close to making his observation. I have elected not to discuss them because they do not mark out a definite interpretive direction. See Malebranche, *The Search after Truth*, Book I, chapters 6–20, esp. pp. 25 and 85 in the Lennon and Olscamp trans., Columbus, Ohio, 1980; *Logic: Or, the Art of Thinking* IV i, p. 369 in the Ozell translation; and Bayle, 'Zeno of Elea', Note G, pp. 365–6 in Popkin's *Selections*, where Bayle refers to both the *Port-Royal Logic* and *The Search after Truth*.

As we saw not long ago, Berkeley sometimes places 'perceive' and 'know' in apposition, and his observation at *Principles* 15 may therefore amount to an admission that relativity arguments prove exactly that Philonous thinks they prove: that we do not 'know by sense'—that is, *perceive* by sense, or immediately perceive—the true qualities of objects.[27] Note, however, that if this is Berkeley's meaning he is using the word 'true' as the materialist does, to pick out the qualities that inhere in outward objects. This use would be consistent with the *ad hominem* character of *Principles* 14 and the first sentence of § 15, but it seems to me that in the second sentence, where Berkeley makes his observation, he is speaking for himself. He is making what he describes as a confession, and his use of 'true' is more plausibly read as a neutral one. He is stating a lesson which even the immaterialist can take to heart: we do not know *merely by sensing* which are the true qualities of an object, because we sense different qualities as circumstances vary, though the object remains the same.

My reading leaves us with a question: How can Philonous move beyond the observation that we *sometimes* perceive our own ideas to the conclusion that we *always* do, even when the colour or extension we perceive is the true one? I can suggest three ways.

First, he might simply appeal to the likeness principle. The true colour of an apple resembles its apparent colours; in some cases the match is very close. But only an idea can be like an idea. Hence the colour we perceive is always an idea in the mind. Philonous might even settle for a weaker principle, along the lines of Cummins's principle *A*: 'All qualities which are determinates of the same determinable have the same ontological status.'

A second way is to appeal to the desire, felt by many materialists, for a uniform account of the perception of colour. If the colours we immediately perceive are *sometimes* ideas caused by outward objects it makes theoretical sense to say that that they *always* are. When we perceive the true colour we immediately perceive an idea that matches the object, rather than a quality inherent in the object itself.

Third, Philonous can argue that if a true quality is supposed to inhere in an outward object, we cannot avoid being arbitrary when we single out the situation in which that quality is immediately perceived. It is not implausible to say that the true colour of an object is the one we see when we view it near at hand in normal circumstances.[28] (This

---

[27] This is how the passage is interpreted by Stroud, 'Berkeley *v.* Locke', pp. 162–3.

[28] It is not plausible in the case of figure or extension. See Bennett, *Locke, Berkeley,*

is probably the view that Hylas has in mind on p. 184.) Defining
proximity and normalcy is no easy task, as Philonous in effect shows on
pp. 184–5, but supposing they have been defined, what reason do we
have for thinking that the circumstances *we* deem normal somehow
enable the object to present itself as it really is, when in every other
situation a potentially misleading appearance intervenes? This is,
perhaps, merely another version of the previous point, but Philonous
can use it to cast suspicion on the materialist's understanding of what it
is for a quality to be true. The materialist's understanding invites the
attempt to identify the situation in which the object's true colour
reveals itself. And Philonous does not see how the identification of a
privileged situation can be anything but arbitrary. He suggests that we
stop searching for a privileged situation, and that we notice the
connection between knowing an object's colour and being able to
anticipate its appearance in a variety of circumstances. Wrong
judgments about the qualities of objects concern the ideas we take to
be connected with those we immediately perceive (Third Dialogue,
p. 238). The truth of such a judgement lies 'in ideas, fleeting indeed,
and changeable; however not changed at random, but according to the
fixed order of Nature' (Third Dialogue, p. 258). Knowing what colour
will appear in the circumstances we deem normal is not unimportant,
because this is often all it takes to enable us to predict how the object
will appear at other times. The materialist can of course agree that
knowing an object's colour is nothing over and above a certain
predictive capacity. But at the risk of being arbitrary he cannot say that
any of the colours the object appears to have is the true one, as he or
she understands *true*. Berkeley's observation that we cannot know true
qualities by sense suggests that we know them in another way. If we *do*
sometimes know them—if the distinction between the person who
knows the true colour and the person who does not is a just one—then
we cannot accept the view that the true quality inheres in the object.
The argument can be summarized as follows:

1. We do not know by sense which are the true qualities of an
   object.
2. Yet we sometimes know this.
3. If a true quality is (a) inherent in an outward object and (b)

Hume, pp. 94–100, and Pitcher, *A Theory of Perception*, Princeton, 1971, pp. 223–30. For
an argument that the proposal fails in the end even for colour see Edward Wilson Averill,
'The Primary–Secondary Quality Distinction', *Philosophical Review* 91 (1982), 343–61,
esp. pp. 351–4.

immediately perceived in some privileged situation, then we cannot help but be arbitrary when we identify that situation.

4. If we cannot help but be arbitrary when we identify that situation, then we cannot know which quality is the true one.

5. Because we do know which quality is the true one, a true quality cannot satisfy both (a) and (b).

Philonous provides an alternative way of understanding what it is for a quality to be true—or, more precisely, another way of understanding what it is to know which qualities of an object are the true ones. It involves rejecting both (a) and (b), and replacing them with the view that we always immediately perceive our own ideas, and that knowing the true qualities of objects is a matter of knowing what course our experience will take. Because the future course of experience is a large thing, more or less of which might be predicted, knowledge of objects becomes a matter of degree, as Philonous acknowledges in the Third Dialogue: 'The more a man knows of the connexion of ideas, the more he is said to know of the nature of things.' (p. 245.)

I conclude that Berkeley accepts the relativity strategy, but believes that it can be used to show that we *always* perceive our own ideas only if it is joined to one of the three lines of thought just reviewed. Unfortunately, the strategy faces two more serious objections.

In the *Theory of Vision* Berkeley responds to the difference between visible extension and tangible extension by concluding that 'the objects of sight and touch are two distinct things' (§ 49). He responds to a kind of relativity by *multiplying* the objects of perception. A materialist might respond in the same way to the instances of relativity brought forward by Philonous. 'I was wrong to say that the outward world is unchanging. The outward world is as Heraclitean as Berkeley takes the world of ideas to be, but it remains a material and mind-independent world.' The materialist will, of course, have an awkward time explaining why outward objects change in apparent synchrony with changes in us. But in his defence he can plead that even if the properties of outward objects are causally dependent on us, it doesn't follow that they have no existence apart from us. In fact the instances of relativity brought forward by Philonous suggest there is causal dependence on the state of our *bodies*; perhaps our minds do not enter in at all. This last point brings us to the second objection.

Philonous assumes that the qualities we perceive must be in mind if they are not in body, a reasonable enough assumption in an eighteenth-century context. But he does not succeed in showing that they are not *in body*; the most he shows is that they are not in *external* bodies. They might nevertheless be in our own. In order to show that they are not in body at all, Philonous needs examples where the qualities we immediately perceive are varied while our bodies remain unchanged. But he has no such examples. As he seems to acknowledge on p. 205, his examples all involve 'motions in our bodies, suspending, exerting, or altering our faculties or organs of sense'.

Our long discussion of the argument of *Principles* 4 can be summarized as follows. The argument gives rise to a structural objection of which Berkeley was certainly aware, and his strategy for turning aside the objection rests heavily on the views discussed in Chapter 1. A defence of the premiss that we immediately perceive nothing but our own ideas can be drawn out of the First Dialogue, but the defence, despite the ingenuity with which Berkeley conducts it, is open to serious objection.

4. *The argument of* Principles *3*

In the third section of the *Principles* Berkeley appeals to the meaning of the word *exist*:

That neither our thoughts, nor passions, nor ideas formed by the imagination, exist without the mind, is what every body will allow. And it seems no less evident that the various sensations or ideas imprinted on the sense, however blended or combined together (that is, whatever objects they compose) cannot exist otherwise than in a mind perceiving them. I think an intuitive knowledge may be obtained of this, by any one that shall attend to what is meant by the term *exist* when applied to sensible things. The table I write on, I say, exists, that is, I see and feel it; and if I were out of my study I should say it existed, meaning thereby that if I was in my study I might perceive it, or that some other spirit actually does perceive it. There was an odour, that is, it was smelled; there was a sound, that is to say, it was heard; a colour or figure, and it was perceived by sight or touch. This is all that I can understand by these and the like expressions. For as to what is said of the absolute existence of unthinking things without any relation to their being perceived, that seems perfectly unintelligible. Their *esse* is *percipi*, nor is it possible they should have any existence, out of the minds or thinking things which perceive them.

This passage seems not so much an argument as a series of assertions. We can approach it by considering a way in which Berkeley, as a careful reader of Locke, might have arrived at the views he presents here. As we saw in Chapter 1, Locke holds that all significant words, other than particles such as *is* and *is not* and 'negative Names' such as *barrenness*, stand for ideas. In his notebooks, Berkeley notes the exception made for particles, and follows Locke in suggesting that particles signify operations of the mind. (Negative names can then be treated as words signifying a complex of idea and operation.) This gives us a way into the argument of *Principles* 3. Every significant word must stand for something present to the mind. The word *exist*, however, does not stand for an idea. There is nothing sensible that the word can be said to signify. The claim that existence is not an idea but an operation of the mind is as close as one can come, in the vocabulary available to Berkeley, to the Kantian observation that existence is not a real predicate. Now if existence is an operation of the mind, what operation can it be? It must be perception, the only candidate with the requisite generality. Not only does it follow that we have no conception of 'the absolute existence of unthinking things without any relation to their being perceived'; it follows as well that there are two basic kinds of things, the things perceived and the spirits who do the perceiving. Out of a Berkeleyan amendment to a Lockean conception of meaning we generate not only the claim that existence is the same as perception, but also the two basic categories of Berkeley's metaphysics.

But from the fact that the word *exist* has a mental operation as its immediate signification, it cannot be inferred that existence and perception are the same. The materialist believes that the idea of red represents a quality outside the mind even though the idea can exist only in the mind. Why not suppose that in much the same way, the operation of perception represents an 'external' quality?

Whether or not this doubt can be removed, I do think the argument helps to explain why *Principles* 3 appealed to Berkeley. But it cannot be the whole story. The problem with the argument is that it does not accord with Berkeley's belief that we cannot always seek the meaning of a word in isolation. He argues for this very forcefully in *Alciphron* VII, and if we compare the word *exist* with the expressions that figure most prominently in his argument there—*force, grace, the square root of minus one*—it appears to be a perfect candidate for the same kind of treatment. And at *Principles* 3 Berkeley handles the word *exist* just as *Alciphron* VII suggests he should. He does not ask what the word itself stands for, but asks for the meaning of statements in which it plays a part. The requirement he imposes is that the meaning of a statement about sensible things be exhausted by its implications for experience, potential as well as actual. It follows that the word *exist* neither involves nor imparts a conception of the 'absolute existence' of unthinking things 'without any relation to their being perceived'.

But it does not follow that unthinking things must actually be perceived in order to exist. At one point Berkeley seems to reaching toward this bolder conclusion. His premiss is that to say an unthinking thing exists is to say that it is perceived ('there was an odour, that is, it was smelled; there was a sound, that is to say, it was heard; a colour or figure, and it was perceived by sight or touch'), but he undermines this by providing an analysis of what it means to say that a table exists which is more liberal and more plausible. To say that a table exists is sometimes to say that it would be perceived if certain conditions were fulfilled. Berkeley drops the liberalizing clause when he considers odours and sounds. This is understandable, because 'there was an odour' and sentences like it are less likely to be used by someone who has not actually had the perceptions Berkeley names. But if we change the tense of these sentences from past to present, and say a bit more about the qualities—if we give them locations, for example—then the counterfactual treatment becomes more natural. 'There is a foul odour in the hallway', 'there is a strange sound in the basement', 'there is a bright light on the horizon'—if they tell us anything about perception they tell us what we *would* perceive in the hallway, in the basement, or on the horizon. If this more liberal analysis is closer to the truth Berkeley can no longer claim that an unthinking thing cannot exist unperceived. He has to say instead that an unthinking thing cannot exist unless it is perceivable. Hylas entertains this weaker conclusion in the Third Dialogue, but Philonous convinces him that it leads back to the conclusion he hopes to avoid:

HYLAS. I grant the existence of a sensible thing consists in being perceivable, but not in being actually perceived.
PHILONOUS. And what is perceivable but an idea? And can an idea exist without being actually perceived? These are points long since agreed between us.   (p. 234.)

By this time Hylas has agreed that only ideas can be perceived, and Philonous is right to remind him of that. But Berkeley cannot offer a similar defence of *Principles* 3. In *Principles* 3 he needs to argue that nothing but ideas are perceivable; he cannot rely on it.[29]

[29] Note, however, that if *Principles* 3 succeeded in proving that the *esse* of sensible qualities is *percipi*, Berkeley would have an argument that sensible qualities are ideas. And on the assumption that sensible qualities are the only objects of immediate

Of the arguments for immaterialism reviewed in this chapter, the argument of *Principles* 3 is the only one which does not rest explicitly on Berkeley's views about intentionality, necessity, and intelligibility. But it is also, as we glimpsed at the outset, the least argumentative. Berkeley simply assumes a general view about the meaning of sentences or statements, and then reaches the only conclusion about the meaning of the word *exist* that is consistent with that view. Perhaps he thinks he is appealing to pre-theoretical intuitions no one would deny. It is clear, in any case, that *Principles* 3 provides very little that can be used against the materialist who affirms the kind of absolute existence Berkeley so confidently denies.

5. *Against matter*

In Berkeley's writings matter is a moving target: he knocks it down only to have his interlocutors prop it up somewhere else, at another location in philosophical space. Berkeley argues that the notion of matter is either contradictory or empty: contradictory if matter is meant to be the unperceiving substratum of qualities whose *esse* is *percipi*; empty if it is a substratum of qualities as unknown to us as colours are to a man born blind, a substance or occasion in general, or an unknown something-or-other. Berkeley is sensitive to the difficulty of proving the non-existence of something so variable. His case against it can only be a series of responses to things said on its behalf; he cannot hope for the elegance of a demonstration, where a settled definition is reduced to contradiction. Yet what he produces comes close to matching a demonstration in persuasive force. We watch as the notion of matter shrinks before him, from something robust enough to be proven inconsistent to something so vague it becomes hard to imagine anyone wanting to defend it. Berkeley finds even the most robust understanding too vague or sketchy to count as a real understanding, but it is definite enough, he thinks, to allow for a decisive refutation.

The word *matter* does not appear in the *Principles* until § 9, where it is introduced along with the distinction between primary and secondary qualities. But the *notion* of matter appears as early as § 7,

perception (an assumption it may be the job of *Principles* 1 to articulate), Berkeley would then have an argument that we immediately perceive only our own ideas. It may therefore be a mistake to say that Berkeley offers no defence of this premiss in the *Principles*.

where Berkeley speaks of an 'unthinking substance or *substratum*' of the sensible qualities, and rests his argument against it on his proof in §§ 3 and 4 that the sensible qualities are ideas:

Now for an idea to exist in an unperceiving thing, is a manifest contradiction; for to have an idea is all one as to perceive: that therefore wherein colour, figure, and the like qualities exist, must perceive them; hence it is clear there can be no unthinking substance or *substratum* of those ideas.

At *Principles* 9 'matter' is defined as an unthinking or inert and senseless substance in which the primary qualities—extension, figure, and motion—'do actually subsist'. The argument against matter in this sense closely resembles the argument in § 7, but in § 9 Berkeley also appeals to the likeness principle, introduced in the previous section:

It is evident from what we have already shewn, that extension, figure and motion are only ideas existing in the mind, and that an idea can be like nothing but another idea, and that consequently neither they nor their archetypes can exist in an unperceiving substance. Hence it is plain, that the very notion of what is called *matter* or *corporeal substance*, involves a contradiction in it.

The argument here may not appear as tight as the argument in § 7, because Berkeley has not even asserted that it is a contradiction to deny the likeness principle. But it is clear that he holds the principle to be a necessary truth, and even the arguments of § 7 rest on the premiss that the *esse* of an idea is *percipi*. The transition from § 8 to § 9 reflects Berkeley's belief that the impossible and the contradictory are one and the same.[30]

At *Principles* 16 and 17 Berkeley argues that there is no distinct meaning attached to the word 'matter'. He asks what is meant by the claim that matter supports extension. 'It is evident *support* cannot here be taken in its usual or literal sense, as when we say that pillars support a building: in what sense therefore must it be taken?' (§ 16.) His answer probably borrows from both Malebranche and Locke:[31]

If we inquire into what the most accurate philosophers declare themselves to mean by *material substance*; we shall find them acknowledge, they have no other meaning annexed to those sounds, but the idea of being in general, together with the relative notion of its supporting accidents. The general idea of being

---

[30] The argument of §§ 7 and 9 also makes several brief appearances in the *Three Dialogues*, on pp. 190 (in a passage added to the *Dialogues* in 1734), 216, and 224–6.

[31] For Locke see *Essay* II xiii 19, II xxiii 2, and I iv 18. For Malebranche see *The Search after Truth*, Bk. III, pt. ii, chap. 8, § ii, pp. 244–5 in the Lennon and Olscamp trans.

appeareth to me the most abstract and incomprehensible of all other; and as for its supporting accidents, this, as we have just now observed, cannot be understood in the common sense of those words; it must therefore be taken in some other sense, but what that is they do not explain. So that when I consider the two parts or branches which make the signification of the words *material substance*, I am convinced there is no distinct meaning annexed to them.   (*Principles* 17.)

It is noteworthy that despite the indistinctness in meaning, the argument of §§ 7 and 9 (which is among the 'foregoing arguments' Berkeley refers to in § 15) still stands. The meaning of 'support' is clear enough to tell us that a substratum has whatever it supports. But to have an idea is to perceive.

But why should we trouble ourselves any farther, in discussing this material *substratum* or support of figure and motion, and other sensible qualities? Does it not suppose they have an existence without the mind? And is not this a direct repugnancy, and altogether inconceivable? (§ 17.)

The argument is repeated in the First Dialogue (pp. 197–9), where the expressions *matter* and *material substance* figure in the discussion from the very outset (p. 172).

In both the *Principles* and the *Dialogues* Berkeley considers attempts to modify the characterization that allows for the argument that matter is contradictory, and to do so without draining the notion of matter of all its meaning. The leading attempts and Berkeley's main objections to them are as follows:

1. *Matter as the cause of our ideas* (*Principles* 19 and 54; Second Dialogue, pp. 216–17): The only true causes are spirits (Second Dialogue, p. 217), and even if we were not sure of this, no one claims to understand how matter can act upon spirit to produce ideas.

2. *Matter as an instrument God needs to produce ideas* (Second Dialogue, pp. 217–19): Dependence on an instrument runs counter to God's omnipotence.

3. *Matter as an occasion at the presence of which God produces our ideas*: How can a thing without extension or place be present (*Principles* 68)? If its presence is its being perceived by God, it no longer merits the title of *matter* (*Principles* 70–6; Second Dialogue, pp. 219–20).

4. *Matter as a substratum of qualities as unknown to us as colours are to a man born blind* (*Principles* 77–8): Matter in this sense doesn't

concern us. And it could become our concern only if its unknown qualities became ideas.

5. *Matter as substance or occasion in general* (*Principles* 79); *as an unknown something-or-other or indeterminate something* (*Principles* 80–1 and Second Dialogue, p. 221); *as an entity we cannot positively characterize* (*Principles* 67–8): All these notions of matter are vacuous. Matter as they portray it comes to nothing (Second Dialogue, p. 223). They do not even afford a *relative* notion of matter (Second Dialogue, p. 223; see also pp. 197 and 199 of the First Dialogue, as well as *Principles* 16, where Berkeley writes that 'if you have any meaning at all, you must at least have a relative idea of matter').

The variety of conceptions calls for a variety of responses: matter as defined may be pointless, too vague to be worth confuting, or inconsistent with some belief to which the interlocutor is bound. The plasticity of the notion may have dashed Berkeley's hopes for the closure of a demonstration, but Philonous brings the discussion to a satisfying end in the closing paragraphs of the Second Dialogue. He has been complaining about Hylas's 'shifting unfair method', which has drawn out the discussion 'to an unnecessary length'. Philonous has proven the impossibility of matter in every particular sense in which Hylas understands it, and that, Philonous thinks, should be enough. But Hylas isn't sure that in its 'most obscure abstracted and indefinite sense' matter hasn't been left standing:

PHILONOUS. When is a thing shewn to be impossible?

HYLAS. When a repugnancy is demonstrated between the ideas comprehended in its definition.

PHILONOUS. But where there are no ideas, there no repugnancy can be demonstrated between ideas.

HYLAS. I agree with you.

PHILONOUS. Now in that which you call the obscure indefinite sense of the word *matter*, it is plain, by your own confession, there was included no idea at all, no sense except an unknown sense, which is the same thing as none. You are not therefore to expect I should prove a repugnancy between ideas where there are no ideas; or the impossibility of matter taken in an *unknown* sense, that is no sense at all. My business was only to shew, you meant *nothing*; and this you were brought to own. So that in all your various senses, you have been shewed either to mean nothing at all, or if any thing, an absurdity. And if this be not sufficient to prove the impossibility of a thing, I desire you will let me know what is. (pp. 225–6.)

Here Berkeley acknowledges that only a notion with meaning can be proven inconsistent. Yet the argument of *Principles* 16 and 17 shows that meaningfulness comes in grades: meaning can be distinct enough to allow for a proof of inconsistency, but too indistinct to justify the confidence that the notion is really understood. An impossibility proof can do no more than show that every conception with any currency is either contradictory (even if somewhat indistinct) or wholly empty. The one conception of matter left standing at the end is matter only in name, applied as it is to the objects of sense, and implying no substance distinct from being perceived (Third Dialogue, pp. 261–2).

In the midst of Berkeley's case against material substance there is an argument that even if matter exists it cannot be known. The existence of matter cannot be known by the senses, by which 'we have the knowledge only of our sensations, ideas, or those things that are immediately perceived by sense, call them what you will' (*Principles* 18). It must therefore be known by reason, inferring the existence of matter from objects immediately perceived by sense. But the inference cannot rest on a necessary connection, since everyone agrees 'that it is possible we might be affected with all the ideas we have now, though no bodies existed without, resembling them' (*Principles* 19). The illusions of dreams and frenzies put this point beyond dispute. But the prospects for a probable inference are just as bleak. All probable reasoning takes the form of an inference to the best explanation. If it were easier to 'conceive and explain' the production of ideas on the hypothesis of external things it would then be reasonable to believe in their existence. But the manner in which body acts upon spirit is a mystery.

Berkeley's case against matter confirms many of the interpretive contentions of Chapter 4. Berkeley's inability to conjure up an *image* of matter plays no role in his case against it. His primary argument is that matter is impossible because the very notion of an unperceiving substratum of sensible qualities is contradictory or repugnant. Berkeley's proof of this falls short of twentieth-century standards of formality: he appeals to premises (such as the claim that only spirits can be causes) without even trying to show it is a contradiction to deny them. But he appeals consistently to premises he takes to be necessary: if our analytical tools were perfected, he believes, the requisite contradictions would be revealed. At times he has to settle for saying that some notion of matter is empty; at other times he makes the even more modest point that matter on some understanding is pointless or of no concern. As a result his case against matter falls short of a demonstration, but we should not let ourselves forget that demonstrations are usually considered apart from the context that gives them their life and point. Even in a demonstration, a crucial notion may be defined in one way rather than another simply because the preferred definition is more useful. Every demonstration of any concern to us is, perhaps, *ad hominem* in the end; it is just that in certain cases, where meanings are settled and agreement on premisses is universal, their *ad hominem* character can be suppressed.

6. *The master argument*[32]

In both the *Principles* and the *Dialogues* Berkeley says he will surrender if the materialist can so much as *conceive* of a substance, body, or mixture of qualities existing without the mind. 'Surely there is nothing easier than to imagine trees, for instance, in a park, or books existing in a closet, and no body by to perceive them', the interlocutor in the *Principles* replies (§ 23). 'If it comes to that,' Hylas boasts, 'the point will soon be decided. What more easy than to conceive a tree or a house existing by itself, independent of, and unperceived by any mind whatsoever? I do at this present time conceive them existing after that manner.' (First Dialogue, p. 200.) But Berkeley and Philonous point out that trees, books, or houses must be conceived by the person who puts them forward as examples. Any attempt to meet Berkeley's challenge is therefore bound to defeat itself, as the following arguments, paraphrases of the passages cited, purport to show:

In the *Principles* (§ 23):

1. In order to conceive it possible that the objects of our thought exist without the mind, we must conceive of them unconceived or unthought of.
2. But it is a manifest contradiction to conceive of them in that manner.
3. Hence we cannot conceive it possible that the objects of our thought exist without the mind.

In the *Dialogues* (p. 200):

---

[32] I borrow this label from André Gallois, 'Berkeley's Master Argument', *Philosophical Review* 83 (1974), 55–69.

1. We can conceive of a house or a tree existing independent of and out of all minds whatsoever only if we can conceive of the house or tree existing unconceived.

2. But it is a contradiction to speak of conceiving a thing which is unconceived. An unconceived thing can no more be conceived than an unseen object can be seen.

3. Hence we cannot conceive of a house or a tree (or anything else, for that matter) existing independent of and out of all minds.

My paraphrases follow Berkeley's own formulations very closely: attending to his word-choice and to differences between the formulations highlights steps in the argument which might otherwise pass unnoticed. It is certainly a manifest contradiction to say that I am conceiving of a thing which is in fact unconceived, as the second premiss of the *Dialogues* version alleges. But notice the difference between the first sentence of that premiss and the closing words of the first one: we can conceive of a tree existing out of all minds whatsoever, Philonous maintains in premiss 1, only if we can conceive of a house existing unconceived. He does not say that we must conceive of a house *which is* unconceived, or is *in fact* unconceived, and he seems right to refrain from doing so. It is enough to conceive of a house which *we represent as* unconceived. It will be conceived *in fact*, but that by itself is no obstacle to our representing it as unconceived.

Because of the way in which it is put, the second premiss in the *Principles* version of the argument lacks the persuasive force of the corresponding premiss in the *Dialogues* version. In the *Principles* we are told it is a manifest contradiction to conceive of the objects of our thought existing unconceived. But it is natural to read the closing words of this premiss in the same way that we read the closing words of the first premiss in the *Dialogues* version: it is a manifest contradiction to conceive of the objects of our thought *as* existing unconceived. And it is not a manifest contradiction. It is true that we conceive of the object, but it need not be unconceived in order for us to represent it as unconceived.[33]

Berkeley would perhaps reply that there cannot help but be a conflict between representing an object as unconceived and conceiving of it. If we attend to our conceiving of it, he might say, we will see that

---

[33] This criticism has been made by many others, among them A. N. Prior, 'Berkeley in Logical Form', *Theoria* 21 (1955), 117–22; Bernard Williams, 'Imagination and the Self,' reprinted in his *Problems of the Self*, Cambridge, 1973, p. 27; Tipton, *Berkeley: The Philosophy of Immaterialism*, pp. 158–78; and Pitcher, *Berkeley*, pp. 113–15.

we do not in fact succeed in representing it as unconceived. But to establish this Berkeley needs to explain why we cannot *insulate* the content of our thought—the proposition or state of affairs we entertain—from the fact of our entertaining it. If contradiction or repugnancy is to serve as our standard of possibility, it seems fair to propose initially that we can entertain any proposition which is not *itself* contradictory. Putting his earlier immaterialist arguments aside (as seems to be Berkeley's intention in *Principles* 23 and in the First Dialogue), the propositions entertained by Berkeley's interlocutors—*there is a tree of which no one is thinking*, for example—seem to be perfectly consistent. If Berkeley wants to show that it is impossible to entertain such propositions he needs to show that their being entertained somehow spills over into their content, and this he fails to do.

As it turns out Berkeley is as deeply committed to the insulation of content as his materialist opponents. Not only are all the things of which I am thinking thought of, they are thought of *by me*, and *at the present moment*. If we are prevented from representing something as unthought of because the fact that we are thinking it somehow enters into the content of what is thought, we will be prevented from representing something as unthought of *by our own selves*, or by our own selves *now*. We will be unable to stop with immaterialism, and will be driven instead to solipsism, or to a solipsism of the present moment, prospects as distressing to Berkeley as they would be to anyone else. Unlike many commentators who make this charge against Berkeley, I think he does have a way of explaining how I can conceive of an object unconceived by me, or unconceived by me at the present moment.[34] I will discuss it in Chapter 9, but for now I can say that in Berkeley's view our route to such conceptions must always run through other minds—through our conceptions of the minds of others or of our own mind at other times.

I now want to ask why Berkeley found the master argument so compelling. It is not at all easy to explain: the usual explanations are either unsympathetic to Berkeley or hopelessly distant from the texts.[35]

[34] Those who make this criticism include Armstrong, in his editor's introduction to *Berkeley's Philosophical Writings*, London, 1965, pp. 9–11; Pitcher, *Berkeley*, pp. 112–13; and Tipton, *Berkeley: The Philosophy of Immaterialism*, p. 161.

[35] I think the best attempts at an explanation are to be found in Tipton, *Berkeley: The Philosophy of Immaterialism*, pp. 166–78, and in Ayers's introduction to Berkeley's *Philosophical Works*, pp. xii–xiii. Tipton reviews some recent attempts in 'Berkeley's Imagination', in Sosa, *Essays on the Philosophy of George Berkeley*, pp. 85–102.

What I have to offer is not an explanation but something more modest. I think the master argument can be better understood if we realize that it is more dependent on what comes before it than Berkeley's manner of presenting it suggests.

Berkeley does suggest that the argument can conquer immaterialism on its own. But there are also indications that the argument is designed to place a burden on the materialist, who is already weighed down with assumptions touched on earlier in the *Principles* and the *Dialogues*. In both works the argument takes the form of a challenge: show me that you can conceive of a mind-independent object, Berkeley says, and I will give up the case. Berkeley assumes, I think, that the materialist believes we conceive of objects by calling up mind-dependent images of them. That Berkeley makes these assumptions is suggested both by his statement of the challenge in the *Principles*, and by his response to the interlocutor's contention that the challenge is easy to meet. The challenge is to 'conceive it possible for one extended moveable substance, or in general, for any one idea *or any thing like an idea*, to exist otherwise than in a mind perceiving it' (§ 22, emphasis mine). This suggests that the materialist is assumed to agree that representation involves resemblance. And Berkeley's response to the interlocutor's attempt is that he or she has done no more than frame 'certain ideas' in the mind, which suggests that the materialist is assumed to agree that to conceive of a thing is to call up a mind-dependent object. With these assumptions assigned to the materialist, the challenge of the master argument becomes forbidding. 'You have called up a mind-dependent object,' Berkeley can say. 'Tell me how it can represent something mind-independent, something whose existence cannot be cashed out in terms of actual and possible perception.' I do not think Berkeley wants to make the crude point that an idea, being mind-dependent, cannot mirror the independence of its intended object. There is no evidence that he has such an argument in mind. But he would like to know how mind-independence is supposed to be represented. How can it be thought?

It cannot be thought by framing an idea that mirrors a mind-independent quality. No idea could perform such a feat of mirroring. But can an idea mirror a quality that has both mind-dependent and mind-independent instances? Perhaps it can, but we would be in no position to tell whether the instance it happened to be mirroring was one or the other. Hence we could not be sure that we had answered Berkeley's challenge. Can we dispense altogether with the mirroring of qualities, and represent the independence of the object on its own? Here it is hard to know what to say. How can existence be represented apart from the qualities of an existing thing?

The last question gains force if we recall that existence is not according to Berkeley a sensible quality; it is not among the qualities listed in *Principles* 1, and Locke's assurance that existence is an idea of both sensation and reflection would fare no better in Berkeley's eyes than his co-ordinate claim about unity, addressed at *Principles* 13. The word *existence*, Berkeley holds, does not owe its meaning to an idea. How then does it acquire a signification? Here Berkeley turns inward, somewhat as Locke had done when he accounted for the signification of particles. To exist is to be perceived or perceivable (*Principles* 3). Nothing *in* an idea can be said to represent existence. This means that whenever we frame an idea of a purportedly mind-independent object, what we have managed to do is, as far as the idea is concerned, no different from what we do when we conceive of something mind-dependent. All there is left to say about the idea is that we perceive it, or that some other spirit does or would perceive it; but why should *this* give us a conception of mind-independence, of a kind of existence having nothing to do with being perceivable or perceived?

I have suggested that we restore the master argument to the context furnished by earlier passages in the *Principles* and the *Dialogues*, even though Berkeley himself encourages us to remove it. Restoring it does not clear away the reservations expressed above, but it does enable us to understand why the moral Berkeley extracts from the master argument is so easily related to the themes of *Principles* 1 through 9:

It is very obvious, upon the least inquiry into our own thoughts, to know whether it be possible for us to understand what is meant, by the *absolute experience of sensible objects in themselves, or without the mind.* To me it is evident those words mark out either a direct contradiction, or else nothing at all. And to convince others of this, I know no readier or fairer way, than to entreat they would calmly attend to their own thoughts: and if by this attention, the emptiness or repugnancy of those expressions does appear, surely nothing more is requisite for their conviction. It is on this therefore that I insist, to wit, that the absolute existence of unthinking things are words without a meaning, or which include a contradiction. This is what I repeat and inculcate, and earnestly recommend to the attentive thoughts of the reader. (§ 24.)

7. *Materialism and abstraction*

At *Principles* 5 Berkeley writes that materialism depends on the doctrine of abstract ideas:

If we throughly examine this tenet [that sensible objects have an existence natural or real, distinct from being perceived] it will, perhaps, be found at bottom to depend on the doctrine of *abstract ideas*. For can there be a nicer strain of abstraction than to distinguish the existence of sensible objects from their being perceived, so as to conceive them existing unperceived?

The passage suggests that Berkeley has yet another argument against materialism: materialism depends on the doctrine of abstract ideas; that doctrine is false; hence materialism is false. According to my account of Berkeley's attack on abstraction, however, no such argument is available. Before we can say an idea is abstract, we need to know that its object cannot exist. This means that before we can condemn the idea of a mind-independent object as an abstract idea, we must know that such an object is impossible. But if we already have a way of showing *that*, why take a detour through the notion of abstraction? Berkeley may be entitled to *infer* that the idea of mind-independent object is abstract, but he cannot, it seems, offer an allegation of abstraction as a premiss. But the claim that materialism depends at bottom on abstraction can be understood, I think, in another way.

   In the seventeenth and eighteenth centuries it was not unusual to speak of either matter of the laws describing its behaviour as *abstract* or *abstracted*. This way of speaking was as common among the champions of matter as it was among its critics, because abstraction was viewed in at least two different ways. Some saw it as a process that penetrates superficial and distracting detail, putting the mind in touch with the reality underlying appearance. Others saw it as a process leading to airy notions with little or no foundation in fact. John Keill expressed the first view when he described the laws of motion as 'the easiest and most abstracted things in nature'.[36] Francis Bacon, whose misgivings about abstraction are registered at *Philosophical Commentaries* 564, expressed the second view when he condemned the belief in 'potential and uninformed matter' (the prime matter of the scholastics, which Berkeley compares to the corporeal substance of the moderns in a

---

[36] *An Examination of Dr. Burnet's Theory of the Earth*, Oxford, 1698, p. 14.

section—*Principles* 11—that reasserts the connection between materialism and abstraction):[37]

Hence it is that men cease not from abstracting nature till they come to potential and uninformed matter, nor on the other hand from dissecting nature till they reach the atom; things which, even if true, can do but little for the welfare of mankind.

Robert Green, whose *Principles of Natural Philosophy* was published two years after Berkeley's *Principles*, calls matter 'a Creature of the Mind' which 'receives its Stamp and Character from the Arbitrary Composition or Abstraction of the Will, which takes in or leaves out what Properties it thinks fit.'[38] The so-called essential properties of matter, Green argues, are 'Abstracted Ideas' which, like all such ideas, 'terminate in the Mind' and represent nothing in the world.

Keill, Bacon, and Green are concerned either with the formation of general ideas or with the isolation of the primary or original qualities of interest to natural philosophers. Berkeley discusses these abstractive processes in the Introduction to the *Principles* and in *Principles* 10, but in *Principles* 5 his target is the abstraction of being from being perceived, a far more fundamental offence, and one in which the vulgar share the guilt of the natural philosophers. The real novelty of § 5 lies here, but here too there is a precedent. In the *Elements of Philosophy* Hobbes argued that the doctrine of abstraction is to blame for the belief in *immaterial* substance. 'The abuse' he explains,

proceeds from this, that some men seeing they can consider, that is (as I said before) bring into account the increasings and decreasings of quantity, heat and other accidents, without considering their bodies or subjects (which they call *abstracting*, or making to exist apart by themselves), they speak of accidents, as if they might be separated from all bodies. And from hence proceed the gross errors of writers on metaphysics; for, because they can consider thought without the consideration of body, they infer there is no need for thinking-body; and because quantity may be considered without considering body, they think also that quantity may be without body, and body without quantity; and that a body has quantity by the addition of quantity to it.[39]

[37] *Novum Organum* I lxvi, p. 65 in F. H. Anderson (ed.), *The New Organon and Related Writings*, Indianapolis, 1960. See also I lx, where Bacon traces certain misconceptions to 'a faulty and unskillful abstraction' (p. 57).

[38] *The Principles of Natural Philosophy*, Cambridge, 1712, p. 119. The following quotations appear on pp. 123 and 124.

[39] I iii 4, pp. 33–4 in vol. I of Molesworth. Also noteworthy is Hobbes's use of the word 'consider', which plays a similar role in *Commentaries* 254, 318, and 440, in the First Dialogue (p. 193), and in a 1734 addition to § 16 of the Introduction to the

The first of the metaphysical errors listed by Hobbes was committed by Descartes in his argument for the real distinction between mind and body, an argument to which Hobbes objected along the very lines indicated here.[40] I want to suggest that although their eventual conclusions are diametrically opposed, the view Berkeley expresses in *Principles* 5 has the same form as the view Hobbes expresses in the *Elements*. Hobbes believes that abstraction is an important source of the belief in immaterial substance. Berkeley believes that abstraction is an important source of the belief in *material* substance.

After completing his attack on abstraction, Berkeley traces the doctrine to 'language'—more specifically, to the assumption that every significant name stands for a particular idea (Introduction 20). This assumption is stated more fully at *Principles* 116, where Berkeley writes that 'we are apt to think every noun substantive stands for a distinct idea, that may be separated from all others'. Berkeley thinks this assumption has disastrous consequences when it is applied to two words in particular: *existence* and *perception*. For if each of these words stands for an idea 'that may be separated from all others'—including the idea associated with the other word in the pair—then existence and perception can be conceived apart. But whatever is conceivable is possible. It therefore follows that there can be existence without perception, and this, of course, is materialism. Relations among words, Berkeley thinks, are an unreliable guide to relations among things. If we want to know whether there can be existence without perception, it is a mistake to ask whether the words *existence* and *perception* can occur apart, or even whether the definition of the first includes the second. The aim of Berkeley's attack on abstraction is to diminish our faith in such crude linguistic tests of possibility. When he urges us to 'draw the curtain of words' (Introduction 24) he is not recommending a vague stare at our ideas and mental operations, but a concentration on their separability and inseparability, in the hope that when he tells us in

Principles. The word and its cognates had been used in this way by many others, for example Aquinas.

[40] See his Second Objection, pp. 122–3 in Cottingham, *Philosophical Writings of Descartes*, vol. 2. Hobbes may have been encouraged in his diagnosis by the use of 'abstract' to mean *separate or separable from matter*. See pp. 311, 320, and 321 in the selections from Cudworth's *True Intellectual System* included in C. A. Patrides (ed.), *The Cambridge Platonists*, Cambridge, 1969. Berkeley uses 'abstract' in this sense in certain passages in *Siris*. I discuss them in Chap. 7. In this sense an abstract thing is a spiritual thing. What Berkeley calls 'pure intellect' is confined to the apprehension of these objects. This view of pure intellect runs from the *Commentaries* (see entry 531) all the way to *Siris* (see Chap. 7).

Part I of the *Principles* that existence and perception are inseparable, we will look past words and agree. The importance of this concentration is brought out in both the master argument and in the argument of *Principles* 3.

There is at least one more precedent for the connection Berkeley draws between matter and abstraction, and this one is especially interesting because it leads its author to warn against abstraction in terms that foreshadow Berkeley's. The warning even comes in a discussion entitled 'Of the Abuse of Words'. At *Essay* III x 15, Locke investigates the difference between the notion of matter and the notion of body. 'Though *Matter* and *Body*, be not really distinct, but wherever there is one, there is the other;' he explains, 'Yet *Matter* and *Body*, stand for two different Conceptions, whereof the one is incomplete, and but a part of the other.' Body—the complete notion—stands for a solid and extended substance. Matter, though, is 'used for the Substance and Solidity of Body, without taking in its Extension and Figure'. Locke then blames the obscure and unintelligible disputes concerning prime matter on a tendency among philosophers to ignore the difference between real existence and existence 'under Precision'—that is, under abstraction.[41]

But since Solidity cannot exist without Extension, and Figure, the taking *Matter* to be the name of something really existing under that Precision, has no doubt produced those obscure and unintelligible Discourses and Disputes, which have filled the Heads and Books of Philosophers concerning *Materia prima*.

8. *Berkeley's phenomenalism*

Immaterialism can be stated in the language of substance or in the language of ordinary objects. In the language of substance, immaterialism is the view that matter does not exist: there is 'not any other substance

---

[41] Locke uses the word *precise* in connection with abstraction at *Essay* II xi 9. Berkeley speaks of precision as well as abstraction at Introduction 9, and he uses the word 'prescind' at Introduction 10. Suarez speaks of 'precisive abstraction' in *On the Various Kinds of Distinctions*, p. 19 in Cyril Vollert's trans., Milwaukee, 1947. For a definition of 'Precisive Abstraction' as the act whereby 'we consider those Things apart which cannot really exist apart' see Isaac Watts, *Logick*, London, 1725, p. 200. In *De Motu* Berkeley defines abstraction as 'the division of things truly inseparable' (§ 47). 'Abstraction' and 'precision' are treated as synonyms in the *Port-Royal Logic*; see e.g. the heading of pt. I, chap. v, p. 52 in the Ozell trans.

than *spirit*, or that which perceives' (*Principles* 7). In the language of ordinary objects, immaterialism is the view that houses, mountains, and rivers have no existence 'natural or real, distinct from their being perceived by the understanding' (*Principles* 4), or the view that houses, mountains, and rivers are ideas (*Principles* 4, 33, and 38–9), or collections, combinations, or congeries of ideas (*Principles* 1 and 37, Third Dialogue, p. 249). This relation between ideas and spirits can itself be described in more or less learned terms. The more learned description is that ideas *exist in* spirit; the allusion to the technical notion of inherence implies that ideas can no more exist apart from spirit than an accident or mode can exist apart from the substance it modifies.[42] The less learned description is that ideas are *perceived by* spirit. The two descriptions come to the same thing because *being in* and *being perceived by* are (for ideas) one and the same: 'the existence of an idea consists in being perceived' (*Principles* 2); 'qualities are in the mind only as they are perceived by it' (*Principles* 49). My aim in this final section is to clarify statements of immaterialism in the language of ordinary objects. Just what does it mean to say that houses, mountains, and rivers are ideas, or combinations of ideas?

The two responses to this question which I will consider do not exhaust the possibilities, but in my opinion they are the only ones with a fair chance of being correct. Each attempts to take account of Berkeley's respect for common sense; one of his primary commitments, on either construal, is his belief in the truth of some statements asserting the existence of ordinary objects. The two lines of response also agree in supposing that Berkeley takes the language of substance seriously, both as a vehicle for stating his own view and a device for achieving clarification. He does not resort to it merely for the sake of making out a contrast with the materialists, but willingly employs it both to state immaterialism and to clarify the common-sense truths he takes for granted. Both lines of response, then, take Berkeley to operate at two levels: at the level of common sense, where he accepts the existence of houses, mountains, and rivers; and at the deeper level of philosophy, where he uses the language of the learned to speak a deeper (and by no means incompatible) truth about what there is.

The two responses have the following element in common. It qualifies each of them as a version of immaterialism:

---

[42] See *Principles* 49 for evidence that Berkeley was aware of the allusion. There Berkeley takes pains to show that an idea is not an accident or mode, but in my view he takes ideas to resemble modes in their dependence on spirit.

1. Ordinary objects have no existence natural or real, distinct from being perceived. They are not substances. The only substances are spirits, and ordinary objects depend for their very existence on being perceived by spirits.

The first of the two responses, which I will label the *idealist* version of immaterialism, supplements (1) with (2*i*) and (3*i*):

2*i*. Ordinary objects are identical with collections or combinations of ideas.

3*i*. Words such as 'house', 'mountain', and 'river' refer to discriminable entities which can be identified not only at the level of common sense (where they are spoken of as houses, mountains, and rivers) but also at the level of philosophy, where they can be picked out by a different set of co-referential expressions. It is possible, in other words, to arrive at truth-value preserving translations of statements in the language of common sense merely by substituting for terms such as 'house', 'mountain', or 'river' certain referring expressions employed at the level of philosophy.

The second of the two responses, which I will label the *phenomenalist* version of immaterialism, adds three propositions to (1):

2*p*. The truth-conditions of statements about ordinary objects—including statements asserting the existence of such objects—can, as a matter of what these statements *mean*, be expressed in the language of minds and their ideas.

3*p*. The translations referred to in 2*p* are not simply a matter of substituting terms in the language of mind and their ideas (terms referring, for example, to collections of ideas) for terms in ordinary language.

4*p*. The translations referred to in 2*p* typically involve subjunctive or counterfactual conditions. A fragment of such a translation appears in the *Principles*: 'the table I write on, I say, exists, that is, I see and feel it; and if I were out of my study I should say it existed, meaning thereby that if I was in my study I might perceive it, or that some other spirit actually does perceive it.' (§ 3.)

These statements call for a number of clarifications. First, the phenomenalist version of immaterialism includes a weakened form of what has sometimes been called *linguistic* or *analytical phenomenalism*. It is a weakened form because the statement does not require that a translation into the language of minds and their ideas preserve the *meaning* of the statement in ordinary language. It is enough if the two statements are necessarily equivalent—true in exactly the same circumstances. But the availability of such a translation is, according to the phenomenalist version, a matter of what the statement in ordinary language *means*. The meaning of statements in ordinary language is such that an equivalent statement in the language of minds and their ideas will always be available (in principle if not in practice). Second, the phenomenalist version is in other respects much stronger than linguistic or analytical phenomenalism, because it includes an unabashedly ontological component: proposition (1), the component it has in common with the idealist interpretation. Third, the idealist version of immaterialism is, like the phenomenalist version, committed to (2*p*). The idea behind both is that things are *nothing but* ideas. On either view things are constructed out of, reducible to, or supervenient on, ideas. The difference between the two versions lies in the differing forms taken by the translations they seek: according to the idealist version translation will always be term-by-term, and an appeal to subjunctive or counterfactual conditionals will therefore be unnecessary. According to the phenomenalist version term-by-term translation will not in general be possible, and translations will typically include conditionals which are subjunctive or contrary-to-fact. The idealist and phenomenalist versions of immaterialism, then, share a common core, constituted by (1) and (2*p*) (which is entailed by (3*i*)). Fourth, phenomenalism is more modest than idealism in placing fewer constraints on acceptable translations, but at the same time it is more sophisticated in invoking the notion of a subjunctive or counterfactual conditional. These qualities exert pulls in different interpretive directions: it is a rough and ready maxim of interpretation that imputing a weaker claim is less risky than imputing a stronger one; but it is an equally useful rule of thumb that in the absence of indications of sophistication, imputations of naïve views are to be preferred. Fifth, neither idealism nor phenomenalism takes Berkeley at his word when he identifies things with single ideas, as he seems to do in many places, most notably at *Principles* 4, 33, and 38–9. I will assume they are right in this; Berkeley's tendency to shift from formulations referring to single ideas to formulations referring to collections of ideas is not, I think, a sign of uncertainty, but evidence of his willingness to treat a collection or congeries as a single idea.

There is ample textual evidence that Berkeley himself follows the idealist path of development. There are, to begin with, numerous passages in which objects are baldly identified with ideas or collections of ideas:

The ideas imprinted on the sense by the Author of Nature are called *real things*.   (*Principles* 33.)

But, say you, it sounds very harsh to say we eat and drink ideas, and are clothed with ideas. I acknowledge it does so, the word *idea* not being used in common discourse to signify the several combinations of sensible qualities, which are called *things*.   (*Principles* 38.)

PHILONOUS. The ideas perceived by sense, that is, real things, are more vivid and clear, and being imprinted on the mind by a spirit distinct from us, have not a like dependence on our will.   (Third Dialogue, p. 235.)

Moreover, one of Berkeley's central arguments for immaterialism—the argument of *Principles* 4, which lends its structure to the *Dialogues* as a whole—has the identity of things and ideas as its apparent consequence:

For what are the forementioned objects [that is, houses, mountains, rivers, and in a word all sensible objects] but the things we perceive by sense, and what do we perceive by sense besides our own ideas or sensations?   (*Principles* 4.)

PHILONOUS. I do not pretend to be a setter-up of *new notions*. My endeavours tend only to unite and place in a clearer light that truth, which was before shared between the vulgar and the philosophers: the former being of opinion, that *those things they immediately perceive are the real things*; and the latter, that *the things immediately perceived, are ideas which exist only in the mind*. Which two notions put together, do in effect constitute the substance of what I advance.   (Third Dialogue, p. 262.)

The idealist interpretation of Berkeley owes much of its appeal to the ease with which statements of idealism can be drawn from his writings. But it is difficult to take these statements as signs of a commitment to idealism deep enough to count as a thoughtful rejection of the phenomenalist alternative. Defenders of the idealist interpretation would perhaps agree that Berkeley never faces a considered choice between the two positions, but they would probably blame this on his failure to appreciate the subtleties of phenomenalism. As a first step in defence of the phenomenalist interpretation I want to show that the complexities of a developed idealism are at least as great. If the subtlety of phenomenalism is a reason for supposing that Berkeley could not have considered it, the same can be said of idealism.

The complexities of idealism have to do with the principles according to which ideas are combined into things, and with the individuation of the items entering into the combinations. Berkeley addresses these problems briefly in the Third Dialogue. Principles of combination are discussed in the following passage:

Strictly speaking, Hylas, we do not see the same object that we feel; neither is the same object perceived by the microscope, which was by the naked eye. But in case every variation was thought sufficient to constitute a new kind of individual, the endless number or confusion of names would render language impracticable. Therefore to avoid this as well as other inconveniencies which are obvious upon a little thought, men combine together several ideas, apprehended by divers senses, or by the same sense at different times, or in different circumstances, but observed however to have some connexion in Nature, either with respect to co-existence or succession; all which they refer to one name, and consider as one thing. (p. 245.)

This account is affirmed in Philonous's subsequent characterization of a cherry as a congeries of ideas.

A *cherry*, I say, is nothing but a congeries of sensible impressions, or ideas perceived by various senses: which ideas are united into one thing (or have one name given them) by the mind; because they are observed to attend each other. (p. 249.)

This is, of course, not a carefully worked out theory of combination but a casual sketch, which tells us little more than that the mind joins ideas together into things. What is important is Philonous's insistence that in strictness of speech, the 'objects' of different senses—that is, the ideas impressed on them—are not the same. Here Philonous insists on speaking strictly, but in a nearby passage, where the topic is the individuation of ideas, and the question is whether two minds can perceive the same thing, he is willing to speak more loosely. 'If the term *same* be taken in its vulgar acceptation,' he tells Hylas,

it is certain (and not at all repugnant to the principles I maintain) that different persons may perceive the same thing; or the same thing or idea exist in different minds. Words are of arbitrary imposition; and since men are used to apply the word *same* where no distinction or variety is perceived, and I do not pretend to alter their perceptions, it follows, that as men have said before, *several saw the same thing*, so they may upon like occasions still continue the same phrase, without any deviation either from propriety of language, or the truth of things. But if the term *same* be used in the acceptation of philosophers, who pretend to an abstracted notion of identity, then, according to their sundry definitions of this notion (for it is not yet agreed wherein that philosophic identity consists), it may or may not be possible for divers persons to perceive the same thing. (p. 247.)

I see the attitude toward sameness expressed here as part of an attempt to streamline the description of the process of combination Philonous elaborates on p. 245. If we are permitted to say that the ideas entering into combinations exist in many minds at once, we are free to say that an apple is a combination of 'a certain colour, taste, smell, figure and consistence', as Berkeley does at *Principles* 1. We can avoid dissecting the constituent ideas into their further components; a 'certain colour'—understood as an idea which can exist in many minds provided they 'agree in their perceptions' (p. 247)—is something we can treat as a unit. Philonous believes that in the strictest sense of *same* 'the same idea which is in my mind' (to quote Hylas) 'cannot be in yours' (p. 247).[43] But working with this sense of *same* in describing the process of combination would yield an account of bewildering complexity. Objects would, at one level of analysis, be reduced to combination of ideas, and these ideas, at a deeper level of analysis, would themselves be reduced to combinations, not (as at the first level) combinations of ideas of several senses, but combinations of ideas of a single sense in several perceivers.

The complexities of the idealist interpretation can be exhibited without descending to the deeper level. Suppose that we stop with the first level; what does it mean to identify ordinary objects with collections of ideas at that level? If two things are identical they must exist at all and only the same times. It follows that if an ordinary object is identified with a collection of ideas, it must be true to say that the collection exists if, and only if, it is true to say that the object does. The existence of a particular collection must therefore tolerate a good deal of shifting in the members of the collection that exist from moment to moment. I spend the early morning working at my typewriter; the machine exists throughout. Yet at one moment I have a visible idea of nothing but its back, at another I have a visible idea of nothing but its side, at still another I have no visible ideas at all, but tangible ideas of

---

[43] Pitcher defends this reading of the passage in *Berkeley*, pp. 146–50. Odegard points out that Philonous raises no objection to Hylas's assertion that the same idea in my mind cannot be in yours. He objects only to the inference that no two people can see the same thing ('Berkeley and the Perception of Ideas', *Canadian Journal of Philosophy* 1 (1971), p. 168). I discuss this exchange in greater detail in Chap. 9, where I develop Odegard's point. See also C. C. W. Taylor, 'Berkeley on Archetypes', *Archiv für Geschichte der Philosophie* 67 (1985), 65–79, esp. pp. 73–4.

several of its keys, and as I leave the room I am aware of nothing but the purring of its motor. On the idealist interpretation all of the ideas mentioned are members of a collection which *is* the typewriter, and the collection (like the typewriter) must be able to exist at a given time even though only a handful of its constituents is likely to exist then.

It is noteworthy that we find in Berkeley's writings no explicit recognition of the ability of a collection to persist as its members go in and out of existence. This by itself is an indication that the idealist version may impute more sophistication to Berkeley than its adherents realize. But perhaps it is an obvious fact about collections that their existence-conditions are flexible in the way described. Can we suppose that Berkeley recognized this, and that he took account of it by making the existence at a time of one or more members a sufficient condition of the existence of the collection at that time? Here we come into conflict with the account of real existence Berkeley develops with greatest care at *Principles* 30–4. He says there that ideas of sense owe their reality to their strength, coherence, and regularity. The last two characteristics are a function of an idea's relation to other ideas. This means that if an ordinary object is identified with a collection, the collection must depend for its existence at *t* not only on the existence at *t* of some of its members, but on the existence at *other* times of *other* members, suitably related to the ideas existing at *t*.[44]

Our developing understanding of collections is now complex enough to call the apparent simplicity of the idealist version into question. What evidence is there that Berkeley wants to *identify* objects with collections whose existence at a time rests on the way in which ideas later develop? It is true that Berkeley often says that things are ideas, but why should this be taken to mean that every thing is identical with a distinct collection of ideas, a collection that exists when and only when the thing does? Berkeley may instead mean that the existence of anything is nothing over and above the existence of certain ideas, suitably related. The suggestion that objects *supervene* on ideas, instead

---

[44] The same point can be made in another way. Just as several minds can see the same thing, one mind can see what another mind merely imagines. The similarity between the two ideas may actually exceed that between the ideas of two percipients. The imagined idea will be fainter, but we know from 'dreams, phrensies, and the like' (*Principles* 18) that not even this is necessary. Given that the ideas are the same (natural assumption in view of the simplifying manœuvre of p. 245), does it follow that the same collection of ideas exists in each case? If the reply is yes, it looks as if imagining an ordinary object will be enough to bring it into being. If the reply is no, it looks as if the existence of a collection depends on more than the ideas existing at a given time.

of standing in the relation of identity to distinct collections of them, brings us closer to the phenomenalist interpretation of immaterialism, because it amounts to rejection of ($2i$) and ($3i$) in favour of the weaker ($2p$) and ($3p$).

But we have yet to arrive at the phenomenalist interpretation because we have so far made no progress at all toward ($4p$), which injects a subjunctive or counterfactual component into the account of what it is for an object to exist. Yet once we have gone as far as ($2p$) and ($3p$), the step to a subjunctive or counterfactual account is entirely natural. Why, after all, should the existence of an object rest on the ideas that *actually* come to pass? If we break off our investigation, or if the object goes out of existence before we have an opportunity to press on, should this count against the existence of the object? That it should not count is perhaps not obvious, but there are several passages suggesting Berkeley believes that it should not. The most notable is *Principles* 3, where Berkeley includes a counterfactual clause in his account of what it means to say there is a table in his study. The same emphasis on what would be perceived (as opposed to what is in fact perceived) can be found elsewhere in the *Principles* and in an entry in the *Commentaries*:

The question, whether the earth moves or no, amounts in reality to no more than this, to wit, whether we have reason to conclude from what hath been observed by astronomers, that if we were placed in such and such circumstances, and such or such a position and distance, both from the earth and sun, we should perceive the former to move among the choir of the planets, and appearing in all respects like one of them: and this, by the established rules of Nature, which we have no reason to mistrust, is reasonably collected from the phenomena. (*Principles* 58.)

+   Bodies taken for Powers do exist w^n not perceiv'd but this   293a
     existence is not actual. w^n I say a power exists no more is meant
     than that if in ye light I open my eyes & look that way I shall see it
     i.e ye body &c.

For one reason or another, each of the passages I have cited is defective as a statement of phenomenalism. The passage from *Principles* 58 concerns an unperceived property of a *perceived* object, though it certainly suggests the form that a phenomenalist account of unperceived existence would take. The passage from *Principles* 3 speaks of my 'meaning thereby that if I was in my study I might perceive it, *or* [my emphasis] that some other spirit actually does perceive it', and we cannot be sure that what follows the 'or' is not meant to tell us that satisfying the counterfactual clause would not, by itself, secure the existence of the table. Even the entry from the *Commentaries*, in telling us that the existence of bodies is 'not actual', is insensitive to the difference in levels of discourse which the sophisticated phenomenalist exploits. At one level—the level of discourse that the phenomenalist sets out to analyse or understand— the existence of unperceived bodies *is* actual, because to say that bodies are actual is just another way of saying they exist. But at a deeper level—at the level of discourse to which the phenomenalist resorts in an attempt to clarify common sense, a level at which he reveals his or her own ontological commitments—the existence of bodies is not actual, because there are no expressions denoting either bodies or collections with which bodies can be identified.[45] These imperfections are to be expected, I think, in the writings of a philosopher who was one of the first to see the promise of phenomenalism. And the promise seems to have been clearest to Berkeley when we wrote about creation in the Third Dialogue:

HYLAS. What shall we make then of the Creation?
PHILONOUS. May we not understand it to have been entirely in respect of finite spirits; so that things, with regard to us, may properly be said to begin their existence, or be created, when God decreed they should become perceptible to intelligent creatures, in that order and manner which he then established, and we now call the laws of Nature? You may call this a *relative*, or *hypothetical existence* if you please.   (Third Dialogue, p. 253.)

(See also the Third Dialogue, p. 254 and *Works* VIII, pp. 37–8.) These passages show that Berkeley had the sophistication to formulate (4*p*), and the idealist interpretation has no choice but to leave them dangling. The phenomenalist interpretation allows us to gather them up, and although the view it imputes to Berkeley is undeniably a subtle one, the idealist interpretation, when pressed, calls for an under- standing of the existence-conditions of collections which is nearly as subtle, and which cannot be discerned in Berkeley's writings. The passages that invite the idealist interpretation should therefore be seen, I think, as shorthand statements of the phenomenalist view.

We are left, then, with two basic lines of response. We can seek a

---

[45] The suggestion that Berkeley's thought moves at various levels is elaborated by A. C. Grayling in *Berkeley: The Central Arguments*, London, 1986. See in particular pp. 22–9, 42–4, 60–2, and 131–2.

single coherent view behind the conflicting statements, or we can read those statements as expressions of two competing tendencies. Jonathan Bennett takes the second line. He speaks, for example, of Berkeley's account of real existence as 'a vehicle of a kind of phenomenalism which runs, presumably entirely unrecognized' through both the *Principles* and the *Dialogues*.[46] I prefer the first line of response, largely because I am troubled by an unrecognized phenomenalism that is insistently repeated and developed with considerable care. If we respond in the first way, of course, we must decide whether the coherent view underlying the conflicting statements is phenomenalism or idealism. My own decision is influenced by a long list of reasons which are not, I admit, decisive even in the aggregate. In the first place, phenomenalism coheres more firmly with Berkeley's account of real existence, and with his account of creation in the *Dialogues*. Second, phenomenalism is the more sophisticated view, and since the texts and notebooks entries convince me that Berkeley has the sophistication required to formulate that view and appreciate its subtleties, I think it is unlikely that he would offer it as an 'unofficial' statement of idealism. Third, it seems to me that idealism needs to be developed beyond what Berkeley provides if it is to meet some of the difficulties confronting immaterialism. In Berkeley's texts the sense in which objects are 'collections' or 'combinations' is left entirely unexplicated. It is true that Berkeley offers no real account of the way in which phenomenalist relations or equivalence are established, any more than he offers a real account of the way in which ideas are collected or combined into objects. But there is no defect in Berkeley's statements of phenomenalism as glaring as his failure to say what it is to be a *collection* or *combination* of ideas. In this connection it may be helpful to recall how many of Berkeley's pronouncements (those at *Principles* 3, 24, and 133, for example) fall between idealism and phenomenalism. Berkeley's aim as an author allows for some variation in his statements of immaterialism. He wants to rid his readers of their tenacious believe in the existence of unthinking things 'without any relation to their being perceived'; he cares very little whether the reader who turns away from materialism is a convert to idealism or phenomenalism. Yet he cares enough about the difference, I think, to choose phenomenalism for himself.

I want to conclude with a word about phenomenalism and scepticism. Berkeley's belief that materialism is hopelessly exposed to

---

[46] *Locke, Berkeley, Hume*, p. 152.

scepticism was discussed briefly above near the end of section 5. Berkeley held firmly to this belief, and it was an important motive behind his rejection of materialism; in the *Principles* he actually traces the strength of scepticism to the materialist's distinction between things and ideas (*Principles* 86–7). He goes on to promise that doubtfulness regarding the existence of sensible things will vanish once we take that existence to consist in being perceived (§ 88), but in virtue of its phenomenalism Berkeley's immaterialism is itself exposed to a definite sceptical threat. If the reality of an idea of sense depends on the ideas that will follow—if our judgements about the present have a hidden inductive component—then uncertainty about the future will infect the present. Berkeley is well aware that our knowledge of the figure is not absolute; *Principles* 58, quoted just above, is only one of several passages where Berkeley seems to recognize either that God may change the laws of nature, or that the laws of which we speak may not be laws at all, but rules of thumb reliable only for the most part. This suggests that Berkeley is not concerned about everything that might be described as scepticism. Entry 221 in the *Commentaries* reads, 'All our ideas are adequate, our knowledge of the Laws of nature is not perfect & adequate.' I do not know what led Berkeley to attach a plus sign to this entry, but its distinction between the adequacy of our ideas and the adequacy of our knowledge of the laws of nature is useful, I think, in understanding his mature attitude toward scepticism. Although our knowledge of nature's laws is imperfect, and our judgements of real existence are therefore fallible, there is nothing inherently misleading in the ideas we perceive. If God wanted to perfect our knowledge our ideas could be left unchanged. They do not aspire to represent something better or more real; they are all there is to things themselves. Wholesale scepticism about 'the reality of sensible things'—the kind of scepticism at issue in the *Dialogues*—is thereby avoided, even if other kinds of scepticism are not. There is room, Berkeley can say, for more or less reasonable conjecture about the ideas we will have in the future, and in many cases our conjectures—even if fallible—deserve to be counted as knowledge. After a certain point, he can say, once the train of ideas has been followed far enough into the future, doubt simply ceases to be reasonable.[47]

[47] See Anthony Quinton, 'The Problem of Perception', reprinted in Swartz, *Perceiving, Sensing, and Knowing*, pp. 513–14, for a discussion of the extent to which our knowledge of the past and present depends on our predictions about the future.

In my defence of phenomenalism as the proper interpretation of
immaterialism I have said nothing about the ideas in the mind of God.
It might be thought that adverting to divine ideas makes it possible to
eliminate the complexities met with in our attempt to identify objects
with collections of ideas. If, for example, God's ideas are favoured
components of these collections, perhaps the collections exist if, and
only if, God has the appropriate ideas. In the chapter that follows I
offer an account of Berkeley's views on unperceived objects; I hope it
will show that God's ideas fit Berkeley's scheme most comfortably
when they are introduced and understood by means of the phenomenalist interpretetation I have defended here.

7

UNPERCEIVED OBJECTS

A T the beginning of *The Longest Journey*, E. M. Forster portrays a group of Cambridge undergraduates sitting in the dark, lighting matches, and asserting or denying the existence of a cow that none of them perceives. The cow 'was so familiar, so solid, that surely the truths that she illustrated would in time become familiar and solid also'.[1] Lighting the matches is not an attempt to catch the cow rushing back into existence; the cow (when it exists) is in a pasture, not a college living room. Instead the match, like the cow, is a familiarizing prop: just as the cow represents existence and non-existence, the lighted match represents perception, and the darkness the absence of perception'.[2] Forster does not say that the students are discussing Berkeley, but the question he has them asking—'Do [objects] exist only when there is some one to look at them? Or have they a real existence of their own?'[3]—has long been thought to present Berkeley with a problem: if he believes that objects exist only as long as they are perceived, how can he avoid denying that they continue to exist when we do not perceive them? In this chapter I show how the problem can be solved. Although I am confident that the solution I propose is the one Berkeley *should* have adopted, I cannot be certain that he *did* adopt it. Yet the evidence that it is Berkeley's own solution has a peculiar kind of strength, because any evidence in favour of *either* of the two familiar interpretations turns out to be evidence in favour of the interpretation I propose here. My proposal, roughly put, is that the famous limerick by Ronald Knox is right to suggest that Berkeley's God keeps objects in existence by perceiving them.[4] But it is also true that Berkeley is a phenomenalist, who understands statements about unperceived objects as statements about the actual and possible perceptions of finite minds. These claims are consistent because the divine perception responsible for real existence is not mere intellection. It

---

[1] E. M. Forster, *The Longest Journey*, New York, 1962, p. 2.
[2] Ibid., p. 1.　　　　　　　　　[3] Ibid., pp. 1–2.
[4] The closing words of the limerick are: 'And that's why the tree/Will continue to be,/Since observed by/*Yours faithfully*, GOD.'

is, instead, the inevitable cognitive accompaniment of the divine acts of will responsible for our sensations.

1. *Two interpretations*

The first familiar interpretation of Berkeley on the unperceived is that unperceived objects continue to exist because there is 'some other spirit that perceives them, though we do not' (*Principles* 48). That other spirit is God, who on this interpretation preserves every object we fail to notice by an act of universal attention. Some hesitate to accept this interpretation because God, as Philonous points out, 'perceives nothing by sense as we do' (Third Dialogue, p. 241). When we perceive an object we suffer something; whether or not it has our approval, an idea enters our mind. 'To know every thing knowable', Philonous explains, 'is certainly a perfection; but to endure, or suffer, or feel any thing by sense, is an imperfection. The former, I say, agrees to God, but not the latter. God knows or hath ideas; but His ideas are not convey'd to Him by sense, as ours are.' (p. 241.)

At *Siris* 289 Berkeley affirms what Philonous says:

There is no sense nor sensory, nor anything like a sense or sensory, in God. Sense implies an impression from some other being, and denotes a dependence in the soul which hath it. Sense is a passion; and passions imply imperfection. God knoweth all things as pure mind or intellect; but nothing by sense, nor in nor through a sensory.

But these passages tell us only that God does not perceive *by sense*.[5] They do not rule out divine perception of another sort: the mere presence of ideas in the divine understanding. The passages are therefore consistent with what Pitcher calls the 'conception theory', according to which 'God preserves [objects] in existence by thinking of them—i.e., by having ideas of them in His understanding.'[6] I will call the assignment of this theory to Berkeley the *perception interpretation*, because Berkeley does not confine his application of the word

---

[5] Commentators who realize that Berkeley's God does not perceive by sense include H. W. B. Joseph, 'A Comparison of Kant's Idealism with that of Berkeley', British Academy Lecture, 1929, p. 16; G. Dawes Hicks, *Berkeley*, London, 1932, p. 207; George Stack, *Berkeley's Analysis of Perception*, The Hague, 1970, p. 131; George H. Thomas, 'Berkeley's God Does not Perceive', *Journal of the History of Philosophy* 14 (1976), 163–8; and Pitcher, *Berkeley*, London, 1977, pp. 163–79.

[6] Pitcher, p. 175.

'perception' to perception by sense.[7] In this he follows both Locke and Malebranche, who regard every act of the understanding as a perception.

The second familiar interpretation of Berkeley on unperceived objects is the *phenomenalist interpretation*. It rests on passages such as *Principles* 3, *Commentaries* 293a, and *Principles* 58, all of them quoted in Chapter 6. The distinctive feature of phenomenalism is that it dispenses with natural objects without putting anything in their place. Instead of identifying the table in my study with my idea, your idea, God's idea, or a collection of ideas that somehow embraces them all— instead of supplying a denotation for the expression 'the table in my study'—the phenomenalist concentrates on *statements about* the table, and proposes to replace them with statements that demand no more for their truth than the actual and possible existence of ideas. To say that an object exists when none of us perceives it is, on the phenomenalist view, to say something about the perceptions we would have if we turned our attention in a certain direction. The truth of the statement does not depend on the existence of an isolable object called 'the table'.

Phenomenalism, as I have characterized it so far, says nothing about God. But if Berkeley is a phenomenalist he is a theocentric one, who grounds the existence of perceptions, actual and possible, in the will of God.[8] The difference between the perception and phenomenalist interpretations of Berkeley's views on unperceived objects—provided the phenomenalist interpretation is properly developed—is not that the former assigns a role to God while the latter does not, but that the former emphasizes God's role as perceiver, and the latter his role as agent. The perception interpretation emphasizes the contribution to real existence made by the divine understanding, while the phenomenalist interpretation emphasizes the contribution made by the divine will.

The usual reaction to the familiar interpretations is that the

[7] Pitcher makes the point himself on pp. 178–9. There are times, however, when Berkeley uses the word 'perception' to *exclude* non-sensory perception. See e.g. *Philosophical Commentaries* 582. For Pitcher's defence of the perception interpretation see pp. 172–9.

[8] I believe the expression 'theocentric phenomenalism' was first used in connection with Berkeley by J. O. Wisdom, *The Unconscious Origin of Berkeley's Philosophy*, London, 1953, p. 21. See also J. D. Mabbott, 'The Place of God in Berkeley's Philosophy', reprinted in C. B. Martin and David M. Armstrong (eds.), *Locke and Berkeley*, Notre Dame, 1968, particularly pp. 367–9, and Jonathan Bennett, *Locke, Berkeley, Hume: Central Themes*, Oxford, 1971, pp. 176–7.

perception interpretation is better supported by the texts, while the phenomenalist interpretation, considered purely as a philosophical view, is more adequate or attractive.[9] This situation is generally regarded as unfortunate—at least for Berkeley—because the two interpretations are assumed to be incompatible. There is, it seems, no consistent interpretation of Berkeley that is both faithful to the texts and philosophically impressive. I want to show that this is not the case. It turns out that we do not really have to choose between the two interpretations. In a sense, we can have them both.

2. The denial of blind agency

To see how the two interpretations can be brought together requires a brief survey of the views Berkeley inherited from his seventeenth century predecessors on the relationship between perception and volition. Descartes, Malebranche, and Locke were unanimous in their judgement that volition is inseparable from perception. Descartes, for example, writes in the Third Meditation that in willing, 'there is always a particular thing which I take as the object of my thought'.[10] He writes in a letter to Mersenne that 'We cannot will anything without knowing that we will it, nor could we know this without an idea', and he adds that 'I do not claim that the idea is different from the action itself.'[11] In a letter to Regius, written in the same year, he insists that 'We cannot will anything without understanding what we will.' In *The Search after Truth*, Malebranche claims that 'willing presupposes perception'.[12] He argues that the human soul could not create its own ideas even if it had the raw power of creation, because it would need the ideas themselves to serve as the standards or paradigms of its creative acts. For the same reason not even God can create without ideas.[13] But the most explicit claims about the intentionality of volition come in Locke's correspon-

[9] For such a verdict see John Stuart Mill, 'Berkeley's Life and Writings', in the *Collected Works of John Stuart Mill,*, vol. 11, Toronto, 1978, pp. 460–1, and Pitcher, pp. 166–7, 171.

[10] John Cottingham and others (eds.), *The Philosophical Writings of Descartes*, Cambridge, 1985, vol. 2, p. 26. For Berkeley's remarks on the *Meditations* see *Commentaries* 784–5, 790, and 794–8.

[11] *Philosophical Letters*, trans. by Anthony Kenny, Oxford, 1970, p. 93. The following quotation comes from p. 102. Both letters were published in the 17th cent.

[12] Bk. III, Pt. i, chap 1 § 1; Bk. III, pt. ii, chap. 3. I quote from the trans. by Lennon and Olscamp, Columbus, Ohio, 1980, pp. 199 and 223–4.

[13] *Search* III ii 6, p. 230 in Lennon and Olscamp.

dence with Limborch, published in 1708 in *Some familiar letters between Mr. Locke and several of his friends.* In one letter Locke writes,[14]

If you say that the judgement of the understanding, or cogitation, is not one of the 'requisites for acting'. Please consider whether, while you want in this way to make a man free, you are not simply making him a blind agent; and whether, in order to make him free, you are not taking away from him understanding, without which any sort of Liberty cannot exist or be supposed to exist. For liberty does not belong in any way whatsoever to things destitute of cogitation and understanding.

Following Locke, we can call the view he articulates here the *denial of blind agency.* It is reaffirmed later on in the same letter, where Locke speaks of 'that judgement which in every volition immediately precedes Volition', and claims that 'An action of willing this or that always follows a judgement of the understanding by which a man judges this to be better for here and now.'[15]

Berkeley's notebooks show an interest in Locke's treatment of liberty—the occasion of the exchange with Limborch—as early as entry 145a, and the Limborch correspondence is itself discussed at entries 709 and 743–5. Berkeley's concern with the relationship between volition and perception first surfaces at entry 645, where he writes, 'There can be perception wthout volition. Qu: whether there can be volition without perception.' By entry 674 he has his answer—the denial of blind agency: 'Distinct from or without perception there is no volition.' The denial is repeated later on:

S   It seems to me that Will & understanding Volitions & ideas   841
       cannot be severed, that either cannot be possibly without the
       other.

E.S.   Some Ideas or other I must have so long as I exist or Will. But no   842
       one Idea or sort of Ideas is essential.

The most dramatic endorsement of the denial of blind agency, one that will play an important role in my later argument, comes at entry 812: 'The propertys of all things are in God i.e. there is in the Deity Understanding as well as Will. He is no Blind agent & in truth a blind Agent is a Contradiction.' Locke's own denial of blind agency may well have influenced this entry. At entry 708, which immediately precedes

---

[14] *The Correspondence of John Locke*, vol. 7, ed. E. S. De Beer, Oxford, 1982, p. 408.
[15] *Correspondence*, pp. 411, 410. The denial of blind agency is also prominent in the *Essay* (see II xxi 6–16), and in § 1 of *Of the Conduct of the Understanding*, in *The Works of John Locke*, London, 1823, vol. 3, pp. 205–6.

the first entry referring to the Limborch correspondence, Berkeley writes that 'The will & the Understanding may very well be thought two distinct beings.' Entry 743, the second to refer to the correspondence, reads,

Locke to Limborch etc Talk of Judicium Intellectus preceding the Volition I think Judicium includes Volition I can by no means distinguish these Judicium, Intellectus, indifferentia, Uneasiness so many things accompanying or preceding every Volition as e.g. the motion of my hand.

Here Berkeley is not disputing Locke's denial of blind agency, though he is unhappy with Locke's claim that judgement *precedes* volition, which suggests that the two are distinct. Berkeley wants to strengthen the denial by emphasizing the intimacy of the connection between will and understanding, much as Descartes had done when he warned Mersenne that the idea 'accompanying' an action is not distinct from the action itself. Berkeley's emphasis on this intimacy is closely connected with the view of the relationship between the understanding and will as faculties that emerges on the penultimate page of the *Commentaries*:

S   I must no say the Will & Understanding are all one but that they are   871
    both Abstract Ideas i.e. none at all. they not being even ratione
    different from the Spirit, Qua faculties, or Active.

As Berkeley writes at *Principles* 27, 'A spirit is one simple, undivided, active being: as it perceives ideas, it is called the *understanding*, and as it produces or otherwise operates about them, it is called the *will*.'

We can conclude from our survey of Berkeley's predecessors, and from his notebooks entries on volition and perception, that in the *Philosophical Commentaries* Berkeley denies blind agency, and in doing so affirms a commonplace of seventeenth century philosophy of mind. It is, in fact, difficult to locate a philosopher or theologian studied by Berkeley who did *not* deny blind agency. The denial is issued by William King (referred to at entries 142 and 159) and also by John Sergeant (referred to at entry 780). It is also voiced by John Norris.[16]

---

[16] For King, who was strongly influenced by Locke, see *An Essay on the Origin of Evil* (a trans. of *De Origine Mali*, originally pub. in 1702), London, 1731, I.iii.8. and II.i.2.2.; for Sergeant, *Solid Philosophy Asserted*, London, 1697, pp. 219, 225; for Norris, *The Theory and Regulation of Love*, Oxford, 1688, Appendix. It might be objected that blind agency was affirmed by philosophers and theologians who denied that the will always follows the last judgement of the understanding. But even the 'voluntarists' who denied the primacy of the understanding agreed with Locke that the understanding (viewed now as a faculty of simple apprehension) provides the will with its content or

The denial of blind agency will be the central principle in my interpretation of Berkeley's views on unperceived objects. I want to emphasize not only the fact that Berkeley issues the denial in his notebooks, but also its commonplace character, because Berkeley does not make the denial explicit in either the *Principles* or the *Dialogues*. It fails to appear, though, not because he abandons it, but because he takes it for granted. My evidence for this is its enthusiastic acceptance in the notebooks, its re-appearance in works published after the *Dialogues*, and the illumination it provides for several texts in the *Dialogues* and the *Principles*, quite apart from the problem of unperceived objects.

There is actually at least one point in the *Dialogues* where Berkeley comes very close to an explicit denial of blind agency. In the Third Dialogue, Philonous says that 'a thing which hath no ideas in itself, cannot impart them to me' (p. 239), and this, were it not for the context, might be taken to rest on the denial. The context, unfortunately, suggests that Philonous is appealing instead to the scholastic principle that no cause can impart what it does not itself possess. Philonous states this causal maxim earlier in the dialogue (p. 236)—though it is noteworthy that the maxim appears only in the first two editions. The maxim, when applied to the causation of ideas by spirits, entails the denial of blind agency, and it could well be the clarity of the denial, when compared to the obscurity of the scholastic maxim, that accounts for the maxim's disappearance from the third edition. It is very characteristic of Berkeley to favour replacing an obscure principle, regarded by others as an axiom, with a simpler and clearer one which, in the setting of immaterialism, does the same work. At *Commentaries* 831, for example, he says that to assign 'Ex nihilo nihil fit' a 'positive signification', we 'should express it thus. Every Idea has a Cause i.e. is produced. by a Will'. Even more striking in this connection is entry 780:

S.G.   Nihil dat quod non habet or the effect is contained in ye Cause is an axiom I do not Understand or believe to be true.

This should be read along with entry 177a, on Jean Le Clerc:

G.   omnes reales rerum proprietates continentur in Deo w^t means Le Clerc &c by this?

'specification'. For an illustration of this point in a 17th cent. context see Norman L. Fiering, *Moral Philosophy at Seventeenth Century Harvard*, Chapel Hill, 1981, pp. 104–46.

In these entries we are presented with two Latin principles Berkeley cannot understand. But in entry 812 we are told—this time in English—that 'The propertys of all things are in God i.e. there is in the Deity Understanding as well as Will.' This strongly suggests that, in Berkeley's view, the denial of blind agency condenses and clarifies whatever truth there is in the two obscure principles. If so, the scholastic maxim appears in the first two editions of the *Dialogues* only because Berkeley thinks it might be useful to Philonous in snaring Hylas, who has had some philosophical experience. What really lies behind the claim that an unthinking thing cannot impart ideas is not some obscure maxim, but the more lucid denial of blind agency.[17]

Whatever its role in the *Dialogues*, the denial reappears in both *Alciphron* and *Siris*. In a remark reminiscent of entry 743 on the Limborch correspondence, Berkeley's spokesman Euphranor says at *Alciphron* VII 18 that 'I cannot discern nor abstract the decrees of the judgment from the command of the will.' (*Works* III, p. 314.) At *Siris* 254 Berkeley writes,

And it must be owned that, as faculties are multiplied by philosophers according to their operations, the *will* may be distinguished from the intellect. But it will not therefore follow that the Will which operates in the course of nature is not conducted and applied by intellect, although it be granted that neither will understands, nor intellect wills.

He repeats the point at *Siris* 322:

Now although, in our conception, *vis*, or spirit, might be distinguished from mind, it would not thence follow that it acts blindly or without mind, or that it is not closely connected with intellect.

Although it is not stated in the *Dialogues*, the denial of blind agency can help us understand some of the texts Jonathan Bennett points to in support of his contention that Berkeley conflates causation and

---

[17] The denial of blind agency may also be at work in an exchange on p. 220 of the Second Dialogue, where Philonous says that 'those things which you say are present to God, without doubt he perceives.' 'Certainly', Hylas replies, 'otherwise they could not be to Him an occasion of acting.' Hylas's reply probably rests on the denial of blind agency. But since it is *Hylas's* remark, and part of a proposal to which Philonous is hostile, I am unwilling to count it as evidence that *Berkeley* denies blind agency in the *Dialogues*. Note, however, that Philonous's hostility is not directed at the denial of blind agency. It is aroused instead by the implied deprecation of the wisdom and power of God, who has no need of an 'unthinking *substance*' (emphasis mine) to influence or direct him (p. 220). If occasions are viewed not as unthinking substances but as 'certain things perceived by the mind of God', Philonous seems to have no quarrel with them (p. 220).

inherence. Bennett identifies eight occasions on which Berkeley uses 'depend' or related words 'to say something about the ownership of ideas', and eight other occasions on which he uses them 'in discussing what causes ideas to be had by minds'.[18] He then accuses Berkeley of exploiting the ambiguity in the following passage, where Berkeley presents what Bennett calls the 'continuity argument' for the existence of God.[19]

PHILONOUS. When I deny sensible things an existence out of the mind, I do not mean my mind in particular, but all minds. Now it is plain they have an existence exterior to my mind, since I find them by experience to be independent of it. There is therefore some other mind wherein they exist, during the intervals between the times of my perceiving them: as likewise they did before my birth, and would do after my annihilation.

(Third Dialogue, pp. 230–1.)

Bennett writes,[20]

The last two sentences of this, I suggest, exploit the ambiguity of 'independent'. Berkeley takes the premiss that some ideas are independent of (not caused by) my mind, muddles himself into treating it as the premiss that some ideas are independent of (not owned by) my mind, and so infers that some mind has ideas when I do not. How else could we explain his saying that 'I find by experience' that some ideas are 'exterior' to my mind in a sense which implies their existing 'during the intervals between the times of my perceiving them'. The mistake is a bad one anyway; but my diagnosis shows how it could represent not childish incompetence but rather Berkeley's falling into a trap laid by his own terminology.

But there is no muddle, no mistake, and no entrapment. Philonous's premiss is that I am not the cause of my ideas. His conclusion is that they exist in another mind, and his reasoning (suppressed, I suggest, because he finds it so obvious) turns on the denial of blind agency. My ideas must have *some* cause, that cause can only be a spirit, and it therefore follows, by virtue of the denial of blind agency, that the spirit must itself have the ideas it causes, because unless it had them, it could not bring them about. Their existence 'during the intervals between the times of my perceiving them' is, I think, simply assumed at the

---

[18] *Locke, Berkeley, Hume*, p. 168.

[19] Ibid., pp. 170–1. Pitcher agrees with Bennett that Berkeley's argument conflates 'two quite distinct conceptions of an idea's *depending on* a mind' (p. 177). Bennett's accusation is also endorsed by I. C. Tipton, *Berkeley: The Philosophy of Immaterialism*, London, 1974, pp. 323, 383–4.

[20] Bennett, pp. 170–1.

outset, and then carried down to the argument's conclusion, though it could perhaps be thought to follow from the immutability of the mind in which sensible things have been proven to reside. That this reading of the argument does not import a concern with God's will into the passage is made clear by the way the passage ends, in lines Bennett omits from his quotation: 'And as the same is true,' Philonous continues, 'with regard to all other finite created spirits, it necessarily follows, there is an *omnipresent eternal Mind,* which knows and comprehends all things, and *exhibits* [my emphasis] them to our view in such a manner, and according to such rules as he himself hath *ordained* [my emphasis again], and are by us termed the *Laws of Nature.*' (*Works* II, p. 231.)

Bennett is at the very least hasty in supposing that there is no other explanation for Berkeley's inference than the muddle he attributes to him. But are there grounds for preferring my reading over Bennett's, beyond a desire to see Berkeley as subtle rather than confused? My reading is clinched, it seems to me, by some of the passages in which Berkeley presents what Bennett calls the 'passivity argument' for the existence of God, which differs from the continuity argument in appealing, according to Bennett, not to the continued existence of unperceived objects, but to the fact that 'my ideas of sense come into my mind without being caused to do so by any act of my will.'[21] At *Principles* 29, for example, Berkeley says that because ideas of sense 'have not a . . . dependence on my will', there must be 'some other will or spirit that produces them'. In the following section that will or spirit is identified with God. In this case Bennett is not tempted to say that Berkeley exploits an ambiguity. According to Bennett's own compilation, the word 'dependence' here has its causal sense;[22] the argument turns on the premiss that an idea that is not caused by me must be caused by another spirit. Now consider the following passage, which Bennett regards as 'the clearest possible presentation of the passivity argument'.[23]

PHILONOUS. Nor is it less plain that these ideas or things by me perceived, either themselves or their archetypes, exist independently of my mind, since I know myself not to be their author, it being out of my power to determine at pleasure, what particular ideas I shall be affected with upon opening my eyes or ears. They must therefore exist in some other mind, whose will it is they should be exhibited to me.   (Second Dialogue, pp. 214–15.)

---

[21] Ibid., p. 165. For his summary of the continuity argument, see p. 169.
[22] Ibid., p. 168 n. 9.   [23] Ibid., p. 185.

Does Berkeley exploit the ambiguity of 'independently' here? Again, Bennett says 'no; the sense of 'independently' is purely causal.[24] But this version of the passivity argument goes beyond the one at *Principles* 29—which concludes that there is a spirit who *causes* my ideas of sense—in claiming that my ideas or archetypes 'exist in some other mind'. Bennett is surely right to refrain from saying that Berkeley derives this further conclusion by exploiting the ambiguity of 'independently'. But then how does he do it? The answer, of course, is that he exploits the denial of blind agency. In so far as the present argument duplicates *Principles* 29, it establishes the existence of an external spirit that is the cause of ideas of sense. It can go beyond *Principles* 29 only by committing the same mistake Bennett finds in the continuity argument (and, to his credit, fails to find here), or by appealing to the denial of blind agency. So even Bennett needs to attribute the denial to Berkeley. Why not say, then, that the denial is at work even in the so-called continuity argument? Bennett might reply that the two arguments are very different. But if we look closely at the continuity argument (pp. 230–1, quoted above on p. 212), we find that the only difference between the two arguments is that on pp. 230–1, the ideas or objects in 'some other mind' are said to exist 'during the intervals between the time of my perceiving them'.

If Berkeley can derive the *existence* of ideas in another mind without exploiting the ambiguity of 'depend', surely he can derive their *continued* existence without exploiting it—especially if the other spirit in which ideas exist is immutable. *The ambiguity of 'depend' has nothing in particular to do with* continuous *existence.* The continuity argument, far from constituting an independent argument for the existence of God, is simply a modification or elaboration of the passivity argument, or an adaptation of the passivity argument to the problem of intermittency (as the context of its appearance on pp. 230–1 suggests). The passivity argument establishes the existence of God, and the continuity argument merely adds that God continues to perceive whatever continues to exist when we do not perceive it.

It is, incidentally, no objection to this reading that it attributes to Philonous the view that the cause of my ideas has the same ideas that I have. In the Third Dialogue, Philonous endorses a 'vulgar' use of 'same' which allows exactly this (pp. 247–8). Anyone willing to say that the same idea can exist in different minds is free to speak of ideas 'or

---

[24] Bennett, p. 168, n. 9.

their archetypes' existing in the mind of God, as Philonous does at the beginning of the passage on pp. 214–15.

I have argued that the continuity argument provides no evidence for Bennett's hypothesis that Berkeley conflates causation and inherence. Instead the argument shows the influence of the denial of blind agency. Before returning to the problem of unperceived objects, it would perhaps be useful to say a word about the remaining evidence for Bennett's view. Once passages such as the continuity argument are taken away, the only evidence remaining is a passage in which Berkeley is alleged to exploit the ambiguity in another direction, to move from the fact that ideas must have owners to the conclusion that they must have causes.[25]

Those things which are called the works of Nature, that is, the far greater part of the ideas or sensations perceived by us, are not produced by, or dependent on the wills of men. There is therefore some other spirit that causes them, since it is repugnant that they should subsist by themselves. (*Principles* 146.)

As Bennett remarks, in Berkeley's 'normal usage'—exemplified at *Principles* 89, and deriving perhaps from *Essay* II xxiii 1, where Locke accounts for our assumption of a substratum of perceived qualities in terms of our inability to imagine how simple ideas can 'subsist by themselves'—to say that one entity cannot 'subsist by itself' is to say that it must exist in (or be 'owned by') a substance. Yet *Principles* 146 cannot support Bennett's hypothesis on its own, because in this isolated passage Berkeley might not be using 'subsist by themselves' in his normal way. 'It is repugnant that they should subsist by themselves' might mean 'it is repugnant that they should subsist *in virtue of* themselves—that is, without a cause', a possibility supported by the fact that the lines Bennett quotes from § 146 are immediately followed by a cross-reference to § 29, where Berkeley offers the confusion-free version of the passivity argument we reviewed just a moment ago. It is, moreover, implausible to suggest that Berkeley would feel a need to argue that ideas must have a cause in the manner Bennett suggests.[26] Berkeley already has an argument that ideas must have a cause, based on the observation that ideas are changeable and temporary (see *Principles* 26). It is noteworthy that Locke, after observing that we cannot imagine how simple ideas can 'subsist by themselves', goes on

[25] Ibid., pp. 166–7.
[26] Bennett himself admits that Berkeley may not 'seriously regard' the principle as needing proof (p. 166).

to say that 'we accustom our selves, to suppose some *Substratum*, wherein they do subsist, and from which they do result'. This suggests that at times, even for Locke, the ambiguity Bennett finds in Berkeley's use of 'depend' might extend to 'subsist by themselves'.[27]

I conclude that although there may perhaps be *some* evidence for Bennett's hypothesis, it is very weak, and there is *no* evidence that the ambiguity of 'depend' is exploited in any argument of importance to Berkeley. I hope my argument establishes the interpretive power of the denial of blind agency, even for the understanding of texts in which it is not explicit. I now return to the problem of unperceived objects.

3. *Unperceived objects*

I begin with what Pitcher sees as the main fault of the perception interpretation, considered as a philosophical view.[28]

I have to remark that I think the doctrine is by no means an attractive one. Anyone who wants to, or does, believe that objects continue to exist when no finite creature is observing them—and this includes at least all of mankind who are sane—should not be satisfied with the statement that they merely continue to exist in God's mind. It is, in the first place, little more than a bad joke to claim that a thing exists simply in virtue of the fact that someone has an idea of it in his undertanding—i.e., is thinking of it. . . . The weakness of Berkeley's position can be seen, too, if we remember that God must have ideas of all possible worlds in His mind, in addition to ideas of this actual world. The kind of existence that Berkeley accords to unperceived objects of this world,

---

[27] Bennett traces the ambiguity in Locke's use of 'subsist by themselves' to the ambiguity in his use of 'idea', which, as Locke himself acknowledges at *Essay* II viii 8, sometimes means *idea* (in the sense of *Essay* II i 8) and sometimes means *quality*. To say that ideas (in the strict sense) cannot 'subsist by themselves' is to say they need a cause; to say that qualities cannot subsist by themselves is to say they need a substance in which to inhere (Bennett, pp. 78–9). I am suggesting that when Berkeley says an idea cannot subsist by itself, he may have in mind *either* the need for a cause *or* the need for a substratum. For Berkeley, after all, the commitment to the double use of 'idea' goes even deeper than it does for Locke. Ayers (in 'The Ideas of Power and Substance in Locke's Philosophy', reprinted in Tipton (ed.), *Locke on Human Understanding*, Oxford, 1977, pp. 77–104) has proposed a reading of *Essay* II xxiii 1 that differs from Bennett's. According to Ayers, Locke is in effect replacing the traditional relation between a dependent quality and its independently existing substratum with a causal relation between an object's observable qualities and its real essence. (But see Jonathan Bennett, 'Substratum', *History of Philosophy Quarterly* 4 (1987), 197–215.) I take it that on Ayer's view 'subsist by themselves' remains capable of ambiguity, even if Locke in no way succumbs to it. This is precisely the point I want to make about Berkeley.

[28] *Berkeley*, pp. 171–2.

then, is precisely the kind that objects in merely possible, but non-actual worlds, have—e.g., the kind and amount that a purple man with three heads has. No one, I say, should be satisfied with so little.

Pitcher thinks that according to Berkeley, 'God preserves [objects] in existence by thinking of them—i.e., by having ideas of them in His understanding.' He does not suppose that Berkeley thinks the existence so preserved is 'the usual, first-class kind of existence that belongs to things that are actually perceived' (Pitcher cites *Commentaries* 473, where Berkeley confesses—though in a different context—that he uses the word 'existence' in 'a larger sense than ordinary'), but he does imply that Berkeley regards this second-class kind of existence as enough to satisfy anyone who believes in the existence of unperceived objects.[29] Otherwise there would be no 'bad joke', and Pitcher's claim that 'no one . . . should be satisfied with so little' would not be a criticism of Berkeley.

Pitcher's objection uncovers, I think, the real motivation behind the view that Berkeley's God must perceive in some way that resembles perception by sense. Because God is aware of all possible objects as well as all actual ones, merely being thought of by God cannot be sufficient for the real existence of an object. If divine perception is going to establish real existence, it seems that God has to *register* or somehow *respond* to actual existence—but this is exactly what he cannot do. Any form of awareness that 'waits on' its object is incompatible with God's omnipotence.

If we examine the passages Pitcher offers in support of the perception interpretation, however, we find no evidence that Berkeley thinks merely being thought of by God is sufficient for existence in any sense strong enough to impress or satisfy those who believe in the existence of unperceived objects. Pitcher presents nine selections from the *Dialogues* which, he thinks, support his view.[30] We can divide the selections into two groups. The following passage is typical of the first:

PHILONOUS. Mark it well; I do not say, I see things by perceiving that which represents them in the intelligible substance of God. This I do not understand; but I say, the things by me perceived are known by the understanding, and produced by the will, of an infinite spirit.

(Second Dialogue, p. 215.)

The remaining passages in the first group are the passivity argument in

---

[29] Ibid., pp. 175; 171.
[30] The passages, arranged in three groups, are presented on pp. 175–8.

the Second Dialogue (pp. 214–15, discussed above in connection with Bennett), and the closing words of the continuity argument (Third Dialogue, p. 231, quoted above on p. 213). What unites all three is that they make reference not only to God's understanding, but to his will. The passivity argument concludes that ideas 'must . . . exist in some other mind, whose *will* it is they should be exhibited to me'; 'there is an *omnipresent eternal Mind*,' we are told in the final sentence of the continuity argument, 'which knows and comprehends all things, and *exhibits* them to our view in such a manner, and according to such rules as he himself hath *ordained*.' The vocabulary of volition I have emphasized in quoting these passages—'will', 'exhibits', 'ordained', and in the passage on p. 215, 'produced by the will'—makes them completely unsuitable as evidence for the perception interpretation. Instead of saying that merely being thought of by God is sufficient for existence, the passages in the first group suggest just the opposite.

The six passages in the second group say nothing about God as the cause of our ideas, but they still fail to support the perception interpretation. The following passages are typical:

PHILONOUS. Besides, is there no difference between saying, *there is a God, therefore he perceives all things*: and saying, *sensible things do really exist: and if they really exist, they are necessarily perceived by an infinite mind: therefore there is an infinite mind, or God.* This furnishes you with a direct and immediate demonstration, from a most evident principle, of the *being of a God.*
(Second Dialogue, p. 212.)

PHILONOUS. Every unthinking being is necessarily, and from the very nature of its existence, perceived by some mind; if not by any finite created mind, yet certainly by the infinite mind of God.   (Third Dialogue, p. 236.)

These passages say not only that God perceives all things, but that divine perception is a necessary condition of real existence. They do not, however, say that it is a sufficient condition. It might be replied that they strongly suggest it, but even if they do, we cannot conclude that according to Berkeley, *merely being thought of* by God is sufficient for real existence. It may be that the divine perception sufficient for real existence is not mere intellection, but the perception which, according to the denial of blind agency, must accompany every act of will.

None of the nine passages from the *Dialogues* is a response to the objection that in Berkeley's world, objects lead an intermittent life, and because it is in Berkeley's response to that objection that we would expect to find the strongest support for the perception interpretation, it is natural to turn to *Principles* 45–8, the only place in Berkeley's writings where the intermittency objection is discussed. As stated at *Principles* 45, the objection is 'that from the foregoing principles it follows, things are every moment annihilated and created anew. The objects of sense exist only when they are perceived: the trees therefore are in the garden, or the chairs in the parlour, no longer than while there is some body by to perceive them.' The ensuing responses are carefully graded. First Berkeley challenges the reader to conceive of an idea or archetype existing without the mind (§ 45). He then observes that received principles are 'chargeable with [the same] pretended absurdities' (§ 46). Even if matter exists, he says, it will follow from received principles that particular bodies do not exist when unperceived (§ 47). At § 48 he writes,

If we consider it, the objection proposed in *Sect.* 45 will not be found reasonably charged on the principles we have premised, so as in truth to make any objection at all against our notions. For though we hold indeed the objects of sense to be nothing but ideas which cannot exist unperceived; yet we may not hence conclude they have no existence except only while they are perceived by us, since there may be some other spirit that perceives them, though we do not.

Several commentators have remarked on Berkeley's cageyness here: he does not say that there definitely is another spirit that perceives things when we do not, only that there *may* be one.[31] I think the cageyness is due not to any doubt that God perceives all things, but to doubt about the position that the perception interpretation would have us ascribe to him.[32] Berkeley obviously wants to meet the intermittency objection in the most economical way; this is typical of his dialectical style. He grants that things exist only if they are perceived, but he does not think it follows from this that they exist only if they are perceived *by us*. This is because *being perceived* does not entail *being perceived by us*, and to point out that the entailment fails Berkeley has to say no more than that there *may* be some other spirit that perceives them, though we do not—which is exactly what he does say. Had he said that there *is* such a spirit, he certainly would have succeeded in denying the entailment, but he would also have suggested—in view of the concern with real existence that prompts the intermittency objection—that

[31] See Bennett, pp. 174–5, and Pitcher, p. 174.

[32] For an alternative explanation see Bennett, pp. 174–5, and Pitcher, p. 174.

merely being thought of by God, mere presence in the divine understanding, is all it takes to establish the existence of an object. This, I think, he was unwilling to suggest. A similar point can be made about *Principles* 6, where Berkeley writes, 'So long as [bodies] are not actually perceived by me, or do not exist in my mind or that of any other created spirit, they must either have no existence at all, or else subsist in the mind of some eternal spirit.' Here Berkeley emphasizes the *necessity* of perception for a body's existence; he says nothing about the *sufficiency* of perception for existence—at least not in the sense of 'existence' that he so carefully delineates just a few lines before in § 3.

There is, then, no support for the perception interpretation in the passages usually claimed for it. And there is an even more serious problem: there are some passages plainly inconsistent with it.

HYLAS. What shall we make then of the Creation?
PHILONOUS. May we not understand it to have been entirely in respect of finite spirits; so that things, with regard to us, may properly be said to begin their existence, or be created, when God decreed they should become perceptible to intelligent creatures, in that order and manner which he then established, and we now call the laws of Nature? You may call this a *relative*, or *hypothetical existence* if you please.   (Third Dialogue, p. 253.)

PHILONOUS. What would you have! do I not acknowledge a twofold state of things, the one ectypal or natural, the other archetypal and eternal? The former was created in time; the latter existed from everlasting in the mind of God.   (p. 254.)

The most important point in these passages about creation—and the one hardest to grasp, because it runs counter to our natural assumptions—is that *real* existence is *relative, hypothetical*, and *ectypal*. Existence that sounds as if it is really 'first-class' (to borrow an expression from Pitcher)—existence that is absolute, non-hypothetical, and archetypal—turns out on Berkeley's view to be insufficient for 'real' existence. These passages indicate that if we hope to understand Berkeley, we have to turn the Platonic associations of the word 'real' on their heads. 'Real' existence is not the kind of existence that every eternal entity automatically enjoys. Real existence for Berkeley is something that is entirely *relative to us*.

In the passages about creation it is God's will that is responsible for the existence of things. Far from representing a 'brief interlude' or passing flirtation, as Pitcher alleges,[33] they express a view that Berkeley

---

[33] Pitcher, p. 172.

affirms in an important letter to Percival, who had conveyed to Berkeley Lady Percival's concern that the immaterialism of the *Principles* might be inconsistent with the Mosaic story of creation. Berkeley writes,

I do not deny the existence of any of those sensible things which Moses says were created by God. They existed from all eternity in the Divine intellect, and then became perceptible (*i.e.* were created) in the same manner and order as is described in Genesis. For I take creation to belong to things only as they respect finite spirits, there being nothing new to God. Hence it follows that the act of creation consists in God's willing that those things should be perceptible to other spirits, which before were known only to Himself. Now both reason and scripture assure us there are other spirits (as angels of different orders, &c.) besides man, who, 'tis possible might have perceived this visible world according as it was successively exhibited to their view before man's creation. Besides, for to agree with the Mosaic account of creation it is sufficient if we suppose that a man, in case he was then created and existing at the time of the chaos, might have perceived all things formed out of it in the very order set down in Scripture, which is no ways repugnant to our principles. (*Works* VIII, pp. 37–8.)

The date of the letter—6 September 1710, just four months after the publication of the *Principles*, and more than two years before Berkeley arrived in London with the manuscript of the *Dialogues*—suggests that Berkeley held Philonous's view of creation when he wrote the earlier book. This is no brief interlude. Pitcher might reply that even if Berkeley held this view of creation throughout his life, it need not have influenced his views on unperceived objects when considered outside of a Biblical context. But this is very unlikely—and not only because of the close connections between Berkeley's religious and philosophical opinions. Note for example how well the passages about creation fit in with Berkeley's account of the reality of ideas of sense. Ideas of sense, he explains, are stronger, livelier, and more distinct than ideas of imagination (*Principles* 30). They 'have likewise a steadiness, order, and coherence' that ideas of imagination lack (§ 30), and exceed them in their regularity, vivacity, and constancy (§ 33). All these properties are a function of God's will (see §§ 29–33). On the perception interpretation, this account of reality and real existence must be called incomplete. It tells us what real existence is when it comes to ideas of sense—it provides, in other words, an account of real existence 'in respect of finite spirits'—but a complete theory would require the addition of an account of real existence 'in respect of God'. But there is no evidence that Berkeley regards *Principles* 29–33 as anything but a complete account. It gives a full theory of real existence, and just the one that the passages about creation call for.

The same passages about creation that rule out the perception interpretation give the phenomenalist interpretation its most convincing support. For they not only affirm that existence depends on the will of God, but assert the existence of objects when there is no human mind to perceive them. They share this second feature with the continuity argument, but that argument, unlike the passages about creation, does not ground the existence of unperceived objects in a kind of perceptibility—dependent only on the will of God—that can obtain even in the absence of finite spirits. The main obstacle to the phenomenalist interpretation has always been the large number of passages that seem to support the perception interpretation. But now that we have seen that they do not in fact support it, the way has been cleared for my own interpretation, which enables the phenomenalist interpretation to take account of the passages that once seemed to favour its rival.

I agree with the phenomenalist interpretation that according to Berkeley, an object exists if and only if God intends to cause certain ideas in the minds of finite spirits. Because God's intentions do not depend on the existence of finite spirits, objects can exist even if we do not. But when they do, they are not unperceived. Thanks to the denial of blind agency, God perceives every idea *by virtue of his intention to cause it.* If God did not perceive the idea, he could not intend to bring it about. Objects owe their existence to divine volitions, but those volitions cannot exist apart from the appropriate divine perceptions. The texts usually offered on behalf of the perception interpretation are therefore consistent with the phenomenalist interpretation, once it has been supplemented by the denial of blind agency. The mistake of the perception interpretation lies not in thinking that being perceived by God is necessary for the existence of an idea or object, or even in thinking that divine perception of some sort is sufficient, but in supposing that the contribution of perception to the reality of things is distinct from its role in constituting a volition, so that it seems as if the perception—quite apart from the volition—might support the real existence of an object on its own. On my interpretation, God certainly perceives all things, but his perception—in so far as it contributes to real existence—is nothing more than the perception inevitably involved in his volition. God's knowledge of real existence therefore derives entirely from his acquaintance with his will. As Malebranche says of God, 'He sees in His essence the ideas or essences of all possible beings, and in His volitions (He sees) their existence and all its circumstances.'[34] Berkeley does not share Malebranche's views on God's vision of essence, but he agrees with him, I think, that God's knowledge of real existence is acquired by attending to his will, and to his ideas only in so far as they are involved in his will.

A standard objection to including divine ideas in Berkeley's system is that they are superfluous. 'There seems', as J. D. Mabbott writes, 'to be no need whatever in such a system for the realm of God's ideas.'[35] Mabbott is right to hold that because God's ideas are, like all ideas, passive and inert, they can make no *causal* contribution to the reality of things. And if the phenomenalist interpretation is correct in holding that Berkeley does not identify objects with ideas or collections of them, then divine ideas are not required so that we will have suitable entities with which to identify objects. But despite all this divine ideas are not, on my view, superfluous, because without them God would not only be unable to perceive, but unable to will.

Perhaps the strongest support for my interpretation is the dramatic denial of blind agency at *Philosophical Commentaries* 812, already quoted on p. 208 above.

G.S.   The propertys of all things are in God i.e. there is in the Deity Understanding as well as Will. He is no Blind agent & in truth a blind Agent is a Contradiction.

Although this is not the only way to read the entry, it seems to me that Berkeley is deriving the conclusion that God perceives the properties of all things from the fact that he is the cause of all things. This is exactly what my interpretation requires. A similar inference may also be at work between *Commentaries* 674, where the denial of blind agency makes its first appearance in the notebooks, and entry 675. I quoted part of 674 above; I now quote it in its context.

[34] *The Search after Truth*, Bk. IV, chap. 11, § 3, p. 319 in Lennon and Olscamp. See also the Tenth Elucidation (p. 617, trans. by Lennon): 'It is certain that God contains within Himself in an intelligible fashion the perfection of all the beings He has created or can create, and that through these intelligible perfections He knows the essences of all things, as through His volitions He knows their existence.'

[35] 'The Place of God in Berkeley's Philosophy', p. 369. I too have suggested (mistakenly, I now believe) that God's ideas are superfluous. See my introd. to the *Principles*, Indianapolis, 1982, pp. xxxii–xxxiii.

S   Things are two-fold active or inactive, The Existence of Active   673
        things is to act, of inactive to be perceiv'd.

S.E.   Distinct from or without perception there is no volition; therefore   674
        neither is their existence without perception.

G   God May comprehend all Ideas even the Ideas wch are painfull &   675
        unpleasant without being in any degree pained thereby. Thus we
        our selves can imagine the pain of a burn etc without any misery
        or uneasiness at all.

The word 'their' in 674 refers back to the active things of 673. The
conclusion of 674, then, is that active things cannot exist 'without
perception'—that is, without perceiving, because perceiving is required
for their volitional activity. In the next entry Berkeley goes on to suggest
that God comprehends all things, inferring it, I think, from the
conclusion of 674. Entry 675 then says, in effect, 'God may
comprehend all ideas—including pain—without thereby being
pained, because he perceives pain not as its subject but as its cause.'[36]

4. Two objections

My modification of the phenomenalist interpretation helps to solve or
clarify a number of difficulties in the interpretation of Berkeley. But
before I go on to consider some of its advantages I want to take up two
objections that might be made against it. The first takes issue with the
extent to which I agree with the phenomenalist interpretation, and the
second with the extent to which I deviate from it.

According to the first objection, if Berkeley is a phenomenalist about
unperceived objects, then presumably he is a phenomenalist generally.
But, the objection continues, he is not: his frequent identifications of
objects with ideas or collections of ideas show that he is unprepared to
dispense with objects as entities, and unwilling to treat statements
about objects as the proper subject of analysis. Now I cannot deny that

---

[36] For interpretations similar to the one proposed in this section but differently
developed see Charles J. McCracken, 'What *Does* Berkeley's God See in the Quad?',
Archiv für Geschichte der Philosophie 61 (1979), 280–92, esp. pp. 288–90; and Noel
Fleming, 'The Tree in the Quad', *American Philosophical Quarterly* 22 (1985), 25–36.
Tipton anticipates all three interpretations in n. 12 on p. 385 of *Berkeley: The Philosophy
of Immaterialism*. The interpretations are all very close to the view Pitcher says Berkeley
should have adopted; see Pitcher, *Berkeley*, p. 169. A. C. Grayling gives a persuasive
defence of a somewhat different interpretation in *Berkeley: The Central Arguments*,
London, 1986, pp. 95–117.

there is in Berkeley a tendency to view objects as collections of ideas. But not even the most militant defenders of the idealist interpretation deny the presence of the phenomenalist tendency I have focused on,[37] and if Berkeley's comments on creation are the controlling texts for his views on unperceived objects—as I think they must be, in view of my modification of the phenomenalist interpretation and my re-reading of the apparently recalcitrant passages usually regarded as support for the perception interpretation—then instead of saying that the phenomenalist interpretation of Berkeley on unperceived objects is *wrong*, we should say, at the very least, that his views on unperceived objects are inconsistent with his views on objects generally. I argued in Chapter 6 that phenomenalism can be defended as Berkeley's considered view on objects in general. It has at least as strong a claim on the basis of the texts, and a stronger claim if we attempt to draw from the texts the philosophical view that gives them the greatest coherence. In Chapter 6 I did confess that Berkeley's statements of phenomenalism are, by contemporary standards, defective. In the passages about creation there is some improvement, but even here we see him appealing to the existence of 'angels of different orders' before he settles on the position that phenomenalism so clearly recommends. But it would be unreasonable to expect Berkeley's grasp of phenomenalism to be as firm as our own, strengthened as it is by years of familiarity with a distinction between levels of discourse which finds, in Berkeley's famous remark about thinking with the learned and speaking with the vulgar (*Principles* 51), one of its most striking anticipations.

The second objection is directed against my modification of the phenomenalist interpretation. 'No doubt the denial of blind agency *would* allow Berkeley to derive God's perceiving all things from his causing all things,' the objection runs. 'But outside of his notebooks, where it *may* appear at 812 and 673–5, the derivation simply cannot be

---

[37] See Bennett, *Locke, Berkeley, Hume*, pp. 135–9, for a discussion of the differences between 'idealism' and 'phenomenalism'. Bennett's acknowledgements of the phenomenalist tendency are scattered throughout his book: p. 146, on the phenomenalist passages I quote from the *Principles* on p. 199 above; p. 152, where Bennett recognizes in Berkeley's theory of real existence 'a vehicle of a kind of phenomenalism which runs, presumably entirely unrecognized, all through' both the *Principles* and the *Dialogues*; pp. 176–7, on Berkeley's published views on creation. Bennett discusses Berkeley's theory of real things on pp. 160–4; see in particular p. 162, where Berkeley is said to 'move towards phenomenalism when discussing "real things"'. Another recent commentator who reads Berkeley as an idealist but nevertheless recognizes his phenomenalist tendencies is John Foster, *The Case for Idealism*, London, 1982, pp. 17–32. See in particular pp. 22–6.

found. In the *Dialogues*, for example, Philonous often says that God perceives all things, but he never says what your interpretation requires him to say, that God perceives all things *because* he wills them.' Not only does Philonous never say this, but he passes up two perfect opportunities to do so. One opportunity comes in the Third Dialogue, where Hylas says,

We agree in the thing, but differ in the name. That we are affected with ideas from without is evident; and it is no less evident, that there must be (I will not say archetypes, but) powers without the mind, corresponding to those ideas. And as these powers cannot subsist by themselves, there is some subject of them necessarily to be admitted, which I call *matter*, and you call *spirit*. This is all the difference. (p. 239.)

Philonous responds by trying to convince Hylas that the external powers they both acknowledge reside not in matter or some mysterious '*third nature*' but in spirit or mind. Philonous first establishes the existence of will in the external power. From his ideas ('the effects I see produced') he infers actions; from actions, volitions; and from volitions, will. Then in an apparently separate argument he establishes the existence of an external understanding. 'Again, the things I perceive have an existence, they or their archetypes, out of my mind: but being ideas, neither they nor their archetypes can exist otherwise than in an understanding: there is therefore an understanding.' (p. 240.) It is only at this point—with an external will and an external understanding established by separate means—that Philonous goes on to assert the existence of an external spirit. 'But will and understanding constitute in the strictest sense mind or spirit. The powerful cause therefore of my ideas, is in strict propriety of speech a *spirit*.' (p. 240.) Now if the interpretation I have been defending is correct, why doesn't Philonous make explicit use of the denial of blind agency to move directly from the external power as will to the external power as understanding? Such a use of the denial would not only make his separate argument for an external understanding unnecessary, but would secure the unity of the external will and understanding, something the existing argument assumes but does not justify.

The second opportunity comes in the following exchange, which also takes place in the Third Dialogue.

HYLAS. Yes, Philonous, I grant the existence of a sensible thing consists in being perceivable, but not in being actually perceived.

PHILONOUS. And what is perceivable but an idea? And can an idea exist without being actually perceived? (p. 234.)

Bennett calls this an 'anti-phenomenalist skirmish',[38] but in its general drift—from being perceivable to being perceived—it is not inconsistent with the phenomenalist interpretation, modified as I propose. In fact such a drift is just what my modification demands, but here too, Philonous passes up a perfect opportunity to make explicit use of the denial of blind agency. Why?

Such passed opportunities are not necessarily a stumbling block for my interpretation. The passages are, after all, consistent with the denial of blind agency, and although the denial is not explicit in either one, it could be what moves each of them along. In the first passage, for example, the denial—applied to the sub-conclusion that there is an external will—could be the source of the first premiss in the argument for an external understanding. As the passage stands, this premiss seems to come out of nowhere. And the denial would explain Philonous's confidence that the external will and understanding belong to a single spirit. But however the passed opportunities are handled, by interpretation still does better than its rivals. The perception interpretation is inconsistent with Berkeley's considered view of creation. Its most distinctive element—the claim that according to Berkeley, God preserves objects in existence simply by thinking of them—is not supported by a single passage in the *Principles* or the *Dialogues*. The phenomenalist interpretation, in its familiar form, cannot take account of the passages usually offered as evidence for the perception interpretation, and it cries out for supplementation by a denial of blind agency which is obviously true, accepted by the philosophers Berkeley studied most carefully, enthusiastically endorsed in Berkeley's notebooks, and reaffirmed in works published after the *Dialogues*. All the textual evidence for either of the familiar interpretations becomes evidence for my interpretation, which, unlike the others, attributes to Berkeley a position of considerable power and coherence. It is true that in his published works, Berkeley never says that the contribution of God's perception to real existence is exhausted by its contribution to divine volition; nor does he explicitly derive

---

[38] Bennett, p. 150. I think Bennett gets off on the wrong foot when he describes this passage as 'Berkeley's only explicit, published consideration of phenomenalism as a theoretical alternative to idealism' (p. 150). The passage shows no explicit concern with the *meaning* of statements such as 'There is a table in my study'; it says nothing about statements and nothing about meanings.

God's perceiving all things from his causing all things. But the materials of the derivation—the belief that God is the cause of all things in nature, and the denial of blind agency—are available to Berkeley in the *Principles* and the *Dialogues*, and if we add to them the account of real existence contained in the passages about creation (which is simply the account of *Principles* 29–33, regarded as a complete account), they yield what my interpretation requires, the conclusion that God's perception of all things, in so far as it contributes to real existence, is an inescapable component of his creative acts.

5. *Archetypes*

I want to close this chapter by indicating some of the ways in which my proposal helps to solve or clarify long-standing problems in the interpretation of Berkeley. One of the most prominent of those problems is the existence and nature of archetypes. On my interpretation, to say that divine ideas are archetypes is just to say that God has ideas of the ideas he causes in us, or (taking into account Berkeley's relaxed attitude towards sameness) that he has the *same* ideas he causes in us. Because God is the cause, it is appropriate to speak of his ideas as patterns, originals, or archetypes. There is no need to be troubled over further details of the relationship between God's ideas and our own. If we understand the relation between cause and effect, as well as the relation of idea to action in a spiritual cause, there is no separate relation of idea to archetype that remains to be understood. Berkeley is presumably committed to the view that God's ideas are in some way resemblances of our own (how else could they be ideas 'of' ours?), but this should occasion no difficulty. Any difficulty it does occasion can be put down to the limitations of a finite mind. In view of the inescapability of the conclusion that ideas of sense have a spiritual cause who knows and comprehends all things, it would be rash to respond in any other way. As Locke says, 'God is a simple being, omniscient, that knows all things possible; and omnipotent, that can do or make all things possible. But how he knows, or how he makes, I do not conceive: his ways of knowing as well as his ways of creating, are to me incomprehensible.'[39]

---

[39] *An Examination of P. Malebranche's Opinion* § 52, in *Works*, London, 1823, vol. 9, p. 255.

This is a modest view of the archetypes. But there is no text outside of *Siris*, which I take up below, that calls for a bolder construal. That Berkeley was reluctant to commit himself to an elaborate view on archetypes comes out very clearly in his correspondence with Samuel Johnson. In Johnson's first letter there are several questions about archetypes, but in his reply Berkeley says nothing about them. In the next letter Johnson brings up the issue again, this time as the first item in his list of difficulties. Here is all that Berkeley has to say in response:

I have no objection against calling the ideas in the mind of God archetypes of ours. But I object against those archetypes by philosophers supposed to be real things, and to have an absolute rational existence distinct from their being perceived by any mind whatsoever; it being the opinion of all materialists that an ideal existence in the Divine Mind is one thing, and the real existence of material things another. (*Works* II, p. 292.)

We should not be led by this to suppose that if the materialists throw matter out of their systems, they will be left with divine archetypes that Berkeley would embrace. Take for example the case of Malebranche. If we eliminate the Malebranchean material world, we are still left with the divine ideas of the objects in that world—ideas that represent the essences of the departed objects. We have, as it were, the Malebranchean God as he existed before creation, a God whose mind represents objects as they really are, or really would be. Malebranchean divine ideas are ideas of 'intelligible extension', and in their exclusion of secondary qualities they resemble the ideas of corpuscular real essences that would be possessed by a Lockean God, or the clear and distinct idea of matter that would be possessed by a Cartesian one. Berkeley has no use for such ideas, not because he has no use for the distinction between primary and secondary qualities, but because he has no use for the notion of essence, or for the primary/secondary quality distinction in connection with the notion of essence.[40] Berkeley, then, eliminates not only the Malebranchean material world, but the divine ideas representing such a world.

In his first letter, Johnson proposes a more modest, non-Malebranchean kind of archetype.

Is it not therefore your meaning, that the existence of our ideas (*i.e.* the ectypal things) depends upon our perceiving them, yet there are external to any created mind, in the all-comprehending Spirit, real and permanent archetypes

[40] On this see Chap. 8 below.

(as stable and permanent as ever matter was thought to be), to which these ideas of ours are correspondent, and so that (tho' our visible and tangible ideas are *toto coelo* different and distinct things, yet) there may be said to be external to my mind, in the divine mind, an archetype (for instance of the candle that is before me) in which the originals of both my visible and tangible ideas, light, heat, whiteness, softness, etc., under such a particular cylindrical figure, are united, so that it may be properly said to be the same thing that I both see and feel? (*Works* II, p. 275.)

Berkeley says nothing about archetypes in his reply, and Johnson, as we have seen, is forced to repeat his questions in his second letter. In the second letter he is again concerned with sameness—not, however, the sameness of the objects of sight and touch, but the sameness of objects perceived by distinct observers.

For it is as evident that your idea is not mine nor mine yours when we say we both look on the same tree, as that you are not I, nor I you. But in having each our idea, we being dependent upon and impressed upon by the same almighty mind, wherein you say this tree exists, while we shut our eyes (and doubtless you mean the same also, while they are open), our several trees must, I think, be so many pictures (if I may so call them) of the one original, the tree in the infinite mind, and so of all other things. Thus I understand you—not indeed that our ideas are in any measure adequate resemblances of the system in the divine mind, but however that they are just and true resemblances or copies of it, so far as He is pleased to communicate His mind to us. (*Works* II, p. 286.)

Berkeley's reaction was, as we have seen, hardly enthusiastic: 'I have no objection against calling the ideas in the mind of God archetypes of ours.' Johnson's second letter was inspired, no doubt, by the answer Philonous gives to Hylas's observation that the external archetypes supposed by the materialists allow them to say that distinct observers perceive the same thing. Philonous says,

And (not to mention your having discarded those archetypes) so may you suppose an external archetype on my principles: *external*, I mean, to your own mind; though indeed it must be supposed to exist in that mind which comprehends all things; but then this serves all the ends of identity, as well as if it existed out of a mind. (Third Dialogue, p. 248.)

Here Philonous displays the same cageyness Berkeley displays in dealing with the intermittency objection. Philonous does *not* endorse archetypes for the sake of securing 'all the ends of identity'. He merely tells Hylas that external archetypes are consistent with immaterialist principles, and that they serve the ends of identity as well as material

ones. Just a page before Philonous had said that if we use the word
'same' in its 'vulgar acceptation', we can say that distinct observers
perceive the same thing, simply because their ideas are alike. His
disparaging remarks about the philosopher's 'abstracted notion of
identity' make it clear that the vulgar acceptation—and the method of
securing the 'ends of identity' that goes along with it—is the one he
favours. As for Johnson's earlier interpretation of the archetypes—as
objects that somehow unify the ideas of sight and touch—there is no
evidence that Berkeley has any interest in it at all.

Berkeley's archetypes, then, are not Malebranchean divine ideas, or
Johnsonian unifiers of the ideas of distinct observers or different
senses. It is interesting that in the following passage from his *Elementa
Philosophica*, a book dedicated to Berkeley and '*in a particular Manner
beholden to that excellent Philosopher*', Johnson's archetypes conform to
the minimalist interpretation that I have proposed for Berkeley.[41]

Indeed [God] may be said to have a Form, Idea, or *Archetype* in His infinite,
all-comprehending Mind, conformable to which He acts; but this can mean no
more than that all Things which He produceth are always present with Him,
and perfectly known to Him, with all their Relations and Connections,
antecedent to their Production, and that He produceth them conformable to
His own Knowledge, Design and Contrivance, being the Plan which He hath
formed.—And that Existence of Things in the divine eternal Mind (if it may
be so called) as being perfectly known to Him, antecedent to their Production,
is called their *Archetypal State*; and their Existence in *Rerum Natura*, as being
actually produced by His Will and Power, and thereby perceived and known to
us, is called their *Ectypal State*.

In thinking about Berkeleyan archetypes it is important to bear in
mind Berkeley's belief that experience is a text, authored by God in the
language of ideas for the sake of our well-being. In view of this belief it
would be odd for Berkeley to have any view of the divine archetypes, in
so far as they contribute to the ectypal state of things, that goes beyond
the interpretation I have recommended here. H. W. B. Joseph once
remarked on a peculiarity of Berkeley's language of nature: it is a
system of signs which do not refer to a realm of things beyond
themselves.[42] The signs refer instead to one another, though the
language as a whole may be said to signify the presence of God. The
signs of the divine language, then, convey information, *but it is*

[41] *Elementa Philosophica*, Philadelphia, 1752, 'Noetica', p. 23. The acknowledgement
of Berkeley's influence is on p. vii of the 'Noetica'.
[42] Joseph, p. 10. He considers the peculiarity a 'fault' or 'confusion'.

information about other ideas of sense. To see the divine archetypes as something more than whatever is required for God to cause our ideas is to suppose that the archetypes embody information which even *God* takes to be interesting. *But in Berkeley's world there is no such interesting information.* Such information does exist in a Malebranchean world, even if we drive matter out of it, because the divine ideas that remain represent matter as it really as, or would really be if only it existed. For Berkeley there is no such thing as the essence or nature of the material world, and therefore nothing for God's ideas to represent, apart from the ideas of sense he intends to cause in us.

6. *Archetypes in* Siris

It has been suggested that the divine ideas of Berkeley's *Siris* are the archetypes of the *Three Dialogues*.[43] Because what Berkeley says about divine ideas seems to go beyond what my interpretation requires, it might be thought that my interpretation is too modest after all, or that I must at any rate admit that *Siris* represents a development beyond the view of archetypes I find in the earlier works.

I do think *Siris* represents a development of Berkeley's earlier views, but *not* of his views on archetypes. The divine ideas that interest Berkeley in *Siris* are ideas 'such as being, beauty, goodness, likeness, parity' (§ 308), or 'goodness, beauty, virtue, and suchlike' (§ 335). These are not archetypes of natural objects in any sense that connects them with the archetypes of the earlier works. They are not natural essences, Johnsonian unifiers of diverse ideas, or perspective-free representations of objects. At *Siris* 306 Berkeley does report that Plato's scheme includes 'a form or species that is neither generated nor destroyed, unchangeable, invisible, and altogether imperceptible to sense'. But if Berkeley endorses the existence of such forms or species, the surrounding texts make it clear that they are forms or species of *spiritual* objects, not natural ones.

It is also a mistake to suggest that the divine ideas of *Siris* are abstract ideas in the sense at issue in the *Principles* and the *Dialogues*.[44]

---

[43] See Peter S. Wenz, 'Berkeley's Two Concepts of Impossibility: A Reply to McKim', *Journal of the History of Ideas* 43 (1982), 673–80, and the refs. he provides on pp. 679–80.

[44] The suggestion has been made by Wenz, 'Berkeley's Christian Neo-Platonism', *Journal of the History of Ideas* 37 (1976), 537–46.

It has been argued that they are, and that the endorsement of divine ideas in *Siris* is consistent with the attack on abstraction in the *Principles* because the attack is meant only to show that abstract ideas are impossible *for us*, not that they are impossible for God.[45] This is misguided in two respects: first, the abstraction Berkeley attacks in the *Principles* is, he thinks, impossible for any mind, finite or infinite;[46] second, the ideas Berkeley endorses in *Siris* exist not only in the divine mind, but exist—even if only as something glimpsed—in finite minds (see, for example, §§ 330 and 336).

In *Siris*, Berkeley does speak with approval of abstract entities, but they are said to be abstract in a way that is deliberately contrasted with the abstraction attacked in the *Principles*. At *Siris* 323 Berkeley reports and apparently accepts the view that

God is a Mind, χωριστὸν εἶδος—not an abstract idea compounded of inconsistencies, and prescinded from all real things, as some moderns understand abstraction; but a really existing Spirit, distinct or separate from all sensible and corporeal beings.

This is meant to recall § 307, where Berkeley says of Aristotle that by 'abstracted, χωριστόν, he understands separable from corporeal beings and sensible qualities'. Berkeley then makes it clear in the following section that if the divine ideas of *Siris* are to be linked with anything in his earlier works, it is with *notions*. § 308 is a survey of opinions on innate ideas. There are some, Berkeley reports, who think the mind is a *tabula rasa*; Plato, on the other hand, 'held original ideas in the mind'. 'Some', however, 'may think the truth to be this',

that there are properly no ideas, or passive objects, in the mind but what were derived from sense: but that there are also besides these her own acts or operations; such are notions.

If we return to Berkeley's examples of divine ideas, we find that they are either 'ideas' we tend to associate with spirit, 'ideas' that might be derived from our notion of spirit, or 'ideas' of relations capable of existing among spirits. They are, in other words, not ideas at all, but

---

[45] See the articles by Wenz.

[46] The suggestion that abstraction might be possible for God betrays a serious misunderstanding of the context of Berkeley's attack on abstraction. The defenders of abstraction regarded the need for abstract ideas as a mark of our *imperfection*. This is made clear by Locke (*Essay* II vii 9), Norris, and Suarez (see Chap. 2, p. 35 above). For a generally sound reply to Wenz see Robert McKim, 'Wenz on Abstract Ideas and Christian Neo-Platonism in Berkeley', *Journal of the History of Ideas* 43 (1982), 665–71. For Wenz's rejoinder see the article cited in n. 43.

notions or aspects of notions. The divine idea of being may look dangerously close to the abstract ideas ridiculed in the *Principles*, but there is no reason to suppose that the author of *Siris* thinks that having the idea is anything other than considering or attending to the being of a spirit—perhaps to the being of one's own self. The divine idea of being, so understood, is as unobjectionable as selective attention to a figure 'merely as triangular', or to Peter 'so far forth as man' (Introduction to the *Principles* 16). None the less it is abstract in the sense of *Siris* 307, 'separable from corporeal beings and sensible qualities', and derived from the mind's own existence, acts, and operations.

My minimalist interpretation of the archetypes, then, is not inconsistent with anything in *Siris*. And even if it were, I must admit that I would not be too disturbed. The aim of the metaphysical sections of *Siris* is to give us 'a glimpse of another world, superior to the sensible, . . . to teach [us] not to neglect the intellectual' (§ 330), and Berkeley is not particularly fussy about how this aim is accomplished: the 'hoary maxims, scattered in this essay', he writes, 'are not proposed as principles, but barely as hints to awaken and exercise the inquisitive reader, on points not beneath the attention of the ablest men' (§ 350). If we can arrive at an interpretation of *Siris* that is consistent with the best interpretation of Berkeley's earlier works, fine; if not, then it is *Siris*, composed of hints rather than principles, that ought to give way.

7. *Mabbott's objections to divine ideas*

Mabbott, in his well-known paper 'The Place of God in Berkeley's Philosophy', gives a number of reasons why divine ideas can have no place in Berkeley's system. One of them I have already considered and rejected, but I want to take up several of the others, and show why they cannot be urged against Berkeley on the interpretation I have proposed.

Mabbott claims that the question of the relationship between God's ideas and our own 'raises all the difficulties of a correspondence theory against which Berkeley fought so persistently'. For example, 'If the reality our ideas represent is the world of God's ideas, Berkeley's principal claim for his theory must fall—his claim that it is a direct theory of perception.'[47] But my interpretation allows Berkeley to

---

[47] Mabbott, pp. 370, 371.

accommodate divine ideas without saying that they constitute the reality our ideas represent. If a direct theory of perception requires that perceivers be in contact with entities called 'objects', then on my interpretation Berkeley's theory is not, of course, direct, because there are (at the deepest level) no 'objects' with which to be in contact.[48] Yet it is not an *indirect* theory either, and this, it seems to me, is what matters most to Berkeley.

Scepticism follows inevitably, Mabbott claims, 'from supposing a difference between our ideas and God's'.[49] But sceptical conclusions of the kind that worry Berkeley cannot be generated by anyone who accepts the view that our ideas are caused by a benevolent and all-powerful being. It is true that a kind of doubt remains possible on my interpretation, but it is not a doubt that Berkeley seeks to eliminate. Berkeley, as we saw in Chapter 6, observes of arguments from perceptual relativity that they do not 'so much prove that there is no extension or colour in an outward object, as that we do not know by sense which is the true extension of colour of the object'. (*Principles* 15.) We do not know the true extension of color *by sense* because our current ideas depend for their truth or reality on how they cohere with ideas we do not at the moment have. We can *reason* our way to conclusions about the truth or reality of current ideas, but such conclusions will be based on what we gather from past experience— and this creates a chance for error and leaves room for doubt. This doubt, however, does not worry Berkeley, for the reasons I gave at the end of Chapter 6.

Finally, Mabbott objects that because all ideas are inert and passive, a purely active God cannot possess them.[50] It is this that accounts, I think, for Mabbott's contention that the denial of blind agency is precluded by Berkeley' main tenets, even though he is aware that Berkeley issues the denial at *Commentaries* 812.[51] Mabbott quotes Philonous's claim that 'I do not understand how our ideas, which are things altogether passive and inert, can be the essence, or any part (or like any part) of the essence or substance of God, who is an impassive, indivisible, purely active being',[52] but this remark, which is directed specifically at Malebranche, does not rule out something Malebranche himself was unwilling to consider: the possibility that ideas exist in the mind of God without being part of his substance or essence. The

---

[48] We are, of course, in direct contact with ideas.
[49] Mabbott, p. 372.   [50] Ibid.   [51] See Mabbott, pp. 377, 370.
[52] Second Dialogue, pp. 213–14. Quoted by Mabbott on p. 372.

presence of ideas in God's mind can be troublesome, I think, only if
that presence demands that the *predicates* of those ideas—'passive', for
example—be predicated in turn of God himself. But if, as Berkeley
maintains at *Principles* 49, perceived qualities need not be predicated of
the perceiving mind, surely the qualities of such qualities need not be.
And the objection can be turned aside in yet another way if we recall
that a divine idea contributes to real existence by providing a volition
with its content or specification. The idea is therefore an essential part
of something active.

8. *Conclusion*

In his second contribution to his correspondence with Clarke, Leibniz
writes that 'the reason why God perceives every thing, is not his bare
presence, but also his operation. 'Tis because he preserves things by
an action, which continually produces whatever is good and perfect in
them.'[53] Leibniz repeats the point several times (see for example pp. 41
and 83), and some of his statements could be inserted into Berkeley's
Principles without disturbing the flow of the argument:

> He perceives them, because they proceed from him; if one may be allowed to
> say, that he *perceives* them: which ought not to be said, unless we divest that
> word of its imperfection; for else it seems to signify, that things act upon him.
> They exist, and are known to him, because he understands and wills them; and
> because what he wills, is the same as what exists. (p. 84.)

Clarke's response is that the belief 'God perceives and knows all
things, not by being present to them, but by continually producing
them anew; is a mere fiction of the schoolmen, without any proof'
(p. 109). No doubt Leibniz was aware of the scholastic precedent, but
he approved of the view because it served to unite two great truths: the
first that God perceives the actual in a way he does not perceive the
merely possible; the second that actual things owe their existence to
the will of God. In this chapter I have tried to show how the denial of
blind agency allows Berkeley to combine the same two truths. If we
accept the perception interpretation, we cannot say that what actually
exists depends on the will of God; this brings us up against Berkeley's
insistence that it does. If we accept the unmodified phenomenalist

---

[53] H. G. Alexander (ed.), *The Leibniz–Clarke Correspondence*, Manchester, 1956, p. 17.
All page refs. in this paragraph are to this edn.

interpretation, we have no reason to say that God's perception of the actual differs from his perception of the merely possible; this brings us up against the criticisms so forcefully expressed by Pitcher. My interpretation offers a way out.

I do not mean to suggest that Berkeley's position is completely free from difficulties. But I do think it is fair to say that Berkeley would not be ruffled by the ones that remain. Some—such as the creation of the world in time—are genuine, but cut equally against materialism (see the Third Dialogue, p. 254). Others call for choices—'Does God have one idea for every idea he causes, or one idea for every family of ideas?'—that Berkeley thinks we needn't make. 'If in every inference we should not agree,' he tells Johnson, 'so long as the main points are settled and well understood, I should be less solicitous about particular conjectures.' (*Works* II, pp. 293–4.) A final feature—I will not say virtue—of my interpretation is that it not only makes this attitude understandable, but shows that it is largely justified.

8
CORPUSCULARIANISM

BERKELEY can see his table simply by returning to his study. Forster's students can see what their rooms look like 'in the vac' simply by cutting short their vacations, and they can see trees in an empty quad just by looking out the window. My concern in the present chapter lies with a more elusive kind of unperceived object—the microscopic parts and submicroscopic particles of seventeenth and eighteenth century science. To perceive parts and particles as diminutive as these it isn't enough to move to a certain location, or turn one's attention in a certain direction. The animalcules in rain-water, the organs of a mite, or the corpuscular constitution of cork cannot be perceived without some kind of sensory enhancement. To the naked senses they are not just unperceived but unperceivable.[1]

1. *The corpuscularian background*

There is no room for doubt that Berkeley accepted the existence of objects already revealed by the magnifying glass or microscope. When he responds to the objection that immaterialism renders 'the clockwork of Nature' vain and useless, Berkeley never questions his interlocutor's view that a great part of that clockwork is 'so wonderfully fine and subtle, as scarce to be discerned by the best microscope' (*Principles* 60). He describes the parts and organs of plants and animals as 'ideas' or '*inefficacious perceptions*'; they are 'discernible only to the curious eye of the philosopher' (§ 64), but they are none the less discernible (and therefore real). Philonous is equally receptive to the testimony of the microscope, which resembles the telescope in

---

[1] In this chap. I deal only incidentally with corpuscularian themes in *Alciphron* and *Siris*. They are discussed by Tipton in 'The "Philosopher by Fire" in Berkeley's *Alciphron*', pp. 159–73 in Turbayne, *Berkeley: Critical and Interpretive Essays*, Minneapolis, 1982, and by Gabriel Moked in 'A Note on Berkeley's Corpuscularian Theories in *Siris*', *Studies in History and Philosophy of Science* 2 (1971), 257–71, and 'Two Central Issues on Bishop Berkeley's "Corpuscularian Philosophy" in the *Siris*', *History of European Ideas* 7 (1986), 633–41.

disclosing objects inaccessible to the naked senses: 'if you take the telescope', he tells Hylas, 'it brings into your sight a new host of stars that escape the naked eye.' (Second Dialogue, p. 211.) These stars are part of a system whose reality only a sceptic would deny. 'What treatment . . . do those philosophers deserve,' Philonous asks, 'who would deprive these noble and delightful scenes of all reality? How should those principles be entertained, that lead us to think all the visible beauty of the creation a false imaginary glare?' (p. 21.) In *Siris* Berkeley approvingly recounts the discoveries of Malpighi and Grew:

Those who have examined the structure of trees and plants by microscopes have discovered an admirable variety of fine capillary tubes and vessels, fitted for several purposes, as the imbibing or attracting of proper nourishment, the distributing thereof through all parts of the vegetable, the discharge of superfluities, the secretion of particular juices. They are found to have ducts answering to the tracheæ in animals, for the conveying of air; they have others answering to lacteals, arteries, and veins. They feed, digest, respire, perspire, and generate their kind, and are provided with organs nicely fitted for all those uses. (§ 29.)

Berkeley probably regarded a belief in the existence of objects disclosed by the microscope as part of educated common sense.[2] Robert Hooke's *Micrographia*, published in 1665, presented its readers with more than thirty plates lavishly delineating such objects as the hooks or bristles on the sole of a fly's foot. Hooke spoke without hesitation of the existence of those objects, and he was equally sure that they were *seen*. Advances in optics, he surmised, may enable us to see even more:[3]

'Tis not unlikely, but that there may be yet invented several other helps for the eye, as much exceeding those already found, as those do the bare eye, such as by which we may perhaps be able to discover living Creatures in the Moon, or other Planets, the figures of the compounding Particles of matter, and the particular Schematisms and Textures of Bodies.

Pope followed Locke in arguing that microscopical eyes would be a danger, but his reason was not that microscopic objects do not exist:

[2] On the penetration of microscopical discoveries into the rest of English culture see Marjorie Hope Nicolson, 'The Microscope and English Imagination', *Smith College Studies in Modern Languages* 16 (1935), particularly pp. 39–44 (on the 'scientific Lady'), 50–6 (on Swift), 56–62 (on the role of the microscope in the quarrel between ancients and moderns), and 67 and 75–7 (on Addison).

[3] Robert Hooke, *Micrographia*, London, 1665, reprinted as vol. 13 of R. T. Gunther (ed.), *Early Science at Oxford*, Oxford, 1938. I quote from the Preface, eighth page.

'Why has not man a microscopic eye?', he asked. 'For this plain reason, man is not a fly.'[4] Microscopical eyes are highly useful to a fly or mite, because they are helped and hindered by objects—*real* objects—too small to be of practical concern to us.

Berkeley's views on what Hooke calls '*the compounding Particles of matter*'—the corpuscular building blocks still beyond the reach of our instruments—are more difficult to determine. At times he is certainly willing to *speak* as if they exist. One reason the moon appears larger on the horizon than in the meridian, he explains, is that the rays of lunar light pass through a wider expanse of atmosphere when the moon is low. The greater the quantity of atmosphere the larger the number of the 'particles' which compose it (*Theory of Vision* 68). The denser sea of particles intercepts a larger number of the moon's rays, producing a fainter appearance which is suggestive of greater size. But does Berkeley really believe in the existence of insensible particles of atmosphere? Or is this just another 'vulgar error' in which he is pretending to share, because it is 'beside [his] purpose to examine and refute it' in a book about vision?[5]

Berkeley refers to a wide range of scientists and philosophers who can be classified as corpuscularians, among them Galileo, Hobbes, Descartes, Boyle, Gassendi, Cudworth, Malebranche, and Newton. Yet the corpuscularian whose voice can be heard most clearly in Berkeley's writings, the one whose book seems to be at Berkeley's side as he fills his notebooks or composes the early entries of the *Principles*, is John Locke. I have chosen to focus on Locke in this chapter partly for this reason, and partly because Berkeley has long been blamed for misinterpreting Locke, and for misleading readers of the *Essay* who came after him. In recent years Berkeley has been defended against this accusation, but he deserves to have it shown in a somewhat different way that his anti-corpuscularian arguments retain their power even when Locke is read in what is now widely held to be the proper way.[6]

I will be treating Locke as a representative corpuscularian. In

---

[4] For Locke see *Essay* II xxiii 12; for Pope see *Essay on Man*, Epistle I, l. 193 f.

[5] The quoted words are taken from *Principles* 44.

[6] Defenders of Berkeley's interpretation of Locke include M. R. Ayers, 'Substance, Reality, and the Great, Dead Philosophers', *American Philosophical Quarterly* 7 (1970), 38–49; Barry Stroud, 'Berkeley *v.* Locke on Primary Qualities', *Philosophy* 55 (1980), 149–66; and Margaret Wilson, 'Did Berkeley Completely Misunderstand the Basis of the Primary–Secondary Quality Distinction in Locke?', in Turbayne, *Berkeley: Critical and Interpretive Essays*, pp. 108–23.

developing his views I will make use of corpuscularian passages from the writings of Boyle, Cudworth, Descartes, and Malebranche. In *Some Thoughts concerning Education*, where he recommends natural philosophy as a study 'necessary for a gentleman in this learned age . . . to fit himself for conversation', Locke says that it makes no difference whether 'Des Cartes be put into his hands' or the young gentleman is exposed instead to 'a short view of that and several others also'.[7] Locke differs from Descartes on a long list of interlocking issues: on the nature or essence of matter, where Locke's agnosticism is opposed to Descartes's confidence that the essence of matter is extension; on the existence of empty space, which Locke affirms and Descartes denies; and on the primary qualities, where Locke follows Boyle in adding solidity to Descartes's list. Despite these disagreements Locke includes Descartes among the 'modern corpuscularians' who 'talk, in most things, more intelligibly' than the scholastics.[8]

But to return to the study of natural philosophy: though the world be full of systems of it, yet I cannot say, I know any one which can be taught a young man as science, wherein he may be sure to find truth and certainty, which is what all sciences give an expectation of. I do not hence conclude, that none of them are to be read; it is necessary for a gentleman in this learned age to look into some of them to fit himself for conversation: but whether that of Des Cartes be put into his hands, as that which is the most in fashion, or it be thought fit to give him a short view of that and several others also; I think the systems of natural philosophy that have obtained in this part of the world, are to be read more to know the hypotheses, and to understand the terms and ways of talking of the several sects, than with hopes to gain thereby a comprehensive scientifical and satisfactory knowledge of the works of nature: only this may be said, that the modern corpuscularians talk, in most things, more intelligibly than the peripatetics, who possessed the schools immediately before them.

His solidarity with Descartes—his recognition that their differences cannot begin to compare with their agreements—makes Locke a perfect target for Berkeley, who cares very little whether extension is seen as the essence of matter or merely as an affection, and who is no less troubled by the belief that space is a void punctuated by solid masses than he is by the belief that space is an extended plenum. From Berkeley's point of view there are two central and unifying corpuscularian doctrines, and Descartes and Locke embrace them both. The first is

---

[7] § 193, p. 185 in vol. 9 of *The Works of John Locke*, London, 1823. Berkeley was familiar with *Some Thoughts* and recommended it; see *Works* VIII, p. 46.
[8] *Some Thoughts concerning Education* § 193, p. 185.

the distinction between primary and secondary qualities. The second is the existence of corpuscles, tiny pieces of matter, too small to be seen or felt, which affect one another by impact or impulse. This broad characterization papers over several differences in addition to the ones already mentioned. Some corpuscularians believed that impact or impulse could explain everything in nature; others doubted that it could, and many who were influenced by Newton were sure that it could not.[9] These differences, like the others, play no important role in Berkeley's argument.

Locke's reason for accepting corpuscularianism is that it goes farther than other hypotheses in giving an intelligible account of the world and our place in it. There is a hint of this belief in the index Locke prepared for the second edition of the *Essay*. Aside from an entry keyed to a definition of *atom*, there is only one entry on corpuscularianism, mechanism, or atomism, and it reads as follows:[10]

CORPUSCULARIAN Philosophy most intelligible.

The passage to which the entry refers praises the corpuscularian philosophy for going farther than any other 'in an intelligible Explication of the Qualities of Bodies' (IV iii 16). Locke's interest in the explication of qualities is primarily an interest in change and the sources of change, in what he describes in the indexed passage as '*the Powers of Substances* to change the sensible Qualities of other Bodies'. This interest extends to the powers of bodies to produce sensations. As Locke employs it, the 'Explication of Qualities' covers both the explication of change in the natural world and the explication of change in the minds of those who perceive that world.

The chief alternative to the corpuscularian philosophy was the scholastic philosophy of substance and accident. 'They who first ran

---

[9] Writers influenced by Newton who opposed the view that mechanism can explain everything in nature included George Cheyne, *Philosophical Principles of Religion, Natural and Revealed*, London, 1715, p. 43; William Whiston, *Astronomical Principles of Religion, Natural and Reveal'd*, London, 1717, pp. 45, 46; and Colin MacLaurin, *An Account of Sir Isaac Newton's Philosophical Discoveries*, London, 1748, p. 95. Some writers influenced by Newton took a position on the powers of matter akin to Malebranche's or Berkeley's. In *A Discourse Concerning the Unchangeable Obligations of Natural Religion*, 6th edn., London, 1724, Samuel Clarke writes that matter is 'evidently not at all capable of any *Laws* or *Powers* whatsoever' (p. 221). 'So that all those things which we commonly say are the Effects of the *Natural Powers of Matter*, and *Laws of Motion*; of *Gravitation, Attraction*, or the like; are indeed (if we will speak strictly and properly) the Effects of *God's* acting upon Matter continually and every moment, either immediately by himself, or mediately by some created intelligent Beings.' (pp. 221–2.)

[10] The entry appears on p. 725 of Nidditch's edn. of the *Essay*.

into the Notion of Accidents, as a sort of real Beings, that needed something to inhere in,' Locke writes at *Essay* II xiii 19, 'were forced to find out the word *Substance*, to support them. Had the poor *Indian* Philosopher (who imagined that the Earth also wanted something to bear it up) but thought of this word *Substance*, he needed not to have been at the trouble to find an Elephant to support it, and a Tortoise to support his Elephant: The word *Substance* would have done it effectually.' In the section that follows he again claims that the scholastics substitute words—related to one another, but cut off entirely from anything beyond them—for understanding:

> Whatever a learned Man may do here, an intelligent *American*, who enquired into the Nature of Things, would scarce take it for a satisfactory Account, if desiring to learn our Architecture, he should be told, That a Pillar was a thing Supported by a *Basis*, and a *Basis* something that supported a Pillar. Would he not think himself mocked, instead of taught, with such an account as this? . . . But were the Latin words *Inhærentia* and *Substantia*, put into the plain English ones that answer them, and were called *Sticking on*, and *Under-propping*, they would better discover to us the very great clearness there is in the Doctrine of *Substance and Accidents*, and shew of what use they are in deciding of Questions in Philosophy.

These passages are usually read as attacks on explanatory appeals to the notion of substance, and they are that in part. But the passages are also aimed at similar appeals to the correlative notion of an accident, conceived of 'as a sort of real Being'. What it means to conceive of an accident in this way can be gleaned from Locke's brief discussion of the privative causes of positive ideas. This discussion, which paves the way for the distinction between primary and secondary qualities, is designed to show that an object can give rise to a positive idea even though there is nothing positive in the object to which the idea corresponds. 'Thus the *Idea* of Heat and Cold, Light and Darkness, White and Black, Motion and Rest,' Locke writes, 'are equally clear and *positive Ideas* in the Mind; though, perhaps, some of *the causes* which produce them, are barely *privations* in those Subjects, from whence our Senses derive those *Ideas*.' (II viii 2.) So much is in fact common ground between Locke and his scholastic opponents.[11] To treat accidents as a sort of real being is, in part, to assign *too many* of our ideas of sense to distinct qualities in bodies, and to attribute *too many* of a body's powers to distinct qualities in which those powers are

---

[11] See Rom Harré, *Matter and Method*, London, 1964, p. 62.

realized. To some extent the common man is guilty of the same mistake:

For if Sugar produce in us the *Ideas*, which we call Whiteness, and Sweetness, we are sure there is a power in Sugar to produce those *Ideas* in our Minds, or else they could not have been produced by it. And so each Sensation answering the Power, that operates on any of our Senses, the *Idea* so produced, is a real *Idea*, (and not a fiction of the Mind, which has no power to produce any simple *Idea*;) and cannot but be adequate, since it ought only to answer that power: and all simple *Ideas* are adequate. 'Tis true, the Things producing in us these simple *Ideas*, are but few of them denominated by us, as if they were only the causes of them; but as if those *Ideas* were real Beings in them. For though Fire be call'd painful to the Touch, whereby is signified the power of producing in us the *Idea* of Pain; yet it is denominated also Light, and Hot; as if Light and Heat, were really something in the Fire, more than a power to excite these *Ideas* in us; and therefore are called *Qualities* in, or of the Fire. (II xxxi 2.)

The common man is guilty of the same mistake, but at least he does not claim to have an explanatory theory. The scholastics do. Their theory fails, Locke thinks, because they do not provide an intelligible account of the way in which the crowd of real qualities is attached to the thing itself. Nor do they explain how the qualities of one thing bring about a change in the qualities of another.

The defects in the scholastic view stand out vividly, Locke thinks, in their theories of perception. Because I am more concerned with the way in which the corpuscularians understood those theories than I am with the theories themselves, I propose to work with the following sketch, offered by Malebranche in *The Search after Truth*. Locke accepts the sketch as an accurate summary of at least one version of the scholastic view.[12]

The most commonly held opinion is that of the Peripatetics, who hold that external objects transmit species that resemble them, and that these species are carried to the common sense by the external senses. They call these species *impressed*, because objects impress them on the external senses. These impressed species, being material and sensible, are made intelligible by the *agent*, or *active intellect*, and can then be received in the *passive intellect*. These

---

[12] The sketch appears in *The Search after Truth*, Bk. III, Pt. ii, chap. 2, p. 220 in Lennon and Olscamp. Locke endorses it in *An Examination of P. Malebranche's Opinion* §§ 9–14, pp. 215–18 in *The Works of John Locke*, vol. 9. For a brief sketch of scholastic views of perception see John Yolton, *Perceptual Acquaintance from Descartes to Reid*, Minneapolis, 1984, pp. 6–10. For a Malebranchean dismissal of real accidents see the *Search*, IV ii 3, p. 446 in Lennon and Olscamp.

species, thus spiritualized, are called *expressed* species, because they are expressed from the impressed species, and through them the *passive intellect* knows material things.

Locke agrees with Malebranche that the scholastics do not intelligibly explain how material species voyage through space to the external senses. But Locke and Malebranche are, I think, committed to finding an even deeper defect, one that fills out our so far partial understanding of what it means to treat an accident as a sort of real being. According to the scholastic theory as Malebranche presents it, a species is capable of a kind of dual existence, first in matter (where it is a *material* species) and then in mind (where it is an *expressed* or *spiritualized* species). A species, then, is more than a modification of matter, for if it were a modification—a determinate way in which matter exists—it could not possibly exist in a spiritualized form. To treat an accident of body as a sort of real being is not only to treat it as a positive quality, as the corpuscularians themselves treated the primary qualities, but to treat it as an entity that can exist apart from matter. In the writings of John Sergeant, a seventeenth-century scholastic, the ability of qualities to lead a double life—one in matter, the other in mind—is quite explicit. The same being or thing, Sergeant writes, has 'diverse *Manners* of Existing; one Corporeal, the other Intellectual or Spiritual'.[13] When we perceive a thing we have what Sergeant calls a *notion* of it. '*A Notion*', he writes, '*is the very thing it self existing in my understanding.*'[14] '*Notions* are the very *Natures* of the Thing, or the *Thing* it self existing in us *intellectually*.'[15] A notion is not to be confused with an idea or phantasm:[16]

For a *Phantasm*, and a *Notion*, differ as widely, as *Body* and *Spirit*; the one being a *Corporeal*, the other a *Spiritual* Resemblance; or rather, the one being a resemblance, or a kind of *Image*, or Picture, the other being the *thing Resembled.*

Sergeant argues that the Lockean view of perception leads to scepticism. 'If I have *only* the *Idea*, and not *the Thing*, in my Knowledge or Understanding,' he writes, then 'I can only know the *Idea*, and *not the Thing*; and, by Consequence, I know nothing *without me*, or nothing in Nature.'[17] We cannot know that an idea resembles a thing, he writes

---

[13] *The Method to Science*, London, 1696, p. 3.
[14] *Solid Philosophy Asserted*, London, 1697, p. 27.
[15] *The Method to Science*, p. 2.   [16] *Solid Philosophy Asserted*, p. 3.
[17] *Solid Philosophy Asserted*, p. 30.

in an argument anticipating Berkeley's defence of the likeness principle in the *Commentaries*, 'unless they be *both* of them *in our comparing Power*'.[18] 'But,' he continues, 'this necessitates that the *Thing it self*, as well as the *Idea*, must be in the Understanding.'[19] 'No Relation', he insists, 'can be known without knowing both the Correlates.'

It is this feature of scholastic theories of perception to which Boyle is objecting in the following passage from 'The Origin of Forms and Qualities':[20]

One thing the modern Schools are wont to teach concerning accidents is too repugnant to our present doctrine to be in this place quite omitted: namely, that there are in natural bodies store of *real qualities* and other *real accidents*, which not only are no moods of matter, but are real entities distinct from it, and, according to the doctrine of many modern schoolmen, may *exist separate* from all matter whatsoever.

By allowing the accidents of body to exist in a spiritualized form, scholastic theories purport to explain how bodies are perceived or known. But from the corpuscularian viewpoint that unites Locke, Malebranche, and Boyle, this is no explanation at all, because too little is said about the way in which these accidents exist in body, and about the manner in which they bring about changes in other bodies and in perceiving minds.

Locke's alternative to the scholastic explication of qualities and the perception of qualities rests on the distinction between primary and secondary qualities, which is presented in Book II, chapter viii of the

---

[18] Ibid., p. 32. Berkeley refers to this book at *Commentaries* 840. Sergeant is discussed by G. A. Johnston in *The Development of Berkeley's Philosophy*, London, 1923, pp. 383–96, and by H. M. Bracken in *Berkeley*, London, 1974, pp. 82–5. I am not suggesting that Sergeant was Berkeley's source. Locke himself argues that whether Malebranchean ideas are the 'true representation of any thing that exists, that, upon his principles, neither our author [Malebranche] nor anybody else can know'. 'How can I know that the picture of any thing is like that thing, when I never see that which it represents?' Locke asks (*Examination of Malebranche*, § 51, p. 250). Idea and original cannot be 'immediately compared by juxta-position' (§ 52, pp. 250–1).

[19] *Solid Philosophy Asserted*, p. 32. The following quotation appears on the same page.

[20] Robert Boyle, 'The Origin of Forms and Qualities According to the Corpuscular Philosophy', originally pub. in 1666, in M. A. Stewart (ed.), *Selected Philosophical Papers of Robert Boyle*, Manchester, 1979, p. 21. Hobbes makes a similar point in a passage quoted in Chap. 6, p. 189. Boyle's care in his choice of words—his preference for 'mood' or 'modification' over 'quality'—is characteristic of the corpuscularians. Newton for example contrasts 'the Peripatetick terms *Quality, Subject, Substance, Sensible qualities*' with 'the Mechanick ones *Body, Modes, Actions*' (*The Correspondence of Isaac Newton*, ed. H. W. Turnbull, vol. 1, Cambridge, 1959, p. 106). In the *Essay* Locke sometimes shows the same preference for 'mode' over 'accident'.

Essay. The subtleties in Locke's discussion are not always fully appreciated. For example, when Locke first defines the primary qualities as those qualities 'utterly inseparable from the Body, in what estate soever it be; such as in all the alterations and changes it suffers, all the force can be used upon it, it constantly keeps; and such as Sense constantly finds in every particle of Matter, which has bulk enough to be perceived, and the Mind finds inseparable from every particle of Matter, though less than to make it self singly be perceived by our Senses' (II viii 9), the qualities he has in mind are *general* or *determinable*.[21] No body keeps the same determinate figure or size 'in all the alterations and changes it suffers'. What it 'constantly keeps' are solidity, figure, extension, and mobility—that is, solidity, some figure or other, some size or other, and some degree of motion or rest. I will refer to these general or determinable qualities as the *primary affections* of body.

There is a second subtlety in Locke's claim that the mind finds the primary affections inseparable from every particle of matter. The claim is not analogous to Descartes's statement that nothing but extension in length, breadth, and depth can be found in the idea of matter or body in general.[22] Locke is saying instead that in view of the fact that our senses find the primary affections in every particle of matter large enough to be perceived, we cannot seriously suppose that further division does away with them. 'For division', as he goes on to say, 'only makes two, or more distinct separate masses of Matter, of that which was but one before.'

To Locke's list of the primary affections we can join his belief that everything that exists is particular (III iii 1, 11). Locke applies this belief to qualities or affections as well as to things themselves: 'Whatsoever is in Peter exists in Peter', Locke writes in his 'Reply to the Right Reverend the Lord Bishop of Worcester's Answer to his Letter', 'and whatever exists in Peter, is particular.'[23] It follows that solidity, extension, figure, and mobility cannot exist apart from their determinate modifications. What I will call the *primary qualities* of a body are therefore the determinate modifications—the determinate modes or manners of being—of what I earlier called the primary

---

[21] This feature of Locke's discussion is noticed by Peter Alexander, *Ideas, Qualities and Corpuscles: Locke and Boyle on the External World*, Cambridge, 1985, p. 133.
[22] For Descartes's claim see *Principles of Philosophy* II, articles 4 and 11, pp. 224 and 227–8 in vol. 1 of Cottingham, *The Philosophical Writings of Descartes*.
[23] *The Works of John Locke*, vol. 4, p. 166.

affections of a body. Every one of a body's remaining qualities is *secondary*. They 'are nothing in the Objects themselves, but Powers', either 'to produce various Sensations in us by their *primary Qualities*, i.e., by the Bulk, Figure, Texture, and Motion of their insensible Parts, as Colours, Sounds, Tasts' (II viii 10), or powers to bring about changes in other bodies. By *texture* I take it Locke has in mind what Boyle defines as 'a certain disposition or contrivance of parts in the whole'.[24] We have already met with this use of the word *texture* in a passage from Hooke.

Earlier I said that in Locke's opinion the scholastics endow bodies with *too many* qualities. Locke is not unimpressed, I think, with the economy of his own view, but I hope it is clear by now that his objection to the scholastic philosophy is not primarily quantitative. The great advantage of the distinction between primary and secondary qualities is that it makes way for the view that bodies act on one another largely by impact or impulse. In the first edition of the *Essay*, II viii 11 reads as follows:

The next thing to be consider'd, is how *Bodies operate* one upon another, and that is manifestly *by impulse*, and nothing else. It being impossible to conceive, that Body should operate on what it does not touch, (which is all one as to imagine it can operate where it is not) or when it does touch, operate any other way than by Motion.

This passage was revised in the fourth edition to take account of Newton's law of attraction, which convinced Locke that God could endow bodies with powers of operation beyond our comprehension:[25]

The next thing to be consider'd, is how *Bodies* produce *Ideas* in us, and that is manifestly *by impulse*, the only way we can conceive Bodies operate in.

'That the size, figure, and motion of one body should cause a change in the size, figure, and motion of another body,' Locke writes at IV iii 13, 'is not beyond our Conception; the separation of the Parts of one Body, upon the intrusion of another; and the change from rest to motion, upon impulse; these, and the like, seem to us to have some *connexion* one with another.' Boyle had ridiculed the schoolmen for

---

[24] For Boyle's definition of *texture* see 'The Origin of Forms and Qualities', p. 30. In ch. 3 of 'An Introduction to the History of Particular Qualities' Boyle defines texture as 'a certain manner of existing together' of the corpuscles united in a body (Stewart, p. 106).

[25] For Locke's account of what prompted the revision see 'Mr. Locke's Second Reply to the Right Reverend Lord Bishop of Worcester', *Works*, vol. 4, pp. 467–8.

explaining why snow comes to dazzle the eyes by pointing to 'a *quality of whiteness that is in it*'.[26] By reducing bodily action to mechanical impact or impulse, Locke and Boyle are in a position to offer explanations of events in nature that are simultaneously informative and intelligible, despite their lack of detail. And the same strategy can be applied to the changes bodies cause in the organs of sense.[27]

But what about the action of the senses on the mind? Can Locke improve on the scholastics here? In the *Examination of Malebranche* Locke makes a candid confession which seems to call his preference for corpuscularianism into question:[28]

Impressions made on the retina by rays of light, I think I understand; and motions from thence continued to the brain may be conceived, and that these produce ideas in our minds, I am persuaded, but in a manner to me incomprehensible. This I can resolve only into the good pleasure of God, whose ways are past finding out.

This might be taken as an admission that corpuscularianism fails to improve on scholasticism, but Locke would insist, I think, that corpuscularianism is better off in at least two ways: the corpuscularian is more successful in explaining what human beings are able to explain, and more candid about the limits likely to be encountered by any theory of our devising. It is true that sensations or ideas 'have not any apparent Congruity, or conceivable Connexion' with the texture or motion of bodies (II viii 25; see also IV iii 13), and that we cannot help but suppose that God annexes certain ideas to certain textures and motions, just as he annexes the idea of pain to the motion of steel dividing our flesh (II viii 13). But until the chain of causes reaches the mind, Locke's account of perception can dispense with God without lapsing into unintelligibility. According to Locke's account all that needs to be transmitted to the brain is motion. He can welcome the fact that the trace produced in the brain will depend not only on the object perceived but on the object's setting, the intervening medium, the state of the sense organ, and the condition of other parts of the perceiver's body. This allows him to deal with perceptual relativity in a way not readily available to the scholastics, whose material species

[26] 'The Origin of Forms and Qualities', p. 16 in Stewart.

[27] See not only II viii 11 in the 4th and 5th edns., quoted just above, but the more explicit discussion at IV ii 11.

[28] § 10, p. 217 in vol. 9 of the *Works*. Locke does go on to say that although he does not understand 'how it is that I perceive', it is plain that motion 'has to do in the producing' of ideas.

must somehow retain their character as they travel from the object to the brain. 'We may be able to give an Account,' Locke writes, 'how the same Water, at the same time, may produce the *Idea* of Cold by one Hand, and of Heat by the other: Whereas it is impossible, that the same Water, if those *Ideas* were really in it, should at the same time be both Hot and Cold.' (II viii 21.) Perceptual relativity does not prove that primary and secondary qualities should be distinguished in the way Locke favours, but it does draw attention to facts the scholastic cannot easily explain. The two hands in the lukewarm tub of water play roughly the same role as the pounded almond at II viii 20, whose clear white colour becomes dirty and whose sweet taste becomes oily. We find it intelligible that the impact of the pestle on the nut should cause a breakdown of its texture. But it is not readily intelligible that it should bring about the departure of one real accident and its replacement by another. 'What real Alteration can the beating of the Pestle make in any Body,' Locke asks, 'but an Alteration of the *Texture* of it?' And what alteration can a tub of water make in my hand, other than a change in the motion of its parts?

The deliberate caution in Locke's praise of corpuscularianism has another source. Passages such as II xiii 19–20, where he ridicules the doctrine of substance and accident, may suggest that he wants to make a comparison such as this: while the scholastic view of nature leaves the relationship between a thing and its qualities an utter mystery, the corpuscular hypothesis takes at least the first steps required to make that relationship intelligible. The primary qualities are not accidents mysteriously inhering in an unknown something lying beneath them, but modifications—determinate modes or manners of being—of a body's principal attributes. The primary qualities are attached to body in a manner demanded by reason, because the attributes inseparable from body must be modified or determined in definite ways.

The problem with attributing this reasoning to Locke is that when he is not dismissing it as a verbal matter (as at III vi 5–6, for example), Locke disavows knowledge of the essence of body. He writes at II xiii 24 that extension is 'but an affection of Body, as well as the rest discoverable by our Senses, which are scarce acute enough to look into the pure Essence of things'. This does not go against his earlier contention that extension and body are inseparable, because that claim tells us only that our senses find extension in every body large enough to come to their attention, and that the mind has no reason to suppose that continued division into parts would do away with it. The mind

finds the primary qualities inseparable from body not because it is
defeated when it attempts to imagine a separation—Locke disputes
the relevance of such attempts at II xiii 24—but because it is aware that
division only makes two where before there was one. But if the primary
qualities are mere affections of body, rather than parts or aspects of its
essence, then the ultimate constitution of matter is, after all, *something
we know not what*, and the relationship between that constitution and its
'primary' affections, though we may clothe it with labels suggestive of
causation, is no less mysterious than inherence. The obscurity of this
relationship threatens even the intelligibility of impact. One idea we
have of body, Locke writes at *Essay* II xxiii 28, is 'the power of
communication of Motion by impulse'. But if we ask how this is done we
are '*in the dark*':

For in the communication of Motion by impulse, wherein as much Motion is
lost to one Body, as is got to the other, which is the ordinariest case, we can
have no other conception, but of the passing of Motion out of one Body into
another; which, I think, is as obscure and unconceivable, as how our Minds
move or stop our Bodies by Thought; which we every moment find they do.

Locke's problem in this passage is similar to one that troubled
Newton. We must 'universally allow that all bodies whatsoever are
endowed with a principle of mutual gravitation', Newton writes, but he
insists that this is not to say that gravity is essential to bodies.[29] The
word 'essential', as Newton understands it, conveys immediacy as well
as universality. An essential property is immediately attached to matter;
because no quality is more fundamental, the presence of an essential
property cannot be explained. Newton links the notion of essence with
that of explanatory opacity in the Preface to the second English edition
of the *Opticks*:[30]

And to shew that I do not take Gravity for an Essential Property of Bodies, I have
added one Question concerning its Cause, chusing to propose it by way of a Question,
because I am not yet satisfied about it for want of Experiments.

Newton is notoriously unwilling to commit himself to a particular
explanation of attraction; he is equally unwilling to declare attraction
essential, because that would rule out even the possibility of
explanation. Locke refuses to describe the primary qualities as
essential for the same basic reason: for all he knows there may be a

---

[29] Bk. III, Rule iii, pp. 399–400 in *Sir Isaac Newton's Mathematical Principles of Natural
Philosophy*, Andrew Motte and Florian Cajori (trans.), Berkeley, 1934.
[30] New York, 1952, p. cxxiii. The 2nd edn. appeared in 1717.

reason why a body exhibits one of the primary affections, though he is thoroughly pessimistic about our prospects of finding that reason out. Newton and Locke are both agnostic about the essence of matter, and this means that if Locke plans to defend the corpuscular hypothesis as a more intelligible substitute for the scholastic doctrine of substance and accident, he cannot hope for much support from his conception of the relationship between matter and its most basic affections. Locke may be able to account for the secondary qualities more intelligibly than his scholastic competitors. He may be able to make it clear why an extended, solid body must have a determinate size, shape, motion and share of solidity. But at bottom, in his portrayal of the innermost recesses of body, there is ignorance as deep as the ignorance of the scholastic. Yet this does not undercut his defence of the corpuscular hypothesis. He approves of that hypothesis because it *goes farther* in accounting for the powers of body; he does not say that it makes them fully perspicuous. And when the corpuscularian comes up against the limits of what we can understand he is willing to admit it.

The views of Ralph Cudworth may help to illuminate those of Locke. Cudworth regards corpuscularianism as an ancient invention, recently revived by Descartes and Gassendi. In *The True Intellectual System of the Universe* he praises the 'Ancient Physiologers' for taking away 'all Forms and Qualities of Bodies (as Entities really distinct from the Matter and Substance)' and for resolving them not merely into mechanism but into '*Mechanism* and *Fancy*'.[31] In Cudworth's view mechanism and fancy go hand in hand: it was, in fact, the recognition of fancy or consciousness that convinced most of the ancient atomists 'also [to] assert Incorporeal Substances' (p. 35), and it was the misfortune of the atheists among them not to recognize fancy as a principle, an omission which led to an absurdity as great as the opinion their atomism overthrew. Cudworth realizes that in explaining the production of fancy we must have recourse to God, but it is one thing, he thinks, to bring God in at a certain point, and quite another to bring him on the stage 'with his Miraculous extraordinary Power, perpetually at every turn'.[32] Like Cudworth, Locke is not committed to saying that corpuscularianism makes everything intelligible; his claim is merely that it goes farther in accounting for things, or staves off our ignorance a little longer. The text from the *Examination of Malebranche* quoted above suggests that there is a difference between knowing *that*

---

[31] London, 1678, I xxvii, pp. 32–3.
[32] *True Intellectual System*, p. 33.

something happens and knowing *why* it happens. Locke's point at *Essay* II xxiii 28 may then be that motion is transmitted by impulse—we see it happen—even if we do not understand how or why.

It has not been possible to keep the second central and unifying corpuscularian theme—the existence of particles too small to be singly sensed—from intruding into our discussion of the first. Although it is logically possible to distinguish between primary and secondary qualities without admitting the existence of corpuscles, the two beliefs are bound by a common standard of intelligibility.[33] Only if there are insensible particles can motion be mechanically transmitted across apparently empty space, which means that only a philosopher who admits the existence of insensible things can take full advantage of the explanatory strategy of mechanism. For Locke, the existence of insensible particles must be regarded as a hypothesis, but it is a hypothesis with unusually strong support, because the difficulty of conceiving of non-mechanical action to some extent exempts it from the following caution:

Hypotheses, if they are well made, are at least great helps to the Memory, and often direct us to new discoveries. But . . . we should *not take up any one too hastily*, (which the Mind, that would always penetrate into the Causes of Things, and have Principles to rest on, is very apt to do,) till we have very well examined Particulars, and made several Experiments, in that thing which we would explain by our Hypothesis, and see whether it will agree to them all; whether our Principles will carry us quite through, and not be as inconsistent with one *Phænomenon* of Nature, as they seem to accommodate, and explain another. And at least, that we take care, that the Name of *Principles* deceive us not, nor impose on us, but making us receive that for an unquestionable Truth, which is really, at best, but a very doubtful conjecture, such as are most (I had almost said all) of the *Hypotheses* in natural Philosophy. (IV xii 13.)

This is advice about the proper attitude toward relatively specific hypotheses, such as the ones discussed at *Essay* IV xvi 12. Our ground for these, Locke there explains, is always analogy:

We see Animals are generated, nourished, and move; the Load-stone draws Iron; and the parts of a Candle successively melting, turn into flame, and give us both light and heat. These and the like Effects we see and know: but the causes that operate, and the manner they are produced in, we can only guess, and probably conjecture. For these and the like coming not within the scrutiny

---

[33] The many distinctions that might be made between primary and secondary qualities are catalogued by John J. MacIntosh in 'Primary and Secondary Qualities', *Studia Leibnitiana* 8 (1976), 88–104.

of humane Senses, cannot be examined by them, or be attested by any body, and therefore can appear more or less probable, only as they more or less agree to Truths that are established in our Minds, and as they hold proportion to other parts of our Knowledge and Observation. *Analogy* in these matters is the only help we have, and 'tis from that alone we draw all our grounds of Probability. Thus observing that the bare rubbing of two Bodies violently one upon another, produces heat, and very often fire it self, we have reason to think, that what we call Heat and Fire, consists in a violent agitation of the imperceptible minute parts of the burning matter: Observing likewise that the different refractions of pellucid Bodies produce in our Eyes the different appearances of several Colours; and also that the different ranging and laying the superficial parts of several Bodies, as of Velvet, watered Silk, *etc.* does the like, we think it probable that the Colour and shining of Bodies, is in them nothing but the different Arrangement and Refraction of their minute and insensible parts.

It is important to distinguish between the relatively restricted hypotheses discussed in this paragraph—one about the cause of heat and fire, the other about the cause of colour and sheen—and the corpuscular hypothesis itself. The more general hypothesis is supported by the restricted ones. But it is also supported by the unique intelligibility of impact and the accompanying suspicion of unmediated action at a distance. The corpuscular hypothesis rests not only on analogy, but on the obscurity and explanatory impotence of rival views. I think this is why Locke is careful to say that *most* hypotheses in natural philosophy are very doubtful conjectures. 'I had almost said all', he tells us. But he does not say all. In the *Essay*, then, we find a very powerful defence of the two central doctrines of corpuscularianism, a defence that avoids Cartesian appeals to an idea of the essence of body, and uses perceptual relativity to illustrate the flexibility and power of an explanatory strategy.

Commentators on Locke sometimes write as if he accepted corpuscularianism not because of arguments he himself was able to appreciate, but because Boyle and other authorities told him that it was true. Peter Alexander writes that 'Locke was not attempting to *make* the primary/secondary quality distinction but was accepting it, ready-made, from Boyle as an essential part of the corpuscular hypothesis, which was already well on the way to being established.'[34] According to Maurice Mandelbaum, 'What seems missing [in Locke]

[34] 'Boyle and Locke on Primary and Secondary Qualities', reprinted in I. C. Tipton (ed.), *Locke on Human Understanding*, Oxford, 1977, p. 70. In *Ideas, Qualities and Corpuscles* Alexander seems to have modified his earlier view; see e.g. pp. 242 and 118.

is any attempt to justify the acceptance of that atomism which runs throughout his discussion of human knowledge. It is my opinion that Locke did not feel obliged to justify this theory because he not unnaturally viewed it as an empirically based conclusion drawn from the experimental inquiries of his day.'[35] It seems to me that these statements convey a distorted view of the relationship between science and philosophy in the late seventeenth century. They suggest that scientists and philosophers operated within clearly defined spheres of authority, so that a scientist could simply tell a philosopher what sorts of things populate the world. But there was no such division of labour. Alexander and Mandelbaum underestimate the extent to which Boyle himself relied on philosophical considerations which Locke could perfectly well appreciate. When we examine Boyle's writings we do not find an empirical case for the corpuscular hypothesis assembled by Boyle the scientist to be handed over to the philosopher. Instead we find a case for corpuscularianism in which scientific and philosophical considerations are mixed. What would now be described as philosophical considerations are, in fact, the dominant ones, not because Boyle thinks philosophy has a special set of credentials for deciding ontological questions, but because the generality of the corpuscular hypothesis and its fundamental disagreements with competing views call for a generality of outlook characteristic of philosophy.[36] I think I have shown that Mandelbaum is wrong to say that there is no defence of corpuscularianism in the *Essay*. A defence can be found, though it must be pieced together out of remarks Locke scatters throughout the book. It is, I think, a very powerful defence, and no special scientific training is required to appreciate it. I now want to show that it was understood by Berkeley, though unlike Locke he found it wanting.

2. *Primary and secondary qualities*

Berkeley's response to the distinction between primary and secondary qualities is more complex than the largely hostile discussions in the *Principles* and *Dialogues* indicate when taken by themselves. Although he consistently rejects the distinction as a vehicle for materialism,

[35] 'Locke's Realism', *Philosophy, Science, and Sense Perception*, Baltimore, 1964, p. 60.
[36] The prominence of philosophical considerations is especially clear in Boyle's unpublished MS. 'Notes on a Good and an Excellent Hypothesis', p. 119 in Stewart. I do not mean to suggest that the line between philosophical and empirical considerations is hard and fast.

Berkeley accepts it in *Siris* as a delineation of the qualities of greatest predictive value to the student of nature. *Siris* is a very late work, published in 1744, but the views developed there are foreshadowed in *De Motu*, which was published more than twenty years earlier. And the view that extension, figure, and motion are more informative than colour, taste, and smell is in keeping with the account of science developed in §§ 101–10 of the *Principles*.

Berkeley, it will be recalled, introduces the distinction at *Principles* 9. The list of primary qualities he presents there is borrowed from Locke (*Essay* II viii 9), but Berkeley takes himself to be addressing a whole movement of thought:

Some there are who make a distinction betwixt *primary* and *secondary* qualities: by the former, they mean extension, figure, motion, rest, solidity or impenetrability and number: by the latter they denote all other sensible qualities, as colours, sounds, tastes, and so forth. The ideas we have of these they acknowledge not to be the resemblances of any thing existing without the mind or unperceived; but they will have our ideas of the primary qualities to be patterns or images of things which exist without the mind, in an unthinking substance they call *matter*. By matter therefore we are to understand an inert, senseless substance, in which extension, figure, and motion, do actually subsist.

Berkeley's initial response is to remind us that extension, figure, and motion are 'only ideas existing in the mind', which means that 'neither they nor their archetypes can exist in an unperceiving substance' (§ 9). Only in § 10 are we given anything new:

If it be certain, that those original qualities are inseparably united with the other sensible qualities, and not, even in thought, capable of being abstracted from them, it plainly follows that they exist only in the mind. But I desire any one to reflect and try, whether he can by any abstraction of thought, conceive the extension and motion of a body, without all other sensible qualities. For my own part, I see evidently that it is not in my power to frame an idea of a body extended and moved, but I must withal give it some colour or other sensible quality which is acknowledged to exist only in the mind. In short, extension, figure, and motion, abstracted from all other qualities, are inconceivable. Where therefore the other sensible qualities are, there must these be also, to wit, in the mind and no where else.

Warnock over-reads this passage in an interesting way; he has Berkeley saying that colour and extension are inseparably united:[37]

---

[37] G. J. Warnock, *Berkeley*, 3rd edn., Oxford, 1982, p. 99.

Locke had maintained that external objects are (for example) solid and extended, but are not really (for example) coloured. The former qualities are in the objects themselves, the latter are only 'in the mind'. Berkeley contends that this is inconceivable, on the ground that colour and extension are 'inseparably united'; any object which is solid and extended must have some colour.

If Warnock is right Berkeley must deny the possibility of wholly transparent bodies. Warnock is aware of this, but he thinks Berkeley would have maintained 'that anything which is at all visible is thereby, perhaps in some slightly extended sense, also coloured' (p. 100). There is, in fact, some support for Warnock's speculation in the *Commentaries*, where Berkeley writes, 'Ask a Cartesian whether he is wont to imagine his globules without colour, pellucidness is a colour.' (453.) But Berkeley does not say in § 10 that colour and extension are inseparable. He makes the more modest claim that whenever we conceive of a body extended and moved we must give it some colour *or other sensible quality*. The claim Warnock finds in the passage is deliberately avoided, the same being true of the corresponding passage in the First Dialogue (*Works* II, p. 192). Berkeley's premiss, then, is that the primary qualities cannot be abstracted from *all* other sensible qualities. And his conclusion is that primary qualities, like the others, exist 'in the mind and no where else'.

The interpretation of *Principles* 10 is made more complicated by Berkeley's denial that there are qualities perceived by more than one sense. The list of primary qualities in *Principles* 9 includes four taken by Locke to be common to sight and touch: extension, figure, motion or rest, and number. Berkeley argues against the existence of common sensibles in §§ 46–51 of the *Theory of Vision*; the topic is never introduced by name in the *Principles*, but in § 44 of that work, where he refers to the essay on vision, Berkeley says that 'the ideas of sight and touch make two species entirely distinct and heterogeneous', which in effect repudiates all of the common sensibles recognized by Locke. This repudiation reflects back on § 10 and endows it with a second set of meanings. If the reader thinks of extension as a common sensible the section says that extension cannot be conceived apart from all other sensible qualities: if it is conceived apart from the secondary qualities proper to sight, it must be conceived along with at least one of the qualities proper to touch. But if the reader distinguishes between visible and tangible extension then the section says something else. With regard to visible extension something like Warnock's reading turns out to be correct, though not at all in the way he intended: visible extension, the section tells us, cannot be conceived apart from colour. With regard to tangible extension the claim is similar: tangible extension cannot be conceived apart from the secondary qualities proper to touch—resistance, heat and cold, and hard and soft. Berkeley's intention at *Principles* 10 is no doubt to allow for either of these readings. Otherwise it would be careless of him to postpone the heterogeneity thesis until § 44. On either reading the upshot of § 10 is the same: because the primary qualities cannot be conceived apart from all other secondary qualities, the distinction between them cannot have the ontological significance which Locke and others attach to it.

How effective is Berkeley's argument? An obvious reply on behalf of Locke is that secondary qualities are not in the mind, but in the very things to which they seem to be assigned. At *Principles* 10 Berkeley writes as if the corpuscularians all agree that secondary qualities are ideas, but Locke at any rate is careful to distinguish between the qualities in things and the ideas to which they give rise:

Whatsoever the Mind perceives in it self, or the immediate object of Perception, Thought, or Understanding, that I call *Idea*; and the Power to produce any *Idea* in our mind, I call *Quality* of the Subject wherein that power is. (II viii 8.)

Locke then warns that he will sometimes speak of ideas 'as in the things themselves', but he asks that we take him to be referring in such cases not to ideas but to 'those Qualities in the Objects which produce them'. If even the secondary qualities exist in things themselves then Berkeley loses the concession he hopes to exploit: Locke admits that primary and secondary qualities exist together, but he locates both of them in things.

Yet there is something disingenuous in this reply. When Locke says that secondary qualities exist in things he is saying only that things are the *causes* of ideas such as whiteness, sweetness, and heat (II xxxi 2). When he says that primary qualities exist in objects he means something more. He spells out the added meaning at II viii 15:

The *Ideas of primary Qualities* of Bodies, *are Resemblances* of them, and their Patterns do really exist in the Bodies themselves; but the *Ideas, produced* in us *by* these *Secondary Qualities, have no resemblance* of them at all. There is nothing like our *Ideas*, existing in the Bodies themselves. They are in the Bodies, we denominate from them, only a Power to produce those Sensations in us: And what is Sweet, Blue, or Warm in *Idea*, is but the certain Bulk, Figure, and Motion of the insensible Parts in the Bodies themselves, which we call so.

An idea of shape or extension, Locke explains, resembles something in the body that gives rise to it; an idea of colour does not. But this seems to commit Locke to the kind of abstraction Berkeley repudiates in § 10. Primary and secondary qualities cannot be conceived apart, and therefore they must, as resemblances, stand or fall together. My idea of extension is supposed to resemble the extension of the particles which constitute the object. (Exact resemblance is not of course in question, and there is no reason to suppose that Berkeley fails to see that.) But a striking feature of my idea of extension is that I cannot separate it from my ideas of colour and texture. Anything that is held to resemble my idea must therefore resemble the idea in its resistance to such separation; it must be a quality which is inseparable from qualities which my ideas of colour and texture resemble. To put the point another way, once it is conceded that ideas of colour and texture are not resemblances, it follows that ideas of extension are not resemblances either, since nothing could resemble the idea of extension if it did not have a place in a system of relationships corresponding to the system that obtains among ideas. Ideas and qualities needn't be alike in every respect in order for one to resemble the other, but the difference Locke describes is simply too extreme.

Locke's talk of resemblance might be reinterpreted: when he says that ideas of primary qualities are resemblances and those of secondary qualities are not, perhaps he is making a point about causal or explanatory role. 'My idea of extension resembles something in the object' may mean only that extension must be ascribed to the object if we hope to account for change. But there are two obstacles to this. The first is that Berkeley is ready to argue that the prospects for such an account are hopelessly bleak. He is well aware of the corpuscularian conviction that sensations of colour, sound, heat, and cold 'depend on and are occasioned by the different size, texture, and motion of the minute particles of matter' (*Principles* 10). The problem is that, as Locke himself admits, the mechanical affections of body have 'no affinity at all' with the ideas they produce in us (IV iii 28; see also IV iii 29). The second obstacle is even more fundamental, because it calls into question our ability to *think* of the corpuscular constitutions Locke describes. If Locke's talk of resemblance is to tell us something about things themselves—if it is to be more than a comment about the words we find ourselves using when we attempt to account for change in the natural world—we need to have some assurance that in saying corpuscular textures are responsible for our ideas we are thinking of things that are really there. If he reinterprets resemblance in the way proposed, Locke can no longer hope to provide such assurance. His appeals to resemblance are an indication that he, like Berkeley, believes that awareness of an object's effects will not by itself provide us with a conception of the object as it really is. He says that bodies resemble our ideas of extension, figure, and motion because he believes that these ideas do in fact provide us with such a conception.

In §§ 11 through 13 of the *Principles* Berkeley considers some specific cases of allegedly primary qualities. The selection of cases is a strange one (great and small, swift and slow in § 11; number in § 12; unity in § 13), but Berkeley thinks he can show in each case that the quality is either relative, and therefore 'dependent on men's understanding' (*Principles* 12), or illegitimately abstract. In § 14 he observes that arguments from perceptual relativity are as convincing when applied to primary qualities as they are when applied to secondary ones, but in § 15 he insists that they do not work at all. (These sections were discussed in Chapter 6.) The discussion in the *Principles* then concludes with a reminder that 'the arguments foregoing plainly shew it to be impossible that any colour or extension at all, or other sensible quality whatsoever, should exist in an unthinking subject without the mind, or in truth, that there should be any such thing as an outward object.' (*Principles* 16.) The 'arguments foregoing' are plainly the arguments of §§ 1 to 8.

Despite the criticisms of the distinction presented in the *Principles* (and repeated for the most part in the First Dialogue), in *Siris* Berkeley actually allows for a distinction between primary and secondary qualities, and this allowance is foreshadowed by a neglected passage in *De Motu*. His reinstatement of the distinction strengthens his earlier attack by showing that we can give progress in science its due without making a *metaphysically significant* distinction between two kinds of qualities.

Siris defends the same view of cause and effect as Berkeley's early works, with one qualification: the author of *Siris* allows us to describe a mere sign as a cause, albeit a 'physical' one. Berkeley's endorsement of a distinction between primary and secondary qualities comes in § 266, where he praises the Pythagoreans and Platonists—with what justice I will not enquire—for their recognition of mechanical principles, and their subordination of matter to spirit:

The Pythagoreans and the Platonists had a notion of the true system of the world. They allowed of mechanical principles, but actuated by soul or mind; they distinguished the primary qualities in bodies from the secondary, making the former to be physical causes, and they understood physical causes in a right sense.

To understand physical causes in 'a right sense' is to treat them as *signs*, or indications of the future; to distinguish the primary qualities from the secondary is to recognize that the primary qualities are particularly useful signs.

The developments in *Siris* are foreshadowed in *De Motu*, where Berkeley argues that 'all that . . . to which we have given the name *body* contains nothing in itself which could be the principle of motion or its efficient cause', because 'impenetrability, extension, and figure'—all of them primary qualities—'neither include nor connote any power of producing motion' (§ 22). The secondary qualities are not even mentioned because the physicist is interested in the causes—the *signs*—of motion, and colour, taste, and smell tell us nothing about it. In the following section Berkeley says that the term *body* covers nothing but 'solid extension and its modes'. To borrow a useful way of speaking from the 1734 version of the Introduction to the *Principles*, the natural philosopher *considers* only the primary qualities of body; the word 'body' as he or she uses it is tailored to fit the primary qualities and no more. The natural philosopher is not guilty of abstraction as long as he or she abstains from ontological conclusions, and understands that the truncated conception of body he or she employs is a reflection not of a distinction written into things themselves but of the utility of the primary qualities in predicting the events that interest us.

Berkeley's recognition of the distinctive predictive opportunities afforded by the primary qualities is in keeping with the account of science he elaborates in later sections of the *Principles*. There he explains that the natural philosopher surpasses the bulk of humanity in his or her ability to 'extend our prospect beyond what is present'; the natural philosopher is especially well-equipped to make 'very probable conjectures, touching things that may have happened at very great distances of time and place, as well as to predict things to come' (§ 105). These conjectures and predictions generally concern the primary qualities of bodies—the orbits and positions of the planets, for example, or the height of the tides—and even when they do not, the observations on which they rest are almost always observations of primary qualities. John Dewey was perhaps the first of Berkeley's readers to recognize that Berkeley has no quarrel with the natural philosopher who chooses to concentrate on some qualities rather than others, and to enshrine that choice in a 'distinction'. Dewey ends an essay on Locke with a self-consciously Berkeleyan treatment of the difference between primary and secondary qualities. Treated in such a way, Dewey explains,[38]

Primary qualities cease to be the counterparts of traditional essential attributes and the efficacious causes of secondary; they are those qualities of things which serve as the most accurate, dependable, and comprehensive signs. . . . Sweetness has turned out to be a much less valuable *sign* than is the 'bulk, number and texture' of extended parts.

Dewey's proposed treatment allows for a mechanistic 'explication' of secondary qualities such as colour and taste. If it turns out that the shape and arrangement of a body's superficial parts are reliable indicators of its colour, we can provide a mechanical 'account' of the body's colour which will be as secure as mechanical accounts of its motion. That 'abundance of information is conveyed unto us, concerning what we are to expect from such and such actions, and what methods are proper to be taken, for the exciting such and such ideas', Berkeley writes as he closes *Principles* 65, is '*all that I conceive to be distinctly meant*, when it is said that by discerning the figure, texture, and mechanism of the inward parts of bodies, . . . we may attain to know the several uses and properties depending thereon, or the nature of the thing' (emphasis mine).

But it does not follow from this that our predictive power would be enhanced by assigning primary qualities to unperceived or unperceivable corpuscles. The bodies Berkeley has in mind in the *Principles* are *signs*, or things which are perceived. In the *Theory of Vision* Berkeley actually expresses doubts about the utility of the microscope in making predictions. Like other writers on microscopy he marvels at the 'new world' to which the microscope transports us, but the 'new scene of visible objects' is not as useful, he thinks, as the one presented by the naked senses:

---

[38] 'Substance, Power and Quality in Locke', *Philosophical Review* 35 (1926), p. 38.

Herein consists the most remarkable difference, to wit, that whereas the objects perceived by the eye alone have a certain connexion with tangible objects, whereby we are taught to foresee what will ensue upon the approach or application of distant objects to the parts of our own body, which much conduceth to its preservation, there is not the like connexion between things tangible and those visible objects that are perceived by help of a fine microscope. (§ 85.)

This is Berkeley's way of explaining why microscopical eyes would be of little use, providing only 'the empty amusement of seeing' and being 'utterly unserviceable' when we try to find our way in the tangible world (§ 86). This is not to say, of course, that submicroscopic particles do not *exist*, but it may intensify the problem of construing them immaterialistically. It is that problem to which we now turn.

3. *Immaterial corpuscles*

The notion of an immaterial corpuscle, on the surface at least, is a contradiction in terms: if a corpuscle really exists—if it enjoys the kind of existence which is, according to Berkeley, relative to us—then it must be something we could sense, even if we happen not to. But a corpuscle *cannot be perceived*. So it is tempting to say that if there is any hope for the notion at all, it must be construed instrumentally, as a notion with a settled place in a fruitful theory or way of speaking but without a referential role. As Warnock says, the scientist as Berkeley understands him 'has not really discovered that *there are* "insensible particles"; it is rather that it suits his purpose as a theorist to *say* so. We may indeed say of them whatever we please, so long as some theoretical purpose is served by what we say. If our theories can be most easily formulated by supposing all such particles to be spherical, let us by all means say they are spherical; but this is to simplify our theory, and not to "set forth the nature of things".'[39]

Warnock proposes that Berkeley should deal with corpuscles in the same way that he deals with forces—as hypotheses or fictions rather than as real beings. Berkeley's approach to force is developed in greatest detail in *De Motu*:

Force, gravity, attraction and terms of this sort are useful for reasonings and reckonings about motion and bodies in motion, but not for understanding the

[39] *Berkeley*, p. 203.

simple nature of motion itself or for indicating so many distinct qualities. As for attraction, it was certainly introduced by Newton, not as a true, physical quality, but only as a mathematical hypothesis. (§ 17.)

Plausible as Warnock's proposal is, Berkeley never says about particles what he says about forces. And he has at least two reasons for being reluctant to do so. First, particles (unlike forces) are very much like the houses, mountains, and rivers whose existence Berkeley readily admits. According to the corpuscularians, the only real difference is that particles are very much smaller. Second, particles are even more like the parts and organs of plants and animals which were once inaccessible to sense but are now laid before our eyes by the microscope, and it would be rash to deny that advances in microscopy might disclose even smaller entities. As Henry Power (Hooke's leading predecessor in promoting microscopical discoveries) wrote in his *Experimental Philosophy* of 1664, 'Who can tell how far Mechanical Industry may prevail: for the process of Art is infinite, and who can set a *non-ultra* to her endeavors?'[40] Power and Hooke were inclined to set no limits at all: while they couldn't be sure that the shape of the ultimate particles would one day be revealed, it would be reckless, they suggested, to insist that it could not be. Because Berkeley acknowledges the existence of entities invisible to the naked eye, it would be reasonable for him to grant the possibility of further discoveries of the same kind. If he wants to draw a line at the existence of ultimate particles he needs a good reason for doing so. Unless he can point to some difference between ultimate particles and grosser parts which were once concealed but are no longer, he should not insist that ultimate particles are mere hypotheses or fictions.

Warnock believes that Berkeley acknowledges the existence of observable physical objects but treats corpuscles instrumentally, in the same way he treats physical force. Some more recent commentators take an approach that differs markedly from Warnock's. Gerd Buchdahl proposes that 'Berkeley does *not* deny the existence of micro-entities in principle, provided they are regarded as "ideas".'[41] He criticizes Berkeley for failing to provide an explicit account of what it is for such an entity to be an idea, but it presumably means, according to Buchdahl, that the entity is unperceived 'simply as an accidental matter of fact'. Daniel Garber argues for the strong

---

[40] Quoted in Nicolson, 'The Microscope and English Imagination', p. 59.
[41] *Metaphysics and the Philosophy of Science*, Cambridge, Mass., 1969, p. 309. The following quotation is taken from p. 308.

conclusion that Berkeley is prepared 'to accord corpuscles the same real existence that he gives to the inner mechanism of the watch, the parts of a tree, and the organs of an animal'.[42]

In defending their interpretations Buchdahl and Garber appeal to the seven sections of the *Principles* where Berkeley replies to the objection that immaterialism makes the parts and organs of plants and animals superfluous. This series of texts has a complex structure, so it will be necessary to work through it very carefully. There are several layers to Berkeley's reply, and we encounter his final position only after several more superficial responses have been tried.

In § 60 the objection is stated. 'If it be a spirit that immediately produces every effect by a *fiat*, or act of his will, we must think all that is fine and artificial in the works, whether of man or Nature, to be made in vain.' By this doctrine, the objection continues, a watchmaker must think that the works of a watch are superfluous. Why can't the divine intelligence move the hands on the dial-plate without putting the watchmaker to all the trouble of contriving internal parts? Why wouldn't an empty case serve just as well? Why is it that whenever a watch breaks down, there is a corresponding disorder in the parts which, once fixed, solves the problem? 'The like may be said of all the clockwork of Nature, great part whereof is so wonderfully fine and subtle, as scarce to be discerned by the best microscope. In short, it will be asked, how upon our principles any tolerable account can be given, or any final cause assigned of an innumerable multitude of bodies and machines framed with the most exquisite art, which in the common philosophy have very apposite uses assigned them, and serve to explain abundance of phenomena.'

It is noteworthy that as Berkeley states the objection, it does not accuse him of having to deny the existence of parts and organs. The claim is only that on his view they have no point. It may seem odd that doubts about their point would not develop into doubts about their being, but Berkeley keeps the two kinds of doubt apart. Thus it is common ground between Berkeley and his interlocutor that the parts and organs of plants and animals exist. The interlocutor's assertion that some of those parts are 'scarce to be discerned by the best microscope' is therefore highly significant; we can assume that Berkeley holds the same view.

---

[42] 'Locke, Berkeley, and Corpuscular Scepticism', in Turbayne, *Berkeley: Critical and Interpretive Essays*, p. 184. See also Tipton, 'The "Philosopher by Fire" in Berkeley's *Alciphron*', pp. 167–9.

Berkeley's first level of response, in § 61, is to admit that even if there were some difficulties 'relating to the administration of providence'—difficulties which immaterialism could not solve—the objection 'could be of small weight against the truth and certainty of those things which may be proved *a priori*, with the utmost evidence'. His second reply in § 61 is that the same problem arises for the materialist, because Berkeley has shown that the qualities of things have no efficacy. 'Whoever therefore supposes them to exist (allowing the supposition possible) when they are not perceived, does it manifestly to no purpose; since the only use that is assigned to them, as they exist unperceived, is that they produce those perceivable effects, which in truth cannot be ascribed to any thing but spirit.'

The opening of § 62—'to come nearer the difficulty'—marks a descent to a deeper level of response. Here Berkeley observes that although parts and organs 'be not absolutely necessary to the producing any effect, yet it is necessary to the producing things in a constant, regular way, according to the Laws of Nature'. In a passage that foreshadows *Siris* 266 he writes that 'a particular size, figure, motion and disposition of parts are necessary, though not absolutely to the producing any effect, yet to the producing it according to the standing mechanical Laws of Nature.' He points out that God could have chosen to bring about all the motions on the dial-plate of a watch, though no one had ever made the parts. In general, God could produce the same ideas of observable objects that we have now, even if the insides of everything were hollow. 'But yet if he will act agreeably to the rules of mechanism, by him for wise ends established and maintained in the Creation, it is necessary that those actions of the watchmaker, whereby he makes the movements and rightly adjusts them, precede the production of the aforesaid motions.' Berkeley does not say *why* God chooses to act according to the laws of mechanism (he assures us only that it is for some good and wise end), nor does he say that God *always* chooses to act according to those laws. In § 63 Berkeley admits that God sometimes overrules his laws, in order to surprise and awe us into an acknowledgement of him. Of course irregularity will have this effect only if laws are abrogated 'but seldom'. In any case God prefers to convince us of his attributes by the works of nature, rather than by miraculous ('anomalous and surprising') events.

With § 64 we move to the deepest level. The objection is restated 'to set this matter in a yet clearer light'. The objection 'amounts in reality to no more than this: ideas are not any how and at random produced, there being a certain order and connexion between them, like to that of cause and effect: there are also several combinations of them, made in a very regular and artificial manner, which seem like so many instruments in the hand of Nature, that being hid as it were behind the scenes, have a secret operation in producing those appearances which are seen on the theatre of the world, being themselves discernible only to the curious eye of the philosopher'. Yet if the parts behind the scenes are neither causes nor instruments, but '*inefficacious perceptions in the mind*', what is their point? § 65 contains Berkeley's reply. First, the regularities among ideas do not imply the relation of cause and effect, but that of a mark or sign and the thing it signifies. Second,

the reason why ideas are formed into machines, that is, artificial and regular combinations, is the same with that of combining letters into words. That a few original ideas may be made to signify a great number of effects and actions, it is necessary they be variously combined together: and to the end their use be permanent and universal, these combinations must be made by *rule*, and with *wise contrivance*. By this means abundance of information is conveyed unto us, concerning what we are to expect from such and such actions, and what methods are proper to be taken, for the exciting such and such ideas.

It is true that God could have created hollow watches that would work as well as watches filled with springs and gears, but if it were not for the rules of mechanism watches would never have been built *by us*. The curious eye of the philosopher discerns regularities which escape the notice of the vulgar, and which allow both the philosopher and those he or she instructs to control and anticipate the future. Anyone can observe that 'food nourishes, sleep refreshes, and fire warms us' (*Principles* 31), but it is the natural philosopher who identifies a small number of regularities of much wider application. *Principles* 62 assures us of a 'wise and good end' served by the rules of mechanism; in § 65 that end emerges as the benefit of human life. Berkeley's reply to the objection of *Principles* 60 becomes a defence of the minute attention to the parts of bodies that distinguishes natural philosophy.

Garber takes Berkeley's reply to the objection in § 60 as an endorsement of the existence of insensible corpuscles. 'For one,' Garber explains, 'the argument that is meant to render the existence of internal mechanisms compatible with his immaterialism works as well for corpuscles as it does for the wheels of a watch. It would seem as difficult to explain magnetic and chemical phenomena, and phenomena clearly relating to heat and fire on mechanical principles without corpuscles, as it would be to explain the movements of a watch dial on mechanical principles without wheels and springs.'[43] Garber also calls attention to the prominence of corpuscularian language and metaphor in *Principles* 60 through 65: the word 'parts', often used by Locke to designate insensible corpuscles; the mention of mechanisms 'scarce to be discerned by the best microscope'; the characterization of parts and organs as 'instruments . . . behind the scenes', 'discernible only to the curious eye of the philosopher'; and the metaphor of nature as clockwork. But even if these corpuscularian devices were not more characteristic of the statement of the objection than they are of Berkeley's reply, their use cannot serve as evidence that Berkeley believes in corpuscles. By 'parts' Berkeley is most likely to mean parts just large enough to be detected by a microscope, not parts so small that no one has perceived them. The objector, after all, is not explicitly concerned with insensible parts, but with the 'curious organization of plants, and the admirable mechanism in the parts of animals' (*Principles* 60). He wants the immaterialist to explain why 'God should make us, upon a close *inspection* into his works, *behold* so great variety of *ideas*, so artfully laid together' (§ 64, emphasis mine). For the purposes of the objection the interlocutor is assuming that all things are ideas, or '*inefficacious perceptions* in the mind' (§ 64). He refers not to parts which have never been perceived (had he done so his objection would not be that parts, being ideas, are unnecessary and pointless, but that some parts of things seem not be ideas), but to the 'great variety of ideas' which dissection and microscopy bring before us. 'Scarce to be discerned by the best microscope' means *just barely discerned* by the best microscope.[44]

But Garber is on the right track when he says that the argument meant to show that internal mechanisms are compatible with immaterialism works as well for corpuscles as it does for the parts of a watch. A Berkeleyan case for corpuscles can be constructed, it seems, along somewhat Lockean lines; the crucial difference will be that where the Lockean appeals to the intelligibility of mechanism—its power to explain—the Berkeleyan will appeal to its universality—its status as a 'grammar' in which everything (or everything of a certain kind) finds a place. A watch owes its behaviour to its springs and

[43] 'Locke, Berkeley, and Corpuscular Scepticism', p. 184.

[44] Some of the points I make in the paragraph are also made by Margaret Wilson, 'Berkeley and the Essences of the Corpuscularians', in John Foster and Howard Robinson (eds.), *Essays on Berkeley: A Tercentennial Celebration*, Oxford, 1985, pp. 137–8.

wheels. A louse depends for its nourishment on organs seen only through a microscope. If mechanism is universal the operation of an insect's organs should depend on even smaller parts which we may never see. This kind of hypothesizing is an expression of a tendency of which Berkeley cautiously approves, a tendency to seek general rules under which the analogies and uniformities we observe in nature can be subsumed (*Principles* 105).

But Berkeley's approval is deliberately cautious, and it is here that we may discover a difference between the parts and organs of plants and animals seen only through a microscope and the ultimate particles we have not yet been fortunate enough to see. At *Principles* 65 Berkeley describes the connections among ideas as 'permanent and universal', and in § 146 he admires the 'constant regularity, order, and concatenation of natural things'. Yet in § 106, just after approving of our search for general rules, he warns that we should 'proceed warily':

for we are apt to lay too great a stress on analogies, and to the prejudice of truth, humour that eagerness of mind, whereby it is carried to extend its knowledge into general theorems. For example, gravitation, or mutual attraction, because it appears in many instances, some are straightway for pronouncing *universal*; and that to *attract, and be attracted by every other body, is an essential quality inherent in all bodies whatsoever.*

The regularities we observe, he continues, depend entirely 'on the will of the *governing spirit*, who causes certain bodies to cleave together, or tend towards each other, according to various laws, whilst he keeps others at a fixed distance; and to some he gives a quite contrary tendency to fly asunder, just as he sees convenient'. The same warning is delivered in *Siris* 235–46, where Berkeley repeats his earlier point that the regularities we believe in may not be universal, and adds that the rules of mechanism cannot be used to explicate every phenomenon in nature: 'Nature seems better known and explained by attractions and repulsions than by those other mechanical principles of size, figure, and the like; that is, by Sir Isaac Newton, than Descartes.' (§ 243.) A related warning appears in *Principles* 107:

By a diligent observation of the phenomena within our view, we may discover the general laws of Nature, and from them deduce the other phenomena, I do not say *demonstrate*; for all deductions of that kind depend on a supposition that the Author of Nature always operates uniformly, and in a constant observance of those rules we take for principles: which we cannot evidently know.

The implication of these passages is that we need to exercise caution in applying such principles as Newton's third rule of philosophizing, which says that '*the qualities of bodies, which admit neither intension nor remission of degrees, and which are found to belong to all bodies within the reach of our experiments, are to be esteemed the universal qualities of all bodies whatsoever.*'[45] It follows that no argument from the universality of mechanism can be risk-free, and it follows too, it seems to me, that the Lockean argument sketched above cannot be one that Berkeley is obliged to accept. I suspect that Berkeley wants to avoid too definite a position on the existence of entities not yet perceived, whether or not those entities are corpuscles. He wants his position to 'float', its level to be determined by the kind of evidence that would strike both materialists and immaterialists with at least roughly equal force. Evidence might be provided by analogies between the phenomena to be explicated and phenomena already known to depend on mechanisms which were once covert, but there can be little doubt that Berkeley, like most of his contemporaries, would be especially impressed by observations of the entities inferred. He might be criticized for failing to see that the decision to count microscopical scenes as observations of the imperceptibly small is itself laden with mechanism. In a moment I will explain why I do not believe this is the case, but even if it is—even if so-called microscopical observations are not observations at all but additional data to be accounted for—microscopical scenes can strengthen the case for a hypothesis by adding to the list of phenomena it might be used to explicate.

So much for what Berkeley seems to have intended. I now want to ask how microscopic and sub-microscopic immaterial entities are to be construed, because even if Berkeley harboured no doubts about the universality of mechanism, he would be unable to accommodate unperceived parts and particles if they ran counter to his declaration that unthinking things cannot exist out of all relation to their being perceived.

Granting for the moment that a microscopical scene we are inclined to call an observation can in fact be said to be one, unperceived parts and particles will presumably pose no problem at all, so long as advances in instrumentation would permit them to be perceived. On the account of unperceived existence I defended in Chapter 7, an unperceived thing exists at a time if, had certain conditions then been met, it would have been perceived. In Chapter 7 I said relatively little

---

[45] *Principia*, Bk. III, Rule iii, p. 398 in Motte and Cajori.

about those conditions, but it is clear that they must be conditions in which the standing laws of nature entail that the thing in question would be perceived. Thus if the laws of nature entail that an unperceived part or particle would be perceived under certain circumstances, Berkeley's phenomenalism permits the part or particle to exist, even if it is beyond the power of the best microscopes. An example of the kind of circumstances I have in mind is the construction of a microscope with certain optical properties. It must be possible, of course, to specify these properties without referring to the object whose existence is in question.

Suppose, though, that the laws of nature (either alone or together with some very basic facts) give us reason to believe that the part or particle can never be perceived. Consider the particles by which we perceive other things—the particles of light, or of the ether that transmits light. Suppose that advanced microscopists have harnessed these particles and use them to display the outline or figure of the larger corpuscles that combine to form things. If the powerful microscopes by which we perceive these corpuscles can be explicated mechanically, the particles of light must presumably be very small: only if they were considerably smaller than the other corpuscles would they be able to carry information about their outline or figure. Can we perceive the outline or figure of the tiny particles of light? There might, of course, be particles even smaller than the particles of light, and it might be possible—that is, consistent with the laws of nature—for a machine to use these particles as the microscope uses light, 'illuminating' the particles of light themselves. Even if these smaller particles are not *normally* the ones by which we see, they might in fact be used to see. But this merely postpones the difficulty.[46] Whatever turns out to be the smallest particle cannot, it seems, be perceived, at least not without sacrificing the universality of mechanism.[47] Can we

[46] But this line of reasoning does show that observing the particles of light is not inconsistent with mechanism. There might be smaller particles on hand, and we might be able to manipulate them in the required way.

[47] In fact the most we are entitled to conclude is that we cannot perceive the *shape* of these particles without sacrificing the universality of mechanism. Perhaps we could detect their presence (and even count them) by means of particles too gross to register their shape. It is not clear to me whether Berkeley and his contemporaries could be brought to say that this would amount to perceiving them. But I am not in fact certain that an exceptionless mechanism makes it impossible to perceive even the smallest particle; perhaps someone with more imagination than myself will find a way in which larger particles, responding only to impact, can register (in a form available in the end to our sense organs) the properties of the smallest particles.

suppose that God simply turns away from mechanism at precisely this point, vouchsafing us ideas of the smallest particles? We would then have to wonder, with Margaret Wilson, whether 'on this understanding, the "perceivability in principle" of corpuscles is sufficient to ground their actuality, or *only* their possibility'.[48] If the laws of nature, together with the admittedly contingent claim that the particles in question happen to be the smallest ones, tell us that no machine could enhance our senses dramatically enough to permit us to perceive their shape, then the best account of their existence we could provide would come to something like this: 'If God makes them perceivable (in certain circumstances) then we will perceive them (in those circumstances).' But why is this a comment about the actual world, as opposed to the observation (quoting Wilson again) that 'in some possible world, different from the actual one, human beings perceive [the smallest] corpuscles, which therefore exist in that world'? Why wouldn't the particles be *created* at the first moment we perceived them?

The problem Wilson identifies can be overcome, however, if the non-mechanistic principle, though never activated, has been in force from the very beginning. Unknown though it is, the principle entails that under certain conditions the smallest particles must be perceived. The conditions may include the invention of a device which mechanism cannot explicate, or an exercise of our own faculties that strikes the committed mechanist as magical or superstitious.

But should views displayed by non-mechanistic or magical means be treated as observations of something really there? We cannot address this worry, it seems to me, without returning to the question of whether the microscopical scenes already available to Berkeley and his contemporaries were properly regarded as observations. Suppose that the microscope reveals animalcules when applied to milk that later spoils, or troubles the digestion of the baby who drinks it for breakfast. Suppose too that as our experience accumulates, we are able to separate safe from unsafe milk by using a microscope. The connection between the views afforded by the microscope and events we can observe without it makes it reasonable to say that the animalcules are in the milk. For the phenomenalist, relations we naturally take to be spatial (such as the part/whole relation, or the relation of physical containment) are simply a matter of such connections. If, then, non-

---

[48] 'Berkeley and the Corpuscularians', p. 143. The next quotation appears on the same page.

mechanistic or apparently magical methods enable us to make predictions we could not make without them, it can likewise be reasonable to say the view these methods afford are observations of the smallest particles. The decision to count microscopic scenes as observations is not, then, laden with mechanism; it does depend, however, on the existence of reliable connections between the scenes disclosed and the observations we make by other means. This gives us a way of correcting an over-simplification in my statements of phenomenalism in Chapter 7. In order for a table to exist in an unoccupied study it is not in fact enough that I should have an idea of a table when I go there. The idea must bear the kind of relations to other ideas that make it a real idea; an observation of a table is not merely having a table-like idea, but having a table-like idea that satisfies certain conditions. In the same way, in order for an unperceived part to exist it is not enough that I should have an idea of that part when I dissect an organism or place it under a microscope. In order for my observation to be 'of' the part my idea must in certain ways be fruitful; if it bears no fruit my idea is nothing more than an engaging scene.[49] In much the same way, the part's 'inwardness' is nothing over and above its fruitfulness:

By this means abundance of information is conveyed unto us, concerning what we are to expect from such and such actions, and what methods are proper to be taken, for the exciting such and such ideas: which in effect is all that I conceive to be distinctly meant, when it is said that by discerning the figure, texture, and mechanism of the inward parts of bodies, whether natural or artificial, we may attain to know the several uses and properties depending thereon, or the nature of the thing. (*Principles* 65.)

I conclude, then, that Berkeley can construe particles immaterialistically, though the case of the smallest particles probably calls for an abandonment of universal mechanism. Yet the perceivability of even the smallest particles depends on laws or regularities. For a particle to be perceivable—for a particle to exist—it isn't enough to say that it is logically possible to perceive it. A standing regularity must entail that in certain circumstances it would be perceived.

[49] This may destroy the contrast between particles and forces. A contrast might still be drawn by saying that there are no force-like ideas, but I am not sure that Berkeley has a way of defending this. Note, though, that if the contrast is destroyed and the interpretation I offer here is the correct one, Berkeley does not become an instrumentalist about particles, but a non-instrumentalist about forces.

As Garber and Tipton have both noted, particles which are perceivable in principle must have some secondary qualities.[50] But it remains true that these qualities need not play a scientifically important role. As Garber points out, Berkeley can even explicate the manifest colours of bodies in terms of the primary qualities of particles.[51] It is also possible for ultimate corpuscles to be transparent or pellucid, as many corpuscularians in fact suspected. Berkeley's claim at *Commentaries* 453 that pellucidness is a colour may seem outrageous, but in my view he is rightly calling attention to our experience of transparent things. These things can be seen because they reflect the objects around them; even if we hesitate to say they have a colour of their own, the play of light on their surfaces plays the role of colour. And Berkeley, when he specifies the proper objects of sight at *Principles* 1, includes light as well as colour, as Philonous does in the First Dialogue (p. 175).[52]

In this chapter I have tried to show that Berkeley addresses the kind of corpuscularianism advocated by Locke. I have suggested that Berkeley was aware of the corpuscularian standard of intelligibility, a standard Hylas in fact represents when he tells Philonous that 'the only action of bodies is motion; and motion cannot be communicated otherwise than by impulse' (First Dialogue, p. 186). Unlike Hylas, Berkeley does not believe that the appeal to corpuscular substructures can explain anything. He proposes another way of understanding the importance of unperceived parts, one that undercuts the attempt to rest a metaphysically significant distinction between primary and secondary qualities on the authority of science. He does this by showing that we can respect the success of science without using the distinction to mark anything more than the difference between more or less useful signs. The secondary qualities are the signs of impending pleasure and pain that we exploit in our primitive state. God has arranged things so that we can get along quite well without knowing very much. But in the end, the primary qualities may be more useful to us than the secondary, because they allow for predictions of larger scope. We have been doubly equipped for getting along in life—first

[50] Garber, 'Locke, Berkeley, and Corpuscular Scepticism', pp. 193–4; Tipton, 'The "Philosopher by Fire" in Berkeley's *Alciphron*', p. 173.

[51] Garber, 'Locke, Berkeley, and Corpuscular Scepticism', p. 194.

[52] For another reading of entry 453 see Arnold I. Davidson and Norbert Hornstein, 'The Primary/Secondary Quality Distinction: Berkeley, Locke, and the Foundations of Corpuscularian Science', *Dialogue* 23 (1984), p. 301.

with ideas of secondary qualities linked in obvious ways with pleasure and pain, later with the means of detecting subtler and more extensive connections involving the primary qualities. For Berkeley, this would further testify to God's providence.

9
SPIRIT

EARLY in the Third Dialogue, when Philonous admits that we have no idea of God, it dawns on Hylas that Philonous may be double-dealing. 'If you can conceive the mind of God without having an idea of it,' Hylas asks, 'why may not I be allowed to conceive the existence of matter, notwithstanding that I have no idea of it?' (p. 231.) In response Philonous offers a long explanation of why 'the case of *matter* [is] widely different from that of the *Deity*', describing our use of reflection and reasoning to arrive at 'some sort of an active image' of God (p. 232). In the first two editions Hylas pronounces himself satisfied with this explanation, and he moves on to a different point. But in the third edition his worry is not so easily shaken, and he presents it in another way:

You say your own soul supplies you with some sort of an idea or image of God. But at the same time you acknowledge you have, properly speaking, no idea of your own soul. You even affirm that spirits are a sort of beings altogether different from ideas. Consequently that no idea can be like a spirit. We have therefore no idea of any spirit. You admit nevertheless that there is spiritual substance, although you have no idea of it; while you deny there can be such a thing as material substance, because you have no notion or idea of it. Is this fair dealing? To act consistently, you must either admit matter or reject spirit. What say you to this? (p. 232.)

Hylas is undeterred by Philonous's first attempt at a reply. 'Notwithstanding all you have said,' says Hylas,

to me it seems, that according to your own way of thinking, and in consequence of your own principles, it should follow that you are only a system of floating ideas, without any substance to support them. Words are not to be used without a meaning. And as there is no more meaning in spiritual substance than in material substance, the one is to be exploded as well as the other. (p. 233.)

Hylas is mainly concerned with the problem of how we can think of spirits, but if we cannot think of them we cannot know them, and in his reply Philonous tries to show that we can manage both. Berkeley's right to say that he knows there are minds other than his own can be challenged, of course, even if his claim that he can think of other minds is taken for granted. Thomas Reid writes,[1]

Although [Berkeley's system] leaves us sufficient evidence of a supreme intelligent mind, it seems to take away all the evidence we have of other intelligent beings like ourselves. What I call a father, a brother, or a friend, is only a parcel of ideas in my own mind; and, being ideas in my mind, they cannot possibly have that relation to another mind which they have to mine, any more than the pain felt by me can be the individual pain felt by another. I can find no principle in Berkeley's system which affords me even probable ground to conclude that there are intelligent beings, like myself, in the relations of father, brother, friend, or fellow-citizen. I am left alone, as the only creature of God in the universe, in that forlorn state of *egoism* into which it is said some of the disciples of Des Cartes were brought by his philosophy.

Like Hylas, Reid is demanding parity of treatment, but he is thinking less of Berkeley's attack on matter as empty or incoherent than he is of *Principles* 18–20, where Berkeley maintains that 'If there were external bodies, it is impossible we should ever come to know it; and if there were not, we might have the very same reasons to think there were that we have now.' (§ 20.) A few simple changes in the rest of § 20 are all it takes to adapt it to the case at hand:

Suppose, what no one can deny possible, an intelligence, without the help of *other finite minds*, to be affected with the same train of sensations or ideas that you are, imprinted in the same order and with like vividness in his mind. I ask whether that intelligence hath not all the reason to believe the existence of *other finite minds*, disclosed by his ideas, and exciting them in his mind, that you can possibly have for believing the same thing? Of this there can be no question; which one consideration is enough to make any reasonable person suspect the strength of whatever arguments he may think himself to have, for the existence of *finite minds besides his own*. [The three italicized phrases have been substituted for 'external bodies', 'corporeal substances', and 'bodies without the mind'. After the second phrase I have also substituted 'disclosed' for 'represented'.]

In this chapter I hope to defend Berkeley against the objections of Hylas and Reid. I think it can be shown that Berkeley accounts for our ability to think of spirits without compromising his attack on matter. Once he provides such an account it is comparatively easy for him to meet the challenge thrown down by Reid, partly because Reid asks

---

[1] *Essays on the Intellectual Powers of Man*, II x, p. 285 in vol. 1 of the Hamilton edn.

only to be shown that the existence of other minds is probable, and partly because he accepts a case for God's existence which is bound up with the case for other created minds. Each case lends support to the other. Yet it remains true that the evidence of God's existence is more copious and compelling than the evidence for any single created mind other than one's own.

1. *The parity objection*

Philonous responds to Hylas's third edition objection in two separate speeches, the first on pp. 232–3, and the second on pp. 233–4. In the first speech Philonous identifies three ways in which the notion of matter falls short of the notion of spirit. The notion of matter is first of all inconsistent: 'I do not deny the existence of material substance, merely because I have no notion of it, but . . . because it is repugnant that there should be a notion of it.' There is no inconsistency in the notion of spirit. Second, although it is sometimes reasonable to believe in the existence of things we do not perceive, there has to be some reason for such a belief. 'I have no reason for believing the existence of matter', Philonous says. 'I have no immediate intuition thereof: neither can I mediately from my sensations, ideas, notions, actions or passions, infer an unthinking, unperceiving, inactive substance, either by probable deduction, or necessary consequence.' But my own soul, he explains, is known by reflection, and the existence of others can be inferred from their signs and effects. Finally, we know what we mean when we affirm the existence of a spiritual substance who knows and perceives ideas. The claim that there is a material substance in which ideas or qualities inhere has no meaning, or no meaning that is consistent: 'I do not know what is meant, when it is said, that an unperceiving substance hath inherent in it and supports either ideas or the archetypes of ideas.' In view of the wide differences in coherence, evidence, and clarity, Philonous concludes that 'there is . . . upon the whole no parity of case between spirit and matter.' (All quotations in this paragraph are from the Third Dialogue, pp. 232–4.)

Hylas receives all this as docilely as he had received the earlier material is meant to uphold. 'I own my self satisfied', he says, and in view of his prior commitments this is, after all, as it should be. Hylas has accepted Philonous's case against material substance, and virtually every consideration earlier brought against matter seems to argue for the existence of spirit. The notion of matter is repugnant because an inactive and unperceiving substratum cannot support an idea or quality whose *esse* is *percipi*. But this is just to say that if ideas or qualities stand in need of support, it can only be provided by a perceiving substance or spirit. The notion of matter is drained of content when, in an attempt to avoid incoherence, the relation of matter to its qualities is characterized as inherence. The notion of spirit, which invites us to fill out the abstract notion of inherence with the concrete operations of willing and perceiving, could hardly be more clear.

Philonous closes the first of the two speeches in the third edition by invoking a distinction between ideas and notions. 'I say lastly, that I have a notion of spirit, though I have not, strictly speaking, an idea of it. I do not perceive it as an idea or by means of an idea, but know it by reflexion.' The distinction had in fact been respected by Hylas in stating his objection. Hylas had said that Philonous denies the existence of matter because he has 'no notion or idea of it', yet affirms the existence of spirit despite having 'no idea of it'. The point of the distinction is that the case against matter turns not on a narrow claim about ideas, but on a wider claim about what we are able to think of or understand. According to Philonous we have a notion of spirit—we are able to think of it—even though we have no idea of spirit. The same, he thinks, cannot be said for matter.

The distinction between idea and notion also appears in the second edition of the *Principles*, which was published along with the third edition of the *Dialogues* in 1734. In the first edition of the *Principles* the two notions had been pretty much interchangeable , though even there the word 'notion' often suggested something that did not merely reproduce ideas impressed on the senses. Among Berkeley's predecessors in the writing of philosophical English—in Locke, Cudworth, and Sergeant, for example—the word 'notion' was often used for a thought or representation which involves more in the way of mental activity than a mere reproduction of something sensed, or for a thought whose object is intelligible rather than sensible.[2] These two uses of

---

[2] According to Locke's official definition of 'idea' (*Essay* I i 8) there is no difference between an idea and a notion; in this Locke follows Gassendi (see Howard P. Jones (ed.), *Pierre Gassendi's Institutio Logica 1658*, Assen, 1981, pp. 83–4) and the authors of the *Port-Royal Logic* (*Logic: Or, the Art of Thinking* I i, p. 35 in the Ozell trans., London, 1723). Yet at *Essay* II xxii 2, when introducing mixed modes, Locke writes that '*The Mind* often *exercises an active Power*' in combining ideas. 'For it being once furnished with simple *Ideas*, it can put them together in several Compositions, and so make variety of complex *Ideas*, without examining whether they exist so together in Nature. And hence, I

'notion' were connected, because the mind was taken to be passive in sensation, and many writers took it to be passive even in the reproduction of sensation, as in Hobbes's characterization of imagination as decaying sense.[3] In the second edition of the *Principles* Berkeley added the following sentence to the end of § 27, where he had argued that a soul or spirit cannot be represented by an idea:

Though it must be owned at the same time, that we have some notion of soul, spirit, and the operations of the mind, such as willing, loving, hating, in as much as we know or understand the meaning of those words.

In the first edition version of § 140 he had said that 'in a large sense indeed, we may be said to have an idea of *spirit*'; in the second edition this was amended to read 'an idea, or rather a notion of *spirit*', though Jessop explains that this marked a return to a formulation crossed out in the original manuscript.[4] In § 142 in the second edition Berkeley added the following:

We may not I think strictly be said to have an idea of an active being, or of an action, although we may be said to have a notion of them. I have some knowledge or notion of my mind, and its acts about ideas, inasmuch as I know or understand what is meant by those words. What I know, that I have some notion of. I will not say, that the terms *idea* and *notion* may not be used convertibly, if the world will have it so. But yet it conduceth to clearness and propriety, that we distinguish things very different by different names. It is also to be remarked, that all relations including an act of the mind, we cannot so

think, it is, that these *Ideas* are called *Notions*: as if they had their Original, and constant Existence, more in the Thoughts of Men, than in the reality of things.' In the *True Intellectual System*, London, 1678, Cudworth contrasts 'Sensible Ideas' with 'Intelligible Notions' (p. 636). For Sergeant see the passages from *The Method to Science* and *Solid Philosophy Asserted* quoted in Chap. 8. The distinction between ideas and notions was by no means strict or absolute. Henry More, for example, freely alternates between them. See the selections from *An Antidote Against Atheism*, I vi 3, 6 in Flora MacKinnon (ed.), *Philosophical Writings of Henry More*, New York, 1925, pp. 16, 17. Samuel Johnson's *Elementa Philosophica*, Philadelphia, 1752, testifies to the influence of the Lockean usage. Idea 'has been commonly defined and used by the Moderns', he explains, to signify 'any immediate Object of the Mind in Thinking, whether sensible or intellectual, and so is, in Effect, synonymous with the word *Thought*, which comprehends both' ('Noetica', p. 3). 'It may be best', he suggests, 'to confine the Word *Idea* to the immediate objects of Sense and Imagination, which was the original Meaning of it; and to use the Word *Notion* or *Conception*, to signify the Objects of Consciousness and pure Intellect' ('Noetica', p. 4).

[3] *Leviathan*, Pt. 1, chap. 2, pp. 4–5, Sir William Molesworth (ed.), *The English Works of Thomas Hobbes*, London, 1839, vol. 3.

[4] See the textual apparatus on p. 105 of *Works* II, as well as the n. on p. 53.

properly be said to have an idea, but rather a notion of the relations or habitudes between things. But if in the modern way the word *idea* is extended to spirits, and relations and acts; this is after all an affair of verbal concern.[5]

It is important to understand that Berkeley's notions—in the narrow sense of 1734—are not representations which stand to minds in anything like the way in which ideas, as the materialist views them, stand to bodies. When Berkeley says that we have a notion of mind or spirit, he means that we are able to think and speak of mind and spirit. For Berkeley, to say that we have a notion of spirit is not to explain our understanding of it. The words *soul*, *spirit*, and *substance*, he writes at *Principles* 139, 'do mean or signify a real thing, which is neither an idea nor like an idea, but that which perceives ideas, and wills, and reasons about them. What I am my self, that which I denote by the term I, is the same with what is meant by *soul* or *spiritual substance*.' If *having a notion* means anything more than *understanding*, it is merely that the understanding is not acquired through the senses.[6]

But if to say that we have a notion of spirit is to say nothing more than that we are able to think and speak of it, Berkeley seems to be *asserting* that spirit is conceivable instead of proving that it is. Can the materialist simply assert that matter is conceivable? This can help the materialist only if we are given some reason to believe that the appropriate route to a conception of matter does not involve having an idea of it. If it appears that we can conceive of matter only by way of idea, then the distinction between ideas and notions will be of no use to the materialist. Berkeley is in a better position because he has at least the outline of a way in which we can arrive at a non-sensed-based

[5] See also § 89 for another passage introduced in 1734 in which the word 'notion' plays an important role. There were also a number of smaller changes, all of them documented by Luce and Jessop. The 'modern way' of using idea, incidentally, is probably an allusion to such writers as Descartes, Gassendi, Arnauld and Nicole, and Locke. At *Theory of Vision* 45 Berkeley takes the word 'idea' to stand for 'any the immediate object of sense or understanding, in which large signification it is commonly used by the moderns'.

[6] It is also important to realize that a notion is not necessarily 'relative.' At *Principles* 89 and 142 Berkeley counts relations as objects of knowledge of which we have notions rather than ideas, but this is because relations always include an act of mind (§ 142). Berkeley's reasoning on this point was perhaps inspired by Locke, who wrote that relations are 'not contained in the real existence of Things' but are 'superinduced' (II xxv 8) by the comparing mind. One of Berkeley's most prominent examples of a notion is that of one's own self, which is not constructed by exploiting a relation that terminates in known ideas, but acquired by reflecting on a soul with which we are immediately acquainted. Berkeley's belief that we have notions of relations is derived from his belief that we have notions (rather than ideas) of the mind and its operations.

conception of mind and spirit. We arrive at a notion of spirit by turning inward, by reflecting on our own selves. Philonous recognizes the importance of this method when he uses it to support the distinction between notions and ideas. 'I say . . . that I have a notion of spirit, though I have not, strictly speaking, an idea of it. I do not perceive it as an idea or by means of an idea, but know it by reflexion.' (p. 233.) Even in the first two editions of the *Dialogues* Philonous calls attention to the importance of the 'reflex act' by which we know our own selves, a mode of apprehension to be carefully distinguished from our objective perception of inactive beings or ideas (p. 232). This is further evidence for Jessop's already well-fortified contention that the modifications of 1734 do not reflect a change in view.

In the texts we have discussed there are unacknowledged shifts in the apparent focus of concern. This is particularly clear in *Principles* 139, where Berkeley begins with the terms *soul*, *spirit*, and *substance*, but later shifts to 'the term I'. In the passages from the Third Dialogue he seems to be concerned for the most part with the words *soul* and *spirit*, and with the notion of spirit-in-general they might be said to express, though in the passage last quoted from the *Dialogues* his concern seems to have shifted once again to the notion of *one's own* self, and to the 'reflex act' that allegedly provides it.

Berkeley has to do more than establish his right to think and speak of his own self, but self-awareness plays a central role in his account of our ability to think and speak of other minds. 'The being of my self, that is, my own soul, mind or thinking principle, I evidently know by reflexion', Philonous says on p. 233, and Berkeley hopes to use this knowledge or acquaintance to show that we can both think of other minds and know that they exist, even if our grounds for this knowledge are merely probable. Philonous carefully distinguishes between knowledge of his own soul and knowledge of the souls of others. His own existence is disclosed by reflection or 'immediate intuition' (p. 233). The existence of others is known only by argument. Reflection not only assures Philonous of his own existence, but equips him with a notion of mind or spirit (a notion of them in general) which he can proceed to apply—with somewhat diminished assurance—to the case of others. When he moves from his own case ('the being of my self, . . . I evidently know by reflexion') to the case of other finite minds (known by their 'signs and effects'), and then returns to reflection ('I say lastly, that I have a notion of spirit, though I have not, strictly speaking, an idea of it') as the source of his understanding of spirit in general, Philonous is giving voice to the dual role of reflection in Berkeley's account of our conception and cognition of spirit. Reflection assures us that our own soul can be both conceived and known to exist. But it also supplies us with a notion of spirit that can be extended to others. The extension is accomplished with the help of the ideas which are the 'signs and effects' of other spirits. To conceive of another finite spirit is to conceive of an entity like oneself who is associated, as occasion or cause, with a certain body of ideas. To know that such a spirit exists is to be justified in inferring its existence from that body of ideas. How powerful such a justification can be is a question I will take up in just a moment; the important point for now is that I am able to conceive of another person without coming into direct contact with his or her soul, and I owe that ability to my capacity to conceive of my own self. My soul serves, then, as an image of the souls of others:

We know other spirits by means of our own soul, which in that sense is the image or idea of them, it having a like respect to other spirits, that blueness or heat by me perceived has to those ideas perceived by another. (*Principles* 140.)

In the case of God a bit more work is required, and even after all the work the resulting image is less adequate than in the case of other finite spirits, but according to Philonous the basic process is the same:

Taking the word *idea* in a large sense, my soul may be said to furnish me with an idea, that is, an image, or likeness of God, though indeed extremely inadequate. For all the notion I have of God, is obtained by reflecting on my own soul heightening its powers, and removing its imperfections. I have therefore, though not an inactive idea, yet in my self some sort of an active thinking image of the Deity. And though I perceive Him not by sense, yet I have a notion of Him, or know Him by reflexion and reasoning. (Third Dialogue, pp. 231–2.)

Philonous sums up the process as follows: 'My own mind and my own ideas I have an immediate knowledge of; and by the help of these, do mediately apprehend the possibility of the existence of other spirits and ideas.'

Berkeley's way of establishing our capacity to conceive of other minds has two notable attractions. First, it gives Berkeley a way of reconciling his belief that other minds are not present to our own with the assumption (made for example by Malebranche) that perception or understanding requires presence to the mind, not merely what Arnauld called 'objective presence', which is just a way of referring to an object's being perceived or understood, but something more. Although other minds are not present to my mind, my own mind certainly is, and I can think of other minds by means of it. Second, Berkeley's approach explains how we can claim to conceive of God without exaggerating the limits of our intellect. God is conceived as an entity like us who is responsible for an especially rich and orderly system of ideas. This removes at least some of the abstraction found in an account such as Locke's, according to which we arrive at our idea of God by 'enlarging' simple ideas derived from reflection or sensation until they achieve the 'vastness' appropriate to the Deity (*Essay* II xxiii 34). Philonous also speaks of 'heightening our own powers', but Berkeley gives us a concrete way in which such heightening can be accomplished, because much of God's vastness is mirrored in the system of ideas he has created.

I turn now to our knowledge of the existence of other minds. One of Berkeley's most dramatic proofs of God's existence comes near the end of the *Principles*:

But though there be some things which convince us, human agents are concerned in producing them; yet it is evident to every one, that those things which are called the works of Nature, that is, the far greater part of the ideas or sensations perceived by us, are not produced by, or dependent on the wills of men. There is therefore some other spirit that causes them, since it is repugnant that they should subsist by themselves. See *Sect.* 29. But if we attentively consider the constant regularity, order, and concatenation of natural things, the surprising magnificence, beauty, and perfection of the larger, and the exquisite contrivance of the smaller parts of the creation, together with the exact harmony and correspondence of the whole, but above all, the never enough admired laws of pain and pleasure, and the instincts or natural inclinations, appetites, and passion of animals; I say if we consider all these things, and at the same time attend to the meaning and import of the attributes, one, eternal, infinitely wise, good, and perfect, we shall clearly perceive that they belong to the aforesaid spirit, *who works all in all*, and *by whom all things consist.* (*Principles* 146.)

In his own commentary on the proof Berkeley calls attention to the rich variety of evidence for God, whose existence is more evident than that of any being other than oneself:

Hence it is evident, that God is known as certainly and immediately as any other mind or spirit whatsoever, distinct from our selves. We may even assert, that the existence of God is far more evidently perceived than the existence of men; because the effects of nature are infinitely more numerous and considerable, than those ascribed to human agents. There is not any one mark that denotes a man, or effect produced by him, which doth not more strongly evince the being of that spirit who is the *Author of Nature*. For it is evident that in affecting other persons, the will of man hath no other object, than barely the motion of the limbs of his body; but that such a motion should be attended by, or excite any idea in the mind of another, depends wholly on the will of the Creator. He alone it is who *upholding all things by the Word of his Power*, maintains that intercourse between spirits, whereby they are able to perceive the existence of each other. And yet this pure and clear light which enlightens every one, is it self invisible. (*Principles* 147)

Now despite its grandeur there is something disturbing in Berkeley's argument, and the effect is actually heightened by his commentary. The argument ends by proclaiming that God's existence is more evident than that of other men and women, yet the argument itself seems to depend on a separation between 'the works of Nature' and the works of humankind, a separation which could not be made if the existence of men and women had not already been established. The argument of *Principles* 146 begins by putting aside those things 'human agents are concerned in producing'. In much the same way, a similar argument at *Alciphron* IV 5 begins with the observation that 'The soul of man actuates but a small body, an insignificant particle, in respect of the great masses of nature, the elements, and heavenly bodies, and system of the world', and the ensuing argument urges that we infer 'power and wisdom incomparably greater than that of the human soul' from the motions 'independent of ʏan's will' (*Works* III, p. 146). Although Reid lets it pass, Berkeley's argument for God's existence seems to depend on the very belief in other created minds which he accuses Berkeley of failing to establish.

There are dialectical reasons for distinguishing between the works of nature and those of human beings before beginning an argument for God's existence, and these reasons might appeal even to a philosopher who is convinced that the argument might be presented in another way. Scepticism about the existence of God was far more likely to be encountered than scepticism about one's fellow humans; the 'problem of other minds' was far from the stock philosophical conundrum it has become. And mention of human skill and intelligence is useful to the argument because it provides those who hear it with a standard against which God's superior perfections can be measured.[7] But would the

[7] A third force working on behalf of the distinction is the way in which Berkeley's writings are *addressed*. An audience of many finite minds is simply (and unsurprisingly)

argument survive if the distinction between the natural and the artificial had not been made?

Without the distinction the argument would, I think, lose a fair amount of power, because a good part of human behaviour is not so regular—or not so obviously regular—as the behaviour determined by what Berkeley calls the 'laws of pain and pleasure'.[8] And even if its regularity were both striking and exceptionless, a great deal of human behaviour is neither virtuous nor good. This means that the meditation Berkeley recommends on the attributes infinitely wise, good, and perfect would not lead to the result he hopes for. A god who is responsible for all of human behaviour would be somewhat less wise and a good deal less perfect than Berkeley's God.

Yet I do not think it follows that Berkeley's argument for God's existence can be commenced only after the existence of other finite minds has been established. It would be better to say that the existence of God and other finite minds should be inferred *simultaneously*, as the best total explanation of our ideas of sense. In a world bespeaking both vast goodness and significant evil, an inference to a complex cause may be the most reasonable response. In the end the argument cannot of course succeed, if only because the evidence will not be enough to convince us that the existence of an infinitely wise and perfect God is even part of the best explanation of ideas of sense. The attributes named simply go too far beyond the ideas they are invoked to explain. But the outline of the argument should be clear enough to show that Reid cannot reasonably draw a line between Berkeley's case for God's existence and his case for the existence of other created minds. Other minds can be conceived as readily as the mind of God, and the existence of both can be inferred, with some plausibility, by the same kind of probable argument.

Berkeley would not be entirely happy with my contention that the grounds for God's existence are probable at best. In the Third Dialogue, for example, there are indications that in Berkeley's opinion we can infer God's existence by 'necessary consequence'. In a passage that appears in all three editions of the *Dialogues*, Philonous says that

assumed. The 'I' of the *Principles* then becomes a *we*, and the distinction between the works of man and the works of nature is reduced to the distinction between what is brought about by me and what is not.

[8] It is conceivable that the hedonism of the *Philosophical Commentaries* carried over into the *Principles*; in that case the 'laws of pain and pleasure' would encompass the laws of human behaviour, and Berkeley would perhaps not agree with the claim I have just made.

'from my own being, and from the dependency I find in my self and my ideas, I do by an act of reason, necessarily infer the existence of a God, and of all created things in the mind of God.' (Third Dialogue, p. 232.) This echoes the argument for God's existence presented in the Second Dialogue, an argument Philonous describes as 'a direct and immediate demonstration' (p. 212). The fact that 'an infinite mind should be necessarily inferred from the bare existence of the sensible world' had there been cited as a singular advantage of immaterialism (p. 212). It cannot be supposed that Berkeley is using the modal modifier in a loose sense; Philonous's claim in the Third Dialogue that he infers God's existence necessarily is followed in the third edition by a passage identifying 'probable deduction' and 'necessary consequence' as distinct modes of inference (p. 233). Philonous goes on to say that 'we have neither an immediate evidence nor a demonstrative knowledge of the existence of other finite spirits', and he claims that their existence is probable (p. 233). All this suggests that Berkeley's proof of God's existence is not, at least in intention, a merely probable argument, and that there is an asymmetry between the case for God and the case for other minds, where probability is avowedly all that Berkeley seeks.

In this connection it may be useful to take a brief look at *Alciphron* IV. The main argument there is not the blend of cosmological and teleological considerations that we find in earlier works, but an ingenious adaptation of Berkeley's belief that our visual ideas are the language of the Author of Nature. Berkeley's representative Euphranor first offers a conventional argument for the existence of God, then challenges Alciphron to find (as Alciphron puts it) 'an argument which will prove the existence of a free-thinker, the like whereof cannot be applied to prove the existence of God' (IV 6, *Works* III, p. 148). Alciphron replies,

At first methought a particular structure, shape, or motion was the most certain proof of a thinking reasonable soul. But a little attention satisfied me that these things have no necessary connexion with reason, knowledge, and wisdom; and that, allowing them to be certain proofs of a living soul, they cannot be so of a thinking and reasonable one. Upon second thoughts, therefore, and a minute examination of this point, I have found that nothing so much convinces me of the existence of another person as his speaking to me. It is my hearing you talk that, in strict and philosophical truth, is to me the best argument for your being. And this is a peculiar argument, inapplicable to your purpose; for you will not, I suppose, pretend that God speaks to man in the same clear and sensible manner as one man doth to another? (pp. 148–9.)

But Euphranor does think that God speaks to man. 'The great Mover and Author of Nature constantly explaineth Himself to the eyes of men by the sensible intervention of arbitrary signs, which have no similitude or connexion with the things signified', and which therefore constitute a language of nature (IV 12, *Works* III, p. 157). Crito sums up the exchange between Euphranor and Alciphron with an appeal to necessary connection reminiscent of the *Three Dialogues*:

I think it plain this optic language hath a necessary connexion with knowledge, wisdom, and goodness. It is equivalent to a constant creation, betokening an immediate act of power and providence. It cannot be accounted for by mechanical principles, by atoms, attractions, or effluvia. The instantaneous production and reproduction of so many signs, combined, dissolved, transposed, diversified, and adapted to such an endless variety of purposes, ever shifting with the occasions and suited to them, being utterly inexplicable and unaccountable by the laws of motion, by chance, by fate, or the like blind principles, doth set forth and testify the immediate operation of a spirit or thinking being; and not merely of a spirit, which every motion or gravitation may possibly infer, but of one wise, good, and provident Spirit, who directs and rules and governs the world. (IV 14, pp. 159–60.)

It is hard to know how strictly Berkeley takes Crito's claim of necessary connection. When he presents his first, more conventional argument, Euphranor claims only that sensible signs 'suggest, indicate, and demonstrate an invisible God, as certainly, and with the same evidence, at least, as any other signs perceived by sense do suggest to me the existence of your soul, spirit, or thinking principle' (p. 147). Even his statement of the argument from the natural language of vision ends with the modest conclusion that 'you have as much reason to think the Universal Agent or God speaks to your eyes, as you can have for thinking any particular person speaks to your ears' (p. 157). He suggests that his evidence for God's existence is greater than his evidence for the existence of the free-thinker Alciphron, but the evidence he adduces for God is of the same basic type. I conclude from all this that although God's existence is something Euphranor certainly claims to demonstrate, the claim is not, when literally understood, central to his presentation; it seems more accurate to read him not as someone who hopes to convert the atheist by irresistible argument, but as a philosopher proposing a view of the world in which the Christian God finds a place.

The text of the *Dialogues* makes it difficult to play down Philonous's remarks about demonstration and necessary consequence as I have played down Crito's and Euphranor's. But my treatment of *Alciphron* IV does mark out a way of closing the gap between the text of the *Dialogues* and my reading of Berkeley's proof. Euphranor deliberately conducts the argument of *Alciphron* IV along lines laid down by Alciphron. 'O Alciphron,' he says before the argument begins, 'to content you *we* must prove . . . and we must prove upon your own terms.' 'What sort of proof', he asks, 'do you expect?' (p. 144.) Perhaps the *ad hominem* character of the first dialogue between Hylas and Philonous to some extent carries over into the other two: because Hylas shares the conventional expectation that God's existence will be demonstrated or inferred by necessary consequence, Philonous presents his proof in just those terms. This is not as insincere as it may seem, because Berkeley is convinced that his proof is no less demonstrative or necessary than the proofs of the materialist.[9]

There is another possible source of Berkeley's tendency to present his case for the existence of God as if it is more than a probable argument. Although we cannot agree with Philonous that the existence of God in all his detail is a necessary consequence of the dependency I find in my self and my ideas (p. 233), we can agree that the inference to *some* spiritual cause *is* necessary, at least within the setting of Berkeley's other views. Because they are changeable and perishing our ideas must have a cause; that cause can only be a spirit or a collection of spirits; and because I am unaware of bringing about the effects in question I cannot be among them. We have, then, a 'necessary' inference to what Philonous at first settles for describing as '*some other mind*' (Second Dialogue, p. 212). He promptly expands the description to 'an infinite omnipresent spirit', but the name of God is actually introduced by Hylas, whose reaction to the initial statement of the proof is that it comes to 'no more than I and all Christians hold; nay, and all others too who believe there is a God' (p. 212). Now if Philonous is inattentive to the greater specificity of 'an infinite omnipresent mind' and 'God', he is likely to represent a necessary inference to the existence of 'some other mind' as a necessary inference to the existence of God. Such inattentiveness would be excusable, it seems to me, because it is encouraged by Hylas and in the end makes no difference. The problem presented by the more specific

---

[9] The subtitle of the *Dialogues* promises a demonstration of 'the reality and perfection of human knowledge, the incorporeal nature of the soul, and the immediate providence of a Deity' (*Works* II, p. 147). Claims of almost equal strength are made in the Pref. to the first edn. of the *Principles* (*Works* II, p. 23).

descriptions cuts equally against the materialist, and such a problem, as Philonous repeatedly maintains, cannot be a proof against either side (Third Dialogue, p. 248).

Berkeley's descriptions of God also become progressively more specific in the *Principles*. In later sections there are even some signs of uneasiness over the steps required to make the 'some other will or spirit' of § 29 into the God of Scripture. At *Principles* 146 Berkeley concludes his proof with uncharacteristic vagueness, asking us to 'consider' the argument just offered, and to 'attend' at the same time to the 'meaning and import' of the traditional attributes of God. Perhaps he is aware that the additional steps are not deductive ones; at best there is a relation of fit between the existence of a spiritual cause (established in § 29), the order and beauty of the effects of that cause, and the divine attributes Berkeley enumerates in § 146.

Berkeley's account of how we think of other minds or spirits enables him to solve a difficulty which arose in Chapter 6, in connection with the master argument. I suggested there that Berkeley does have a way of explaining how I can conceive of an object or idea unconceived by me, or unconceived by me at the present moment. We can now see that I do it by conceiving of another mind. As Philonous explains in the Third Dialogue, I can, with the help of my mind and its ideas, 'mediately apprehend the possibility of other finite spirits *and ideas*' (p. 232, emphasis mine).

2. *An alleged incoherence*

S. A. Grave argues that Berkeley's descriptions of the mind combine two incompatible principles.[10] According to the 'distinction principle' (p. 298), the mind and its ideas are entirely distinct; this principle, Grave explains, permits Berkeley to say that two kinds can perceive the same thing. The 'identity principle' identifies an idea with an episode of awareness or act of perceiving; because it 'welds ideas to individual perceivers', Grave holds that this principle does not permit two minds to have the very same idea (p. 297). Two minds might have ideas that are in some ways *similar*, but they cannot be numerically identical if they are the acts or operations of minds which are numerically distinct.

---

[10] 'The Mind and Its Ideas', reprinted in C. B. Martin and David M. Armstrong (eds.), *Locke and Berkeley*, Notre Dame, 1968, pp. 296–313. Page refs. in the text are to this appearance of the article.

Grave insists that the principles are 'quite irreconcilable' (p. 298), and he speculates on the source of Berkeley's fatal attempt to combine them. Berkeley 'was driven', he suggests, 'by two conflicting desires: one, to oblige men to see that if there were no minds there would be nothing at all; the other, to meet the demands of common sense' (p. 298).

Grave believes that Berkeley is in fact committed only to the identity principle. 'The illusion of two conflicting sets of opinions', he writes, 'is generated by the expression of paradoxical opinions in unparadoxical language.' (p. 300.) According to Grave, Berkeley *thinks* with the learned, which means that he embraces the identity principle, but *speaks* with the vulgar, which means that it looks as if he accepts the distinction principle as well. But he does not. His commitment to the 'learned' view reaches down to the very bottom of his thought, and his commitment to the vulgar view is no deeper than his fondness for a common-sense way of speaking.

Pitcher notices the same potential for conflict and resolves it in a similar way.[11] He associates the distinction principle with an *act–object* analysis of perception, according to which perception takes place when the mind enters into a relation with an object wholly distinct from it. He associates the identity principle with an *adverbial* analysis, according to which ideas are not discriminable objects or entities, but contents of mental acts or operations. To perceive a shade of red is, on an adverbial analysis, to 'perceive redly': the perception owes it content—its being 'of red'—not to the redness of a distinct object to which it is related, but to its own nature, to its being a perception of a certain kind. Pitcher believes that Berkeley shifts 'back and forth between the adverbial and act–object points of view', though 'he means to have just *one* view about our awareness of ideas' (p. 199). If the distinction principle is taken to mean that the mind and its ideas are *strongly distinct*, or capable of separate existence (p. 191), Pitcher argues that 'the simplest and best way to preserve the largest bulk of Berkeley's central philosophical doctrines is to have [Berkeley] abandon' it (p. 201). If Berkeley is willing to settle for a *weak distinction* between the mind and its ideas—a distinction which does not permit separate existence, such as the distinction or non-identity between a person and his or her acts or states (pp. 191–2, 203)—then he can take the distinction principle to be true. Yet the identity principle, on

---

[11] *Berkeley*, London, 1977. Page refs. are included in the text.

Pitcher's view as on Grave's, is dominant. Margaret Atherton urges the same basic conclusion: Berkeley's ideas, she writes, are 'ways of perceiving, not . . . discriminable mental objects'.[12]

Pitcher offers the adverbial approach more as a philosopher's recommendation than as a historian's interpretation. But I am far from convinced that the adverbial approach provides 'the simplest and best way to preserve the largest bulk of Berkeley's central philosophical doctrines', and I am troubled by the fact that Berkeley's commitment to the act–object analysis seems to be both deeper and more systematic than either Grave or Pitcher realizes. The textual support for the view that Berkeley accepts the identity principle is surprisingly meagre. Grave, Pitcher, and Colin Turbayne, who gives an interesting discussion of the leading issues in his paper 'Lending a Hand to Philonous', are able to muster only four or five texts.[13] There are, to begin with, some passages from the *Philosophical Commentaries*:

wherein I pray you does the perception of white differ from white. (Entry 585, quoted by Grave on p. 297, by Pitcher on p. 190.)

The Distinguishing betwixt an Idea and perception of the Idea has been one great cause of Imagining material substances. (Entry 609, quoted by Pitcher on p. 190.)

Twas the opinion that Ideas could exist unperceiv'd or before perception that made Men think perception was somewhat different from the Idea perceived. (Entry 656, quoted—but in a different context—by Pitcher on p. 201.)

The central text, quoted by all three, comes from *Principles* 5:

Light and colours, heat and cold, extension and figures, in a word the things we see and feel, what are they but so many sensations, notions, ideas or impressions on the sense; and is it possible to separate, even in thought, any of these from perception? For my part I might as easily divide a thing from it self.

---

[12] 'The Coherence of Berkeley's Theory of Mind', *Philosophy and Phenomenological Research* 43 (1983), p. 395. Other useful essays on this topic include Reinaldo Elugardo, 'An Alleged Incoherence in Berkeley's Philosophy', in Charles E. Jarrett, John King-Farlow, and F. J. Pelletier (eds.), *New Essays on Rationalism and Empiricism*, *Canadian Journal of Philosophy* Supplementary Vol. 4 (1978), 177–89; Robert Muehlmann, 'Berkeley's Ontology and the Epistemology of Idealism', *Canadian Journal of Philosophy* 8 (1978), 89–111; Cummins, 'Berkeley's Ideas of Sense', *Nous* 9 (1975), 55–72; Odegard, 'Berkeley and the Perception of Ideas', *Canadian Journal of Philosophy* 1 (1971), 155–71; and Pappas, 'Ideas, Minds, and Berkeley'. *American Philosophical Quarterly* 17 (1980), 181–94.

[13] Turbayne's paper appears in his *Berkeley: Critical and Interpretive Essays*, Minneapolis, 1982, pp. 295–310.

Turbayne (on p. 299) also quotes a concluding sentence omitted from this section in the second edition:

In truth the object and the sensation are the same thing, and cannot therefore be abstracted from each other.

The assembled evidence can by no means be entirely discounted, but it is not so powerful as Pitcher and the others all suppose. *Principles* 5, for example, does not say that ideas are acts or operations of the mind; it says only that an idea can no more be separated from perception than a thing can be divided from itself. The comparison may not be meant to convey an exact analogy between a thing and itself on the one hand and a perception and its idea on the other; Berkeley may only be calling attention to the *inseparability* of a perception and its idea, as Norris, in a passage discussed in Chapter 2, calls attention to the inseparability of any two things of which we have genuinely abstract ideas. It remains true that at *Commentaries* 609 Berkeley denies that ideas are distinct from perception. But 'distinguishing' here may not mean 'regarding as non-identical' but 'regarding as capable of separate existence'. In the *Principles of Philosophy* Descartes describes three kinds of distinctions, only one of which—*real* distinction—implies the separability of the things distinguished.[14] Berkeley's point in entry 609 may well be that regarding ideas and perceptions of them as *really* distinct 'has been one great cause of Imagining material substances'. As Descartes says in article 60 of the *Principles*, a real distinction 'properly exists only between two or more substances'. Entry 609 may therefore impute the following line of reasoning to the materialists:

1. *An idea and perception of the idea can be distinguished.* Berkeley takes this to be true only if the distinction in question is not a real distinction. But the materialists suppose that (1) entitles them to assert:

2. *An idea and perception of the idea are really distinct.*
Now

3. *A real distinction properly exists only between two or more substances.*
Hence (from (2) and (3))

4. *An idea—the object we immediately perceive—must be an (unthinking) substance.*

Note that in the transition from (1) to (2) one kind of distinction—a

---

[14] Pt. I, articles 60–2, pp. 213–15 in John Cottingham *et al.* (eds.), *The Philosophical Writings of Descartes*, vol. I. Here Descartes may follow Suarez, *On the Various Kinds of Distinctions*, trans. by Cyril Vollert, Milwaukee, 1947.

kind Suarez describes as 'mental'—is mistaken for another.[15] Replacing Suarez's scholastic language with Berkeley's, we can describe the transition as a case of illegitimate abstraction: things to which the mind selectively attends are mistaken for things that can exist apart. Selective attention depends on real non-identities but not on real distinctions. Where there are real distinctions abstraction in the strict sense is unnecessary. When writers of the period use the word 'distinct' without qualification they often mean 'really distinct' (as opposed to 'non-identical'). Berkeley's employment of 'distinct' and related words should, I think, be understood in this way.

This last observation tells us nothing, though, about the line Turbayne quotes from the first edition version of *Principles* 5, where Berkeley says not that a sensation and its object are not distinct, but that they are the *same*. As far as its content is concerned this line does support the conclusion that Berkeley accepts the identity principle. But it was, after all, removed from the second edition, and it may have been lifted precisely because Berkeley refused to accept what it implies.

The evidence that Berkeley accepts the distinction principle is ample. The following passages are the most definite of the five Pitcher quotes on p. 190:

This perceiving, active being is what I call *mind, spirit, soul*, or *my self*. By which words I do not denote any one of my ideas, but a thing entirely distinct from them, wherein they exist, or, which is the same thing, whereby they are perceived. (*Principles* 2.)

Thing or *being* is the most general name of all, it comprehends under it two kinds entirely distinct and heterogeneous, and which have nothing common but the name, to wit, *spirit* and *ideas*. (*Principles* 89.)

The main reason for supposing that Berkeley is committed to the identity principle is that he needs it to support his claim that ideas cannot exist unperceived. Pitcher makes this point very forcefully. On an adverbial account of perception, he observes, it is a necessary truth that ideas cannot exist unless perceived (p. 201). He then asks whether it also turns out to be necessary on an act–object account.

If the act–object analyst construes it . . . as a necessary truth, then, as far as I can tell, he is adopting a view that is indistinguishable from the adverbial analysis. For what is the difference between saying, as the adverbial analyst does, that sense-contents exist, of necessity, only when a mind is aware in a certain mode, and saying, as the act–object analyst does if he accepts [this] as a

---

[15] *On the Various Kinds of Distinctions*, pp. 18–21.

necessary truth, that ideas exist, of necessity, only when a mind perceives them? This is a mere seeming-difference; the act–object analyst's 'object' is nothing but the adverbial analyst's sense-content with a different label. (p. 200.)

I share the view that Berkeley wants it to be a necessary truth that ideas do not exist unperceived. Pitcher argues that for anyone who shares this view, the objects of the act–object account turn out to be nothing but the subjective sense-contents of the adverbial account. But it does not follow from this that Berkeley should be saddled with the identity principle. If the ideas of the act–object account are the same as subjective sense-contents, *and if sense-contents are even weakly distinct from the mind's acts, operations, or states*, then Pitcher's argument becomes an unwitting defence of the distinction principle. But can it be said that sense-contents are distinct—even weakly distinct—from the mind's acts or states of awareness?

Pitcher's characterizations of sense-contents, as well as the analogies he employs, indicate that in his view the answer is no. Sense-contents, he writes, are 'essential aspects of the state of consciousness itself' (p. 197), by which he seems to mean both that the state owes its identity to the contents, and that the contents are nothing over and above the state, but mere aspects of its very being. The second point is supported by Pitcher's analogy between sense-contents on the one hand and somersaults or jigs on the other. 'The awareness of an idea is no more distinguishable from the idea', he writes, 'than the turning of a somersault is distinguishable from the somersault turned' (p. 197). 'The words "a jig" . . . do not designate an object distinct from the dancing of it . . . [but] a way of dancing, whether the dancing is an act, a state, a process, or whatever it is.' (p. 198.)

Despite the remarks just quoted Pitcher's understanding of sense-contents is not entirely clear. At times he writes as if sense-contents are modifications of modifications, a suggestion in keeping with his use of the word 'adverbial': 'sense-contents exist', we are told in the long passage quoted above, 'only when a mind is aware in a certain mode' (p. 200). But this cannot be what Pitcher really intends, since he holds that modifications are weakly distinct from what they modify.[16] Pitcher wants, I think, to make the stronger claim that sense-contents (or ideas) are non-entities, that aside from the substance (the mind or spirit) and its modifications (its acts of states of awareness) there is nothing else. On such a view, all talk of sense-contents or ideas is

[16] See pp. 202–3, where Pitcher argues that even on the adverbial account, the mind remains weakly distinct from its modifications.

nothing more than a way of speaking: the truth-conditions of statements about sense-contents can be expressed in words that make no mention of them, just as the truth-conditions of statements about somersaults can be expressed in words that make no mention of somersaults. Pitcher thinks that a vocabulary making no mention of sense-contents is the correct one for expressing Berkeley's philosophical opinions because it foresakes commitment to a class of entities which are, according to Pitcher, 'metaphysically embarrassing' (p. 197). They are embarrassing because they fall outside the categories of substance and modification, which were held by the tradition to be exhaustive. As Pitcher writes on p. 198, in praise of the adverbial view when applied to the case of pain, 'it certainly makes sense to deny that a pain is one thing and the feeling or awareness of it, another. There is just the feeling of pain.' In general, according to Pitcher, there is just the act or state of awareness; its content might be called an 'essential aspect', but an essential aspect is even ghostlier than a modification, and it reduces in the end to nothing. Pitcher's view might also be put by saying that there is nothing (no such entity) as awareness *simpliciter* (or even sensing *simpliciter*): there are episodes of awareness of certain determinate kinds, and these episodes are metaphysical atoms, rather than complexes of act and distinguishable (even if not wholly separable) content.

If a sense-content is a genuine entity, no matter how undistinguished an entity, it can be proven to be weakly distinct from acts or operations of the mind because the two have (according to Berkeley) different properties. This is why Pitcher has to make the very strong claims discussed in the previous paragraph. His defence of the adverbial account is a defence of the identity principle only if statements ascribing properties to sense-contents are less than basic, and reducible to statements in which no reference is made to sense-contents or their properties.

Pitcher would not be ruffled by the objection that there is no hint in Berkeley of the kind of reductionism he would have us impute to him; nor would he be disturbed by the absence of indications that when Berkeley refers to ideas and their properties he is speaking loosely, or operating at a less-than-basic level which cannot be taken to reflect his ontological commitments.[17] This is because Pitcher is making a

---

[17] One possible exception to these claims is Philonous's speech on pp. 247–8, where he speaks of people who would 'without question agree in their perceptions'. I discuss this passage below.

recommendation; he is, in effect, *advising* Berkeley to accept the identity principle and to repudiate the distinction principle, as opposed to arguing that his advice is actually followed. But Pitcher does claim that his recommendation 'leads to fewer and less embarrassing difficulties, and/or is consistent with more that is essential in [Berkeley's] metaphysical system' (p. 199), so the absence in Berkeley's texts of what might be described as anti-realism regarding ideas or sense-contents should give us pause. And we should further hesitate when we recall, as I argued in Chapter 1, that ideas and their properties play an essential role in Berkeley's explanation of the content of thought. Berkeley thinks he can explain, for example, why a certain idea of imagination represents a chair rather than a table. An anti-realist about ideas can manage perhaps to *mark* the difference between imagining a chair and imagining a table—imagining a chair can be said to resemble sensing a chair in being *of a chair*—but Berkeley sets out to give an enlightening *explanation* of the difference, one that turns on a resemblance between ideas which is distinct from, and in the order of explanation prior to, the resemblance in content. It follows that Berkeley cannot take ideas to be non-entities; he wants to make explanatory use of ideas and their properties at the deepest level of his philosophy. But if they are not non-entities then they are at least weakly distinct from the acts or operations of the mind.

Pitcher might reply that even on his interpretation, an explanatory role for ideas can be found. He can propose that an idea of imagination represents an idea of sense because they are, subjectively, very much alike. Resemblance remains at the heart of Berkeley's account of intentionality, but its terms are episodes of awareness rather than objects distinct *from* the mind. The difficulty here is that Berkeley treats resemblance as if it holds between objects. I develop this point below, where I take up the so-called 'realist' interpretation of Berkeley.

If ideas are weakly distinct from the mind it does not follow that they are modifications of the mind. At *Principles* 49 Berkeley explicitly rejects such a view:

It may perhaps be objected, that if extension and figure exist only in the mind, it follows that the mind is extended and figured; since extension is a mode or attribute which (to speak with the Schools) is predicated of the subject in which it exists. I answer, those qualities are in the mind only as they are perceived by it, that is, not by way of *mode* or *attribute*, but only by way of *idea*.

Nor can sense-contents be modifications of the mind's acts or

operations.[18] If this means that Berkeley faces metaphysical embarrass-
ment then so be it. When John Norris first read Locke's *Essay* he
complained about Locke's failure to clarify the nature of ideas: are
they substances, Norris asked, or modifications of substances?[19]
Berkeley, I want to suggest, is simply not impressed by this kind of
request for clarification, couched as it is in a metaphysical vocabulary
which is itself in need of clarification. Berkeley finds it clearer to say
that extension and figure are in the mind by way of idea. Pitcher might
object that it is clear enough what it means to say that extension and
figure are *perceived by* the mind, but that it is by no means clear why
extension and figure, once classed as ideas, cannot exist without the
mind. In Chapter 6 I have done my best to explain why, on Berkeley's
view, ideas cannot exist unperceived. Here I can only point out that
Pitcher's interpretation faces an equally serious difficulty. It is easy to
see why ideas cannot exist without the mind once they have been
domesticated as essential aspects of the mind's acts or states of
awareness. But it is not at all easy to see why ideas, so understood, can be
treated as things perceived, and thereby held to be identical with the
houses, mountains, and rivers we perceive, as the argument of
Principles 4 demands. Pitcher can explain why ideas cannot exist
without the mind only by making it very difficult for Berkeley to
convince his readers that ideas are perceived in the same way that
ordinary things are.

Up to this point I have argued that Berkeley's ideas are entities, and
that they are weakly distinct from both the mind and its acts or
operations. If I am right we needn't accept Grave's judgement that
Berkeley is led into incoherence by his core beliefs about the mind and
its ideas. I now want to present three further reasons for thinking of
Berkeleyan ideas as objects. In my view their objecthood does not have
to do with their capacity to exist in one mind at widely spaced intervals,
in two or more minds, or outside the mind altogether. Pitcher thinks of
objecthood entirely in these terms, which is natural in view of his
concern with showing that ideas cannot possibly exist unperceived. But
ideas can, I think, be regarded as objects even if they can exist only in
individual minds for relatively brief spans of time.

---

[18] Berkeley would presumably have no objection to classifying these acts or operations
as modifications of the mind, because they *can* be predicated of it.

[19] *Cursory Reflections upon a Book call'd, an Essay concerning Human Understanding*,
London, 1690, pp. 3, 22–4. For Locke's reply see his *Remarks upon some of Mr. Norris's
Books*, in *The Works of John Locke*, London, 1823, vol. 10, p. 256.

The first reason for thinking of Berkeley's ideas as objects is that ideas can remain the same even though the acts of thought directed towards them vary. At one moment the mind may be contemplating an idea in its full particularity; at the next, engaged in the task of partial consideration, the mind may be attending to something the idea has in common with others. In such a case the idea survives a change in the content of thought. The change is brought about by a change on the side of the subject. This shows not only that Berkeley needs the very distinction between object and content Pitcher's proposal would deny him, but that a Berkeleyan idea presents itself as something other, as something on which the mind can go to work in different ways.

The second reason is closely related to the first. The traditional framework of substance and mode cannot convey the fact that a state of sensory awareness has an 'inside', that there is something it is like for the subject to be in it. And it is natural to describe this in objectual terms: the mind confronts ideas, perceives them, attends to them, abstracts from them. As we saw in Chapter 1, Berkeley often speaks in precisely these terms. The vocabulary of 'object', 'imprinting', 'observation', and 'perception' does not suit the mind's relationship to its patience, wit, or generosity. These may be entities—modifications of the mind—but it does not seem appropriate to speak of them as objects.

A final reason is that when ideas play the explanatory role Berkeley assigns to them, they figure as subjects of predication, and Berkeley does not even entertain the possibility of eliminating them from this role. They are, so to speak, ultimate subjects of predication: no way is provided of eliminating them from the role of subjects in remarks such as the following:

The ideas imprinted on the senses by the Author of Nature are called *real things*: and those excited in the imagination, being less regular, vivid and constant, are more properly termed *ideas* or *images of things*, which they copy and represent. (*Principles* 33.).

It is not my intention to quarrel over words: the important point is that ideas are genuine entities, weakly distinct from both the mind and its acts or operations. I do believe it is appropriate to speak of them as objects for the reasons listed, and that Berkeley's decision to speak of them as objects is a response to these reasons, but the reader may want to treat these reasons simply as an account of what I mean when I say that ideas are objects. The insistence that ideas are distinct from

episodes of awareness distinguishes my interpretation from those that
centre on the identity principle; the additional characteristics are
meant to enlarge my picture of what Berkeleyan ideas are like.

The distinction principle is the centrepiece of the so-called *realist*
interpretation of Berkeley, and in closing this section I should perhaps
explain where I depart from that interpretation. (There are, of course,
realist elements in the interpretation I have defended in the last four
chapters, because according to that interpretation common-sense
existence claims are often true.) The main lines of the realist
interpretation are these:

(i) Berkeley's 'in the mind' means nothing more than 'in direct
cognitive relation to the mind'.[20] To exist in the mind is simply to be
perceived, comprehended, or known.[21]

(ii) Ideas or things in the mind can therefore be entirely distinct
from the mind.[22]

(iii) In view of (i), the mind-dependency of ideas or things 'lose[s]
its apparent ontic sting'. *Esse* is *percipi* means 'that there is no aspect of
objects that is insensible ([Berkeley's] negative claim against the
materialists) and that objects as known are *in* the mind'.[23] According to
Luce,[24]

> When Berkeley says that sensible things are or exist in the mind, he does not
> mean that they form part of the perceiving subject; he has just said the very
> opposite; he has just said they are 'intirely distinct' from the mind. He means
> simply that they are objects of attention, like the ribbon or the children. They
> are in the mind because they are significant objects of cognition or volition.
> They are not *in* the mind, as Monday is *in* the week, but as a hippopotamus is
> *in* my mind when I see or imagine him. Existence in the mind is thus existence
> for the mind, existence as object of the mind, existence in relation to the mind,
> existence perceived.
> . . . When Berkeley says, That exists only in the mind, . . . he means that it
> exists, but does not exist in matter. . . . 'Only in the mind,' means 'not in
> matter.'

(iv) 'We can think of or conceive of the world only in experiential
terms',[25] and the corporeal world is therefore 'exactly what it is

---

[20] Luce, 'Berkeley's Existence in the Mind', p. 286 in Martin and Armstrong.

[21] John Yolton, *Perceptual Acquaintance from Descartes to Reid*, Minneapolis, 1984,
pp. 135–7, 209–10.

[22] Luce, 'Berkeley's Existence in the Mind', p. 285, and *Berkeley's Immaterialism*,
London, 1945, p. 55.

[23] Yolton, pp. 210, 134.

[24] *Berkeley's Immaterialism*, p. 55.   [25] Yolton, p. 142.

experienced to be'(Jessop, *Works* II, p. 10). 'Even if with science we suppose a molecular architecture beneath the smooth whiteness of the paper, that architecture itself could only be defined as the stuff of a farther possible experience, a vision, say, of certain vibrating particles with which our acquaintance with the paper would terminate, if it were prolonged by magnifying artifices not yet known.'[26] The corpuscular hypothesis is therefore mistaken, because it calls for a 'specific difference'—a difference in kind—between corpuscles and perceptions.[27] The corporeal world exists only in relation to sensing (Jessop, *Works* II, p. 9); hence a physical thing and its properties must be 'immediately perceived or perceivable'.[28]

(v) Berkeley affirms the mind's direct awareness of the world, repudiates representationalism,[29] and defends a common-sense world populated by 'the ordinary objects of our . . . environment'.[30] 'Our sensations are not small inner duplicates of things, they are the things themselves in so far as the things are presented to us.'[31]

Points (i) to (iii) suggest that ideas are strongly distinct at least from finite minds, and that one and the same idea can exist in more than one mind.[32] Defenders of the realist interpretation do not suppose that ideas are strongly distinct from *God's* mind, but they tend to think that this is consistent with a robust realism; like Hylas in the Second Dialogue, they are inclined to think that 'this is no more than . . . all Christians hold' (*Works* II, p. 212). Yolton, for example, speculates that the dependency of all things on God probably has a theological motive: 'it provides an account,' he writes, 'of the dependency of the world on God'.[33]

---

[26] William James, 'The Knowing of Things Together', in *Essays in Philosophy*, Cambridge, Massachusetts, 1978, pp. 72–3.

[27] Yolton, p. 142; Jessop, *Works* II, p. 11.

[28] Luce, 'Existence in the Mind', p. 289.

[29] Luce, *Berkeley's Immaterialism*, p. 28; Yolton, p. 136.   [30] Yolton, p. 136.

[31] James, 'The Notion of Consciousness', p. 263 in his *Essays in Radical Empiricism*, Cambridge, Massachusetts, 1976. For more on Berkeley's realism see J. Laird, 'Berkeley's Realism', *Mind* 25 (1916), 308–28; Harry M. Bracken, 'Berkeley's Realisms', reprinted as an appendix to his *The Early Reception of Berkeley's Immaterialism*, revised edn., The Hague, 1965, pp. 85–96; and Michael Ayers, 'Divine Ideas and Berkeley's Proof of God's Existence', in Ernest Sosa (ed.), *Essays on the Philosophy of George Berkeley*, Dordrecht, 1987, pp. 115–28.

[32] Pitcher takes Luce to be committed to the first claim; see *Berkeley*, p. 202. Luce seems to accept the second in both 'Existence in the Mind', pp. 291–2, and *Berkeley's Immaterialism*, p. 75. See also *Berkeley and Malebranche*, London, 1934, p. 84.

[33] p. 210. See also Luce, 'Existence in the Mind', p. 290, and *Berkeley and Malebranche*, pp. 100–1, 124–5.

On the realist interpretation, immaterialism is distinguished from other ways of recognizing the dependence of all things on God by a twofold claim—point (iv) above—about things and their qualities. The first part of the claim is that the qualities of things are, through and through, the kinds of qualities we immediately perceive them as having. There is nothing further to them. As Jessop writes, 'The corporeal, from top to bottom, superficially and radically, *is* the visible, tangible, etc.' (*Works* II, p. 9.) The second part of the claim is that all these qualities are, again in Jessop's words, 'relative . . . to sensing as such. . . . The sensible has neither meaning nor existence out of all relation to sensing'. To be corporeal, then, is to be immediately perceived or perceivable. But it does not follow from this that the same idea cannot be in more than one mind; the strong distinctness of mind and idea is left intact.

In the Third Dialogue Hylas says that 'the same idea which is in my mind, cannot be in yours, or in any other mind' (p. 247), and I am unhappy with the realist interpretation primarily because of some textual evidence that Hylas's view is also Berkeley's. Philonous's response to Hylas is that the same idea may well exist in different minds if *same* is taken in its 'vulgar acceptation'. 'Words', he explains, 'are of arbitrary imposition; and since men are used to apply the word *same* where no distinction or variety is perceived, and I do not pretend to alter their perceptions, it follows that as men have said before, *several saw the same thing*, so they may upon like occasions still continue to use the same phrase, without any deviation either from propriety of language, or the truth of things.' He goes on to say that it may or may not be possible for several persons to perceive the same thing if *same* is taken in the acceptation of philosophers. Everything depends on the standard of sameness one chooses: if the standard is 'the uniformness of what was perceived', it will be possible for different minds to perceive the same idea; if the standard is the identity of the perceivers it will not be. 'All the dispute', he says, 'is about a word.' (pp. 247–8.)

These remarks, of course, do not show that Philonous agrees with Hylas. But if the realist interpretation is correct, it is at the very least curious that Philonous does not set Hylas right.[34] Of course the tables might be turned on my own view: if ideas are, so to speak, individual possessions, why doesn't Philonous straightforwardly *approve* of what Hylas has said? It is in fact my view that Philonous's failure to correct

---

[34] On this point see Douglas Odegard, 'Berkeley and the Perception of Ideas', *Canadian Journal of Philosophy* 1 (1971), p. 168.

Hylas is *some* evidence—admittedly weak—that he agrees with him. (A debater is, I think, likelier to correct a mistake than to voice approval of right thinking.) But there is stronger evidence for this conclusion in the closing lines of Philonous's speech:

Take this farther reflexion with you: that whether matter be allowed to exist or no, the case is exactly the same as to the point in hand. For the materialists themselves acknowledge what we immediately perceive by our senses, to be our own ideas. Your difficulty therefore, that no two see the same thing, makes equally against the materialists and me. (p. 248.)

I take it Philonous is saying that according to the materialists, no two people immediately perceive the same idea. Note that the objects we immediately perceive are said by the materialists to be 'our *own* ideas'—our own, we can presume, as opposed to someone else's.[35] No doubt the materialists can deal with any objection this might prompt in just the way Philonous deals with the objection made by Hylas. But Philonous seems to think that the materialists are right in what he says they 'acknowledge'. If this is correct then Philonous's failure to correct Hylas is cast in a new light: Hylas goes uncorrected because he is reporting a view Philonous holds. Hylas, incidentally, also believes that according to the materialists, no two people perceive the same idea. In reply to Philonous's contention that his difficulty makes equally against the materialists and immaterialists, Hylas says, 'But they [the materialists] suppose an external archetype, to which referring their *several* ideas, they may truly be said to perceive the same thing.' (p. 248; emphasis mine.)

There is another very interesting feature of the exchange between Hylas and Philonous, though I am uncertain how much weight should be placed on it. When Hylas first makes his objection he distinguishes between the claim that the same *idea* cannot be in more than one mind and the claim that the same *thing* cannot be perceived by more than one mind. He begins by saying that 'the same *idea* which is in my mind, cannot be in yours, or in any other mind', and then asks—as if he is taking an inferential step—whether it does not *follow* that no two see the same *thing*. (The 'things' he has in mind, incidentally, are the garden, trees, and flowers he mentions at the top of p. 247.) Philonous seems to be respecting the same distinction in reporting the views of the materialists. 'The materialists themselves acknowledge what we

---

[35] Berkeley himself says that we perceive nothing 'but our own ideas or sensations'. See *Principles* 4.

immediately perceive . . . to be our own *ideas*', he says. 'Your difficulty therefore, that no two see the same *thing*, makes equally against the materialists and me.' With one exception, Philonous speaks only of *things* in the rest of his reply, and the one exception comes at the very beginning, where he explains that on the 'vulgar acceptation' of the word *same*—an understanding that permits the word to be applied where no distinction or variety is perceived—the same 'thing or idea' can exist in different minds. Philonous had made a distinction between ideas and things just a page or two earlier (pp. 245–6). He there explains that we combine ideas 'apprehended by divers senses, or by the same sense at different times, or in different circumstances' and 'consider [them] as one thing', even though, 'strictly speaking', they are not the same (p. 245). Now it could well be the case that a similar distinction is at work in the exchange we are discussing. It should come as no surprise that the distinction is unimportant on the common understanding of *same*; Philonous therefore speaks indifferently of things and ideas when discussing the vulgar acceptation. But when he turns to the acceptations of philosophers, Philonous speaks consistently of *things*. It was Hylas's objection, after all, not that no two can see the same idea, but that no two can see the same thing. Philonous's reply is that depending on how they understand the word *same*, philosophers may or may not allow that different people can see the same *thing*. The question whether different people can perceive the same *idea* is never addressed, and this is so, I propose, because all *philosophers* agree that they cannot, a point to some extent confirmed by the remarks about the materialists at the end of Philonous's reply. On this reading it is by no means a verbal matter whether two minds can perceive the same idea. It is, rather, a deep truth that they cannot: the distinction between ideas in different minds is as deep as the distinction between the minds themselves.

However the exchange from the Third Dialogue is read, my view of the nature of ideas is supported by *Principles* 140, where Berkeley, speaking in his own voice, indicates that the same idea cannot exist in more than one mind:[36]

Moreover, as we conceive the ideas that are in the minds of other spirits by means of our own, which we suppose to be resemblances of them: so we know

---

[36] This text is used in a similar way by Ian Tipton, *Berkeley: The Philosophy of Immaterialism*, London, 1974, p. 86. Tipton assesses Yolton's claims about Berkeley in '"Ideas" in Berkeley and Arnauld', *History of European Ideas* 7 (1986), 575–84.

other spirits by means of our own soul, which in that sense is the image or idea of them, it having a like respect to other spirits, that blueness or heat by me perceived hath to those ideas perceived by another.

There are three final points to be made against the realist interpretation. The first is that the interpretation puts finite minds and their ideas on the same ontological footing: each depends on God, but neither depends on the other. Yet Berkeley's statement that 'there is not any other substance than *spirit*, or that which perceives' (*Principles* 7) seems to be a way of saying that ideas are ontologically dependent in a way finite minds are not. If ideas or things are strongly distinct from finite minds, why not say that ideas or things are substances? Realist interpreters emphasize Berkeley's opposition to corpuscularianism, and his even more fundamental opposition to a world conceived in other-than-experiential terms, a world inhabited by things which are bare of all sensible qualities and specifically different from things as known. I agree that Berkeley is opposed to this conception, but beneath this opposition lies a deeper opposition to the view that finite minds and ideas are on an ontological par.

The second point is that the realist interpretation gives too simple a picture of Berkeley's relationship to common sense; the relationship was not in fact as comfortable as point (v) would have us think. It is true that in the *Three Dialogues* Berkeley is very concerned to show that immaterialism and common sense are compatible. But in the *Principles* an inconsistency between the two is openly acknowledged. At *Principles* 4 Berkeley speaks of the opinion that physical objects have an existence natural or real, distinct from being perceived, as 'strangely prevailing amongst men'; in § 44 the belief that tangible objects exist without the mind is described as a 'vulgar error' (though here I must admit that a 'vulgar error' may simply be a common or widespread error—common among philosophers rather than among people at large); and later on in the *Principles* he even takes it upon himself to account for the 'universal concurrent assent' to the existence of external things (§§ 54–6). When he wrote the *Principles* I think he supposed that ordinary people share the view that minds and things are on an equal ontological footing. By the time he wrote the *Dialogues* he had perhaps come to the conclusion that this mistaken view is not part of common sense. (It is, in fact, very hard to state the view without using words such as 'substance' or 'ontological', or catch-phrases such as 'absolute existence without the mind', all of which are foreign to common sense.) But when he wrote the *Principles* it would not have been difficult for Berkeley to believe that these technical notions and the beliefs they make possible had *contaminated* or *invaded* common sense, or that these philosophical beliefs had natural counterparts not easily expressed in ordinary terms. In any case Berkeley at one time held the view that immaterialism and common sense are to some extent at odds; my interpretation explains how this could be so.

My third and final comment brings us back to the first point in my elaboration of the realist interpretation, where *existence in the mind* is reduced to the more docile notion of *being perceived, known, understood, or comprehended by the mind.* Because minds and their operations are among the things known or understood, and yet do not exist in the mind by way of idea, point (i) as it stands is dangerously misleading. Berkeley writes that '*Spirits* and *ideas* are things so wholly different, that when we say *they exist, they are known,* or the like, these words must not be thought to signify any thing common to both natures.' (*Principles* 142.) It follows that existence in the mind 'by way of *idea*' is *one species* of being known or understood; point (i) must therefore be revised to reflect whatever it is that makes it distinctive.

In describing existence in the mind by way of idea, Berkeley lays particular stress on passivity and resemblance. Those who embrace point (i) must take account of these notions, and I see no alternative to the following line of development. To know or understand a house or tree is to *sense* or *imagine* it; sensing is a distinctively passive form of knowing or understanding, and imagining is a form of understanding subjectively very much like sensing. When Berkeley says that ideas of sense are passive, then, all he means is that episodes of sensing are caused by outside agents. And when he says that ideas of imagination resemble ideas of sense, all he means is that conceiving of a house or tree is, subjectively, very much like sensing one.[37] No passive objects or isolable images are involved; passivity is a property of mental acts, and resemblance holds between such acts in their subjective aspects.[38]

[37] This formulation was suggested to me by M. R. Ayers, 'Are Locke's "Ideas" Images, Intentional Objects or Natural Signs?', *The Locke Newsletter* 17 (1986), p. 5.
[38] In referring to the mind's states and their subjective character the realist interpretation touches on the interpretation defended by Pitcher. This may come as a surprise, but the most thorough statements of the realist interpretation do acknowledge that Berkeley sometimes uses 'idea' to describe the mind's states or modifications—'perceptions', according to Yolton, as opposed to things perceived (pp. 138–9, 210). This allows the realist interpretation to make sense of passages that would otherwise be troublesome. At *Principles* 89, for example, Berkeley describes ideas as 'inert, fleeting, dependent beings'. There are similar discriptions in the *Three Dialogues* (pp. 205, 216, and 258). They are all descriptions of *beings*, but they cannot be taken as descriptions of

Note that it would not be enough to say that conceiving of a house and sensing it are alike in what Descartes called their objective reality (or in what we would call their intentional object). If the resemblance went only so far, then conceiving of Whitehall—Berkeley's farmhouse in America—would be too much like conceiving of one's own self: in each case there would be an act or state of mind, and in each case there would be an object. Berkeley of course believes that conceiving of Whitehall has the same objective reality as sensing Whitehall, but conceiving of Whitehall owes its objective reality to the subjective similarity it bears to sensing it, and it is *this* to which Berkeley draws our attention.

We now have to ask whether this way of distinguishing between knowing a house or tree and knowing a mind is Berkeley's way. I think the answer is no. Although a similarity between mind-dependent objects can always be redescribed as a subjective similarity between states or modifications, Berkeley regularly speaks as if the features in question belong in the first place to items that inhabit either the sensory field, or the paler copy of that field which is presented in imagination. In the Third Dialogue, for example, Philonous says that when someone looks at a crooked oar in water, 'what he immediately perceives by sight is certainly crooked' (p. 238). 'The visible moon, or that which I see,' he writes in § 44 of the *Theory of Vision*, is 'only a round, luminous plain of about thirty visible points in diameter'. No doubt these claims could be rewritten as claims about the subjective character of states, but Berkeley himself chooses not to present them in that way. If we suppose that ideas are mind-dependent objects, then we do not have to suppose that in the second sentence of a passage such as the following, Berkeley alternates between talk of modifications of the mind and talk of common-sense things. Instead of lurching from one topic to the other, he is speaking throughout about objects which are weakly distinct from the mind:

That neither our thoughts, nor passions, nor ideas formed by the imagination, exist without the mind, is what every body will allow. And it seems no less evident that the various sensations or ideas imprinted on the sense, however blended or combined together (that is, whatever objects they compose) cannot

the hard and stable world Berkeley shares with ordinary men and women; the descriptions are plainly meant to have what Yolton calls 'ontic sting'. But Yolton and other realists are free to view them as descriptions of the mind's states or perceptions, their subjective character (their 'subjective sense-contents') changing from moment to moment.

exist otherwise than in a mind perceiving them. I think an intuitive knowledge may be obtained of this, by any one that shall attend to what is meant by the term *exist* when applied to sensible things. (*Principles* 3.)

No matter how successfully it accounts for Berkeley's talk of resemblance, the realist interpretation will still have trouble with passivity, which Berkeley attributes to ideas of imagination as well as to ideas of sense. Imagining is not passive in the way sensing is, because we are causally responsible for our ideas of imagination: 'It is no more than willing,' Berkeley writes at *Principles* 28, 'and straightway this or that idea arises in my fancy.' If ideas are passive objects, the passivity of ideas of imagination falls into place. If ideas are passive states—states caused by outside agents—then ideas of imagination lose their passive character, and begin to look more like reflex acts or notions than they should. These points tell not only against the realist interpretation but also against the interpretation defended by Pitcher. The realist interpretation tells us that 'idea' sometimes refers to episodes of awareness. (At other times, of course, it refers to objects strongly distinct from the mind.) Pitcher tells us that it always refers to such episodes, or that it always should. Neither interpretation can plausibly accommodate Berkeley's emphasis on the passivity of ideas, or his way of understanding the resemblance between ideas of imagination and ideas of sense.

In the opening section of this chapter I avoided what many feel is the most troublesome part of the parity objection, the suggestion that an unwavering application of the principles used to dispose of matter degrades minds into systems of floating ideas, unsupported by any substance (Third Dialogue, p. 233). In the *Philosophical Commentaries* Berkeley actually entertained (and eventually rejected) this view of mind. Entry 580 describes the mind as 'a congeries of Perceptions'. 'Take away Perceptions & you take away the Mind', its says, 'put the Perceptions & you put the mind.' In entry 581 Berkeley turns aside the reply that the mind is not a bundle of perceptions but that which perceives: 'you are abus'd by the words that & thing these are vague empty words † w^{th}out a meaning.'[39]

I agree with those critics of Berkeley who say that he is in no position

---

[39] Both 580 and 581 are marked with a plus sign; they should be read along with entries 577–9. Similar views are expressed in 587, 614, and 637. See pp. 125–6 in the Thomas edn. for Luce's useful sketch of Berkeley's developing views on mind or spirit. For a more detailed survey see Charles J. McCracken, 'Berkeley's Notion of Spirit', *History of European Ideas* 7 (1986), 597–602.

to prove by coercive argument that an idea must be perceived by something which can rightfully be called a substance. I think no one is in that position; the Humean who takes ideas to be unowned episodes of awareness cannot be made to surrender. But in their rush to say this, Berkeley's critics have failed to appreciate the plausibility of Berkeley's view when taken alongside certain other of his convictions, and they have underestimated the support that view receives from beliefs about the self which even Hume found it hard to deny. A Berkeleyan idea is not an act of awareness but an object of awareness, and if an object of awareness must be perceived, there must be something that perceives it. Now if there *must* be something by which it is perceived then the perceiver has *something* of the character of a substance, because it is something on which the idea depends for its existence. For all I have said so far, though, a 'perceiver' might be nothing more than one pole or aspect of an indivisible thing: an unowned episode of awareness, one of whose aspects is an object, and one of whose aspects is an act. But according to Berkeley I know that *I* perceive, and I know that I perceive an 'endless variety' of ideas that succeed one another in time, upon which I exercise 'divers operations', among them willing, imagining, and perceiving (*Principles* 2). I am therefore a persisting thing capable of various acts or operations. I am not a fleeting or momentary thing, but something that resembles what substances are widely held to be. 'That which I denote by the term I,' Berkeley writes at *Principles* 139, 'is the same with what is meant by *soul* or *spiritual substance*.' The word 'I' may embody an illusion, but the beliefs it is used to express are very hard to escape, and they lend support to Berkeley's view because the self of which they speak is portrayed as something like a substance, a persisting thing with inherent potentialities, one on which other things (ideas formed by imagination, for example) depend. Other minds must be hypothesized, but we conceive of them on the model of our own. As Berkeley writes at *Commentaries* 752, 'We cannot Conceive of other Minds besides our own but as so many selves.' One's own self imparts an understanding of what it is to be a thinking thing, which can then be extended in the manner earlier described.

3. *The mind and its acts*

I have argued that Berkeley's ideas are objects rather than acts or operations of the mind. If I am right then ideas have no clear place in the framework of traditional ontology. Are acts and operations better off? They could be classified as modifications of the mind, but this will clarify their nature only if the relationship between substance and modification is itself clear. Berkeley's predecessors passed on two basic ways of understanding that relationship, and Berkeley was uneasy about both of them.

The first way portrays the relationship much as the materialist portrays the relationship between matter and its accidents. Berkeley outlines this portrayal at *Principles* 17:

If we inquire into what the most accurate philosophers declare themselves to mean by *material substance*; we shall find them acknowledge, they have no other meaning annexed to those sounds, but the idea of being in general, together with the relative notion of its supporting accidents.

The notions of substance and accident articulated here are all-purpose ones, as handy for spirit as they are for matter. Locke appeals to this notion of substance in arguing that the idea of spiritual substance is no less clear than the idea of matter (*Essay* II xxiii 30), but it is scarcely possible for Berkeley to accept as an account of spirit and its acts or operations the very account he rejects in the case of matter.

The second way of conceiving of this relationship is distinctively Cartesian. This view identifies a substance with its principal attribute. The modifications of the substance are then viewed as modifications of the attribute, as determinate ways in which the attribute exists. This conception dominates Malebranche's *Search after Truth*. Malebranche ridicules the notion of substance as a 'subject' or 'principle' of accidents; in a passage that probably influenced Locke as well as Berkeley, Malebranche traces the notion to an uncontrolled abstractive tendency, a tendency to substitute the 'general ideas and entities of logic' for the 'particular and distinct' ideas of natural philosophy.[40] Yet the notion of substance continues to be of central importance: Malebranche identifies material substance with the attribute of extension, and spiritual substance with the attribute of thought.

It is surprising that Berkeley, a close student of the *Search*, shows no sign in either the *Principles* or the *Dialogues* that he is familiar with the Cartesian view. He discusses it briefly, however, in a letter, where he endorses a friend's opinion that 'Descartes flounders often in his Meditations and is not always consistent with himself.' In particular,

---

[40] *Search after Truth*, III ii 8 § 2, pp. 244–5 in Lennon and Olscamp.

In Med. 3 and in the Answer to the 3: Objection of Hobbes he plainly distinguisheth betwixt himself & Cogitation, betwixt an extended Substance & Extension, and nevertheless throughout his Principles he confounds those Things as do likewise his Followers. (*Works* VIII, p. 26.)

In his reply to Hobbes's Third Objection Descartes writes, 'I do not deny that I, who am thinking, am distinct from my thought.'[41] I cannot be sure just what it is in the Cartesian view that troubles Berkeley, but it is likely that he would sympathize with what Hobbes says in the previous objection: 'M. Descartes is identifying the thing which understands with intellection, which is an act of that which understands. Or at least he is identifying the thing which understands with the intellect, which is a power of that which understands. Yet all philosophers make a distinction between a subject and its faculties or acts, i.e. between a subject and its properties and its essences: an entity is one thing, its essence is another.'[42] But if we call the substance the *subject* of properties as intimately related to it as thought and extension appear to be, how will we avoid thinking of it as something 'in addition' to those properties, something of which we have, as Malebranche argues, 'no other idea . . . than being or substance in general'?

It is disappointing that Berkeley makes no attempt to deal with such questions. Perhaps an account was to be included in Part II of the *Principles*, but by 1730 he had lost whatever confidence he may have had in what he once proposed to say. His response to two pages of penetrating correspondence on the topic by Johnson (*Works* II, pp. 288–90) is a perfunctory paragraph which concludes,

I think it might prevent a good deal of obscurity and dispute to examine well what I have said about abstraction, and about the true sense and significance of words, in several parts of these things that I have published, though much remains to be said on that subject. (*Works* II, p. 293.)

[41] *The Philosophical Writings of Descartes*, vol. 2, p. 125. Descartes immediately adds, 'in the way in which a thing is distinct from a mode'. In article 62 of the *Principles of Philosophy*, Pt. I, he explains that in the Replies to the First Set of Objections to the Meditations he papered over the difference between modal and conceptual distinctions. But Berkeley says that his quarrel is with the *Principles*, and article 63 is probably one of the passages Berkeley has in mind when he accuses Descartes of conflating subject and attribute 'throughout his Principles'. There Descartes writes that thought and extension 'must . . . be considered as nothing else but thinking substance itself and extended substance itself—that is, as mind and body' (*Philosophical Writings*, vol. I, p. 215). Berkeley's criticism will not apply if Descartes holds that an individual substance can be a modification. For an interpretation along these lines see Lennon, 'The Inherence Pattern and Descartes' *Ideas*', *Journal of the History of Philosophy* 12 (1974), 43–52.

[42] Second Objection, in *The Philosophical Writings of Descartes*, vol. 2, p. 122.

In Chapter 4 I said that one mark of Berkeley's greatness is his interest in explaining things that others take for granted. Another aspect of his character as a philosopher is an opposing tendency to lose interest in details once the main point has been agreed on. He follows the conclusion last quoted with a reminder that Johnson has agreed that there is nothing without his mind 'but God and other spirits, with the attributes or properties belonging to them, and the ideas contained in them'. It is agreement on *this* that Berkeley aims at, and one characteristic that has come out several times in this study is Berkeley's tendency, once that aim has been achieved, to come to rest.

INDEX